THE SPIRIT AND THE CROSS, WISDOM, AND COMMUNAL DISCERNMENT:
A CRITICAL EXPLORATION OF 1 CORINTHIANS 2.1–3.4

THE SPIRIT AND THE CROSS, WISDOM, AND COMMUNAL DISCERNMENT:

A CRITICAL EXPLORATION OF 1 CORINTHIANS 2.1–3.4

Carl S. Sweatman

GlossaHouse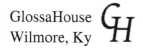
Wilmore, Ky

The Spirit and the Cross, Wisdom, and Communal Discernment:
A Critical Exploration of 1 Corinthians 2.1–3.4

© GlossaHouse, LLC, 2015

GlossaHouse, Inc.
110 Callis Cir.
Wilmore, KY 40390
www.GlossaHouse.com

The Spirit and the Cross, Wisdom, and Communal Discernment:
A Critical Exploration of 1 Corinthians 2.1–3.4
Sweatman, Carl S., 1977-

    p. cm. — (GlossaHouse Dissertation Series; Ref.)

    Includes bibliographical references and indices.

    1.   Biblical Studies – Paul's Letters.   2. Biblical Criticism and Interpretation.

    3. Christian Theology – Pneumatology. I. Title

    II. GlossaHouse Dissertation Series; 1. ISBN:

ISBN: 978-1-942697-02-2 (pb)
        978-1-942697-36-7 (hb)

Library of Congress Control Number: 2015931291

The fonts used to create this work are available from www.Linguistoftware.com/lgku.html

Cover Design by T. Michael W. Halcomb

Text Layout & Book Design by T. Michael W. Halcomb.

THIS WORK IS DEDICATED TO:
MY WIFE, JENN, AND OUR DAUGHTER, ASHLEY

GLOSSAHOUSE DISSERTATION SERIES

VOLUME 1

SERIES EDITORS

FREDRICK J. LONG
T. MICHAEL W. HALCOMB

GLOSSAHOUSE $\mathcal{GH}$

GLOSSAHOUSE DISSERTATION SERIES

The goal of the GlossaHouse Dissertation Series to facilitate the creation and publication of innovative, affordable, and accessible scholarly resources, whether print or digital, that advance research in the areas of both ancient and modern texts and languages.

GLOSSAHOUSE G_H

TABLE OF CONTENTS

The abbreviations used throughout this dissertation follow the standard established by the SBL Handbook of Style (1999). *Those employed that do not appear in the* Handbook *are (listed according to abbreviation):*

21KJV	21st Century King James Version
AYB	Anchor Yale Bible
BECNT	Baker Exegetical Commentary of the New Testament
BMW	Bible in the Modern World
CBR	*Currents in Biblical Research*
CCSS	Catholic Commentary on Sacred Scripture
Cons	*Conspectus*
DARBY	Darby Translation
EBC	Expositor's Bible Commentary
EC	Epworth Commentaries
EGT	Expositor's Greek Testament
ESV	English Standard Version
HCSB	Holman Christian Standard Bible
HTA	Historisch Theologische Auslegung
JPT	*Journal of Pentecostal Theology*
JPTSup	Journal of Pentecostal Theology Supplement Series
JT	*Journal of Theology* (United Theological Seminary)
KNT	Kommentar zum Neuen Testament
LNTS	Library of New Testament Studies
LWC	Living Word Commentary
MSt	*Mission Studies*

NCamBC	New Cambridge Bible Commentary
NColBC	New Collegeville Bible Commentary
NET	The NET Bible
NIBC	New International Biblical Commentary
NIVUK	New International Version, UK Edition
NTC	New Testament Commentary
NTT	New Testament Theology (Series)
PBM	Paternoster Biblical Monographs
PCC	Paul in Critical Contexts
PilNTC	Pillar New Testament Commentaries
PrTMS	Princeton Theological Monograph Series
SBEC	Studies in the Bible and Early Christianity
SHBC	Smyth & Helwys Bible Commentary
SNTW	Studies of the New Testament and Its World
TEF	Theological Education Fund
TGST	Tesi Gregoriana—Serie Teologia
TNIV	Today's New International Version
WYC	Wycliffe New Testament
YLT	Young's Literal Translation
ZBNT	Zürcher Bibelkommentare: Neues Testament

PREFACE

The following study is virtually a carbon copy of my doctoral dissertation, submitted to and accepted by the University of Gloucestershire (Chelteham, England) in 2013. I say "virtually" because this version reflects a few adjustments and corrections that had to be made from the original. By this I mean some clarification in a few sentences, a smattering of additional references, and (it pains me to admit) a handful of tyopographical errors. Moreover, there was also the need to "correct" the British style of writing— e.g. quotation marks, comma usage, and spelling—so that this version fits with US expectations or conventions. However, aside from these rather minor adjustments and corrections, the content and argumentation of the study remain unchanged.

Now for the details. This study explores Paul's teaching on the role of the Spirit in 1 Cor 2.1–3.4, and how that role relates to the (Pauline) themes of cross, wisdom, and (communal) discernment in that passage and the immediate context of 1 Cor 1–4. By providing a close reading of 1 Cor 2.1–3.4, this study focuses on the reasons why Paul articulates and emphasizes the Spirit's essential role in the proclamation of the cross, in the mediation of divine wisdom, and the exercise of communal discernment. This study also investigates how this pneumatological teaching applies to Paul's further assessment of the Corinthian situation, as articulated in 1 Cor 5–15, and thus why the textual unit of 1 Cor 2.1–3.4 occurs at such an early stage in Paul's argument.

After an introductory chapter surveying previous scholarship and situating a study of 1 Cor 2.1–3.4, chapter 2 shows how Paul is addressing a situation in Corinth that emerged after his initial sojourn and in which the Corinthians employ what he sees as faulty criteria of judgment, drawn from the conventions and styles of Greco-Roman rhetoric, in assessing the apostles as heralds of

God's wisdom and themselves as wise, spiritual people. Paul counters these by arguing that the Corinthians' original acceptance of the gospel came not through persuasive speech but by the Spirit working powerfully in the message he proclaimed. Chapter 3 explores Paul's perception that the Corinthians have misconstrued the notion of revelation by defining it as a process by which one comes to know and receive divine wisdom through human ability or effort. This chapter then examines Paul's corrective response and its assertion that divine wisdom can only be known and received through divine mediation, and that the Spirit is the means by which this occurs. Chapter 4 focuses on the topic of (communal) discernment. It investigates Paul's perception that the Corinthians form their assessments by relying on human wisdom, why he holds this to be inappropriate for those who are both in Christ and recipients of God's wisdom, and why he underlines that Spirit-guided discernment is the only appropriate means for judging divine wisdom and those who proclaim it.

A final chapter asks whether and how the issues examined in 1 Cor 2.1–3.4 play out in 1 Cor 1–4 as a whole and then in the rest of the letter. My emphasis here is twofold. The Corinthians' failure to rely on God's wisdom and Spirit-guided discernment and the presence of an internal stratification based on their own perceptions of wisdom and spirituality are seen as contributing to the social and ecclesial problems discussed later in the letter. At the same time what Paul has argued in 1 Cor 2.1–3.4 continues to inform his response, as he appeals for lives shaped by the wisdom of the gospel of the cross and for a community united in its discernment, both made possible by the Spirit.

Before diving into this study, one last detail needs to be addressed: this project would not have seen the light of day had it not been for the encouragement, support, and guidance others. Thus, there is an inescapable to need to express my gratitude.

First and foremost, I cannot express the depth of gratitude for my wonderful wife, Jenn, and her steadfastness during my academic pursuits. She has been (and continues to be) an incredible source of unfailing love and unwavering encouragement, especially when I (more than) occasionally struggled with self-confidence issues and fears of failure. Jenn always knew when to let me rant, when to offer insight, and even when to slap me back into reality.

I am also deeply thankful for my family: Keith and Billye Green; Derek, Micki, Alden and Alex Sweatman; Brennon and Cat Hittner; Scott and Tori Schmitt; Alan and Diane Sams; A.J. and Paige Sams; "Aunt" Pearl and "Cousin" Al Douthit; Paul and Ann Kinder; and my close friends: George and Cassi Frank; Ryan and Shelley Shoaff; Dave and Michelle Parkerson; Alex and Shaleen Fagundo; Brian and Jaylene Howell; Jake and Cari Christian; Chris and Abi Arnold; Mark and Beck Stevens; Tom and Becky Thatcher; Jon and Tammie Weatherly; and Doug and Cheryl McIntosh. All of you have been a reservoir of support.

I am especially grateful for the astute counsel of my Doktoväter, Andrew Lincoln and Lloyd Pietersen. They patiently endured my idiosyncrasies, particularly my near involuntary habit of extremes, and they wisely guided and pushed me to new levels that I could not have achieved on my own. Throughout my program, I learned so much about the rigours and joys of doctoral studies, and I am forever in their debt for all they taught me as well as the personal and intellectual growth I have experienced because of them. Equally, I am thankful for the comments, criticisms, and advice from my two examiners: Adrian Long and Edward Adams. Both provided insightful feedback and encouraging suggestions for how to make the argument better.

Early on I enjoyed the company of a handful of fellow researchers in the office, all of whom were a constant source of empathy and motivation: Jason LeCureux, Robert Thang, Andrew

Lee, and Luke Devine. While I was the "odd man out" amongst these four (i.e. I was the only NT guy), they welcomed me as one of their own. After nearly two years of solitude in the office—the four guys just named finished their PhDs and moved on—I had the pleasure to get to know Cyndi Parker and Mark Arnold, both of whom maintained the tradition of keeping me the "odd man out" yet included, and both greatly encouraged to me in their own ways. I must also mention Matt O'Reilly, who was my NT compadre from a distance. It was a joy to talk with Matt as a fellow aspiring NT scholar, and it was (and still is) comforting to know that he is a pastor at heart (and vocation).

Moreover, I am truly thankful for the impromptu chats with other scholars throughout my program and their willingness to offer their unique insight: Gordon McConville, Pekka Pitkänen, William Large, Todd Klutz, N.T. Wright, Chris Tilling, John Barclay, David Horrell, Jim West, Collin Bulley, Matthew Malcolm, Brian Rosner, and Chris Keith. While I may try, words fail to express how much I appreciate all of you taking the time to listen and be honest with me.

Penultimately, I must extend my deep gratitude to the creators and editors of GlossaHouse: Michael Halcomb and Fred Long. I truly appreciate you not only taking the time to consider this work for the GlossaHouse Dissertation Series but also accepting it. I hope this contribution reflects and furthers the aims of this Series.

Finally, as a way of getting me through long hours in the office and intense research, I am grateful for the music of: Bach, Beethoven, Dvořák, Haydn, Mozart, Vivaldi, Yo-Yo Ma, Howard Shore, Hans Zimmer, Shaun Davey, Beck, Bing Crosby, Civil Wars, Josh Garrels, David Grey, Jack Johnson, Matthew Perryman Jones, Lenny Kravitz, Live, Dave Matthews, John Mayer, Rusted Root, Sting, and U2.

Chapter 1
INTRODUCTION

1.1. Situating the Study

This study explores Paul's teaching in 1 Cor 2.1–3.4 on the role of the Spirit and how that role relates to the (Pauline) themes of the cross, wisdom, and (communal) discernment in that passage and the surrouding context of 1 Cor 1–4. Moreover, this study investigates how this pneumatological teaching applies to Paul's further assessment of the Corinthian situation, as articulated in 1 Cor 5–15, and thus why the textual unit of 2.1–3.4 occurs at such an early stage in Paul's argument.

1.1.1. Immediate Context

The reason for the primary focus stems from three related observations, with the last functioning as the impetus for this study. First, while the themes of Spirit, cross, wisdom, and discernment appear in Paul's extant writings, whether individually or in groups, they pervade the argument of 1 Cor 1–4. Second, the particular concentration of all four themes is found specifically in 1 Cor 2.1–3.4, a passage that speaks directly to Paul's apostolic role, the Corinthians' identity "in Christ," and how they understand and judge both. Finally, while the concentration of the four themes seems to indicate an interrelationship among them, Paul, in this passage, is specifically emphasizing the priority and necessity of the Spirit's role in relation to the other three.

By providing a close reading of the text, this study will show that Paul uses the teaching found in 1 Cor 2.1–3.4 to explain 1) the way in which God's Spirit is essential for the proclamation of the cross, 2) how the Spirit is the unique and necessary mediator of

1

God's wisdom, the reception of which brings with it an epistemological transformation, and 3) how the Spirit is essential for wise, communal discernment, thus enabling right thought and action in the light of the cross and the transformation wrought by God's wisdom. This study will also contend that Paul applies this pneumatological teaching as he assesses the dilemmas noted in the remainder of the letter, thus emphasizing the teaching's rhetorical force and how it shapes the whole of Paul's argument.

What is striking is that with the possible exception of 1 Cor 12–14,[1] this linkage of themes in the context of the Spirit's role is not found anywhere else in the Pauline corpus. This makes 1 Cor 2.1–3.4 an important text for gaining a broader understanding of Paul's theology, 1 Corinthians, notions of Christian identity, and Pauline pneumatology. While the unique concentration of these ideas in 1 Cor 2.1–3.4 would seem to be a sufficient reason for taking on this project, there is a further reason to consider. As will be discussed below, while scholarship has investigated the particular themes of cross, Spirit, wisdom, and discernment (in the Pauline letters in general and 1 Corinthians in particular), and while some have explored the relationship between two or three of these themes, no monographs have been devoted to the specific text of 1 Cor 2.1–3.4, the specific collection of all four themes and their interrelationship, or specifically the Spirit's essential role in that interrelationship. This study seeks to fill that lacuna.

1.1.2. Wider Context

Alongside the two leading reasons for this study, there is a third—one that relates to the conceptual context out of and within

---

[1] While the theme of the proclamation of the gospel is not *explicitly* found in 1 Cor 12–14, a case could possibly be made for its implicit presence, given the specific focus of those chapters. However, making that case is not my intent for this study.

which Pauline thought appears to operate and interact. Here I have in mind the varying (and sometimes competing) ancient notions of divine wisdom and how that wisdom not only is mediated to humanity but also becomes the framework for right or wise living. While this might appear to shift the attention toward wisdom and away from the Spirit, such a consideration is necessary in order to contextualize how Paul's thought relates to notions of wisdom and to recognize what he does specifically with such notions as he presents his argument in 1 Corinthians.

1.1.2.1. Wisdom in the Ancient Near East

Writers of the ancient world express or define the *concept* of wisdom in various ways. For some, wisdom refers to an intangible abstraction external to divine beings, yet sought after by them. For others, wisdom, while still abstract, is not separate from divine beings but represents an essential attribute of divinity. However, in most instances wisdom is elevated to the status of a divine being, placed and revered alongside others in the pantheon.[2] Regardless of these differences, there exists a basic consistency with regard to the *function* of wisdom. As evidenced, for example, in the creation stories of the Sumerians, Babylonians, Egyptians, and Assyrians, most in the ancient world understand wisdom as that which determines and maintains order or balance in the cosmos.

Thus, all beings—divine and human—must adhere to wisdom to maintain harmony in creation.[3] The means for acquiring this

---

[2] E.g. the Egyptian idea of *ma'at*. For the conceptual pre-history of the term, see M. Karenga, *Maat: The Moral Ideal in Ancient Egypt. A Study in Classical African Ethics* (New York: Routledge, 2004), 29-76.

[3] As Lipson points out, in Egyptian mythology the path of the sun god Ra was determined by *ma'at*, and to deviate from that path was an affront to *ma'at*—see C.S. Lipson, "Ancient Egyptian Rhetoric: It All Comes Down to Maat," in *Rhetoric Before and Beyond the Greeks* (eds. C.S. Lipson and R.A. Binkley; Albany: State University of New York, 2004), 81.

wisdom range between a divine gift prior to birth and a learned trait through instruction.[4] Wise living, therefore, comes to be understood as conduct that reflects harmony with the divine, wise, cosmic order. Consequently, those who do not live according to this order are seen as fools and living in direct opposition to the divine—or they are enemies of the divine. Such foolish opponents, therefore, reflect the unbalanced or chaotic forces of creation.

1.1.2.2. Wisdom in the Greco-Roman World

During the Greco-Roman period, the philosophers advocated the goal of life as grasping this (divine) wisdom and allowing it to shape and govern how an individual lives in society. The Ephesian philosopher, Heraclitus, could be seen as one of the first Greek thinkers to articulate this view of human existence.[5] Moreover, Heraclitus is ostensibly the first to suggest the idea that the λόγος is the divine order of the cosmos, and only those who are truly wise can know this λόγος and live in harmony with it.[6] Stoic philosophers would later develop the idea of human existence as being inextricably bound to the created order—or the divine λόγος.

However, because the Stoics hold to cosmological materialism, the λόγος is not divine in the usual abstract, intangible sense. Instead, the λόγος is divine in the sense that it creates, universally permeates, and determines the existence of all creation—obviously including humanity;[7] hence the idea that there are bits of the divine

---

[4] The Egyptians ostensibly struck a middle ground by suggesting a natural endowment within all humans in need of cultivation (see M. Lichtheim, *Moral Values in Ancient Egypt* [Göttingen: Vandenhoeck & Ruprecht, 1997], 15-16).

[5] Whether or not he incorporated it from the ANE, as the Greeks did with virtually everything else, cannot be known for certain.

[6] See Hippolytus, *Haer.* 9.9; Aristotle, *Rhet.* 3.5.6.

[7] Cf. R. Salles, "Introduction: God and Cosmos in Stoicism," in *God and Cosmos in Stoicism* (ed. R. Salles; Oxford: Oxford University Press, 2009), 1-3.

in everything and everyone. For the Stoics, those who find the "divine spark" within their soul and allow it to guide and shape life according to the order of the λόγος will live wisely. Alternatively, those who do not find this "spark" are those who live unethical, disordered, chaotic, and foolish lives. As a result, this latter group forfeits the opportunity and means for obtaining the goal of human existence, which is true happiness or εὐδαιμονία.

1.1.2.3. Wisdom in Second-Temple Judaism

For the Jews in the Greco-Roman world, true wisdom (or חכמה) belongs to Yahweh alone, and it is by this wisdom that Yahweh creates and sustains all of creation.[8] As such, wisdom defines not only a central attribute or characteristic of Yahweh but also how Yahweh operates within creation—i.e. Yahweh *is* wise and *acts* wisely. Accordingly, the people of Yahweh are to be shaped by the wisdom of Yahweh and thus live ordered or balanced lives in Yahweh's creation. The way in which this shaping and living according to wisdom occurred is variously described.

The Old Testament occasionally speaks of wisdom being obtained as a gift from Yahweh,[9] or gained through natural[10] and historical observations,[11] as well as learned by studying from or interacting with wise individuals.[12] Torah instruction would later become the pivotal means for obtaining true wisdom from Yahweh as well as the touchstone for those seeking to live according to Yahweh's wisdom. This might account for why, in several Second-

---

[8] E.g. Job 9.4; 12.13; Ps 104.24; Isa 10.13; cf. Gen 1, 2; Ex 20.11; Neh 9.6; Pss 8, 19; 33.6-9; 102.26; 121.2; Is 40.12-25; 42.5; 45.7-9, 12; Jer 10.12; *Gen. Rab.* 9.2.

[9] E.g. 1 Kgs 3.6-14; 4.29-34; Job 38.36; Prov 2.6; Eccl 2.26; Dan 2.21-23.

[10] E.g. Job 35.11; Prov 6.6.

[11] E.g. Deut 32.39; Ps 78; Prov 19.20; Hos 14.9.

[12] E.g. Job 32.7; Prov 9.9; cf. Deut 1.13, 15; 2 Sam 14.20; 16.23; Prov 12.18; 13.14.

Temple and later Jewish texts, "Torah" and "wisdom" appear to be synonymous—if not necessarily linked.[13] Therefore, for Jews of this period, living a life in harmony with the wisdom of Yahweh requires obedience to Torah because they believe that the Torah mediates the true wisdom of Yahweh. Those who live accordingly are considered to be wise or righteous, while those living contrary to Torah or Yahweh's wisdom are seen as fools, wicked or even enemies of Yahweh.

1.1.3. Controlling Questions

How, then, does the Apostle Paul, as a Jewish believer in Jesus as messiah and one who believes he was called to evangelize the Greco-Roman world, relate to and convey these differing conceptions of wisdom? How do Paul's traditional Jewish beliefs regarding Yahweh's wisdom square with his newfound understanding that this wisdom is now displayed through the death and resurrection of Jesus and mediated by God's Spirit? What differences and similarities exist between how Paul proclaims the role of wisdom and God's Spirit and the Greco-Roman notions of wisdom and speech (or rhetoric) as ways of knowing? What role does Paul see God's Spirit playing in establishing and maintaining the community of believers, as well as the way in which believers learn or know how to live godly, wise, harmonious lives? Specifically, how does Paul understand the Spirit's role in the proclamation of the cross of Christ as God's wisdom, a wisdom that establishes a framework for communal discernment within the community of believers? These questions provide the basic framework around which this study is built.

---

[13] E.g. Sir 17.11; 24.1-29; *T.Levi* 13; *1 En* 42.1-2; *Bar* 3.38-40; *2 Bar* 38.4; 44.16; *4 Esd* 8.12; *Gen. Rab.* 1; Philo, *Mos* 2.3, 9; cf. Prov 8.

1.2. Survey of Scholarship

Before proceeding with this study of Paul's pneumatological teaching, it is necessary to contextualize it within recent studies on 1 Corinthians. However, in the light of the breadth and depth of scholarship on 1 Corinthians—not to mention the Corinthian correspondence—and given the constraints of a focused study such as this one, I must be selective with how much material is surveyed.[14] The results of my selectivity stem from two basic questions: 1) how do scholars define the nature of Paul's response to the Corinthian dilemma, and 2) which scholarly works address the specific Pauline themes of cross, (Holy) Spirit, wisdom, and discernment in 1 Cor 1–4, whether individually, in pairs, or in groups? While I acknowledge the overlap created by these questions, the relevant sources are here divided into two types, each dealing with the specifics of the basic questions.

In the first section of this survey I consider the scholars whose interest lie in 1) locating the problems that Paul confronts in his letter and 2) examining the way in which he goes about it. The contributions here range in focus and levels of coverage, not to mention methodology. In the second section I consider the scholars whose interests lie primarily in understanding particular aspects of Paul's theology as found in 1 Cor 1–4 (e.g. cross, Spirit, wisdom, discernment). Specifically, I focus on those detailed contributions that examine the interrelationship between two or more of the particular aspects or themes. Similar to the first section, the contributions here are diverse in emphasis and approach.

---

[14] Økland's forthcoming work (*1 Corinthians Through the Centuries* [Chichester: Wiley-Blackwell, forthcoming]) will provide a more adequate survey of scholarship on 1 Corinthians than can be given here.

1.2.1. Broad Scope Contributions

Two introductory points repay brief attention, as they relate to how studies of 1 Corinthians often proceed. First, the contents and structure of the letter indicate that Paul is responding to a series of concerns about and even questions from the newly established church in Corinth.[15] In support of this, scholars often appeal to the internal evidence where Paul indicates his awareness of specific topics and concerns—i.e. the report from Chloe's people (cf. 1 Cor 1.11-12), the letter from the Corinthians (cf. 1 Cor 7.1)[16] and the

---

[15] While I cannot provide full justification here, I am operating on the assumptions that 1) Paul's sojourn in Corinth occurs between late-50 or early-51 CE and mid- or late-52 CE, and 2) the time of writing takes place c. 55 CE.

[16] Some argue that since the περὶ δέ formula first appears in connection with the letter from the Corinthians, all subsequent uses of περὶ δέ (i.e. 1 Cor 7.25; 8.1; 12.1; 16.1, 12) indicate that the topics discussed originate from that letter (see e.g. H.L. Goudge, *The First Epistle to the Corinthians: With Introduction and Notes* [London: Methuen & Co., 1911], xxxix; J. Riggs and H. Reed, *Epistles to the Corinthians* [New York: Macmillan Company, 1922], 10; E. Adams, *Constructing the World: A Study in Paul's Cosmological Language* [Edinburgh: T&T Clark, 2000], 86 n.2). However, Mitchell argues that περὶ δέ is a literary device, one that functions as "simply a topic marker, a shorthand way of introducing the next subject of discussion," and that "[i]n itself the formula περὶ δέ gives no information about how the author or reader became informed of the topic, nor does it give information about the order of presentation of topics" ("Concerning ΠΕΡΙ ΔΕ in 1 Corinthians," *NovT* 31.3 [1989]: 234; *contra* Adams, who thinks Mitchell's arguments on this point are not persuasive—see *Constructing the World*, 86 n.2). Moreover, while περὶ δέ precedes the "collection for the saints" in 16.1, it is not clear that it necessarily relates to a discussion-point raised by the Corinthians (cf. G. Voigt, *Gemeinsam glauben, hoffen, lieben: Paulus an die Korinther 1* [Göttingen: Vandenhoeck & Ruprecht, 1989], 159; *contra* A. Robertson and A. Plummer, *A Critical and Exegetical Commentary on the First Epistle of St Paul to the Corinthians* [Edinburgh: T&T Clark, 1911], 383; G.D. Fee, *The First Epistle to the Corinthians* [Grand Rapids: Eerdmans, 1987], 267, 809, 811; M.A. Pascuzzi, *First and Second Corinthians* [Collegeville: Liturgical Press, 2005], 91-92; P. Perkins, *First Corinthians* [Grand Rapids: Baker Academic, 2012], 197. Lang

oral reports (cf. 1 Cor 5.1; 11.18; 15.12[?][17]), possibly transmitted by Stephanas, Fortunatus, and Achaicus (cf. 1 Cor 16.17). [18] Second, 1 Cor 1.11-12 in particular suggests the possible existence of divisions (σχίσματα),[19] which compel some scholars to try and

---

sees it as a possibility—*Die Briefe an die Korinther* [Göttingen: Vandenhoeck & Ruprecht, 1994], 245). As Mitchell points out, if 16.1 does refer to a Corinthian question then we must read the περὶ δέ of 16.12 in the same way, yet nothing in the text requires such a reading for either passage (see *Paul and the Rhetoric of Reconciliation: An Exegetical Investigation of the Language and Composition of 1 Corinthians* [Louisville: Westminster John Knox, 1991], 291-92 n.596). It is instead likely that Paul simply employs the formulaic phrase to indicate a topic change (cf. R.F. Collins, *First Corinthians* [Collegeville: Liturgical Press, 1999], 585, 588; C.S. Keener, *1–2 Corinthians* [Cambridge: Cambridge University Press, 2005], 136; J.A. Fitzmyer, *First Corinthians: A New Translation with Introduction and Commentary* [New Haven: Yale University Press, 2008], 277).

[17] See 5.4.3 below.

[18] While most understand Stephanas, Fortunatus, and Achaicus to be the bearers of the Corinthian letter to Paul (e.g. Robertson-Plummer, *First Epistle*, xx-xxi; Riggs-Reed, *Epistles*, 9-10; J.C. Hurd, *The Origin of 1 Corinthians* [London: SPCK, 1965], 48-50; M.C. de Boer, "The Composition of 1 Corinthians," *NTS* 40.2 [1994]: 230-31; C.D. Stanley, *Arguing with Scripture: The Rhetoric of Quotations in the Letters of Paul* [New York: T&T Clark International, 2004], 79 n.10; Fitzmyer, *First Corinthians*, 43, 138), it is possible that they delivered both the oral reports and the letter from the Corinthians (cf. F.W. Grosheide, *Commentary on the First Epistle to the Corinthians* [Grand Rapids: Eerdmans, 1954], 14).

[19] The existence (or non-existence) of factious groups in Corinth and how to define them have been topics of critical inquiry throughout the history of modern interpretation. For example: while most early commentators accepted the general idea of "factions," Moffatt (*The First Epistle of Paul to the Corinthians* [New York: Harper and Brothers, 1890], xxii, 8-11), Munck (*Paul and the Salvation of Mankind* [trans. F. Clarke; London: SCM Press, 1959], 135-36), and Héring (*The First Epistle of Saint Paul to the Corinthians* [trans. A.W. Heathcote and P.J. Allcock; London: Epworth, 1962], 4) rejected the view in favor of bickering "cliques," each having its own champion. Reitzenstein interpreted the idea along the lines of pagan mystery religions, thus making the

identify the specific groups involved—a pursuit that generally yields varying results but no consensus.[20] Since the identification, description, and even enumeration of the divisions are difficult to ascertain,[21] and allowing for a level of ambiguity in the specific term, σχίσματα, a number of scholars describe the issue in Corinth as an *attitude* or *spirit* of divisiveness.[22] Despite this uncertainty and ambiguity, however, it is usually maintained that Paul's desire for unity within the church (cf. 1 Cor 1.10),[23] and thus the cause for writing, is at least motivated by the *report* of

---

individual parties "guilds," each having its own spiritual leader or progenitor (see *Hellenistic Mystery-Religions: Their Basic Ideas and Significance* [trans. J.E. Steely; Pittsburgh: Pickwick Publications, 1978], 426). Conzelmann, on the other hand, suggests something akin to political parties with competing viewpoints—see *1 Corinthians: A Commentary on the First Epistle of St Paul to the Corinthians* (ed. G.W. MacRae; trans. J.W. Leitch; Philadelphia: Fortress, 1975), 32-34. More recently, Haacker classified the factions as nothing more than "'fan clubs' of different teachers or preachers in Corinth" (*The Theology of Paul's Letter to the Romans* [Cambridge: Cambridge University Press, 2003], 19).

[20] While aged, Alford's critique is still apropos: "Much ingenuity and labour has been spent in Germany on the four supposed distinct parties at Corinth, and the most eminent theologians have endeavoured, with very different results, to allot to each its definite place in tenets and practice" (*The Greek Testament: With a Critically Revised Text* [London: Rivingtons, 1865], 2.49).

[21] See J.D.G. Dunn, *1 Corinthians* (Sheffield: Sheffield Academic, 1995), 27-44; cf. also C.K. Robertson, *Conflict in Corinth: Redefining the System* (New York: Peter Lang, 2001), 1.

[22] Mitchell, *Rhetoric of Reconciliation*, 86.

[23] Ciampa-Rosner disagree with this: "Such a reading puts 'the cart before the horse.' Paul's big goal is not unity, but the sanctification of Gentile believers that they may glorify God....In 1 Corinthians Paul deals with Corinthian factionalism first in order to clear the way for this more important matter" ("The Structure and Argument of 1 Corinthians: A Biblical/Jewish Approach," *NTS* 52.2 [2006]: 214).

divisions or divisiveness.[24] When we consider the history of scholarship on 1 Corinthians we discover the various ways that scholars attempt to explain the relationship between these two points.

1.2.1.1. Identifying the Parties

For some, the emphasis falls on identifying the party-groups mentioned in 1 Cor 1.12. Specifically, are there truly four parties,[25] each having its own champion? Are there only three real parties, those rallying around Paul, Apollos, and Cephas, with the Christ-party being a foil?[26] Or is the Christ-party the leading antagonist?[27] Alternatively, should the specific names be seen as merely illustrating the dialectic within nascent Christianity—i.e. Baur's Jew-Gentile antithesis—thus reducing the true number of parties to two: Petrine and Pauline?[28]

---

[24] Mitchell, *Rhetoric of Reconciliation*, 63; B. Witherington, *Conflict and Community in Corinth: A Socio-Rhetorical Commentary on 1 and 2 Corinthians* (Grand Rapids: Eerdmans, 1995), 28-29; D.E. Garland, *1 Corinthians* (Grand Rapids: Baker Academic, 2003), 6-9. For a fuller treatment of this connection, see C.S. de Vos, *Church and Community Conflicts: The Relationship of the Thessalonian, Corinthian, and Philippian Churches with Their Wider Civic Communities* (Atlanta: Scholars Press, 1999), 179-232.

[25] N.A. Dahl, "Paul and the Church at Corinth According to 1 Corinthians 1:10–4:21," in *Christian History and Interpretation: Studies Presented to John Knox* (eds. W.R. Farmer, C.F.D. Moule, and R.R. Niebuhr; Cambridge: Cambridge University Press, 1967), 322-35.

[26] J. Weiss, *Der erste Korintherbrief* (Göttingen: Vandenhoeck & Ruprecht, 1910), xxx-xxxix.

[27] W. Schmithals, *Gnosticism in Corinth: An Investigation of the Letters to the Corinthians* (trans. J. E. Steely; Nashville: Abingdon, 1971), 114.

[28] F.C. Baur, *Paul: The Apostle of Jesus Christ. His Life and Work, His Epistles and His Doctrines* (trans. E. Zeller; rev. A. Menzies; London: Williams and Norgate, 1876), 1.26-68, 259-97. For a resurrection of Baur's thesis, see G. Lüdemann, *Paul, Apostle to the Gentiles: Studies in Chronology* (trans. E.

Associated with the question of party-groups is the extent to which their respective influence contributed to the issues addressed in Paul's letter. Do each of the topics addressed in the letter indicate specific points of division in the church? Furthermore, since divisiveness is Paul's opening concern, can we assume that if the Corinthians are divided generally they must be divided on the particulars?[29] However, some scholars question this approach on two grounds: 1) nowhere in Paul's argument does he speak directly to one or more of the four (supposed) groups, and 2) Paul nowhere identifies the particular beliefs or doctrines of any group—or even what beliefs or doctrines potentially caused the divisions.[30]

1.2.1.2. Identifying the Issues

For other scholars, the emphasis falls primarily on discovering the types of issues causing trouble in Corinth. Specifically, and based on the contents of the letter, does Paul confront theological, philosophical and/or social issues in the church, and if so what are they precisely? Moreover, does the relationship between the issues discussed indicate groups of "opponents" in Corinth or should we

---

Stanely Jones; Philadelphia: Fortress, 1984); M.D. Goulder, *Paul and the Competing Missions in Corinth* (Peabody: Hendrickson, 2001).

[29] Cf. Polhill: "The first four chapters of 1 Corinthians form an appropriate introduction to the letter. The problems of factionalism treated in them are at the center of the congregational difficulties which surface in the rest of the letter" ("The Wisdom of God and Factionalism: 1 Corinthians 1–4," *RevExp* 80.3 [1983]: 325; cf. Hurd, *Origin of 1 Corinthians*, 96).

[30] See e.g. Hurd, *Origin of 1 Corinthians*, 96-97; C.R. Holladay, *First Letter of Paul to the Corinthians* (Austin: Sweet Publishing Company, 1979), 29; Fee, *First Epistle*, 47-48; L.L. Welborn, "On the Discord in Corinth: 1 Corinthians 1–4 and Ancient Politics," *JBL* 106.1 (1987): 89-90; A.D. Clarke, *Secular and Christian Leadership in Corinth: A Socio-historical and Exegetical Study of 1 Corinthians 1–6* (Leiden: Brill, 1993), 89-91; A.D. Litfin, *St Paul's Theology of Proclamation: 1 Corinthians 1–4 and Greco-Roman Rhetoric* (Cambridge: Cambridge University Press, 1994), 178-80; Collins, *First Corinthians*, 16.

assume a unified antagonism towards Paul?[31] One advantage here is that the analysis proceeds on the basis of textual evidence.

While focusing on this primary emphasis, scholars nevertheless seek to identify the implied "opponents." Traditionally, three (or four!) possibilities are given: Gnostics,[32] Hellenistic enthusiasts or spiritualists,[33] adherents of Hellenistic-Jewish wisdom traditions,[34] or a group of social elite in the church,[35] whether it be comprised

---

[31] Munck, *Paul and the Salvation of Mankind*, 135-67; Fee, *First Epistle*, 6-10, 47-51.

[32] See e.g. Schmithals, *Gnosticism in Corinth*, 137-55, 289-93; G. Theissen, *The Social Setting of Pauline Christianity: Essays on Corinth* (ed. and trans. J.H. Schütz; Edinburgh: T&T Clark, 1982), 132-36 (though with some hesitation); D. Georgi, *The Opponents of Paul in Second Corinthians* (Philadelphia: Fortress, 1986), 317; J.D.G. Dunn, *Unity and Diversity in the New Testament: An Inquiry into the Character of Earliest Christianity* (London: SCM Press, 2006), 297-302. The early work of Wilckens strongly advocated this position (see *Weisheit und Torheit: Eine exegetisch-religions-geschichtliche Untersuchung zu 1 Kor 1 und 2* [Tübingen: J.C.B. Mohr, 1959]), while in a subsequent article he admitted that he could not be as sure (see "Das Kreuz Christi als die Tiefe der Weisheit Gottes: Zu 1 Kor 2,1-16," in *Theologia Crucis-Signum Crucis: Festschrift für Erich Dinkler zum 70 Geburstag* [eds. C. Anderson and G. Klein; Tübingen: Mohr, 1979], 501-37).

[33] Particularly those with an (over-)realized eschatology—see e.g. E. Käsemann, *New Testament Questions of Today* (trans. W.J. Montague; Philadelphia: Fortress, 1969), 82-107; J.L. Sumney, *Identifying Paul's Opponents: The Question of Method in 2 Corinthians* (Sheffield: Sheffield Academic Press, 1990), although, this argument is applied to 2 Corinthians; A.C. Thiselton, "Realized Eschatology at Corinth," *NTS* 24 (1978): 510-26.

[34] B.A. Pearson, *The Pneumatikos-Psychikos Terminology in 1 Corinthians* (Missoula: University of Montana, 1973); R.A. Horsley, "Pneumatikos vs. Psychikos: Distinctions of Spiritual Status Among the Corinthians," *HTR* 69 (1976): 269-88; idem, "Gnosis in Corinth: 1 Corinthians 8.1-6," *NTS* 27.1 (1980): 32-51; J.A. Davis, *Wisdom and Spirit: An Investigation of 1 Corinthians 1.18–3.20 Against the Background of Jewish Sapiential Traditions in the Greco-Roman Period* (Lanham: University Press of America, 1984).

[35] Theissen, *Social Setting*, 73-96; Clarke, *Secular and Christian Leadership*, 45-57; D. Gill, "In Search of the Social Elite in the Corinthian

of Jews, Greeks, or Romans—or a mixture of all three.[36] As will be discussed later,[37] the Gnostic hypothesis has come under criticism and its older formulation is not widely considered to be viable, at least not without serious qualifications (i.e. calling it proto- or incipient gnosticism).[38] While the remaining options are more plausible, two questions arise with regard to their implementation and acceptability: 1) does any one of the three best account for the occasion of Paul's letter—if so which one, and 2) do these options carry the analysis of Paul's argument far enough?

1.2.1.3. Identifying the Cause(s)

For some, and building on the merits of the second approach, the emphasis falls on identifying the cause(s) for the types of issues that characterize the Corinthian situation. Thus, and assuming the report of divisions to be true, the focus is not so much on identifying the particular groups in Corinth or the specific views they espouse as it is on locating the *cause* for divisiveness.[39] How does this differ from the second approach, specifically its emphasis on theological, philosophical, and/or social categories?

Church," *TynBul* 44 (1993): 323-37; R.S. Dutch, *The Educated Elite in 1 Corinthians: Education and Community Conflict in Greco-Roman Context* (London: T&T Clark, 2005). Cf. also L.L. Welborn, *Paul, the Fool of Christ: A Study of 1 Corinthians 1–4 in the Comic-Philosophic Tradition* (London: T&T Clark International, 2005).

[36] See de Vos, *Church and Community Conflicts*, 231.

[37] See 3.2.3–3.2.4 and 4.3.1.1 below.

[38] Conzelmann, *1 Corinthians*, 15; R.P. Martin, *New Testament Foundations: A Guide for Christian Students* (Grand Rapids: Eerdmans, 1978), 173; cf. also R. McL. Wilson, "How Gnostic Were the Corinthians?," *NTS* 19.1 (1972): 74; idem, "Gnosis at Corinth," in *Paul and Paulinism: Essays in Honor of C.K. Barrett* (eds. M.D. Hooker and S.G. Wilson; London: SPCK, 1982), 102-14.

[39] Hurd, *Origin of 1 Corinthians*, 107; Mitchell, *Rhetoric of Reconciliation*, 302.

Whereas the second approach sought to answer questions of "what," this third one, and assuming such categories are legitimate, nuances the inquiry by dealing with questions of "why". Thus, instead of asking, *what* are the specific theological, philosophical, and/or social issues addressed in Paul's letter?, this approach asks: *why* are there theological, philosophical, and/or social issues in the Corinthian church, and is it possible to identify their causes? More to the point, how does identifying such causes affect our understanding of Paul's plea for unity? This approach has much to commend it and the works of key scholars employing it helped fuel and direct my own study. Four contributions should be noted.

1.2.1.3.1. Tübingen Redux

Still adhering to Baur's dialectic—albeit in a slightly modified form—some scholars see divergent or dichotomous theological perspectives as the cause for the dilemma(s) in Corinth (cf. Goulder, Lüdemann). The emphasis here is not so much particular theological precepts or topics addressed in the letter, although such things do play a role. Rather, this approach seeks to locate an overarching theological framework in which such precepts could develop. Therefore, in this instance, since the framework and the details within it are theological and stand contrary to those proposed by Paul, thus creating a division between him and the Corinthians, Paul's desire for unity is *theological* or even doctrinal in nature. While some view this option as untenable or even outdated, [40] and while they might be correct to question the methodological presuppositions of the approach (especially as

---

[40] E.g. W. Schrage, *Der erste Brief an die Korinther* (Neukirchen-Vluyn: Neukirchen Verlag, 1991), 1.38-63; R. Pickett, *The Cross in Corinth: The Social Significance of the Death of Jesus* (Sheffield: Sheffield Academic Press, 1997), 39-40; Keener, *1–2 Corinthians*, 24; cf. also Clarke, *Secular and Christian Leadership*, 89-90, 95.

defined by Baur), I do not think that a theological focus should be so quickly and categorically dismissed, or at least I do not think it should be viewed as necessarily separate from other lines of inquiry. It is simply reductionist to assume that theological ideas played little to no part in how ancient cultures defined the cosmos and society and especially their identity within both.[41]

1.2.1.3.2. Andrew Clarke

Clarke sees the Corinthians as reflecting what occurs in the wider Greco-Roman world: they are fascinated with social status in general and "personality-centered politics"[42] in particular. By this he means the Corinthians are aligning themselves with particular individuals within or related to the community, namely those who possess some level of power and/or influence.[43] Clarke lists three key ways in which this fascination was understood and expressed in the ancient world, and ostensibly in Corinth.[44]

---

[41] Merklein applauds the efforts of sociological studies while at the same time acknowledges the vital connection between theological concepts and sociological realities in the ancient world—see *Der erste Brief an die Korinther: Kaptiel 1–4* (Gütersloh: Gütersloh Verlagshaus Gerd Mohn, 1992), 32. The assumption that we can (or should) study the ancient world, especially its sociological and/or ideological makeup, without recourse to theological ideas or motifs reflects more the state of current historical research than the historical cultures being studied.

[42] Clarke, *Secular and Christian Leadership*, 92.

[43] See Marshall, who highlights the usual direction of esteem: "the inferior who, requiring the aid of a more powerful friend, either committed himself to his protection or received various benefits of services. In return, he was obliged to show gratitude, which consisted of rendering services and providing support in any way his patron required. The patron was morally bound to protect his client, provide for him, and render assistance to him as he had need" (*Enmity in Corinth: Social Conventions in Paul's Relations with the Corinthians* [Tübingen: J.C.B. Mohr (Paul Siebeck), 1987], 143).

[44] See Clarke, *Secular and Christian Leadership*, 93-94.

First, we can define party-loyalty in terms of patronage, where the esteemed leader is believed to have played a vital role in the establishment of the community. The respective groups in Corinth, therefore, elevate the names of Paul, Apollos, and Cephas due to assumptions concerning their role in the community's formation or identity.[45] Presumably mindful of the objection that Cephas most likely did not minister in Corinth, Clarke shows how the *reputation* of an influential leader was enough to justify claims of patronage. Thus, in this case, it would not be necessary for Cephas to have visited Corinth following Paul's departure; all that would be required is his reputation as an original apostle, and presumably his association with James, the leader of the Jerusalem church.

A second way to define party-loyalty is in terms of rhetorical eloquence.[46] Accordingly, the divisions in Corinth are the result of competing opinions on the rhetorical abilities of the named ministers.[47] However, in this case, the list of champions becomes limited to Paul and Apollos;[48] Cephas is not a contender under this

---

[45] For an argument supporting the possibility of Cephas ministering in Corinth, see C.K. Barrett, "Cephas and Corinth," in *Abraham unser Vater: Festschrift für Otto Michel* (eds. O. Betz, M. Hengel and P. Stuhlmacher; Leiden: Brill, 1963), 1-12.

[46] While the topic of rhetoric constitutes its own category of study, recent scholarship has shown an awareness of the fact that rhetorical displays are more appropriately understood when examined in their socio-historical context—see e.g. M.T. Finney, *Honour and Conflict in the Ancient World: 1 Corinthians in its Greco-Roman Social Setting* (London: Bloomsbury T&T Clark, 2012).

[47] Cf. B. Winter, *After Paul Left Corinth: The Influence of Secular Ethics and Social Change* (Grand Rapids: Eerdmans, 2001), 41-43; idem, "Philodemus and Paul on Rhetorical Delivery (ὑπόκρισις)," in *Philodemus and the New Testament World* (eds. J.T. Fitzgerald, D. Obbink and G.S. Holland; Leiden: Brill, 2004), 323-42.

[48] In spite of the repeated mention of Cephas in 3.22 (cf. 1.12), the explicit reference to Paul and Apollos in 3.1-5 and the double explanatory ἵνα-clauses in 4.6 strongly suggest that only the preaching abilities (or styles) of Paul and Apollos are at issue. Relying on the testimony of Acts 18.24, 1 Cor 4.6, and 2

scheme. This is the least developed of Clarke's options; instead he relies on and defers to the findings of Winter. However, a number of studies after Clarke explore the dimensions of this option.

Finally, for Clarke, we can define party-loyalty in terms of political factions, since "[m]uch of the language used by Paul with regard to the situation suggests a political background."[49] In this sense, the Corinthians are behaving like members of competing political parties, each rallying for the supremacy of their chosen leader.[50] Thus, and regardless of which of the three options we choose, since the problems in Corinth affect the social structures of the church, Paul's plea for unity in the church is *social* or *political* concord. Here, Paul exercises his authority as founding apostle in order to re-establish harmony within the community. However, Kim questions this approach since, for him, the social elite are the

---

Cor 10.10, Winter sees the Corinthians recognizing Paul's abilities in writing, even though they fail to impress in person, but favoring Apollos due to his strength as a debater (see Winter, *After Paul Left Corinth*, 41).

[49] Clarke, *Secular and Christian Leadership*, 94. Significant influence from Mitchell's work can be detected in this proposal.

[50] Clarke and others are quick to emphasize that similar to the political rallies of the day, these factions were characterized and even identified by the champion and not the ideas or teachings that the champion promotes (see Clarke, *Secular and Christian Leadership*, 94; cf. Welborn, "On the Discord in Corinth," 91). If we assume that Paul, Apollos, and Cephas ministered in Corinth, and if we further assume that each proclaimed the same gospel (in terms of essential content), the elevation of person over teaching would certainly account for the Corinthians failing to see the compatibility of content in apostolic teaching. This obviously holds true even if we assume the ministerial work of only Paul and Apollos. However, even if we accept the idea of factions identified by leaders rather than ideas/teaching, we should not overlook the perceived significance or influence of the teaching. In other words, we cannot fully separate the individual from the ideas they espouse, for both would have been under the scrutiny of the audience. Moreover, it would be the perceptions or interpretations of the audience that would spark acclaim for a chosen speaker, which would potentially lead to party formation.

ones advocating harmony; true harmony cannot exist where levels of status are maintained and those on higher levels continue to define the nature of harmony for those on lower levels.[51]

1.2.1.3.3. Edward Adams

While the work of Clarke sheds light on the context to which Paul writes, especially with regard to the nature of the problem(s) addressed, it seems to leave one basic question unanswered: why and/or how did this framework of thought make its way into the Corinthian community? More specifically: why and/or how is it that the Corinthians continued to operate in former ways of thinking post-belief in the gospel? The work of Adams provides a helpful explanation:[52] the Corinthians rely on a faulty view of (what Berger calls) "world-construction"[53] by which identity and life are defined, both individually and collectively. Moreover, the Corinthians have failed to distinguish between the "world" defined by the gospel and the "world" defined by their surrounding culture (i.e. weak boundaries),[54] and it is both this faulty view and this failure that create space for the issues in Corinth to develop.

Specifically, as Adams argues, "[t]he Corinthian 'aberrations' are largely failures in boundary maintenance. The Corinthians were insufficiently distinguishing themselves from the surrounding society in their social practices and attitudes. Virtually every

---

[51] Y.S. Kim, *Christ's Body at Corinth: The Politics of a Metaphor* (Minneapolis: Fortress, 2008), 39-49. Admittedly, Kim's work does not engage with treatments that promote a modified version of a unified body, one that embraces diversity and does so in a harmonious and Christ-like manner—see e.g. M. Volf, *Exclusion and Embrace: A Theological Exploration of Identity, Otherness, and Reconciliation* (Nashville: Abingdon Press, 1996), 48.

[52] Adams' approach is indebted to Clarke (see *Constructing the World*, 89).

[53] *Ibid.*, 3-4.

[54] Or, as Adams describes it: the "sociological distinction between 'church' and 'sect' " as developed primarily by Weber and Troeltsch (*ibid.*, 7-8).

Corinthian 'irregularity' stems from the social and cultural environment of the church."[55] Adams goes on to categorize and delineate the various "aberrations" as representative of the Corinthians conforming to either "social practices" or "cultural values" (or both).[56] In this case, the Corinthians' life and behavior resembled more the wisdom and ways of the world than the life defined by God's wisdom, and as a result they were failing to live the distinctive "in Christ" existence that is to follow the acceptance of God's wisdom as proclaimed in the gospel.

Paul's argument, therefore, seeks to correct these "aberrations," and thus solve the internal problems by exhorting the Corinthians to strengthen their boundaries so as to distinguish themselves clearly from the outside world.[57] Specifically, Adams sees Paul encouraging the Corinthians to (re-)translate existing definitions of life and behavior (i.e. "uncoding and recoding"[58]) so as to make appropriate sense of their new life "in Christ." Moreover, the Corinthians must recognize that in (re-)establishing appropriate boundaries via redefinition, they are not capable in themselves to maintain their distinctiveness from the world; for that they must rely on the Spirit as the means by which they can "resist the world's pull on their lives."[59] Given the competing frameworks of thought and the social consequences that follow, Paul's exhortation for unity—or "group solidarity"[60]—in this case is at once *conceptual* and *social* in nature.

While I have relied on much of Adams' contribution, my research differs in two related ways. First, Adams "attempts to relate Paul's socio-rhetorical usage [of κόσμος and κτίσις

---

[55] *Ibid.*, 87-88 (cf. 93).

[56] *Ibid.*, 88-92.

[57] *Ibid.*, 93, 97-99.

[58] *Ibid.*, 113.

[59] *Ibid.*, 117.

[60] *Ibid.*, 99.

language] to the sociological process of 'world-construction' in Pauline Christianity and to the question of the type of 'response to the world' we encounter in the Pauline letters."[61] My emphasis is not primarily on the language used or even how it is used, rather it is on the substance of Paul's teaching on the Spirit's role in accepting God's wisdom, as found in the gospel message, and applying it to life. Thus, I am not disputing the likely use of "world-constructing" language; I am simply emphasizing how Paul sees "world-construction" as possible. Second, while it is certainly an element of Adams' wider argument, the role of the Spirit receives minimal attention,[62] especially as it relates to community formation, believing existence, and conformity to God's wisdom in the cross. My study examines 1) why Paul emphasizes the role of the Spirit in the preaching, acceptance/believing, and living out the gospel, and 2) why this emphasis appears so early in the letter.

1.2.1.3.4. J. Brian Tucker

Relying on the efforts of Adams[63] yet differing in key ways, Tucker nuances the discussion by arguing that "some in Corinth were continuing to identify primarily with key aspects of their Roman social identity rather than their identity 'in Christ' and that this confusion over identities contributed to the problems within the community."[64] As he develops the case in chapter 6, and similar to the conclusions of other sociological readings, Tucker sees the Corinthians' confusion over identity and its disruptive consequences as a social problem and not a theological one.[65] For Tucker, the specific social problem that Paul confronts is an

---

[61] *Ibid.*, 3.

[62] *Ibid.*, 116-18.

[63] See esp. J.B. Tucker, *You Belong to Christ: Paul and the Formation of Social Identity in 1 Corinthians 1–4* (Eugene: Pickwick, 2010), 27, 102, 170.

[64] *Ibid.*, 2.

[65] *Ibid.*, 152-80.

improper hierarchy for defining social-identity. Specifically, not only is the Roman civic identity being elevated as the primary factor and the "in Christ" identity is being marginalized, but the former is also influencing how believers understand the gospel's effect on social or communal identity.[66] One of the consequences is "an over-reliance on the world's wisdom and power (i.e. Roman imperial ideology)," which then creates obstacles for the proper formation of the assembly of believers.[67] For Tucker this hierarchy simply needs to be reversed. Thus, the solution to the problem is the Corinthians' need to rely on the revelation of wisdom via God's Spirit, who is able to assist believers in knowing how to form appropriate social relationships.[68]

Two related aspects of Tucker's work should be noted, the first being a relatively minor point. First, while Tucker identifies the "Roman imperial ideology" as "Paul's primary interlocutor,"[69] it is not immediately clear what he means by that descriptor. All we know is that the Corinthians held to this ideology and it was contributing to their dilemma, as seen, according to Tucker, in 1 Cor 4.8-13; 6.1-11; 8.7-13; 10.27–11.1; and 14.1-25.[70] We must wait until chapter 4 (i.e. more than 100 pages in) before obtaining a glimpse of what Tucker means by "Roman imperial ideology".

This brings me to the second aspect, which deals with both Tucker's definition of Roman imperial ideology and his underlying assumptions about it. With regard to the former, Tucker defines the

---

[66] *Ibid.*, 80-81.

[67] *Ibid.*, 181; cf. 205-08.

[68] *Ibid.*, 193-205.

[69] *Ibid.*, 13; cf. 63.

[70] See *ibid.*, 119-21. In each of these instances, Tucker sees 1) the Corinthians as on good terms with the wider civic community of Corinth, and 2) Paul as viewing this contact as ideally positive but potentially damaging to the needed salient "in Christ" identity.

Roman imperial ideology as characterized by:[71] 1) a reliance on honor and shame to define social boundaries, 2) a patron-client system to govern authority and those under authority, and 3) the use of kinship language to encourage "a sense of belonging while providing a nurturing environment in which group norms could be encultured."[72] With regard to the underlying assumption, while it may be the case that these characteristics comprise Tucker's understanding of Roman imperial ideology, it is not clear how or why Roman imperial ideology is the only framework in which these characteristics must be understood. Morever, Tucker does not make it sufficiently clear why the "three status-oriented cultural phenomena (honor, patronage, and kinship) combined with the urban environment, Roman religion, and allegiance to the emperor to support the local construction of Roman social identity"[73] is the most likely candidate for Paul's critique.[74]

Where Tucker's research and mine intersect is in understanding the Spirit's role in establishing and reprioritizing the Corinthians' identity in Christ.[75] Tucker is right to recognize the mediatorial role of the Spirit in providing the Corinthians with God's wisdom and forming in them a new identity in Christ.[76] Moreover, as Tucker points out, "the work of the Spirit is that which allows for correct categorization of social realities within the community of faith."[77] This correct categorization involves assessments of those "outside" the body of believers—i.e. those not identified as "in Christ"—and those already "within" the body—i.e. those who are "in Christ." Once again, for Tucker, the issue is that the Corinthians have over-

---

[71] See *ibid.*, 105-17.

[72] *Ibid.*, 113.

[73] *Ibid.*, 116.

[74] Cf. *ibid.*, 3, 13.

[75] See *ibid.*, 194-209.

[76] See *ibid.*, 194-96.

[77] *Ibid.*, 198; cf. 202-03.

identified with Roman imperial ideology, which is characteristic of those "outside" the body, instead of allowing the Spirit to filter that ideology through the mind of Christ. This becomes a part of the larger reprioritization process, or the reversal of social hierarchy.

However, while I agree with Tucker's basic conclusion that the reprioritization "creates an alternative community with a distinct ethos,"[78] I see that distinction not in terms of degree but of kind: Tucker argues for an inversion and integration of identity-forming systems of thought, whereas I argue for the replacement of the old (i.e. wisdom of the world) for the new (i.e. God's wisdom).[79]

1.2.2. Specific Contributions Related to this Study

All of the studies noted above presuppose a literary or rhetorical relationship between Paul's critique of divisions in chapters 1–4 and the discussion of other matters in chapters 5–15. Thus, scholars tend to see the topics found in 1 Cor 1–4 as indicating something about the framework of thought held by the Corinthians that Paul opposes in the rest of the letter. In the majority of cases the leading themes recognized include the cross, Spirit, wisdom, and/or discernment, although there are differences in nuance and emphasis. While these themes are not unfamiliar to the Pauline corpus, their presence in 1 Corinthians (especially chapters 1–4) is worthy of the attention they have received. The following survey will be divided into two uneven parts: the first deals with treatments related to the Pauline corpus, and the second focuses on those related to 1 Corinthians in particular.

---

[78] *Ibid.*, 124.

[79] Thus, on this point I am in agreement with Adams. On the assumption that "the influence of [the Corinthians'] Hellenistic environment remains the dominant force behind the beliefs and actions criticized by Paul" (*Constructing the World*, 97), Adams sees Paul calling for clear lines of demarcation, while Tucker seems to allow for more fluidity (see *You Belong to Christ*, 170-71 n.73, where Tucker sees Adams as being too rigid in his conclusions).

1.2.2.1. Themes in the Pauline Corpus

With regard to Paul's writings,[80] some scholars have explored the significance of the cross for Paul and his preaching throughout the Greco-Roman world.[81] Moreover, there is a renewed interest in examining the importance of the Spirit's role for Paul and how that role shapes our understanding of both his theology and the identity and life of the believing community.[82] To a slightly lesser extent, though certainly not less valuable, a handful of monographs have analyzed the notion of (divine) wisdom within the Pauline corpus, though this is often linked with Paul's view of the (Jewish) Law,[83] while others have incorporated the categories of knowledge and

---

[80] Since the focus of this study is limited to 1 Corinthians, my remarks will only briefly mention the contributions related to the Pauline corpus as a whole.

[81] E.g. C.B. Cousar, *The Theology of the Cross: The Death of Jesus in the Letters of Paul* (Minneapolis: Fortress, 1990); P.T. O'Brien, *Gospel and Mission in the Writings of Paul: An Exegetical and Theological Analysis* (Grand Rapids: Baker, 1995); B.H. McLean, *Cursed Christ: Mediterranean Expulsion Rituals and Pauline Soteriology* (Sheffield: Sheffield Academic Press, 1996).

[82] See e.g. H. Gunkel, *Influence of the Holy Spirit: The Popular View of the Apostolic Age and the Teaching of the Apostle Paul* (trans. R.A. Harrisville and P.A. Quanbeck II; Philadelphia: Fortress, 1979); G.D. Fee, *God's Empowering Presence: The Holy Spirit in the Letters of Paul* (Peabody: Hendrickson, 1994); idem, *Paul, the Spirit, and the People of God* (Grand Rapids: Baker Academic, 1996); C.F.D. Moule, *The Holy Spirit* (London: Mowbrays, 1978); F. Philip, *The Origins of Pauline Pneumatology: The Eschatological Bestowal of the Spirit upon Gentiles in Judaism and in the Early Developments of Paul's Theology* (Tübingen: Mohr Siebeck, 2005); J.W. Yates, *The Spirit and Creation in Paul* (Tübingen: Mohr Siebeck, 2008). Cf. also D. Coffey, *"Did You Receive the Spirit When You Believed?": Some Basic Questions for Pneumatology* (Milwaukee: Marguette University Press, 2005).

[83] E.J. Schnabel, *Law and Wisdom from Ben Sira to Paul* (Tübingen: Mohr Siebeck, 1985); C.M. Pate, *The Reverse of the Curse: Paul, Wisdom and the Law* (Tübingen: Mohr Siebeck, 2000); B.S. Rosner, *Paul and the Law: Keeping the Commandments of God* (Downers Grove: InterVarsity, 2013).

prophecy in their treatments of Paul's views of wisdom.[84] This inclusion of ideas invited further discussions on the topic of discernment in Pauline thought and its role in or relationship to the believing community, particularly the question of ethics.[85]

1.2.2.2. Themes in 1 Corinthians

With regard to discussions on Paul's first (canonical) letter to the Corinthians, the situation is similar to scholarly works on the Pauline corpus. To being with, the near parallel studies of Litfin[86] and Bullmore,[87] and the distinctive studies of Pickett[88] and Brown[89] all contribute to our understanding of Paul's preaching of the cross. The works of Litfin and Bullmore stress the rhetorical aspects of Paul's argument as they relate to the Corinthians' assessment of his preaching ministry,[90] while the works of Pickett and Brown emphasize the role of the cross as a standard against which the Corinthians are to understand life.[91]

---

[84] P.W. Gooch, *Partial Knowledge: Philosophical Studies in Paul* (Notre Dame: University of Notre Dame Press, 1987); I.W. Scott, *Implicit Epistemology in the Letters of Paul* (Tübingen: Mohr Siebeck, 2006).

[85] G. Therrien, *Le discernement dans les écrits pauliniens* (Paris: J. Gabalda, 1973); J.M. Gustafson, *Moral Discernment in the Christian Life: Essays in Theological Ethics* (Louisville: Westminster John Knox, 2007); A. Munzinger, *Discerning the Spirits: Theological and Ethical Hermeneutics in Paul* (Cambridge: Cambridge University Press, 2007).

[86] Litfin, *Theology of Proclamation*.

[87] M.A. Bullmore, *St Paul's Theology of Rhetorical Style: An Examination of 1 Corinthians 2.1-5 in Light of First Century Greco-Roman Rhetorical Culture* (San Francisco: International Scholars Publications, 1995).

[88] Pickett, *Cross in Corinth*.

[89] A.R. Brown, *The Cross and Human Transformation: Paul's Apocalyptic Word in 1 Corinthians* (Minneapolis: Fortress, 1995).

[90] An obvious difference between the two is the focus: Bullmore's treatment deals with only 1 Cor 2.1-5, while Litfin considers the whole of 1 Cor 1–4.

[91] The differences between Pickett and Brown are primarily methodological. Pickett approaches the subject from a socio-scientific perspective, while Brown

On the role of the Spirit both in Paul's thinking and in the Corinthian church, the works of Pearson,[92] Winter,[93] Martin,[94] Brodeur,[95] and Tibbs[96] can be fruitfully consulted, although the latter three are confined to later portions of the letter.[97]

In terms of understanding wisdom in 1 Corinthians, the studies of Wilckens,[98] Williams,[99] and Inkelaar[100] make valuable and distinctive contributions. While Wilckens seeks to understand Paul's wisdom-folly contrast against the gnostic background of nascent Christianity and Paul's application of the contrast to the

---

examines things through a rhetorical and theological lens. Another notable difference is the material covered: Pickett selects key passages from both Corinthian letters (i.e. 1 Cor 1–4; 5–15; 2 Cor 4.7–5.19; 10–13), while Brown's treatment is confined to 1 Cor 1.9–2.5.

[92] Pearson, *Pneumatikos-Psychikos*.

[93] M. Winter, *Pneumatiker und Psychiker in Korinth: zum religions-geschichtlichen Hintergrund von 1 Kor 2,6–3,4* (Marburg: N.G. Elwert, 1975).

[94] R.P. Martin, *Spirit and Congregation: Studies in 1 Corinthians 12–15* (Grand Rapids: Eerdmans, 1984).

[95] S. Brodeur, *Holy Spirit's Agency in the Resurrection of the Dead: An Exegetical-Theological Study of 1 Corinthians 15,44b-49 and Romans 8,9-13* (Rome: Editrice Pontifica Universita Gregoriana, 1996).

[96] C. Tibbs, *The Religious Experience of the Pneuma: Communication with the Spirit World in 1 Corinthians 12 and 14* (Tübingen: Mohr Siebeck, 2007).

[97] Most contributions on the popular level reflect the tendency of focusing on the so-called "spiritual gifts" in 1 Cor 12–14 when dealing with the Spirit in the letter—see e.g. D.A. Carson, *Showing the Spirit: A Theological Exposition of 1 Corinthians 12–14* (Grand Rapids: Baker Book House, 1987); R.L. Thomas, *Understanding Spiritual Gifts: A Verse by Verse Study of 1 Cor 12–14* (Grand Rapids: Kregel, 1999). Cf. M.F. Unger, *The Baptism and Gifts of the Holy Spirit* (Chicago: Moody Bible Institute, 1974).

[98] Wilckens, *Weisheit und Torheit*.

[99] H.H.D. Williams, *The Wisdom of the Wise: The Presence and Function of Scripture in 1 Cor 1.18–3.23* (Leiden: Brill, 2001).

[100] H.-J. Inkelaar, *Conflict Over Wisdom: The Theme of 1 Corinthians 1–4 Rooted in Scripture* (Leuven: Peeters, 2011).

message of the cross,[101] both Williams and Inkelaar examine Paul's use of Scripture as a guide for how he advocates divine wisdom for the Corinthians. And finally, the topic of discernment in the letter has received due attention, as seen in the works of McConnell[102] and Pascuzzi,[103] although both of these works focus on particular chapters of 1 Corinthians—i.e. Pascuzzi addresses primarily chapter 5, while McConnell deals with chapter 7.

There is a notable difference between these works on 1 Corinthians and those on the Pauline corpus mentioned above: the works on 1 Corinthians operate with an explicit interest in how the themes of cross, Spirit, wisdom, and discernment might overlap or interrelate. This is not to suggest that the works on the Pauline corpus do not interact with themes outside of their immediate focus. I am simply noting that such an interaction is not the focus of those particular studies. However, there are a few monographs where an examination of the interaction of multiple themes is the intent. For example, both Pogoloff[104] and Kammler,[105] albeit in distinctive ways, seek to understand the role of wisdom in Paul's preaching of the cross; Davis attempts to locate the nature of divine wisdom and the role of the Spirit as the facilitator in

---

[101] In particular, Wilckens reads Paul's wisdom language in the light of the Gnostic Sophia myth, which he sees as traditionally older than the Valentinian form, thus enabling him to make it pre-Pauline.

[102] D.W.M. McConnell, *Paul as Teacher of Discernment: The Ethical Paradigm of 1 Corinthians 7* (New York: General Theological Seminary, 1983).

[103] M.A. Pascuzzi, *Ethics, Ecclesiology and Church Discipline: A Rhetorical Analysis of 1 Corinthians 5* (Rome: Editrice Pontificia Universita Gregoriana, 1997).

[104] S.M. Pogoloff, *Logos and Sophia: The Rhetorical Situation of 1 Corinthians* (Atlanta: Scholars Press, 1992).

[105] H.–C. Kammler, *Kreuz und Weisheit: Eine exegetische Untersuchung zu 1 Kor 1,10–3,4* (Tübingen: Mohr Siebeck, 2003). Cf. also H. Bouter, *Christ the Wisdom of God: Reflections on 1 Corinthians 2* (London: Chapter Two, 1998).

understanding God's work in Christ;[106] and, though not examining 1 Corinthians exclusively, Munzinger draws attention to the necessary relationship between the Spirit and the exercise of right discernment, especially in ethical matters.[107] While each of these works has its merits, none explicitly considers the further overlaps with the other themes in Paul's argument, or the particular and necessary role the Spirit plays in relation to those other themes.

Two recent works, however, do explicitly treat the overlap or interrelationship of more than two themes, and these works deserve special mention as they relate to the aims of my own research.

1.2.2.2.1. Jeffrey Lamp

The work of Lamp[108] deals exclusively with Paul's argument in 1 Cor 1.18–4.21.[109] Lamp attempts first to uncover the specific emphasis on wisdom (σοφία) as held by Paul—rather than the Corinthians—and thus locate the cause for Paul's emphasis on Christ as God's wisdom.[110] Related to this, Lamp seeks to ascertain the particular conceptual or theological background that would allow Paul to make the Christ-wisdom connection.[111] Here Lamp argues for Jewish wisdom or "sapiential" traditions as Paul's source,[112] especially the notions of personified wisdom,[113] which

---

[106] Davis, *Wisdom and Spirit*. Davis' thesis is questionable on several points, not least of which is his claim that the Corinthians were boasting of their strict allegiance to Torah. Also, minimal attention is given to the role of the Spirit in Paul's letter. In fact, despite the title, the Spirit is not a primary concern for Davis' argument.

[107] Munzinger, *Discerning the Spirits*.

[108] J.S. Lamp, *First Corinthians 1–4 in Light of Jewish Wisdom Traditions: Christ, Wisdom and Spirituality* (Lewiston: E. Mellen, 2000).

[109] This excludes Lamp's appendix on 1 Cor 8.6 (see *ibid.*, 201-07).

[110] *Ibid.*, 1-2.

[111] *Ibid.*, 3.

[112] *Ibid.*, 7-51.

[113] *Ibid.*, 52-79.

become a point of contrast when Paul critiques the (assumed) wisdom of the Corinthians.[114]

With regard to the type of wisdom adhered to by the Corinthians, Lamp sees it as the traditions associated with Greco-Roman rhetoric.[115] Accordingly, the Corinthians would define true wisdom as made manifest in persuasive, eloquent speech, whereas for Paul true wisdom is personified in the person of Jesus and it is only by the Spirit that believers can comprehend and accept that truth.[116] While Lamp is to be commended for stressing the links between cross, Spirit, and wisdom, he does not emphasize the specific interrelationship of those topics. Moreover, Lamp's analysis does not address the Spirit's role in discernment.

1.2.2.2.2. John Lewis

The work of Lewis[117] is a theological exegesis of what he calls Paul's "theo-ethical reasoning."[118] While this work covers two Pauline letters (1 Corinthians and Galatians), which would seem to make my analysis of it here out of place, it is nevertheless pertinent, given its emphasis on the interrelationship of the key themes under discussion. One of the three scholarly tendencies that Lewis seeks to correct is the denial of Paul's ability to engage with theological and ethical dilemmas in a constructive way.[119] Relying

---

[114] *Ibid.*, 91-115.

[115] *Ibid.*, 103-04.

[116] *Ibid.*, 155-56, 177-78.

[117] J.G. Lewis, *Looking for Life: The Role of "Theo-Ethical Reasoning" in Paul's Religion* (London: T&T Clark International, 2007).

[118] See *ibid.*, 34.

[119] *Ibid.*, 1; cf. 157. The three specific tendencies: "Interpreters regularly: (1) distinguish Paul's theology from his ethics; (2) emphasize his oral preaching as the sole or primary vehicle for gospel proclamation and divine revelation; and (3) deny that Paul engages in reasoned, ethical reflections" (*ibid.*, 1).

on and developing the work of Gorman, [120] Lewis seeks to demonstrate how the cross of Christ becomes the criterion by which the Corinthians form right theo-ethical decisions—i.e. "the community practice of spiritual discernment."[121] Lewis emphasizes this point on the basis of the two problems he sees at work in Corinth: 1) inappropriate influences from worldly wisdom, and 2) the Corintians' failure to engage in spiritual discernment.[122]

What is important to note here is that Lewis recognizes these problems as central to Paul's argument in 1 Cor 1–4 and that the effect of Paul's response extends to support what he says in the rest of the letter. Thus, the theo-ethical paradigm (a concept that becomes interchangeable with "cruciformity") used in the opening applies throughout the letter. However, the surprising feature of Lewis' argument is the minimal attention given to the role of the Spirit, especially in the early portion of Paul's argument to the Corinthians.[123] This is not to suggest that Lewis marginalizes the Spirit; he does say: "As believers practice spiritual discernment by engaging in theo-ethical reasoning, they are led by the Spirit to identify the connections between experiences of new life and actions that conform to Christ's cruciform pattern."[124] However, beyond this, the Spirit's role is almost tangential to Lewis' analysis of Paul's theo-ethical argument.[125]

---

[120] Cf. *ibid.*, 15-18.

[121] *Ibid.*, 36.

[122] *Ibid.*, 37.

[123] For an elaboration on what Lewis merely suggests, see V. Rabens, *The Holy Spirit and Ethics in Paul: Transformation and Empowering for Religious-Ethical Life* (Tübingen: Mohr Siebeck, 2010), esp. 171-242.

[124] Lewis, *Looking for Life*, 17; cf. 8, 10, 15, 26.

[125] See *ibid.*, 41, 43, 59, 62-63, 65.

1.3. Specific Focus of this Study

While the "Controlling Questions" listed above provide the framework for my research, and in the light of the survey of scholarship, there is a foundational question upon which they are built: when writing to the Corinthians, 1) does Paul confront a myriad of problems, or 2) is he refuting a particular framework of thought and then uses the manifold problems as illustrations of that framework? I will argue that the second option as more likely.

1.3.1. The Argument

In general, I contend that Paul's argument indicates the emergence of a faulty notion of (divine) wisdom and spirituality in Corinth following his apostolic sojourn, and that this faulty notion operates in accordance with the standards of human wisdom. This faulty notion has two basic consequences. First, Paul's apostolic mission and message came under scrutiny, and this scrutiny created an atmosphere of skepticism towards Paul, his message, and the manner in which he presented it. Second, the Corinthians' present sense of (spiritual) identity is congruent not with God's wisdom as displayed in the cross and revealed by the Spirit, but with human wisdom as displayed in pursuits of status and fueled by a spirit of self-interest.

To expose and combat this general problem, Paul appeals first of all to the Corinthians' original experience when they first heard and believed the gospel. The function of this appeal is to remind them of the manner of Paul's preaching, his proclamation of wisdom in the cross, their reception of and belief in that proclamation, and the subsequent reception of their new life "in Christ." Specifically, and this brings me to the thesis of this study, Paul's appeal emphasizes the necessary role of the Spirit in all aspects of that past experience. Therefore, in this study I argue that 1 Cor 2.1–3.4 functions as a pneumatological teaching, where Paul articulates his understanding of the Spirit's necessary role in the proclamation of the cross, the mediation of divine wisdom, and the exercise of communal discernment, and that Paul uses this teaching to correct the Corinthians' present faulty notions of (divine) wisdom and spirituality.

1.3.2. The Chosen Method(s)

In their pursuit to understand the occasion for and content of Paul's letter, scholars have historically employed a number of different methodologies. As intimated already, older scholarship (though not exclusively) tended to favor the history-of-religions approach when attempting to explain key features of Paul's theology. [126] More recently, additional methods such as social-scientific interpretations[127] and rhetorical criticism[128] have yielded insightful results concerning the norms and practices of ancient Corinth, although the latter tends to be more text-centered. Recent modifications have emerged where the social-scientific studies are blended with rhetorical criticism, thus producing a socio-rhetorical

---

[126] See e.g. Wilckens, *Weisheit und Torheit*; Schmithals, *Gnosticism in Corinth*; Pearson, *Pneumatikos-Psychikos*; Winter, *Pneumatiker und Psychiker in Korinth*.

[127] See e.g. Theissen, *Social Setting*; D.G. Horrell, *The Social Ethos of the Corinthian Correspondence: Interests and Ideology from 1 Corinthians to 1 Clement* (Edinburgh: T&T Clark, 1996); Pickett, *Cross in Corinth*; Clarke, *Secular and Christian Leadership*; Tucker, *You Belong to Christ*.

[128] See e.g. M. Bünker, *Briefformular und rhetorische Disposition im 1 Korintherbrief* (Tübingen: Vandenhoeck & Ruprecht, 1983); Mitchell, *Rhetoric of Reconciliation*; Pogoloff, *Logos and Sophia*; Litfin, *Theology of Proclamation*; Bullmore, *Theology of Rhetorical Style*; Collins, *First Corinthians*; Lamp, *First Corinthians*; Keener, *1–2 Corinthians*; cf. also A.C. Thiselton, *The First Epistle to the Corinthians: A Commentary on the Greek Text* (Grand Rapids: Eerdmans, 2000).

analysis,[129] which at least seeks to alleviate the shortcomings of the text-only tendencies in rhetorical criticism.

With regard to the methodology adopted for this study, my priority is to understand Paul's argument as articulated in his letter to the Corinthians,[130] focusing on the interrelationship of cross, Spirit, wisdom, and communal discernment in 1 Cor 2.1–3.4, and specifically the Spirit's essential role in that relationship. Given the emphasis on these themes in 1 Cor 2.1–3.4 in particular and their varying emphasis throughout the letter in general, and given that such themes are historically, rhetorically, theologically, and socially significant for understanding the occasion for and content of Paul's argument, I conduct my exegesis not in accordance with one particular methodology but with an awareness of the benefits that the recent methods provide. As Baird notes: "the conflicts reflected in 1 Corinthians have arisen out of a variety of situations," thus any "analysis of [the] conflict in 1 Corinthians should not be restricted to a single method."[131] Or as Schnelle more recently stated: "The Corinthian church was embroiled in several conflicts springing up from different causes and therefore must be

---

[129] See e.g. D.A. Ackerman, *Lo, I Tell You a Mystery: Cross, Resurrection, and Paraenesis in the Rhetoric of 1 Corinthians* (Eugene: Pickwick Publications, 2006); Adams, *Constructing the World*. Witherington's entire series of commentaries purports to be socio-rhetorical analysis. However, Aune has recently criticized Witherington for "hijack[ing] the term 'socio-rhetorical' for a project that has very little in common with what Robbins describes as 'socio-rhetorical commentary' " ("Introduction," in *The Blackwell Companion to the New Testament* [ed. D.E. Aune; Chichester: Wiley-Blackwell, 2010], 4).

[130] While addressing text-critical questions when they arise, I am following the text of Paul's letter as established in NA[27].

[131] W. Baird, "'One Against the Other': Intra-Church Conflict in 1 Corinthians," in *The Conversation Continues: Studies in Paul and John. In Honor of J. Louis Martyn* (eds. R.T. Fortna and B.R. Geventa; Nashville: Abingdon, 1990), 130-31.

understood methodologically on different planes (sociological, theological, cultural, and the history of religions)."[132]

Moreover, while my approach is primarily exegetical, my concerns in and for this study are also admittedly theological. The reason for this is quite simple: as previous scholarship has demonstrated (cf. Schnelle's observation), Paul confronts religious, social, and rhetorical issues in Corinth. I do not dispute the plausibility that such issues characterized the Corinthian situation to which Paul writes and no doubt contributed to their (internal) struggles in some form. However, my research has led me to two related conclusions. First, Paul's response to the Corinthians appears to be only secondarily related to the religious, social, and rhetorical issues. Second, while scholars may classify many if not all of these problems as being un-theological in nature,[133] Paul's response to these un-theological problems is decidedly theological, specifically the pneumatological teaching found in 1 Cor 2.1–3.4. Therefore, I seek to explain Paul's theological response first before applying it to his assessment of the Corinthian situation.

1.3.3. Limits of the Passage and Rhetorical Placement

Before proceeding, one lingering question must be addressed: why set the limits of the passage to 1 Cor 2.1–3.4, a decision that seems to go against the usual or accepted rhetorical unit(s) for the argument of 1 Cor 1–4? While it is true that such a proposal is unusual or even inconsistent with most readings of 1 Corinthians, it is not unprecedented.[134] In fact, in the late 1970s Hargreaves divided the passage along these same lines, labeling the argument

---

[132] U. Schnelle, *Apostle Paul: His Life and Theology* (trans. M.E. Boring; Grand Rapids: Baker Academic, 2005), 196 n.14.

[133] See those mentioned in n.40 above; cf. also (and almost ironically, given his title) Litfin, *Theology of Proclamation*, 234, 252, 254 (although cf. 17, 193).

[134] In a single passing comment, Fee refers to 2.1–3.4 (see *First Epistle*, 49) but does not identify it as a defined rhetorical unit.

as Paul's explanation of "true wisdom." [135] More recently, Schwager, Fitzmyer, and Mitchell each identified 1 Cor 2.1–3.4 as a distinct unit,[136] although none provides an explicit explanation why. Before offering my reasons for setting the limits to 1 Cor 2.1–3.4, it is important to rehearse scholarly opinions on the wider argument of 1 Cor 1–4 and how that argument is usually divided rhetorically.

Given that 1 Cor 1–4 represents a stand-alone logical unit,[137] some scholars argue that these chapters were intended to circulate as an independent letter,[138] written for a purpose divorced from the rest of the letter.[139] The contents of these chapters address concerns revealed to Paul by Chloe's people, specifically divisions within the community of believers and the effects of such divisions.[140] Advocates of this view further claim that additional reports were delivered to Paul, either near or at the completion of 1 Cor 1–4. In particular, de Boer sees these new reports coming to Paul from two distinct sources: 1) Stephanas, Fortunatus, and Achaicus, relaying

---

[135] See J. Hargreaves, *A Guide to 1 Corinthians* (London: SPCK, 1978), 22.

[136] See R. Schwager, *Must There Be Scapegoats?: Violence and Redemption in the Bible* (trans. M.L. Assad; New York: Crossroads Publishing, 2000), 145; Fitzmyer, *First Corinthians*, 168; M.M. Mitchell, *Paul, the Corinthians and the Birth of Christian Hermeneutics* (Cambridge: Cambridge University Press, 2010), 46.

[137] *Contra* Conzelmann, who asserts: "This part of the letter is not a unity, neither in style nor in content" (*1 Corinthians*, 30).

[138] Fitzgerald sees these chapters as "primarily a letter of admonition" (*Cracks in an Earthen Vessel: An Examination of the Catalogues of Hardships in the Corinthian Correspondence* [Atlanta: Scholars Press, 1988], 117).

[139] de Boer, "1 Corinthians," 229-45. See also L.G. Rylands, *Critical Analysis of the Four Chief Pauline Epistles: Romans, First and Second Corinthians, and Galatians* (London: Watts & Co., 1929), 115-16; Hurd, *Origin of 1 Corinthians*, 43-47, 69-71, 86-89, 131-42.

[140] This is predicated on the assumption that divisions do in fact exist within the church at Corinth.

orally the concerns about immoral behavior, and 2) a non-extant letter from the community raising specific questions about church practices.[141] Accordingly, while chapters 1–4 are said to speak to the issues raised by Chloe's people, chapters 5–6 and 7–16 are taken to be Paul's twofold response to these subsequent reports.[142] Therefore, the structure of the whole letter can be ordered or divided according to the topics discussed in 1–4, 5–6, and 7–16.

Alternatively, some critics read the entire letter as a compositional disunity, given its disjointed structure,[143] or they maintain that the topics discussed are merely treated in an *ad hoc* manner.[144] However, due in large part to Mitchell's work,[145] the majority of scholars now interpret 1 Corinthians as a multi-layered argument held together by a singular aim: unity within the body of believers.[146] The content of 1 Cor 1–4 is thus understood to be a

---

[141] Cf. de Boer "1 Corinthians," 232-34, 240.

[142] This line of argument (i.e. new information emerging in the midst of Paul composing the initial letter occasions an additional letter) is not without precedent; it appears in discussions on the unity of 2 Corinthians and for similar reasons—see e.g. H.D. Betz, *II Corinthians 8 and 9: A Commentary on Two Administrative Letters of the Apostle Paul* (ed. G.W. MacRae; Philadelphia: Fortress, 1985), 90-91, 124-44; R. Bultmann, *The Second Letter to the Corinthians* (trans. R.A. Harrisville: Minneapolis: Augsburg, 1985), 18; M.J. Harris, *The Second Epistle to the Corinthians: A Commentary on the Greek Text* (Grand Rapids: Eerdmans, 2005), 10.

[143] Cf. Weiss, *Der erste Korintherbrief*, xxxix-xliii; W. Schenk, "Der Korintherbrief als Briefsammlung," *ZNW* 60 (1969): 219-43; Héring, *First Epistle*, xiii-xiv.

[144] Fee, *First Epistle*, 2; G.S. Selby, "Paul, the Seer: The Rhetorical Persona in 1 Corinthians 2.1-16," in *The Rhetorical Analysis of Scripture: Essays for the 1997 London Conference* (eds. S.E. Porter and T.H. Olbricht; Sheffield: Sheffield Academic Press, 1997), 356-57.

[145] Mitchell, *Rhetoric of Reconciliation*.

[146] *Ibid.*, 1, 65-68; Collins, *First Corinthians*, xii, 6, 10; V.P. Furnish, *Theology of the First Letter to the Corinthians* (Cambridge: Cambridge University Press, 1999), 12, 15-18; cf. M.J. Gorman, *Apostle of the Crucified*

crucial layer of Paul's argument. In the light of the compositional unity of the letter, whether original or by redaction, [147] most scholars recognize 1 Cor 1–4 to be a sustained argument in its own right but one whose conclusions shape how the rest of the letter is to be read and understood.[148] However, Fee's observation should be noted: "because [the issue of divisions] is the first item to which Paul speaks, most people tend to read the rest of the letter in light of chaps. 1–4; that is, behind every issue (e.g. 7:1-16 or 8:1–11.1) they see the Corinthians divided into parties."[149] Thus, a key concern for me will not be proving the existence and effects or positions of divisions within the community. Instead, I am

---

Lord: A Theological Introduction to Paul and His Letters (Grand Rapids: Eerdmans, 2004), 236-38. However, Kim opposes the idea that unity represents the controlling theme or motivation for Paul's argument (see *Christ's Body in Corinth*, 39-49).

[147] For theories of redaction, see e.g. Héring, *First Epistle*, xiii-xiv; Schenk, "Der Korintherbrief," 219-43; cf. also Schmithals, "Die Korintherbriefe als Briefsammlung," *ZNW* 64 (1973): 263-88.

[148] F. Godet, *Commentary on St Paul's First Epistle to the Corinthians* (vol. 1; trans. A. Cusin; Edinburgh: T&T Clark, 1889), 28-30; Dahl, "Paul and the Church," 317; J.S. Ruef, *Paul's First Letter to Corinth* (Harmondsworth: Penguin Book, 1971), 7; Davis, *Wisdom and Spirit*, 144-48; B. Fiore, "'Covert Allusion' in 1 Corinthians 1–4," *CBQ* 47.1 (1985): 86-87; C.H. Talbert, *Reading Corinthians: A New Commentary for Preachers* (London: SPCK, 1987), 3; Mitchell, *Rhetoric of Reconciliation*, 66-68; R.A. Horsley, *1 Corinthians* (Nashville: Abingdon, 1998), 32, 44; Lamp, *First Corinthians*, 135; J.M.G. Barclay, "1 Corinthians," in *The Oxford Bible Commentary* (eds. J. Barton and J. Muddiman; Oxford: Oxford University Press, 2001), 1108, 1110-11; Keener, *1–2 Corinthians*, 8-11; Fitzmyer, *First Corinthians*, 48-53; cf. Litfin, *Theology of Proclamation*, 147-59; Collins, *First Corinthians*, 27-29; Ciampa-Rosner, "Structure and Argument," 213-14.

[149] Fee, *First Epistle*, 47; *contra* Polhill who argues: "The first four chapters of 1 Corinthians form an appropriate introduction to the letter. The problems of factionalism treated in them are at the center of the congregational difficulties which surface in the rest of the epistle" ("The Wisdom of God," 325).

concerned with the reasons why Paul thinks divisions exist at all and how he responds to those reasons.

As noted above, when examining 1 Cor 1–4 either as a whole or in part, scholars employ various types of analyses in order to make sense of the content and structure of these four chapters. Wuellner, relying upon genre criticism, limits his treatment to 1 Cor 1–3 and reads the argument as a haggadic homily.[150] For Wuellner, a double Old Testament quotation, one in 1.19 and the other in 3.19-20, frames the homily with the core of the homily dealing with "divine judgment on human wisdom."[151] Thus, and incorporating examples from Israel's past, the homily warns the Corinthians about the dangers and consequences of elevating and praising human wisdom over the ways of God.

Branick,[152] using source and redaction criticism, also limits his treatment to 1 Cor 1–3 yet characterizes the unit as a "homiletic midrash."[153] For him, the passage addresses the distinct topics of "the true wisdom of the Spirit" and "the troubles in the church of Corinth."[154] Moreover, for Branick, the topic of wisdom is handled in the homilies of 1.18-31; 2.6-16; and 3.18-23 while the topic of church conflict is dealt with in the homilies of 1.17; 2.1-5; and 3.1-4.[155] According to Branick, the two sets of homilies were intended to be sent independently but were joined only after Paul received the troubling news from Corinth.

---

[150] W. Wuellner, "Haggadic Homily Genre in 1 Corinthians 1–3," *JBL* 89.2 (1970): 199-204.

[151] *Ibid.*, 201.

[152] See V.P. Branick, "Source and Redaction Analysis of 1 Corinthians 1–3," *JBL* 101.2 (1982): 251-69.

[153] *Ibid.*, 258.

[154] *Ibid.*, 252

[155] *Ibid.*, 264. Branick mislabels 3.18-23 as "3:18-33."

Dahl, employing what could be described as an early form of modern rhetorical criticism,[156] reads the whole argument of 1 Cor 1.10–4.21 as an ἀπολογία used by Paul to validate his ministry in Corinth.[157] The core of this defense is framed by the double use of παρακαλῶ in 1.10 and 4.16, which suggests a hopeful response rather than an authoritative expectation, although authoritative action will be taken if necessary.[158] For Dahl, the core of 1.11-4.15 seeks to re-establish Paul's credibility as an apostle and the way in which this apostolic role functioned during his time in Corinth. Inherent to this ἀπολογία are various corrections to false impressions of Paul's message and apostolic role.[159] These corrective statements assist Dahl in isolating the various stages of

---

[156] The hesitancy here stems from the fact that rhetorical criticism, as applied to biblical studies in a programmatic way, is generally held to begin with Muilenburg who suggested such an approach in 1968/1969. Later scholars, especially Kennedy, modified this approach in light of the theories proposed by Perelman and Olbrechts-Tyteca.

[157] Dahl, "Paul and the Church," 313-35; *contra* Fitzgerald, *Cracks in an Earthen Vessel*, 128 n.28. Relying heavily upon Dahl's analysis, Chance extends the ἀπολογία so that it covers 1 Cor 1–6, with chapters 5–6 functioning as a *paraenesis*—see J.B. Chance, "Paul's Apology to the Corinthians," *PRSt* 9.2 (1982): 145-55 (esp. 154-55).

[158] Dahl, "Paul and the Church," 319. See also M.T. Finney, "Honor, Rhetoric and Factionalism in the Ancient World: 1 Corinthians 1–4 in Its Social Context," *BTB* 40.1 (2010): 29. For an incisive critique of how scholars deal with the issue of Paul's authority in 1 Corinthians, see A. Long, *Paul and Human Rights: A Dialogue with the Father of the Corinthian Community* (Sheffield: Sheffield Phoenix Press, 2009), 56-147.

[159] When viewed in conjunction with the rest of the letter, the ἀπολογία is crucial for Paul's ability to respond to the issues raised. Thus, according to Dahl, the argument of 1 Cor 1–4 "has a preparatory function...[in that] before Paul could answer the questions raised, he had to overcome both false appraisals and false objections, and to re-establish his apostolic authority as the founder and spiritual leader of the whole church at Corinth" (Dahl, "Paul and the Church," 326, 329; cf. also Talbert, *Reading Corinthians*, 9-11).

the argument, which results in the following divisions: 1.10-13; 1.17–3.2; 3.5–4.6; and 4.14-21.[160] Litfin, employing the modified form of rhetorical criticism,[161] examines the letter's structure as well as Paul's style and form of public speaking as found in 1 Cor 1–4.[162] While his treatment compares Paul specifically with the Sophistic orators from the Greco-Roman world,[163] Litfin's work essentially substantiates Dahl's apologetic reading of the text and for similar reasons.[164]

When taken together, the views of Wuellner, Branick, and Dahl suggest a conflict between 1) what Paul proclaimed in Corinth during his sojourn, and 2) how it has been interpreted or applied since his departure. In the light of the reports given to him, Paul perceives a faulty understanding of spirituality and divine wisdom in the community, which have engendered wrongful boasting of status.[165] To correct this faulty understanding and subsequent conflict, Paul must reclaim the legitimacy or authenticity of his apostolic role and message. Accordingly, it is possible to see 1 Cor 1–4 as both an apologetic and a polemic.[166] The apologetic elements defend Paul's role as an apostle and the legitimacy of his message (1.10–4.21). The polemical features confront the faulty

---

[160] Dahl allows for fluidity in this regard so that the issues discussed in the respective divisions are not rigidly confined (see "Paul and the Church," 320).

[161] See n.156 above—i.e. the form that emerged with Perelman and Olbrechts-Tyteca, and championed by Kennedy.

[162] Litfin, *Theology of Proclamation*.

[163] *Ibid.*, 153-55, 161, 187, 201-02.

[164] *Ibid.*, 149-50.

[165] Fee, *First Epistle*, 47-50; C.B. Cousar, "1 Corinthians 2:1-13," *Int* 44.2 (1990): 169.

[166] As one scholar notes: "Paul's letters are to be understood against the background of their specific occasion, and that occasion is more than a few times essentially polemical" (J.H. Schütz, *Paul and the Anatomy of Apostolic Authority* [Cambridge: Cambridge University Press, 1975], 3). Thus, Paul responds in kind.

interpretations of Paul's view of spirituality and divine wisdom that have arisen in Corinth (1.18–3.23). Thus, by misconstruing Paul's apostolic role as well as his teaching on spirituality and divine wisdom, a divided community of believers has emerged in Corinth (1.10-11). By providing an apologetic for himself and a polemic against faulty views of his teaching, Paul offers a remedy for the divisions or factions within the community as well.[167] Accordingly, scholars have examined the content and structure of Paul's argument in the light of the features already mentioned.

These scholarly examinations build on recent developments within rhetorical criticism, especially the notion that Paul's letters were "substitutes for oral communication" and "that he shaped them in accordance with formal oral speech, using rhetorical elements recognizable as such by his addressees."[168] However, the

---

[167] Finney takes factionalism to be the leading cause for Paul's argument in 1 Cor 1–4 (see "Honor, Rhetoric, and Factionalism," 28).

[168] Witherington, *Conflict and Community*, 35, 39; cf. 44-48. See also the emphatic assertion of Peterson who claims, "there is never any doubt that the letters [of Paul] are to be read in the context of rhetorical practice" (*Eloquence in the Proclamation of the Gospel at Corinth* [Atlanta: Scholars Press, 1998], 7). Cf. G.A. Kennedy, *New Testament Interpretation Through Rhetorical Criticism* (Chapel Hill: University of North Carolina, 1984), 5-6; R.F. Collins, "Reflections on 1 Corinthians as a Hellenistic Letter," in *The Corinthian Correspondence* (ed. R. Bieringer; Leuven: Leuven University Press, 1996), 39-61; V.P. Furnish, "Letters in the New Testament," in *Eerdmans Commentary on the Bible* (eds. J.D.G. Dunn and J.W. Rogerson; Grand Rapids: Eerdmans, 2003), 1268-76; cf. A. du Toit, *Focusing on Paul: Persuasion and Theological Design in Romans and Galations* (eds. C. Breytenbach and D.S. du Toit; Berlin: Walter de Gruyter, 2007), 23-29. However, this line of argument is difficult to sustain due to the fact that while a small number of rhetorical handbooks do interact with some epistolarly practices, letter-writing and rhetorical instruction were not taught as combined disciplines until at least the Byzantine period (c. 330–1453 CE)—see H.–J. Klauck, *Ancient Letters and the New Testament: A Guide to Context and Exegesis* (Waco: Baylor University Press, 2006), 210. Prior to that period, the two disciplines were viewed and taught separately.

precise rhetorical divisions for 1 Cor 1–4 tend to vary among scholars and the variations depend on how the rhetorical categories are defined by the individual scholar.[169]

For example, Witherington classifies 1 Cor 1.18–4.21 as "argument 1" of the *probatio* (1.18–16.12)[170] and suggests a four-part outline for this first argument: 1.18-31; 2.1-16; 3.1-23; and 4.1-21.[171] While Witherington's reasons for this four-part division are not explicitly clear, one can assume that he means to follow the assumed deliberative nature of the letter and to support the letter's controlling theme of unity within the body of believers. Alternatively, Schnabel isolates six key stages in Paul's argument: 1.10-17; 1.18–2.5; 2.6-16; 3.1-17; 3.18-23; and 4.1-12.[172] These stages collectively speak to the issue of divisions within the community, what Schnabel classifies as the first of four conflicts to be addressed in the letter,[173] and how this issue arose out of a false

Despite this fact, scholars continue to examine the style, form, and function of Paul's letters as substitutes for rhetorical speeches, especially 1 Corinthians.

[169] This phenomenon is certainly not limited to 1 Corinthians. Murphy-O'Connor provides a brief list of the various ways (a sampling of) scholars divide rhetorically the individual letters of the Pauline corpus—see *Paul the Letter-Writer: His World, His Options, His Skill* (Collegeville: Liturgical Press, 1995), 77-79.

[170] Dunn offers a similar outline, although he ends the *probatio* at 15.57, classifies 15.58 as the *peroratio* and 16.1-24 as the epistolary closing (see *1 Corinthians*, 24-25).

[171] See Witherington, *Conflict and Community*, 106-36.

[172] See E.J. Schnabel, *Der erste Brief des Paulus an die Korinther* (Wuppertal: R. Brockhaus, 2006), 79-269. Although, Schnabel does qualify this six-part division: "Der erste Hauptteil des Briefs (1,10–4,21) besteht *aus sieben Abschnitten*" (*Der erste Brief*, 82—emphasis added), which comes from dividing the fourth stage into two: 3.1-4 and 3.5-17 (see *Der erste Brief*, 83; cf. 181-218).

[173] Schnabel's four conflicts are as follows as: 1.10–4.21 ("Spaltungen in der Gemeinde"); 6.1-11 ("Das Prozessieren von Gemeindegliedern"); 11.17-34 ("Die Missstände beim Herrenmahl") and 12.1–14.40 ("Die Gaben des Geistes

understanding of wisdom. On the more elaborate side, Collins defines 1.18–4.21 as the "first rhetorical demonstration" of six within the letter, and he divides this first demonstration into eleven distinct sections: 1.18-31; 2.1-5; 2.6-16; 3.1-9; 3.10-17; 3.18-23; 4.1-5; 4.6-7; 4.8-13; 4.14-16; and 4.17-21.[174] Collins relies heavily on the structuring of rhetorical speeches espoused by Aristotle and Cicero, and he sees the individual parts together as forming a persuasive argument that supports the "statement of purpose" in 1 Cor 1.10.[175]

While intermittent similarities appear in these basic structures, most scholars agree on the structure of a particular segment of 1 Cor 1–4. Further agreement is found with regard to the assumed single argument of 1.18–3.4, which is said to unfold in two stages: 1.18–2.5 and 2.6–3.4.[176] Support for these two stages comes from a detailed analysis of the contents. First, Paul appeals to the cross of

---

in der Gemeinde")—see *Der erste Brief*, 79-269, 301-26, 625-75 and 670-861 respectively. Along with the four conflicts, Schnabel classifies six compromises: 5.1-13 ("Die wilde Ehe eines Gemeindeglieds"); 6.12-20 ("Der Verkehr mit Prostituierten"); 7.1-40 ("Ehe und Verlobung"); 8.1–11.1 ("Götzenopferfleisch und Götzentempel"); 11.2-16 ("Kopfbedeckungen im Gottesdienst") and 15.1-58 ("Der Alltag und die Auferstehung")—see *Der erste Brief*, 270-300; 327-47; 348-425; 426-586; 587-624 and 862-995 respectively.

[174] See Collins, *First Corinthians*, 86-202.

[175] *Ibid.*, 87.

[176] See e.g. Fiore, "'Covert Allusion'," 87-88; Fee, *First Epistle*, 48-51, 66-128; R.B. Hays, *First Corinthians* (Louisville: Westminster John Knox, 1997), 26-50; Horsley, *1 Corinthians*, 47-63; Lamp, *First Corinthians*, 135-79; Thiselton, *First Epistle*, 147-295; Barclay, "1 Corinthians," 1110, 1112-14; Kammler, *Kreuz und Weisheit*, 1-2; Gorman, *Apostle of the Crucified Lord*, 240-43; R.E. Ciampa and B.S. Rosner, "1 Corinthians," in *Commentary on the New Testament Use of the Old Testament* (eds. G.K. Beale and D.A. Carson; Grand Rapids: Baker Academic, 2007), 696; cf. Edwards who moves the starting point to 1.13 (*A Commentary on the First Epistle to the Corinthians* [New York: A.C. Armstrong & Son, 1886], xxxvii) and Talbert who moves the starting point to 1.17 (*Reading Corinthians*, 4).

Christ as an expression of divine wisdom, its significance in human history, Paul's historic role in proclaiming both, and the Corinthians' original reception of all three (1.18–2.5).[177] Second, because he sees the believers as presently divided due to a faulty understanding of spirituality and divine wisdom, Paul defines the source of true wisdom as well as the means by which it is made known to the believers. In this case, the source is God and the means is the Spirit of God. Furthermore, this wisdom, mediated through God's Spirit, defines the Corinthians' relationship with God, Paul, and each other (2.6–3.4).

This type of analysis provides useful clues for establishing the flow and purpose of Paul's argument, especially with the scholarly opinion that 1.18–2.5 and 2.6–3.4 function as distinct units within the argument. And when examining 1.18–2.5 in particular, most scholars follow a threefold division. Schnabel's recent work is representative of this trend: "In drei Gedankengängen behandelt Paulus das Evangelium vom gekreuzigten Messias (1,18-25) die (Orts-) Gemeinde als Gemeinde des gekreuzigten Messias (1,26-31) und die missionarische Predigt als Wort vom Kreuz (2,1-5)."[178] Thus, while 1 Cor 2.1-5 has an individual role within this scheme, its function and purpose are often subsumed under the larger argument of 1.18–2.5.[179]

---

[177] S.C. Barton argues that this rhetorical unit is marked by the apparent *inclusio* of δύναμις θεοῦ in 1.18 and δυνάμει θεοῦ in 2.5 ("1 Corinthians," in *Eerdmans Commentary on the Bible* [eds. J.D.G. Dunn and J.W. Rogerson; Grand Rapids: Eerdmans, 2003], 1320); although, cf. Collins (*First Corinthians*, 90), who moves the boundaries of the *inclusio* to 1.18 and 1.24.

[178] Schnabel, *Der erste Brief*, 83.

[179] See D.L. Stamps, "The Christological Premise in Pauline Theological Rhetoric: 1 Corinthians 1:4–2.5 as an Example," in *Rhetorical Criticism and the Bible* (eds. S.E. Porter and D.L. Stamps; Sheffield: Sheffield Academic Press, 2002), 447.

However, a question arises over whether or not this makes sense in the light of the larger argument of 1.10–4.21. Is dividing the rhetorical units into 1.18–2.5 and 2.6–3.4 the only option, and is such a division reflective of what Paul is doing within the larger argument? Is it possible to shift the boundaries of the rhetorical units, and what would such a shift do for our understanding of Paul's argument? My contention is that the whole of 1 Cor 2.1–3.4 can be read as a distinct unit and one that initiates a new stage within the larger argument. Support for this alternative reading comes first by revisiting the assumed structure of 1.10–4.21 but recognizing a particular pattern that appears to exist within the initial portion of this argument.

Following the epistolary prescript (1.1-9), Paul acknowledges the report about the existence of divisions or factions within the believing community in Corinth (1.10-17). Furthermore, the claim of 1.10 functions as a type of thesis statement for the argument that follows. The post-positive γάρ in 1.11 reads as an explanatory conjunction, thus revealing the source and basic content of Paul's knowledge regarding the Corinthian situation. This situation is then briefly mentioned in 1.12-13, which can be understood as the cause for Paul's remarks in 1.10. When commentators examine the content of 1.14-17, the focus tends to be on Paul's explanation of what he did not do while in Corinth—i.e. he did not baptize many. This becomes pivotal for understanding Paul's conduct and to what he gave priority during his sojourn in Corinth. The interpretations of 1.18–2.5 as noted above then follow. However, a pattern seems to emerge beginning with 1.14 and continuing until 3.4 that has not been explicitly recognized (or explored).[180] The pattern is based on

---

[180] Some have hinted at it in various ways—see e.g. C.K. Barrett, *A Commentary on the First Epistle to the Corinthians* (London: Adam & Charles Black, 1971), 42-49; Conzelmann, *1 Corinthians*, 32-38; Fee, *First Epistle*, 54-66; Horsley, *1 Corinthians*, 44-47; Thiselton, *First Epistle*, 120-47.

a categorization of the contents of Paul's argument, and this pattern is repeated twice in 1.14–3.4.

The first occurrence is found in 1.14-31 where Paul begins with a *historical comment* regarding his original visit to Corinth (1.14-17). The manner in which 1.17 ends prepares the way for the *theological explanation* found in 1.18-25.[181] Similarly, the focus of 1.25 allows for the transition to the *social application* given in 1.26-31, which also unifies the preceding argument. The second occurrence is found in 2.1–3.4 where Paul begins with another *historical comment* about his initial visit to Corinth (2.1-5). The substance of that comment prepares the way for the *theological explanation* that follows in 2.6-16. Finally, Paul supplies a *social application* in 3.1-4, which unifies the foregoing argument.[182] While 1.14-31 and 2.1–3.4 represent two individual occurrences of this threefold pattern, important similarities in content exist between them that must be kept in mind: both sections deal with Paul's original visit to Corinth, both speak to the essential substance of his message, and both refer to the way in which the Corinthians originally responded to Paul and his message. This then forms the backdrop for examining the faulty views of Paul's apostleship and message that arose after his departure and against which Paul gives his defence.

Even if this does not satisfactorily explain the rhetorical units of the argument of 1 Cor 1–4, a focused study on 1 Cor 2.1–3.4 is nevertheless justified for it is in this passage that the themes of

---

[181] Lampe does recognize this as a "fundamental theological unit" within Paul's argument ("Theological Wisdom and the 'Word About the Cross': The Rhetorical Scheme of 1 Corinthians 1–4," *Int* 44.2 [1990]: 124).

[182] While 1 Cor 3.5–4.21 functions as a broad application of what precedes it, the two metaphors of 3.5-9 and 3.10-15, similar to 1.14-17 and 2.1-5, together appear to recall circumstances related to Paul's founding visit—i.e. a *historical comment*.

cross, Spirit, wisdom, and discernment appear together as a part of Paul's wider argument.

1.3.4. Summary and Aims of this Thesis

My study of Paul's pneumatological teaching in 1 Cor 2.1–3.4 proceeds in four steps, each being taken in individual chapters. First, I will investigate Paul's understanding of the Spirit's role in the proclamation of the cross during his initial visit to Corinth. Here I am concerned with 1) how Paul's proclamation relates to Greco-Roman conventions of rhetorical display and notions of persuasion, and 2) why Paul negotiates this relationship by means of a strict contrast. Second, I will examine Paul's teaching on how the Spirit serves as the mediator of divine wisdom for the believers in Corinth, both during and following Paul's proclamation of the gospel. Here I am concerned with 1) the Spirit's role in establishing a new epistemological framework for believers, based on God's wisdom, and 2) why Paul sees this new framework as distinct from existing Hellenistic and Jewish wisdom traditions. Third, I will explore Paul's view of the Spirit as the provider and sustainer of wise, communal discernment for believers. Here I am concerned with 1) how Paul defines the limits and nature of Spirit-led discernment for all believers, and 2) the ways in which Paul demonstrates or exercises the discernment he advocates. Finally, and following a summary of this study's key points, I will address two major topics: 1) how the pneumatological teaching in 2.1–3.4 fits within the immediate argument of 1 Cor 1–4, specifically the issue of the Corinthians' relationship Paul (and Apollos), and, more briefly, 2) the possible ways in which this pneumatological teaching shapes and/or influences the rest of the letter.

Chapter 2
THE SPIRIT'S ROLE IN THE PROCLAMATION OF THE CROSS

2.1. Introduction

As noted in the previous chapter, a key component of 1 Cor 1–4 is the argument of 2.1–3.4, where an intriguing set of references to the role of God's Spirit in relation to Paul's apostolic preaching emerges (see 2.4-5, 8-12, 13-14). These references are intriguing because the way Paul defines the role of the Spirit is unique in the Pauline corpus (although cf. 1 Thess 1.5), and this uniqueness is found not only in what Paul says about this role but also in how he makes his case. What is it that Paul says about this role? In both 1 Cor 2.4-5 and 2.13-14, Paul argues that God's Spirit plays a necessary role in the proclamation of the gospel, a role that has implications for the nature of Paul's apostolic commission, especially in Corinth. Furthermore, in 1 Cor 2.8-12 Paul contends that the Spirit plays an equally important role in the comprehension of the message by those who hear it, which has implications for the nature of the message itself.

How then does Paul make this case, and why is this approach significant? Paul stresses the necessity of the Spirit's role in the proclamation and reception of the gospel in the form of a strict contrast. Specifically, Paul argues that the demonstration of the Spirit powerfully at work in the simple proclamation of the gospel (cf. 2.2-4) stands in opposition to another (expected) form of proclamation, namely, one given in wise, eloquent or persuasive (human) speech. An important result of this contrast is that Paul distinguishes his apostolic mission and message from the cultural expectations for public speakers and the conventions to which they adhered. Crucial to Paul's argument is the fact that the Corinthians believed and accepted the gospel he proclaimed in spite of the simple form in which he proclaimed it. And Paul's explanation for why this is the case points away from any rhetorical ability or persuasiveness on his part and toward the power of the Spirit at work in the messenger and message.

What significance, therefore, does the particular contrast in 1 Cor 2.4 have for our understanding of what Paul is doing with the larger argument? Why does Paul contrast a proclamation given in wise, persuasive (human) speech with one that is a demonstration of the power of the Spirit? What does this contrast say or imply about the cultural expectations and conventions of wise, eloquent or persuasive (human) speech as they relate to his apostolic role and message? Does recognizing the nature of this contrast and its function help us to understand why Paul refers to the Spirit in the way he does at this particular stage of the argument? Moreover, can this contrast and its placement inform our understanding of Paul's other references to the role of the Spirit in the proclamation and reception of the gospel? These questions will guide the exploration of this chapter, which contains two major sections.

First I will consider the historical circumstances to which Paul wrote his letter to the Corinthian church. Here I am concerned with Paul's message and style as compared with contemporaneous traveling orators, thus requiring an examination of the general nature of and expectations about rhetorical speech in the ancient world. Second, I will consider the issues about or criticisms laid against Paul and his message following his departure, after his first visit to Corinth. Here I will focus on the relevant sections of Paul's argument where he responds to this situation, specifically where he contrasts his message and style with both the orators of his day and the expectations held by those who hear them. Moreover, I am concerned with why Paul distinguishes his message and style from the traveling orators in the way he does and why that distinction is vital for his response to the Corinthian situation.

2.2. Exploration of the Context

On five distinct occasions in the opening chapters of 1 Corinthians, Paul refers to wisdom and its mode of expression as they relate to the proclamation of the gospel (see 1.17; 2.1, 4, 5, 13; cf. 4.20). How Paul describes the categories of wisdom and its expression varies, presumably with the differences being shaped by the emphasis he seeks to supply. Paul begins with the simple "wise speech" (1.17)[1] before moving to the slightly more elaborate "superior speech or wisdom" (2.1). Paul then alternates between the specific, "plausible words of wisdom" (2.4)[2] and the general,

---

[1] While some English translations render λόγου as "words" (KJV, NKJV, 21KJV, ASV, NIV, ESV, HCSB, NCV, CEV), the more general rendering, "speech" (see NASB, NLT) or "discourse" (DARBY) agrees with the original "number" of the Greek noun and maintains the more abstract focus of Paul's argument.

[2] While a small number of MSS contain the brief reading, πειθοῖς σοφίας ($\mathfrak{P}^{46}$, F, G, Chrysostom[mss]; although see it[b, f, g] which reads, πειθοῖ σοφίας), the evidence can be divided into two categories: 1) πειθοῖ[ς] σοφίας [λόγοις] (B, D, 0150, 33, 1175, 1506, 1739, 1852, 1881, 1912, it[r], vg[ww, st], geo[1], syr[p], Origen[gr4/7, lat2/3], Eusebius, Didymus[1/3], Chrysostom[1/2], Severian, Ambrose[1/7], Jerome[4/5], Pelagius, Varimandum), and 2) πειθοῖς ἀνθρωπίνης σοφίας λόγοις (א[2], A, C, Ψ, 6, 81, 104, 256, 263, 365, 424, 436, 459, 1241, 1319, 1573, 2127, 2464, Byz [L, P], l592, it[o], vg[cl], geo[2], slav, Origen[gr1/7, lat1/3], Ps-Athanasius, Cyril-Jerusalem, Apollinaris, Didymus[2/3], Chrysostom[1/2], Cyril[2/3], Ambrose[2/7]). Variants in the first category include: πειθοῖς σοφίας λόγος (א*) and πειθοῖ σοφίας λόγων (syr[p], Origen[gr1/7], Ambrose[1/7, [3/7]], Jerome[1/5]). Variants in the second category include: πειθοῖς ἀνθρωπίνης σοφίας (2200), πειθοῖς σοφίας ἀνθρωπίνης λόγοις (1962), πειθοῖς ἀνθρωπίνης σοφίας καὶ λόγοις (131), πειθοῖ ἀνθρωπίνης σοφίας λόγοις (1, 42, 205, 440, Cyril[1/3]) and πειθοῖ σοφίας ἀνθρωπίνης λόγοις (2595). Virtually all scholars reject the second reading and its variants on the basis that it appears to be "an explanatory gloss inserted by copyists...in order to identify more exactly the nuance attached to σοφίας" (B.M. Metzger, A Textual Commentary on the Greek New Testament [Stuttgart: Deutsche Bibelgesellschaft, 1997], 481; cf. Thiselton, First Epistle, 215). See also E.B. Ebojo, "How Persuasive is 'Persuasive Words of Human Wisdom'," BT 60.1 (2009): 10-21.

"human wisdom" (2.5) before returning again to the specific:
"words taught in accordance with human wisdom" (2.13).

Even if we take πειθοῖ[ς] σοφίας [λόγοις] as the accepted reading,
questions remain over the form and function of πειθός and the use or non-use
of λόγος. The noun πειθός and its semantic partner πιθανός appear with
varying frequency in Greek literature and with similar meaning—i.e. persuasion,
plausibility, enticement, assurance. However, Paul uses πειθός in 2.4
adjectivally, a use not found elsewhere in the Pauline corpus or Classical Greek
literature. How, then, is this anomaly best explained? Godet suggests that the
adjectival usage existed in *spoken* Classical Greek, and Paul simply borrowed
that form and employed it for the purposes of his letter (see *First Epistle*, 128-
29). However, no further evidence or examples of this phenomenon exists in
Paul or other Greek texts. Lietzmann and Barrett both suggest the more plausible
explanation that Paul either adapted the nominal form or coined the adjectival
form for the purposes of his argument (see H. Lietzmann, *An die Korinther I-II*
[ed. and suppl. W.G. Kümmel; Tübingen: J.C.B. Mohr (Paul Siebeck), 1969],
11; Barrett, *First Epistle*, 65). Thiselton points out that such a practice
"corresponds with expected grammatical conventions for structural
transformation of the cognate verb πείθω, *I persuade*, into a related adjective"
(*First Epistle*, 216—italics original). The coining of a descriptive term fits with
Paul's intention, which is to distance himself from a particular *type* or *form* of
wisdom—as will be argued later. The decision to render πειθοῖς as "plausible"
is for the purpose of making the contrast with ἀποδείξις explicitly clear.

While the use or non-use of λόγος remains a point of scholarly discussion,
the difference in meaning is primarily one of emphasis. If λόγος is not original
to the text, then the focus of Paul's argument is on the framework of ideas
related to human wisdom and the belief that such things have persuasive power
if and when they manifests themselves in eloquent speech. If, however, λόγος is
original to the text, then the focus of Paul's argument is on the assumed
persuasive power inherent in eloquent speech that flows from the framework of
ideas related to human wisdom. Either option suggests that a decision in this
matter does not greatly affect Paul's meaning or the sense of the passage. The
only possible difference relates to whether Paul is referring to wisdom or
eloquent speech as the means of persuasion. In either case, the primary focus of
Paul's argument is that both belong to human wisdom and its ways of knowing,
and that such things have no influence, power, persuasion, or meaning when it
comes to revealing and understanding God's wisdom in the cross of Christ.

Regardless of how he describes the phenomenon, Paul's tone is decidedly negative in each case. Specifically, he seems to portray it as an invalid means for proclaiming the gospel message. More problematic, at least initially, is the lack of clarity for what Paul has in mind with such descriptions. Can we therefore be more precise about Paul's focus in these references?

By consolidating the various descriptions into a single category, we can tentatively suggest that Paul's object of negative attention is the use of rhetoric in proclaiming the gospel. Pogoloff maintains that this specific focus would have been the obvious conclusion for someone reading Paul's letter: "any Hellenistic reader would have taken his disclaimers to refer to rhetorical practice."[3] However, does this therefore mean that Paul's readers would have taken his statements to mean a complete rejection of rhetorical ability and the use of its devices? Or would they have understood him as rejecting something else? Maybe we need to begin with a more rudimentary question: what is rhetorical ability and what were its practices or conventions, and how would this relate to Paul's apostolic mission in Corinth?

2.2.1. Survey of Greco-Roman Rhetoric

Since a number of scholarly works cover ancient Greco-Roman rhetoric in considerable detail,[4] and many others have examined its

---

[3] Pogoloff, *Logos and Sophia*, 7.

[4] See e.g. D.L. Clark, *Rhetoric in Greco-Roman Education* (New York: Columbia University Press, 1957); S.C. Jarratt, *Rereading the Sophists: Classical Rhetoric Refigured* (Carbondale: Southern Illinois University Press, 1991); J. Herrick, *The History and Theory of Rhetoric: An Introduction* (Boston: Allyn and Bacon, 1997); G.A. Kennedy, *Comparative Rhetoric: An Historical and Cross-Cultural Introduction* (New York: Oxford University Press, 1998); idem, *Classical Rhetoric and Its Christian and Secular Tradition from Ancient to Modern Times* (Chapel Hill: University of North Carolina Press, 1999); B. McComiskey, *Gorgias and the New Sophistic Rhetoric* (Carbondale: Souther

application to the NT and Paul,[5] my treatment here will only be a summary of the relevant points about ancient rhetoric, especially as they relate to Paul's claims in 1 Cor 2.1–3.4. The purpose of this summary is to assist us in determining whether Paul rejects rhetoric categorically or if the object of rejection is something else.

2.2.1.1. Types and Contexts for Rhetoric

Ancient rhetorical instruction varied in content and emphases. Suetonius' summary of the discipline recognizes that not all teachers of rhetoric instructed their students in the same styles or methods. Often, as Suetonius describes it, the topics of instruction were rather individualized or conducted according to the desires of the teacher.[6] In spite of this, a number of general features do appear consistent throughout the history of rhetorical instruction. These features can be divided broadly into two categories: 1) types of rhetorical speeches, and 2) the contexts (or locations) in which the types of speeches were typically given. With regard to types of speeches, and following the divisions laid down by Aristotle, the

---

Illnois University Press, 2001); L. Pernot, *Rhetoric in Antiquity* (trans. W.E. Higgins; Washington D.C.: Catholic University of America Press, 2005).

[5] See e.g. Kennedy, *New Testament Interpretation*; B. Mack, *Rhetoric and the New Testament* (Minneapolis: Fortress, 1990); Mitchell, *Rhetoric of Reconciliation*; D.L. Stamps, "Rhetorical Criticism of the New Testament: Ancient and Modern Evaluations of Argumentation," in *Approaches to New Testament Study* (eds. S.E. Porter and D. Tombs; Sheffield: Sheffield Academic Press, 1995), 129-69; R.D. Anderson, *Ancient Rhetorical Theory and Paul* (Leuven: Peeters, 1999); C.B. Forbes, "Paul and Rhetorical Comparison," in *Paul in the Greco-Roman World: A Handbook* (ed. J.P. Sampley; Harrisburg: Trinity Press International, 2003), 134-71; F.J. Long, *Ancient Rhetoric and Paul's Apology: The Compositional Unity of 2 Corinthians* (Cambridge: Cambridge University Press, 2004).

[6] Suetonius, *Rhet.* 1.1.

primary rhetorical manuals list three options: [7] deliberative, forensic, and epideictic. With each type of speech, two further details should be recognized: 1) the goal of each type of speech, and 2) the type's relationship to past, present, and future time.

In deliberative speeches, the orator attempts to persuade the audience to adopt or abandon a particular course of action at some point in the future—whether immediate or distant. These types of speeches included political proclamations aimed at shaping or changing public policy or social norms. In forensic speeches, the orator seeks to persuade the audience to accept or reject the testimony concerning a past event. These types of speech included court cases where matters of (in)justice were decided. Finally in epideictic speeches, the orator desires to influence current (or present) opinions concerning notable figures—and the ideals they espouse—by lavishing praise or dispensing blame upon them. A key difference between this type and the other two is that epideictic speeches do not necessarily require a decision to be made at a speech's conclusion. Moreover, both in the early periods of rhetoric and from the 3rd century BCE onward, epideictic speeches were primarily used for entertainment. [8] Aeschylus, Sophocles, Aristophanes, Euripides, and Menander are examples of this trend.

With these observations about the types of speeches, we come to the second broad category: writers of rhetorical handbooks in the ancient world often understood each type of speech to be linked with a particular context (or location). Specifically, because deliberative speeches sought to influence public policy they

---

[7] Aristotle, *Rhet.* 1.3.3; 1.4.1–1.15.33; *Rhet. Her.* 1.2; 1.5.1–3.15.27; Cicero, *De or.* 1.137-47; idem, *Inv.* 1.5.7; idem, *Top.* 24.91; Quintilian, *Inst.* 3.3.15; 3.7.1–3.9.9 (see also 3.4.1-16 for Quintilian's perspective on this threefold scheme).

[8] See B. Witherington, *The Paul Quest: The Renewed Search for the Jew of Tarsus* (Downers Grove: InterVarsity, 1998), 116; Long, *Ancient Rhetoric*, 24.

generally occurred in public assemblies or political arenas. Further, since forensic speeches sought to determine matters of legality or justice they were reserved primarily for the law courts. Finally, since epideictic speeches sought to influence general opinions, norms, or values in public life they often occurred in theaters or the public square. Another important difference between the types is that both deliberative and forensic speeches were judged on the basis of the case or arguments given, whereas epideictic speeches were judged on the basis of the speaker's perceived ability or skill.

2.2.1.2. Contents and Assessment of Rhetorical Speeches

In terms of overall structure, Aristotle claimed that a speech comprises two parts: 1) the statement of the case, and 2) the exposition that proves it.[9] Since rhetoric is the art of persuasion, the stress often falls on the manner in which a speaker proves the stated case. Thus, the focus tends to be on the overall structure of the argument and the specific points presented within it. To help guide the students of rhetoric in forming a persuasive speech, instructions related to form and content were typically divided into recognizable parts. As with the classifications of speeches, the individual parts remained fairly consistent throughout the history of rhetorical instruction. Aristotle labelled the parts of a speech as προοίμιον, πρόθεσις, πίστις, ἐπίλογος, and διήγησις[10]—the final part often being reserved for forensic speeches.[11] The variations in this scheme can be found in the works of Cicero, where he begins with six parts but later reduces it to four;[12] the

---

[9] Aristotle, *Rhet.* 3.13.1.

[10] Aristotle, *Rhet.* 3.13.1-4. Scholars tend to view these parts of rhetorical speeches listed above as typical—see e.g. Witherington, *The Paul Quest*, 117-18; Anderson, *Ancient Rhetorical Theory*, 69; Long, *Ancient Rhetoric*, 25.

[11] Aristotle, *Rhet.* 3.13.3.

[12] The six-part scheme: *exordium, narratio, partitio, confirmatio, reprehensio,* and *conclusio* (see *Inv.* 27). The four-part scheme: *exordium,*

anonymous *Rhetorica ad Herennium*, which provides six parts that are similar to Cicero's earlier version;[13] and finally Quintilian, who advocates a fivefold scheme.[14]

A brief summary of the various parts should be noted. The προοίμιον serves as the introduction to the speech and the point at which the orator established himself or herself as an able speaker.[15] According to Aristotle, the establishment of ability deals with the matter of the speaker's character (or ἦθος), and how one goes about this process can dramatically affect the outcome of the speech.[16] On some occasions this part of the speech also became the place for acknowledging one's opponents or the nature of the criticisms raised by them. [17] If the speech is forensic, [18] the διήγησις comes next and it is the place where the speaker lists the facts of the case that are agreed upon by all parties involved in the debate. The purpose here is not to expound upon the details of the facts presented but merely to state them as topics to be addressed. Since διήγησις appears in forensic speeches, the proposal must

---

narratio, confirmatio (with *reprehensio*), and *peroratio* (see *Part. or.* 27). The correspondence between the Greek and Latin divisions: προοίμιον = *exordium*; πρόθεσις = *propositio* (*partitio, divisio*); πίστις = *probatio* (*confirmatio, refutatio*); ἐπίλογος = *peroratio* (*conclusio*); διήγνσις = *narratio*.

[13] I.e. *exordium, narratio, divisio, confirmatio, confutatio*, and *conclusio* (see *Rhet. Her.* 1.4).

[14] I.e. *prooemium, narratio, probatio, refutatio*, and *peroratio* (see *Inst.* 3.9.1; 4.1–4.2; 6.1).

[15] See Aristotle, *Rhet.* 3.14.1-12. However, as Waterfield points out, Greek rhetoric was a discipline predominantly known and practiced by men, especially in the Sophistic period where "there were no female Sophists" ("Introduction," in *The First Philosophers: The Presocratics and the Sophists* [trans. R. Waterfield; Oxford: Oxford University Press, 2000], xxx).

[16] See Aristotle, *Rhet.* 2.12.1–2.17.6.

[17] See *ibid.*, 3.14.7; cf. *Rhet. Her.* 1.6-8.

[18] Quintilian maintains that this element of a speech should "follow immediately" after the προοίμιον (*Inst.* 4.2.1, 24).

"be of a moral character,"[19] which later became understood as true (or truthful).[20]

The πρόθεσις functions as the stated aim or goal of the speech, usually given in a clear and succinct manner.[21] Along with stating the aim or goal of the speech it supplies the framework or boundaries for what will be argued. From this framework the listener will be able to determine the flow of the argument and when the body of the speech reaches its conclusion. Quintilian states that if the aim or goal is complex, then the speaker ought to subdivide it into manageable parts and define the order in which they will be addressed.[22] The πίστις represents the body of the speech or argument, the place where the speaker fulfills Aristotle's second criterion for all speeches (i.e. proving the case). The kinds of proof offered in the speech depend on the type of speech being given.[23] In a deliberative speech, the proof supports the validity of a particular course of action to be adopted or implemented by the people. In a forensic speech, the proof substantiates the credibility of the one giving the testimony and the claims being made by that person. In an epideictic speech, the proof assures the audience that the topic of discussion is either worthy or unworthy of reflection.

Finally, the ἐπίλογος operates as the conclusion of the speech. Often this portion of the speech restates the goal of the speaker and the primary points of the argument. While this feature is occasionally found in the body of the speech, the speaker will typically conclude by seeking the support of the audience through strong appeals to the emotions (πάθος). Quintilian describes such appeals as the place where "the power of oratory shows itself at its

---

[19] Aristotle, *Rhet.* 3.16.8.

[20] *Rhet. Her.* 1.14, 16; cf. also Quintilian, *Inst.* 4.2.52-60.

[21] Cicero, *Inv.* 1.31-33; Quintilian, *Inst.* 4.5.3.

[22] Quintilian, *Inst.* 4.5.1, 22-27.

[23] See Aristotle, *Rhet.* 3.17.1-4; *Rhet. Her.* 2.13-26; 3.8-9, 13-15; Quintilian, *Inst.* 5.1.1–5.14.35.

highest."[24] However, Aristotle provides a word of caution in this regard that should not be overlooked. Early on in his treatment, Aristotle speaks negatively about appeals to the emotions of the audience. This stems from his concern that such appeals might be employed wrongly, thus tainting or steering the response in a negative direction.[25] Later, when dealing with the topic of emotions specifically, Aristotle suggests positively that appeals to emotions should be in agreement with both the argument as a whole and what is honorable and good.[26]

In terms of assessment, the structure of the parts and the method of their delivery often played a crucial role in how the overall speech was judged or measured. Thus, while it was important for an orator to know the types of speeches and their essential components, it was equally vital—if not more so—for the orator to know which speech was the most effective and how to structure it so that it achieves the best result. Virtually the whole of book three of Aristotle's *Rhetoric* is devoted to this feature,[27] and the later rhetorical handbooks provide additional helps for how to be successful in this regard.[28] In terms of forming the structure, Cicero supplies a succinct description:

> The parts of [a speech], as most authorities have stated, are invention, arrangement, expression, memory, delivery. Invention is the discovery of valid or seemingly valid arguments to render one's cause plausible. Arrangement is the distribution of arguments thus discovered in the proper order. Expression is the fitting of the proper language to the

---

[24] Quintilian, *Inst.* 6.2.2.

[25] Aristotle, *Rhet.* 1.2.5.

[26] *Ibid.*, 2.2.1–2.11.7; cf. 1.9.7-12.

[27] *Ibid.*, 3.1–19.

[28] See *Rhet. Her.* 1.3; Quintilian, *Inst.* 3.3.1.

invented matter. Memory is the firm mental grasp of matter and words. Delivery is the control of voice and body in a manner suitable to the dignity of the subject matter and the style.[29]

One underlying assumption is that those witnessing a speech would know the elements of rhetorical speeches, thus enabling them to determine whether or not the speech was in fact successful or persuasive.[30] A further assumption is that orators who proved themselves to be successful or persuasive speakers were also considered wise. Thus, those gifted with wisdom can know the best possible means for not only constructing a speech but also delivering that speech in a way that proves itself beneficial for those who hear it.[31] Proof that wisdom granted the speaker a clear view of reality was found in the clarity of the message proclaimed. Thus, it was nearly axiomatic that wisdom and fine speech were viewed as essentially joined.[32]

2.2.2. Greco-Roman Rhetoric and Paul
2.2.2.1. Historical and Cultural Context

When we approach the time of Paul's ministry, two related details concerning ancient rhetoric must be taken into account. First, as Kennedy shows, Aristotle's comprehensive rhetorical

---

[29] Cicero, *Inv.* 1.9.

[30] Cf. Dutch, who contends for the possibility of elite members of the Corinthian church having such abilities, primarily on the assumption that they were (thoroughly) educated in philosophy and rhetoric in the Greco-Roman gymnasium (see *Educated Elite*, 95-167—esp. 147, 166-67).

[31] Cicero: "wisdom without eloquence is but of little advantage to the states" (*Inv.* 1.1).

[32] Cf. Litfin, *Theology of Proclamation*, 244—noting the observations of E. Norden. It is also worth mentioning that this connection is recognized and emphasized in the wisdom instructions of the ANE.

theory not only went unpublished in complete form until the 1st century BCE but also was not known except by those who studied under Aristotle or were able to read early portions of his work.[33] Thus, as Anderson contends, by the time of Paul the theory of Aristotle, in relation to other rhetorical theories of the time, was not widely known or adopted.[34] In support of this,[35] Anderson specifically points out that later rhetorical theories did not follow Aristotle's view of ἐνθύμημα, nor did subsequent theorists consistently maintain the distinction between ἔντεχνοι and ἄτεχνοι, and the balance between πάθος, ἦθος, and λόγος does not appear in later rhetorical works,[36] although some did emphasize a pair of the three.[37] Anderson also shows that knowledge of and

---

[33] G.A. Kennedy, *A New History of Classical Rhetoric* (Princeton: Princeton University Press, 1994), 62-63, 87-88; cf. also idem, "Historical Survey of Rhetoric," in *Handbook of Classical Rehtoric in the Hellenistic Period: 330 B.C.–A.D. 400* (ed. S.E. Porter; Boston: Brill Academic, 2001), 22.

[34] See Anderson, *Ancient Rhetorical Theory*, 42-48. Earlier in the same work, Anderson argued that Aristotelian rhetoric, as a defined science and systematically taught discipline, was virtually non-existent in Paul's time (*Ancient Rhetorical Theory*, 35). Smit has recently criticized Anderson's conclusions on the awareness and influence of ancient rhetorical categories in Paul's time (see *"About the Idol Offerings": Rhetoric, Social Context and Theology of Paul's Discourse in First Corinthians 8:1–11:1* [Leuven: Peeters, 2000], 41-42).

[35] The following are the first three of seven pieces of evidence as found in Anderson, *Ancient Rhetorical Theory*, 47-48. The remaining four are: Aristotle's distinction between κονιά and τόποι is not repeated; Aristotle's εὕρεσις lacks the στάσις theory and a clear exposition on the parts of speech; when Aristotle does address the parts of speech, he does so under the category of τάξις; and Aristotle's classification of only one ἀπρετή λέξεως is not continued in later theories. Kennedy seems to overlook Anderson's evidence when he asserts that the distinction between ἔντεχνοι and ἄτεχνοι, the use of πάθος, ἦθος and λόγος, and the implementation of ἐνθύμημα are "[t]he most important contributions of Aristotle to rhetorical theory" ("Historical Survey," 20-22).

[36] Although cf. Cicero, *De or.* 2.115.

[37] See e.g. Quintilian, *Inst.* 6.2.8-20.

reliance on Aristotle's theory appear to be limited to specific elements: Theophrastus focuses primarily on λέξις, Cicero develops the idea of τόποι, and Demetrius concerns himself with ἑρμηνεία.[38] However, the most significant feature of Aristotle's theory that does remains throughout later developments is the listing of the three types of speeches, although the emphasis they receive varies among rhetoricians. Furthermore, epideictic speeches became more common beginning with the 3rd century BCE, and Cicero devoted most of his instruction to forensic speeches, primarily because they were the most popular in his day.[39]

Second, in spite of its revival during the latter half of the 1st century BCE, primarily due to the work of Cicero,[40] Suetonius notes that instruction in rhetoric was neither uniform nor consistent. He goes on to say that the instruction provided to students was often determined by the desires of the respective teacher. Thus, while some taught composition of eloquent speeches, others taught students how to praise or censure esteemed Greek texts, and still others gave instruction on the art of elevating certain habits and how to demean others.[41] Moreover, Suetonius alludes to the fact that not all teachers in rhetoric during the 1st century BCE were appreciated or respected,[42] resulting in an unpopular view of rhetorical instruction. It is quite true that it would take the writings of Cicero before a more uniform and consistent treatment of rhetorical instruction could be formulated, thus helping regain its former appeal. However, as Anderson points out, like Aristotle's theory, Cicero's rhetoric would not serve as the influential

---

[38] See Anderson, *Ancient Rhetorical Theory*, 49-55.

[39] See *ibid.*, 70; Long, *Ancient Rhetoric*, 23-31.

[40] Suetonius, *Rhet.* 1.1.

[41] *Ibid.*, 1.1.

[42] See *ibid.*, 1.2-6.

framework during his lifetime.[43] The work of Quintilian would be pivotal in developing Cicero's ideas into what would be considered normative rhetorical practice.[44]

2.2.2.2. General Conventions

In the light of these two details, we need to consider what criteria were available in the time of Paul that would enable people to determine the success of a rhetorical speech. As noted above, epideictic speeches became more common after the start of the 3rd century BCE. Freese pins the cause of this on the fall of Greece and "Athens [losing] her independence" following the battle of Chaeronea in 338 BCE.[45] As Freese continues, "political oratory gradually declined, its place being subsequently taken by the rhetoric of the schools, characterized by a highly artificial and exaggerated style."[46] Those most famous for this new emphasis were the traveling Sophists.[47] Not only did these traveling orators popularize a particular style of rhetoric, they also appear to have popularized a set of expectations for how a successful orator should behave and speak. These expectations or conventions repay brief attention, as they are relevant for examining the social

---

[43] See Anderson, *Ancient Rhetorical Theory*, 87-92.

[44] See *ibid.*, 92-96. Although Quintilian is hesitant to "impose on students of rhetoric a system of laws immutable as fate" (*Inst.* 2.13.1)

[45] J.H. Freese, "Introduction," in *The Art of Rhetoric* (trans. J.H. Freese; London: William Heinemann, 1926), xvi. For similar reasons as those of Freese, Aune recently argued that, "deliberative rhetoric became attenuated into a rhetorical exercise with no real usefulness in the real world" ("The World of Roman Hellenism," in *The Blackwell Companion to the New Testament* [ed. D.E. Aune; Chichester: Wiley-Blackwell, 2010], 22).

[46] Freese, "Introduction," xvi.

[47] See G.A. Kennedy, "The Genres of Rhetoric," in *Handbook of Classical Rhetoric in the Hellenistic Period: 300 B.C.–A.D. 400* (ed. S.E. Porter; Boston: Brill Academic, 2001), 47-48.

context of Paul's ministry, comparing his style with the practices of Sophistic orators.[48]

An orator would first enter a city and then take steps for obtaining a receptive audience. Upon arrival this orator would intimate a desire to contribute to the welfare of the city in some way. To prove the legitimacy of his desires—not to mention his ability or competency—the orator would supply an initial speech for the leading figures of the city.[49] (On some occasions, the orator would advertise his forthcoming speech and invite members of the public to attend). From this initial speech, the leaders would determine if the populace would hear a more detailed presentation from the orator. The leaders' determination was often based on the success or persuasiveness of this first speech, which ostensibly would include the necessary and balanced components of a polished rhetorical display. It is on this point that invention, arrangement, expression, memory, and display are most necessary for the orator. Those able to strike this balance and produce the desired result would be considered both wise in what they profess and worthy to be heard on a larger scale.[50] However, this seemingly formal approach does not appear to be the only means by which a Sophistic orator obtained an audience.

From the writings of Dio Chrysostom we see a number of orators displaying their skill during the time of and in the same proximity as the Olympic and Isthmian games.[51] It is reasonable to assume that many of the orators in these settings had already

---

[48] See Winter, *After Paul Left Corinth*, 36-38; idem, *Philo and Paul Among the Sophists: Alexandrian and Corinthian Responses to a Julio-Claudian Movement* (Grand Rapids: Eerdmans, 2002), 143-64; cf. also Litfin, *Theology of Proclamation*, 206-07; Bullmore, *Theology of Rhetorical Style*, 208-10; Witherington, *Conflict and Community*, 121, 124.

[49] See Schnabel, *Der erste Brief*, 150-51.

[50] See Hays, *First Corinthians*, 37.

[51] See esp. Dio Chrysostom, *Or.* 8–9; 12.

gained acceptance in the city through the process noted above. However, it is equally reasonable to assume that during the time of the games, other traveling orators not vetted by the city's leading figures took advantage of the opportunity to display their skill to a captive audience. Moreover, Dio Chrysostom notes that many citizens where the games took place often ignored orators who were essentially well known and tended to favor the ones "they only see at intervals or have never seen before." [52] In such instances, a type of rhetorical competition would often emerge, although the speeches tended to become negative or derogatory. For example, in reference to the sojourn of Diogenes in Corinth, Dio Chrysostom states:

> That was the time, too, when one could hear crowds of wretched sophists around Poseidon's temple shouting and reviling one another, and their disciples, as they were called, fighting with one another, many writers reading aloud their stupid works, many poets reciting their poems while others applauded them, many jugglers showing their tricks, many fortune-tellers interpreting fortunes, lawyers innumerable perverting judgment, and peddlers not a few peddling whatever they happen to have.[53]

Despite this tendency or potential result, Sophistic orators using this second means of gaining an audience shared one thing with those using the first (i.e. the more formal) means: they sought opportunities to display their skills and receive the acclaim of those who witnessed them.

---

[52] *Ibid.*, 9.4.
[53] *Ibid.*, 8.9.

2.2.2.3. Relevance for Studying Paul

What relevance does this have for our understanding of Paul's ministry, particularly in Corinth? Four basic points repay attention. First, we need to be aware of and allow for developments and adaptations to existing rhetorical theories. Specifically, we need to be cautious in what we assume about Paul's knowledge and use of rhetorical elements during his ministry. This caution must be exercised because we cannot know how much rhetorical training Paul received (assuming that he did at all), which theories influenced him the most, and what topics of instruction were most prominent in that training. Second, if we were going to compare an assumed rhetorical style for Paul with styles popular in his time, then the best option would seem to be epideictic speeches made famous by traveling Sophists prior to and even during his life.[54] However, caution must be exercised here also because, contrary to the aims of such speeches, Paul would certainly expect a decision (of some kind) to be made as a result of the proclamation of the gospel. It is also possible that Paul's style could be compared with judicial speeches, since he would be testifying about the validity of past events—either the Christ-event or his own apostolic work.

This raises a third concern however: we must realise that the contexts (or locations) commonly associated with ancient rhetoric are, in the main, distinct from those in which Paul frequently proclaimed the gospel. Specifically, from what we can gather from his letters, and from recent studies on Paul's missionary strategies, Paul's preaching of the gospel rarely occurred in a public venue,

---

[54] While acknowledging specific differences between Paul's rhetoric and that of the Sophists, Hug confidently asserts: "I look upon [Paul] as a great orator, and I should even be inclined to compare him, as far as regards eloquence, to the renowned orators of antiquity—for instance, to Isocrates, whose address to Demonicus and partly to Nicocles more nearly resemble Paul in design and object" (*Introduction to the Writings of the New Testament* [trans. D.G. Wait; London: C. & J. Rivingtons, 1827], 2.341).

let alone a court of law. Stowers notes that Paul's preaching was predominantly conducted in homes of wealthy citizens of a given city.[55] This difference in location serves as an initial piece of evidence that something is certainly distinct between how Paul proclaims the gospel and how Sophistic orators displayed their rhetorical abilities. This distinction is recognized simply because Paul's manner of preaching, and the locations in which he did it, were not consistent with the known conventions and practices of traveling orators. Therefore, if we accept that Paul's original proclamation took place in private homes and not in the public square, one conclusion becomes viable: those hearing his message would have minimal (if any) reason to compare him with Sophistic orators. To say it differently: very little—if anything—about Paul's preaching strategy would lead those who hear him to the conclusion that he is just another orator, trying to gain an audience and proffer (entertaining) ideas.

Finally, and more pressing is the fact that we do not possess any of Paul's sermons in the form in which he gave them,[56] thus we have no way of knowing how much rhetoric (if any) influenced or shaped his preaching. All we have are his letters to the churches he established, and these writings are primarily responses to issues or questions that emerge following belief in the gospel. Thus, and to state it rather abruptly, Paul's letters are not the gospel message he proclaimed. This means we must be cautious in equating the

---

[55] Cf. S.K. Stowers, "Social Status, Public Speaking and Private Teaching: The Circumstances of Paul's Preaching Activity," *NovT* 26.1 (1984): 59-82 (esp. 70; although cf. 73-74, where Stowers notes that the evidence suggests that Paul might not have limited his preaching platform so exlusively, and 80-82, where the conclusions about this evidence are rather tentative). This is, of course, excluding the portrait in Acts 17.19-32 and 19.9 of Paul proclaiming the gospel on Mars Hill and the "school of Tyrannius" (respectively).

[56] A possible exception is Paul's letter to the Romans, but even that is debatable.

purpose, form, and content of the letters with the purpose, form, and content of Paul's apostolic preaching. Whatever Paul does rhetorically in the letter is not necessarily an exact reflection of his rhetorical style while preaching (assuming he had one).[57] Thus, while rhetorical theory might be useful for analyzing the logic and persuasiveness of his letters, it is ultimately of little benefit for understanding the manner in which Paul proclaimed the gospel. All we can do is examine what Paul says about his proclamation (or even a possible style) and then draw conclusions from those statements. This is especially the case when we examine Paul's letter of 1 Corinthians and specifically the argument of 2.1–3.4.

2.3. Exploration of the Contrast(s)

Earlier it was noted that on five distinct occasions in the opening chapters of 1 Corinthians, Paul refers to wisdom and its expression as they relate to the proclamation of the gospel. In the light of the preceding discussion, it would appear that what Paul has in view specifically are the art of rhetorical speeches and the assumed wisdom possessed by those who are gifted with such speech. It was also noted that with each reference Paul's tone is decidedly negative, treating such things as invalid means for proclaiming the gospel. The obvious implication is that if Paul sees rhetorical speech and its assumed wisdom as invalid means for proclaiming the gospel, then Paul would certainly have rejected them during his apostolic mission in Corinth. The question that remains unanswered, however, is whether Paul rejects rhetoric categorically or if his rejection had a specific focus. Commentators have long since argued that what Paul rejected was the art of

---

[57] Marshall recognizes this distinction but does nothing with it (see *Enmity in Corinth*, 341; cf. 393-94). Schrage, on the other hand, does develop this point (see *Der erste Brief*, 1.81-83).

rhetorical speech, [58] an argument that remains prominent in discussions of Paul's ministry and writing. With regard to 1 Corinthians, Lim says:

---

[58] See e.g. W. Lothian, *Expository Lectures on Paul's Epistles to the Corinthians* (Edinburgh: Waugh & Innes, 1828), 20, 27, 38-44; J. Locke, *A Paraphrase and Notes on the Epistles of Galatians, First and Second Corinthians, Romans and Ephesians* (Cambridge: Brown, Shattuck and Company, 1832), 81, 84; H. Olshausen, *Biblical Commentary on St Paul's First and Second Epistles to the Corinthians* (trans. J.E. Cox; Edinburgh: T&T Clark, 1851), 37-38, 47, 49-50; L. Paige, *First and Second Epistles to the Corinthians* (Boston: Universalist Publishing House, 1867), 17-18, 26-29, 34; C.F. Kling, *The First Epistle of Paul to the Corinthians* (New York: Charles Scribner's Sons, 1868), 24, 41, 50-53; C. Hodge, *An Exposition of the First Epistle to the Corinthians* (New York: Robert Carter & Brothers, 1860), 29, 31-32; H.A.W. Meyer, *Critical and Exegetical Handbook on the Epistles to the Corinthians* (vol. 1; trans. and ed. W.P. Dickson and F. Crombie; Edinburgh: T&T Clark, 1878), 35-36, 54-55; J.A. Beet, *A Commentary on St Paul's Epistles to the Corinthians* (London: Hodder and Stoughton, 1882), 44-46; A. Stanley, *The Epistles of St Paul to the Corinthians: With Critical Notes and Dissertations* (London: John Murray, 1882), 36; Edwards, First Epistle, 44-45, 46-47; E.P. Gould, *Commentary on the Epistles to the Corinthians* (Philadelphia: American Baptist Publication Society, 1887), 15, 21-22; C.J. Ellicott, *Critical and Grammatical Commentary on St Paul's First Epistle to the Corinthians* (Andover: W.F. Draper, 1889), 54-55, 57; M. Dods, *The First Epistle to the Corinthians* (London: Hodder & Stoughton, 1909), 50-51, 58-60; J.E. McFadyen, *The Epistles to the Corinthians with Notes and Comments* (London: Hodder and Stoughton, 1911), 24, 36-38; Robertson-Plummer, *First Epistle*, 15-16, 29-33, 35; Riggs-Reed, *Epistles to the Corinthians*, 30, 32.

While some early commentators do not mention it specifically, the tone of their remarks suggests they had the art of rhetoric in mind—see e.g. J.G. Billroth, *A Commentary on the Epistles of Paul to the Corinthians* (trans. W.L. Alexander; Edinburgh: T&T Clark, 1837), 50-51; Godet, *First Epistle*, 123-24, 128-29; J. Boise, *Four of the Earlier Epistles of the Apostle Paul, viz First and Second Thessalonians, First and Second Corinthians: Greek Text with Explanatory Notes* (New York: Appleton and Company, 1890), 36-37; J.J. Lias, *The First Epistle to the Corinthians* (Cambridge: The University Press, 1897), 42-43 (although Lias does argue that Paul's opponents criticized him for being

When Paul writes in 1 Cor 2:4, καὶ ὁ λόγος μου καὶ τὸ κήρυγμά μου οὐκ ἐν πειθοῖς σοφίας ἀλλ᾽ ἐν ἀποδείξει πνεύματος καὶ δυνάμεως, he appears to be rejecting not human communication in general, but that specific, studied art of persuasive speech as was practised by orators and rhetoricians of the Greco-Roman world and by at least some of the Corinthian preachers.[59]

However, while it might be the case that Paul is rejecting the art of rhetoric categorically (or at least a form of it), it does not appear to be the primary focus of his repudiation.

Closer readings of the relevant passages in 1 Corinthians suggest that Paul rejects the underlying assumption that one must speak eloquently in order for the gospel message to be considered persuasive, meaningful, or worthy of acceptance.[60] Moreover, Paul rejects the assumption that if one is to speak of wisdom then eloquently formed words or arguments are the necessary (or only)

"ignorant of the rules of rhetoric" [xx]); M.F. Sadler, *The First and Second Epistles to the Corinthians: With Notes Critical and Practical* (London: George Bell and Sons, 1898), 28-30; C.R. Erdman, *The First Epistle of Paul to the Corinthians: An Exposition* (Philadelphia: Westminster Press, 1928), 30-32.

[59] T.H. Lim, "'Not in Persuasive Words of Wisdom, But in the Demonstration of the Spirit and Power,'" *NovT* 29.2 (1987): 146 (although cf. 148). Gräbe appears to be repeating Lim's comment (although slightly modified) when he says: "In 1 Cor 2,4 when Paul writes καὶ ὁ λόγος μου καὶ τὸ κήρυγμά μου οὐκ ἐν πειθοῖ σοφίας ἀλλ᾽ ἐν ἀποδείξει πνεύματος καὶ δυνάμεως, he appears to be rejecting that specific, studied art of persuasive speech which was practised by orators and rhetoricians of the Greco-Roman world and by at least some of the Corinthian preachers" (*The Power of God in Paul's Letters* [Tübingen: Mohr Siebeck, 2000], 63). Cf. Fitzmyer who makes a similar claim: "Thus Paul is rejecting explicitly the art of persuasion cultivated by the orators trained in Greco-Roman rhetorical tradition" (*First Corinthians*, 173).

[60] Cf. Litfin, *Theology of Proclamation*, 206 n.83.

means by which that wisdom is made known. To apply this directly to 1 Corinthians: Paul rejects the notions that rhetorical speech and its assumed wisdom have the ability (or power) to reveal God's wisdom, especially in the message of the cross of Christ. The reasons for this conclusion about Paul's rejection will be explored in what follows. However, it is important to consider first why Paul would state this rejection in his letter to the Corinthian church, which will then assist in our understanding of its inclusion in the specific argument of 2.1–3.4. The most appropriate reason why Paul would make this case is related to the historical circumstances that arose after his departure and prior to the time of writing.

2.3.1. Historical Occasion for Paul's Response

Following his departure, Paul's apostolic mission and message came under scrutiny, and this scrutiny created an atmosphere of skepticism towards Paul, his message, and the manner in which he presented it.[61] While debates continue over the precise origin of this skepticism and its subsequent results, scholars agree that Paul's mission and message were being judged according to the conventions or styles of esteemed orators from the Greco-Roman world.[62] As stated above, ancient views of wisdom maintained the idea that persuasive speech was the verifiable proof for one's claims of possessing wisdom or being able to reveal wisdom.

---

[61] While this suggestion obviously runs the risk of "mirror-reading," it is the one that best answers the question of why Paul repeatedly speaks about the manner in which he proclaimed his gospel.

[62] See e.g. Keener, *1–2 Corinthians*, 25; cf. also K. Donahoe, "From Self-Praise to Self-Boasting; Paul's Unmasking of the Conflicting Rhetorical-Linguistic Phenomena in 1 Corinthians," (Ph.D. diss; University of St Andrews, 2008), 86-88; O.–Y. Kwon, "A Critical Review of Recent Scholarship on the Pauline Opposition and the Nature of its Wisdom (σοφία) in 1 Corinthians 1–4," *CBR* 8 (2010): 390-92.

However, and recognized as early as Plato and as late as Tacitus, this view was often exploited to the point where persuasive speech functioned as the necessary condition for proving one's claims of possessing wisdom.[63] Thus, if an orator spoke persuasively about a given subject, then the audience would naturally assume that the orator was wise not only in that subject but also in those related to it.[64] The inverse of this would also be true: if an orator could not speak persuasively about a given subject, then the audience would naturally conclude that the orator was unwise not only in that subject but also in those related to it.

Paul's argument suggests that this view of wisdom is both flawed in what it assumes and inappropriate for assessing the validity of the gospel and the manner in which he proclaimed it. Moreover, the perceptions of wisdom and eloquent speech to which Paul responds are problematic because, as he contends, his proclamation did not rely on these criteria and because such criteria were not influential in the Corinthians' original belief and acceptance of the gospel. I offer this assumption for two reasons. First, if Paul did adhere to expected conventions or styles then his argument in 2.1–3.4 would ultimately collapse. To defend this claim, an important distinction must be recognized. There is a difference between a person 1) downplaying his or her abilities as a rhetorician and 2) clearly stating the non-use of rhetorical devices or methods. The former is a rhetorical device used to disarm an audience's preconceptions about a particular speaker or the use of

---

[63] Cf. Plato, *Gorg.*; Tacitus, *Dial.* 1.32. The complete version of Cicero's prefatory remarks about wisdom and eloquence are worth noting: "wisdom without eloquence is but of little advantage to states, but [also] eloquence without wisdom is often most mischievous, and is never advantageous to them" (*Inv.* 1.1).

[64] This is the assumption upon which Gorgias operates—see Plato, *Gorg.* 456b-c. For more on the philosophical background for Socrates' critique of Gorgias' rhetorical enterprise, see McComiskey, *New Sophistic Rhetoric*, 17-52.

rhetoric in general, and its usage does not result in a contradiction. The latter operates as a statement about a known particular event or occasion, one that can be verified as either true or false. In the case of 1 Corinthians, if Paul did employ rhetoric during his original sojourn in Corinth but, in writing to the Corinthians, denies the use of rhetoric during that original visit, this would not be Paul using an acceptable rhetorical device to downplay his abilities but a logical (and historical) contradiction.

There is a second reason why I contend that Paul did not rely on rhetorical criteria and that such criteria were not influential originally for the Corinthians. If these criteria were influential during Paul's original visit, to the same degree that they were following his departure, then the Corinthians would not have accepted the gospel he proclaimed, especially in the way he proclaimed it, because they would have considered it to be weak, unpersuasive, and foolishness. Thus, while Paul's argument to the Corinthians must show that the conventional criteria for judging an orator were not influential in the decision to accept the gospel, he must also explain why it is that the Corinthians originally accepted his message as God's wisdom. If, therefore, rhetorical devices, methods, or conventions were not the means of demonstrating the wisdom of the gospel, then what was?

2.3.2. Rhetorical Persuasion vs. the Spirit's Demonstration
2.3.2.1. Where It Begins

While the specific contrast is stated in 1 Cor 2.4, we must consider first the logical and theological basis for the contrast, a basis that appears in 1 Cor 1.17. In this latter passage, Paul states that his apostolic commission was not to baptize but to proclaim the gospel. He immediately qualifies this by saying that his proclamation would not be given in accordance with wise (human) speech, and his reason for not relying on wise speech is because to do so would divest the cross of Christ of its power. This qualifier suggests an important cause and effect relationship. If Paul relied on wise (human) speech, then the power of the cross would necessarily be lost. The obvious implication of this would be: if Paul desired to retain the power of the cross, he could not rely on wise speech (or the framework of human wisdom) to articulate the nature of the gospel. Paul must therefore rely on other means for not only proclaiming the gospel but also being assured that it would be understood properly.

We find clues for this notion of proper understanding in 1 Cor 1.18, where Paul notes two responses to the message of the cross: those who see it as foolishness, and those who see it as the power of God. With regard to the former, the message of the cross is viewed as foolishness because of a particular framework of ideas or standards by which wisdom and folly are judged. In 1 Cor 1.20 Paul interprets this framework of ideas as σοφία τοῦ κοσμοῦ. Those who view the gospel through this framework are those who are ἀπολλυμένοις. With regard to the latter, Paul only says one thing in 1.18 about those who see the cross as God's power: they are the ones who are σῳζομένοις. In view of the strict categories in 1.18, we can safely assume that neither σοφία τοῦ κοσμοῦ nor the wise speech of 1.17 were the cause for the Corinthians' original acceptance of the gospel. Moreover, if reliance on wise speech divests the cross of its power, and if Paul did not rely on wise speech when he originally proclaimed the gospel, and if the Corinthians originally accepted the gospel that Paul preached (and in the manner in which he gave it), then something else caused the Corinthians to know the cross of Christ as God's power.

The identification of the "something else" emerges in 1 Cor 2.4-5, where Paul not only strengthens the contrast between the usual styles of proclamation and his own but also reveals why it is the case that Corinthians originally believed and accepted his gospel. In this passage, Paul creates a specific distinction between a message given in wise, persuasive (human) speech and one that demonstrates the power of the Spirit. At stake in this is the proclamation that Paul gave during his initial visit to Corinth, a proclamation that he describes as ὁ λόγος μου καὶ τὸ κήρυγμά μου (2.4a). Moreover, the manner in which he proclaimed the message is also at stake, a manner (or mode) that he describes as οὐκ ἐν πειθοῖς σοφίας λόγοις ἀλλ' ἐν ἀποδείξει πνεύματος καὶ δυνάμεως (2.4b). It will be helpful to consider both sides of this description before seeking to ascertain the relevance of Paul's claim.

2.3.2.2. The Object of Paul's Proclamation

The pairing of λόγος and κήρυγμα in this instance is a point of scholarly dispute worthy of close attention. The focus of this dispute is to determine what Paul means by the phrase. Some have suggested a distinction between the venues in which Paul conducted his ministry, where λόγος refers to private instruction and κήρυγμα public exhortation.[65] This would be useful if one were attempting to view Paul's modes of preaching as comparable to the Sophistic orators of his day. On this reading, Paul's visit to Corinth would be seen as following the convention of obtaining an initial hearing (κήρυγμα) before supplying a more substantial teaching (λόγος) for those who accept him. However, this reading does not account for two basic details. First, the conventional method for an incoming orator was to speak to a select audience in order to gain permission to speak to a more general one. Second, and more importantly, it was argued earlier that Paul's ministry took place primarily in the private sectors, such as homes, rather than open venues or public gatherings. If we accept the private

---

[65] See Hodge, *First Epistle*, 31. Thiselton also notes Aquinas, Grotius, De Layra, Bengel, and Fascher as advocating this position (see *First Epistle*, 217).

venue as Paul's usual location for proclaiming the gospel, and if
we apply this to his ministry in Corinth, we can safely assume that
his proclamation of the gospel in Corinth was more private than
public, which would therefore make the above distinctions
between λόγος and κήρυγμα tenuous.

However, the earlier distinction between public teaching and
private instruction allowed enough hermeneutical space for the
religionsgeschichtliche Schule to examine Paul's teaching with
practices known from the mystery cults, especially Gnosticism.[66]
The comparison between Paul and the mystery cults seemed
straightforward in view of the apparent shared vocabulary—e.g.
wisdom, mystery, knowledge, spirit, perfect, mature.[67] As in these
mystery cults, Paul's message in public was general in content
whereas his private instruction revealed the secret hidden mysteries
of God, which could only be revealed to the initiated.[68] Those
advocating this view conclude that Paul in 2.4 refers primarily to
the public message (κήρυγμα) and secondarily to the private

---

[66] See e.g. R. Bultmann, *Theology of the New Testament* (trans. K. Grodel;
New York: Charles Scribner's Sons, 1951), 1.175-81; Schmithals, *Gnosticism in
Corinth*; Reitzenstein, *Hellenistic Mystery-Religions*.

[67] Wilson shows that the insistence on seeing this pool of terminology as
shared by Paul and the mystery religions is unjustified. Wilson argues that no
credence can be given to the assumption that when terms like μυστήριον or
τέλειος appear in Paul's writing they must be understood according to their use
in the mystery cults (see "How Gnostic," 68). See also H.J. Schoeps, *Paul: The
Theology of the Apostle in the Light of Jewish Religious History* (trans. H.
Knight; Philadelphia: Westminster Press, 1961), 20.

[68] Schmithals argues: "Paul also claims to be able to speak on [the topic of]
'wisdom,' but he does this only for the 'mature.' Thus his talk about wisdom
does not belong to the faith-awakening and church-founding preaching of the
gospel; it occurs, rather, in the reality of a post-baptismal instruction for those
who are advanced" (*The Theology of the First Christians* [trans. O.C. Dean;
Louisville: Westminster John Knox, 1997], 128).

instruction (λόγος),[69] with the latter serving as a segue for what he will say in 2.6-16. However, recent scholarship has shown that the arguments of the *religionsgeschichtliche Schule* prove neither the existence of Gnosticism in Corinth in the 1st century CE nor that its teachings were influential in the city following Paul's departure.[70] More substantial is the fact that these sorts of distinctions, especially those related to supposed levels of instruction, ultimately perpetuate the very issues that Paul seeks to remedy, namely disunity within the community of believers, a disunity rooted in faulty views of divine wisdom, how that wisdom is imparted, and to whom it is given.

Alternatively, in the discussion on the pairing of λόγος and κήρυγμα in 2.4, some have suggested that Paul is referring to the content and form (respectively) of his original proclamation.[71]

---

[69] If κήρυγμα were in fact Paul's primary focus in this passage, one would expect it to be listed first.

[70] See e.g. Wilson, "How Gnostic," 65-75; A.W. Carr, "The Rulers of this Age—1 Cor ii.6-8," *NTS* 23.1 (1976): 20-35 (esp. 28, 35); E.M. Yamauchi, "Pre-Christian Gnosticism, the New Testament and Nag Hammadi in Recent Debate," *Them* 10.1 (1984): 22-27; Fee, *First Epistle*, 11; G.E. Sterling, "'Wisdom Among the Perfect': Creation Traditions in Alexandrian Judaism and Corinthian Christianity," *NovT* 37.4 (1995): 354-84 (esp. 383-84); S.J. Chester, *Conversion at Corinth: Perspectives on Conversion in Paul's Theology and the Corinthian Church* (London: T&T Clark, 2003), 220-224 (esp. 223-24); T.E. Klutz, "Re-Reading 1 Corinthians after *Rethinking Gnosticism*," *JSNT* 26.2 (2003): 193-216 (esp. 194-96); Keener, *1-2 Corinthians*, 2-3; M.F. Bird and P.M. Sprinkle, "Jewish Interpretation of Paul in the Last Thirty Years," *CBR* 6.3 (2008): 355-76 (esp. 357, 360, 372). From a more practical viewpoint, Patte argues that the time between Paul's initial visit and his correspondence with the Corinthian community is too brief for the development of "several different kinds of heresy" (*Paul's Faith and the Power of the Gospel: A Structural Introduction to the Pauline Letters* [Philadelphia: Fortress, 1983], 301).

[71] E.g. Godet, *First Epistle*, 128; Robertson-Plummer, *First Epistle*, 32; Grosheide, *First Epistle*, 61; Fee, *First Epistle*, 94; Litfin, *Theology of Proclamation*, 199.

(However, some have transposed the meanings so that λόγος equals speech and κήρυγμα refers to the content of that speech).[72] While Paul could be describing his initial proclamation in this way, especially since he is contrasting it with conventional rhetorical styles or expectations, it does not appear to be the most likely reason for his pairing of the terms.[73] It is more plausible to see λόγος and κήρυγμα as a hendiadys for the preaching of the gospel of Christ crucified.[74] While Morris contends that "Paul is not differentiating between the two with any exactness (Conzelmann speaks of 'rhetorical duplication'), but simply uses two terms to bring out both the way he preached and the contents of his sermons,"[75] Schrage clarifies this point by saying:

> Dieser Schwachheit des Verkündigers, die die Schwachheit des Gekreuzigten selbst reflektiert, korrespondiert auch die Art und Weise der Verkündigung. Die gemeinsame Beziehung von λόγος und κήρυγμα auf die Verkündigung ist zwar trotz der Wiederaufnahme des καταγγέλειν (V 1) nicht unbestritten. Aber λόγος und κήρυγμα sind ebensowenig auf Form und Inhalt zu verteilen wie auf private und öffentliche Verkündigung. Trotz des doppelten μου ist eher eine umfassende Umschreibung der

---

[72] E.g. Boise, *Earlier Epistles*, 41; Goudge, *First Epistle*, 15; Barrett, *First Epistle*, 65.

[73] Besides, arguing for such a distinction places an unnecessary strain on the terminology. See Bullmore, *Theology of Rhetorical Style*, 216; Thiselton, *First Epistle*, 217.

[74] See Conzelmann, *1 Corinthians*, 54-55; Litfin, *Theology of Proclamation*, 205 n.79; Bullmore, *Theology of Rhetorical Style*, 21; Schnabel, *Der erste Brief*, 155; Fitzmyer, *First Corinthians*, 172.

[75] L.L. Morris, *The First Epistle of Paul to the Corinthians: An Introducton and Commentary* (Leicester: InterVarsity Press, 1986), 51.

apostolischen Tätigkeit beabsichtigt als eine Differen-
zierung, zumal alles auf V 5 zielt.[76]

The aiming at 2.5 is one key point to recognize when seeking to
understand the pairing of λόγος and κήρυγμα; the other is how
Paul uses these terms in the preceding context, which suggests
significant overlap in their respective meaning.

In 1 Cor 1.17-18, Paul employs λόγος to refer to the message
he was commissioned to proclaim, specifically the message of the
cross of Christ. Accordingly, Paul could reasonably describe this
message in possessive terms because it represents the core of his
apostolic vocation. Then in 1.23-24, Paul employs κήρυγμα to
refer to the message of Christ crucified that he originally
proclaimed in Corinth.[77] Here Paul could reasonably lay claim to
this message in the sense that he takes ownership for what he
preached. No matter which term Paul uses in these passages, two
related things are constant. First, the primary subject of Paul's
gospel is the cross of Christ. Second, the cross of Christ is
presented as the essential component of God's wisdom for
bringing about salvation to the world. We find a similar twofold
emphasis in 2.1-5 where Paul recounts his original proclamation of
the gospel of Christ crucified (see 2.2, 4) and where the aim of this
proclamation was belief in the saving power of God in the cross of
Christ (see 2.5).

---

[76] Schrage, *Der erste Brief*, 1.231.

[77] Admittedly, the text reads: ἡμεῖς δὲ κηρύσσομεν (1.23a). The plural
could indicate collaborative preaching either between Paul and Sosthenes or
Paul, Silas, and Timothy (if we allow the description in Acts 18.5).
Alternatively, it could serve as an inclusive statement about all who proclaim the
gospel. However, in view of the larger argument of 1 Cor 1–4, Paul could be
referring to his preaching and the preaching of Apollos in order to stress their
unity of content, despite any supposed differences in form.

2.3.2.3. The Manner (or, Mode)

With λόγος and κήρυγμα being understood as Paul's gospel message, we can now consider why Paul contrasts the manner in which he proclaimed this message with the conventions of ancient rhetoric. The contrast he supplies is given in negative and positive terms. On the negative side Paul emphatically asserts that his message did not rely on persuasive (or plausible) words of wisdom (οὐκ ἐν πειθοῖς σοφίας λόγοις). The most likely cause for this statement is the scrutiny of Paul's message following his departure, where the criteria used to judge rhetorical speeches were applied to his apostolic preaching. This recalls one part of the twofold issue noted above where Paul's message and his role were subjected to criticism. Particularly, also mentioned above, views of rhetoric and wisdom were held in tandem so that one's ability to speak eloquently was a result of possessing wisdom, or eloquent speech proved one's ability to proclaim (or reveal) wisdom.

If the Corinthians are at present judging Paul's original proclamation according to the criteria used for rhetorical speeches, in view of Paul's claims (i.e. he proclaims a simple message [2.2], and does so without relying on superior words or wisdom [2.1]) they would certainly deem his message not only rhetorically inept but also foolish. Or, if it is historically true that Paul did not rely on rhetorical methods to proclaim the gospel, as he asserts, and if the Corinthians judged his proclamation then according to the usual rhetorical criteria, his message would fail to persuade and be accepted as wise. However, Paul's argument reveals a crucial error in this assessment. While the Corinthians might hold to that conclusion now, Paul reminds them that they originally accepted his message of Christ crucified as God's wisdom, and did so in spite of his non-reliance on rhetorical conventions. We must remind ourselves of the significance of this claim and its function in Paul's argument. In saying that his message did not rely on rhetoric and its assumed wisdom, we should not read this as Paul simply using a rhetorical device to downplay any supposed ability on his part while preaching in Corinth;[78] instead we should read it as Paul presenting a verifiable statement about the nature of his original visit and the manner of his preaching.[79]

With λόγος and κήρυγμα remaining the focal point of the argument, Paul asserts positively that his message relied on the demonstration of the power of the Spirit (ἐν ἀποδείξει πνεύματος καὶ δυνάμεως). To grasp Paul's meaning here we must consider the key points of his claim, the first being his use of ἀπόδειξις. While a NT *hapax legomenon*, ἀπόδειξις appears frequently in other Greek texts and an awareness of these occurrences will inform our understanding of Paul's usage. In general, ἀπόδειξις can refer to a collection of ideas or data known to be true,[80] or it can be used to describe the authenticity or truthfulness of a given historical account.[81] Here ἀπόδειξις operates as a categorical statement about various items discussed— i.e. that which is stated is accepted knowledge.

In its more specialized usage, ἀπόδειξις refers to logical proofs made in public discourse or legal argumentation. Specifically, these proofs are based on undisputed data or

---

[78] *Contra* Collins, *First Corinthians*, 119.

[79] This is a point where we must recognize the distinction between what Paul does (rhetorically) in his letter and what he did during his original visit to Corinth. Schnabel is also instructive on this point: "Das Ptz. Präs. καταγγέλων signalisiert, dass Paulus bei seiner missionarischen Verkündigung immer, nicht nur manchmal, auf rhetorische Feuerwerke verzichtet" (*Der erste Brief*, 152-53). Cf. also Long, *Paul and Human Rights*, 85, 94, 114.

[80] E.g. Herodotus, *Hist.* 1.136.1; 1.207.7; 2.148.2; cf. also Josephus, *A.J.* 8.4.1.

[81] E.g. Herodotus, *Hist.* 1.1.0; 2.101.1; 4 Macc 3.19.

established facts, which can be used to refute false testimony.[82] In terms of logic, ἀποδείξις compares with other forms of proof in a specific way. A conclusion can be considered true by virtue of the fact that it follows logically from the premises, regardless of whether or not those premises are in fact true.[83] Alternatively, a conclusion is deemed necessarily or absolutely true not only because it follows the premises but also because the premises are known to be true.[84] Accordingly, ἀποδείξις carries the sense of irrefutable or incontrovertible proof.

What, then, is the irrefutable or incontrovertible proof to which Paul refers in 2.4? To answer that question, we must consider the other key point: the pairing of πνεῦμα and δύναμις. Earlier scholarship viewed πνεῦμα and δύναμις as separate terms referring to different phenomena that result from Paul's preaching. [85] Accordingly, πνεῦμα refers to the experiential presence of God's Spirit upon belief in the message (i.e. conversion), and δύναμις represents the miraculous signs (charismatic gifts?) that confirm the presence of God's Spirit in the believer.[86] This type of reading does seem to maintain an important connection between πνεῦμα and δύναμις that Paul would presumably endorse. In Gal 3.5 we find a similar pairing with a similar meaning: ὁ οὖν ἐπιχορηγῶν ὑμῖν τὸ πνεῦμα καὶ ἐνεργῶν δυνάμεις. However, the passage in Galatians differs from what we see in 1 Corinthians in two related ways. First, in

---

[82] Specifically Polybius, *Hist.* 1.12.6; 3.1.3; 4.86.2; 5.10.3; 10.21.8; 12.5.5; cf. also Pausanias, *Descr.* 10.9.11; Herodotus, *Hist.* 7.50.2; 8.101.2; Josephus, *A.J.* 8.2.8; 3 Macc 4.20.

[83] See Aristotle, *Rhet.* 2.24.

[84] Euclid employs the term as the final word for a mathematical proof—see *Elem.* 5. Prop. 8.

[85] See e.g. Edwards, *First Epistle*, 48.

[86] See John Chrysostom, *Hom. 1. Cor.*, 6.3; Fee, *First Epistle*, 95; idem, *God's Empowering Presence*, 92-93 (see esp. n.38).

Galatians δύναμις is also paired with ἔργον, which more naturally suggests something miraculous (i.e. works of power), especially when both are linked with the Spirit. This pairing of ἔργον with δύναμις is lacking in 1 Cor 2.4.

Second, the Galatians passage has δύναμις in the plural, which further suggests miracles.[87] By contrast, with regard to 1 Cor 2.4, Schrage points out that if miraculous deeds (or charismatic gifts) were in view, one would expect a plural (as seen in 12.10, 12.28) rather than the singular.[88] Moreover, even if we assume that δύναμις in 2.4 refers to miraculous deeds or charismatic gifts in the same way that it does in 12.10, despite the noted differences, another key distinction must be recognized. The context of Paul's remarks in chapter 12 is post-belief whereas the context for the argument of chapter 2 is the foundation for belief, or even that which brings about belief.[89] It could be argued that if this is the case, then Paul's use of δύναμις in 2.4 means something like "attesting signs" or "miracles" to prove the validity of the message proclaimed.[90] Nielsen has argued that such a reading makes the most sense of the text since God's power, in the light of the gospel message, has a visibly verifiable effect—i.e. ἀποδείξις.[91]

---

[87] Where δύναμις appears in the plural throughout the NT, it nearly always refers to miracles.

[88] Schrage, *Der erste Brief*, 1.234. See also Gräbe, *Power of God*, 38.

[89] The Gal 3.5 passage attests to this distinction—see J.D.G. Dunn, *Jesus and the Spirit: A Study of the Religious and Charismatic Experiences of Jesus and the First Christians as Reflected in the New Testament* (London: SCM Press, 1975), 227.

[90] See J. Rickaby, *Notes on Paul: Corinthians, Galatians, Romans* (London: Burns and Oats, 1898), 6, 11.

[91] H.K. Nielsen, "Paulus' Verwendung des Begriffes Δύναμις: Eine Replik zur Kreuzestheologie," in *Die Paulinische Literatur und Theologie* (TS 7; ed. S. Pedersen; Århus: Forlaget Aros, 1980), 154—as cited by Gräbe, *Power of God*, 65. Cf. Fee (*First Epistle*, 95 [esp. n.33]), who argues that πνεῦμα and δύναμις naturally refer to "visible evidences of the Spirit's presence," specifically the

However, this argument operates on a particular assumption about the use of ἀποδείξις, which is not necessarily the only or even primary usage or meaning, as noted above. Also, this argument assumes that miracles or attesting signs must accompany the message in order for the message to be God's wisdom (or true), and thus worthy of acceptance (cf. Paul's remarks in 1.22). Moreover, by favoring a "miraculous" reading for δύναμις this argument overlooks a particular nuance of δύναμις, especially its connections with salvation language in Paul.

Penna has shown that Paul installs a more specific meaning for δύναμις, a meaning that emerges when viewed in relation to a specific two-part event in history: the cross and resurrection of Christ.[92] Accordingly, when δύναμις appears in this context it carries a soteriological meaning, one that cannot be overlooked.[93] This meaning presents itself in 1 Cor 1.18, where Paul explicitly states that, for those who are being saved, the message of the cross is δύναμις θεοῦ. It should be noted that the "power" is not the preaching of the cross but the soteriological power of the cross that the preaching announces. Therefore, the preaching of the cross only reveals the power of God because that power was first revealed in the cross. Then in 1 Cor 6.14 Paul equates the means by which believers will be raised with that which raised Christ, and the shared means is God's power (διὰ τῆς δυνάμεως αὐτοῦ).

---

gift of tongues, otherwise the reference is ambiguous. Contrary to this perspective are Hays (*First Corinthians*, 36) and Keener (*The IVP Background Commentary: New Testament* [Downers Grove: InterVarsity, 1993], 457).

[92] See R. Penna, "The Gospel as 'Power of God' According to 1 Corinthians 1:18-25," in *Paul the Apostle* (vol. 1; trans. T.P. Wahl; Collegeville: Liturgical Press, 1996), 173-80.

[93] Menzies argues that this nuance is entirely unique to Paul—see *The Development of Early Christian Pneumatology with Special Reference to Luke-Acts* (Sheffield: JSOT Press, 1991), 48-49, 282-315.

From other Pauline texts that refer to the resurrected Christ, we learn what significance the resurrection has for the life of the believer. In 2 Cor 13.4 the power that raised Christ is that which will enable believers to live with him. Then, in Phil 3.8-12 the power that raised Christ in the past is the means by which Paul is able to live the righteous life granted by the cross in the present. Since the focus of Paul's argument in 1 Cor 2.4 is the message of the cross, and since this message is about what God has done in and for the world, especially humanity, and given that the goal of Paul's argument in 2.5 is to show the foundation for belief is God's power, it makes better sense of the text to say that δύναμις refers not to miracles but to the essence of the cross—i.e. salvation.[94]

While this might account for δύναμις, we still need to consider the other half of the pairing (i.e. πνεῦμα) and what Paul means by joining the two terms. With regard to meaning, we can reasonably assume that Paul is referring to God's Spirit. Scholars have pointed out that the use of πνεῦμα and δύναμις together in Paul's letters constitute a hendiadys for God's Spirit,[95] and it is only in 1 Cor 2.4 and 1 Thess 1.5 that we find πνεῦμα and δύναμις so joined.[96] The

---

[94] Moreover, as Conzelmann argues, miraculous signs in themselves "beweisen nicht die Wahrheit des Wortes vom Kreuz, sondern sind ihrerseits dem Kriterium des Kreuzes unterworfen" (*Der erste Brief an die Korinther* [Göttingen: Vandenhoeck & Ruprecht, 1981], 77).

[95] See e.g. Bultmann, *Theology*, 156; Litfin, *Theology of Proclamation*, 207; Bullmore, *Theology of Rhetorical Style*, 213-14; Collins, *First Corinthians*, 120; Thiselton, *First Epistle*, 222-23; Schnabel, *Der erste Brief*, 156; Fitzmyer, *First Corinthians*, 173.

[96] While Rom 15.13, 19 and Gal 3.5 do contain πνεῦμα and δύναμις, their syntactical relationship and theological function in those verses are distinct from their usage here in 1 Cor 2.4. In Romans, the relationship between πνεῦμα and δύναμις is a dependent one, where πνεῦμα is a genitive of production and δύναμις is the product. In Galatians, πνεῦμα and δύναμις are depicted as distinct manifestations from the same God: 1) the giving of the Spirit, and 2)

similarities and the differences between these two passages repay close attention, for doing so will assist our understanding of Paul's view of the Spirit in the proclamation. Like 1 Cor 2.1-5, the opening verses of 1 Thessalonians recount Paul's original visit, and the object of discussion is the proclamation of the gospel message. In terms of syntax, πνεῦμα and δύναμις in both texts are linked with the conjunction καί, and the function of the pair is to describe the manner in which Paul proclaimed his message. Moreover, as in 1 Cor 2.1-5, Paul in 1 Thess 1.5 offers a contrast when describing his style of preaching: τὸ εὐαγγέλιον ἡμῶν οὐκ ἐγενήθη εἰς ὑμᾶς ἐν λόγῳ μόνον.[97] Instead, Paul declares that he proclaimed the gospel in Thessalonica ἐν δυνάμει καὶ ἐν πνεύματι ἁγίῳ καὶ [ἐν] πληροφορίᾳ πολλῇ. A final syntactical similarity in both texts is the emphatic correlative conjunctions οὐκ...ἀλλά, which Paul uses to distinguish between what he did and did not do in proclaiming the gospel message.

The differences between the two texts are clear and only require minimal attention. In 1 Thess 1.5 the order of πνεῦμα and δύναμις is reversed; the Thessalonian passage incorporates πληροφορία as a third descriptive term for Paul's preaching, and all three are prefaced with the instrumental preposition ἐν, which might suggest a threefold description for how Paul preached;[98] and πνεῦμα in 1 Thess 1.5 is qualified with ἅγιος, which could be read as "holy spirit" or "spirit of holiness." One further difference between the two passages should be considered. The way in which πνεῦμα and δύναμις stand in relationship with ἀπόδειξις in 1 Cor 2.4 seems to be unlike their relationship with πληροφορία in

---

works of power or miracles (cf. Acts 8.13; 1 Cor 12.10, 28, 29; 2 Cor 12.12; Heb 2.4).

[97] Bruce reads the last phrase as, "speech unaccompanied by the convicting power of the Holy Spirit" (*1 & 2 Thessalonians* [Waco: Word, 1982], 14).

[98] G.L. Green, *The Letters to the Thessalonians* (Grand Rapids: Eerdmans, 2002), 95.

1 Thess 1.5. In the latter text, "complete conviction" appears to be a part of Paul's threefold description, and it is possible that this conviction belongs to Paul's preaching,[99] whereas in 1 Cor 2.4 it is God's Spirit who provides the ἀπόδειξις of the gospel.

However, upon further reflection, the difference between the two texts might not be so pronounced. In 1 Thess 1.5, Paul's stress falls on the fact that the gospel came to the Thessalonians not just in words; they also experienced it as being accompanied by the Spirit in power and complete conviction.[100] A similar emphasis is at work in 1 Cor 2.4 where Paul states that the Spirit was actively and powerfully involved in the proclamation of the gospel. Moreover, for Paul the cross of Christ is the power of God and the message he proclaims not only speaks to but also relies on that power. Thus, Paul does not need human superior speech or wisdom in order to proclaim persuasively the gospel of Christ crucified; to rely on such extraneous devices would only strip the cross of its inherent power (see 1.17).[101] Instead Paul relies on the powerful work of God's Spirit to demonstrate the validity and saving power of the message.

2.3.2.4. The Aim of ἀπόδειξις πνεύματος καὶ δυνάμεως

This brings us to the aim or purpose of Paul's claim to rely on God's Spirit in the proclamation, marked by the ἵνα-clause of 2.5. Paul openly states that he did not want the Corinthians' faith (πίστις) to rest in human wisdom but in God's power.

---

[99] By this it is meant that Paul's manner of preaching revealed his full conviction (or belief) in what he proclaimed to the Thessalonians.

[100] Cf. Long, who contends that "spiritual experiences...accompanied conversion" (*Paul and Human Rights*, 224). However, Long does not elaborate on what those spiritual experiences might be.

[101] Or to cite Lothian: "Foreign ornaments, instead of improving [the preaching of the cross], only obscure its glory, and neutralise its power" (*Expository Lectures*, 20).

Admittedly, reading "faith" for πίστις requires explanation. Some interpret πίστις in 2.5 in light of the assumed rhetorical features of the passage, thus suggesting the idea of logical "proof."[102] However this suggestion not only prioritizes the giving of proof but also downplays the need for any human response to the given proof. This reading also downplays the role of the Spirit working in the message, a work that becomes foundational to the response given. Moreover this interpretation becomes cumbersome when read in light of the argument of 2.4-5, where the "Spirit and power" are the "proof" (ἀποδείξις) that becomes the foundation upon which the Corinthians respond, and that response is "faith" (πίστις).

We must also be careful not to see this faith as merely a general religious belief or as an uncritical acceptance of some abstract idea. The term is much richer and more nuanced than that. As Thiselton notes, πίστις is best "described as 'a polymorphous concept' (like σάρξ, *flesh*, and ἀλήθεια, *truth*) since any attempt at an abstract definition encounters contexts which will not make some *single* meaning or 'essence' of the term."[103] At the very least, we can say that πίστις includes notions of complete "intellectual conviction"[104] about what is proclaimed as truth, thus making πίστις—as a response to the proclamation of the gospel message—something reasonable, justifiable, and worthy to possess. This type of meaning fits with what Paul is doing with his argument in 2.1-5, especially as it relates to the present scrutiny of his message and manner of proclamation. In this case, Paul reminds them that their original faith was not founded upon human eloquence or wisdom, for such things view the gospel as unreasonable, not justifiable and unworthy of acceptance (i.e.

---

[102] Winter advocates this position—see *Philo and Paul*, 159-64.

[103] Thiselton, *First Epistle*, 223.

[104] *Ibid.*, 223.

πίστις).[105] Instead, as Paul reminds them, their original faith was founded upon the power of God in the cross of Christ, a power revealed by God's Spirit.

2.3.3. The Role of the Spirit

From the above comparison, we begin to understand why Paul relies on the power of God's Spirit at work in the proclamation, specifically in the argument of 1 Corinthians where Paul contends that he relied on nothing else. This reliance substantiates not only his present argument in the letter but also the historical validity of his claim about his original visit. It has already been noted that Paul's apostolic mission in Corinth and the manner in which he proclaimed the gospel came under scrutiny. Since his role and message are now seen as inferior to the rhetorical abilities or skills of traveling orators, he is also now viewed as unwise and his message as foolishness. In response, Paul must show that these views are not only false in what they assume but were also not influential in the Corinthians' original decision about the gospel.

Since Paul preached the simple gospel of Christ crucified, a message that declares God's wisdom, and did so without the use of superior speech or (human) wisdom, an explanation must be given for why the Corinthians accepted or believed the gospel in the manner in which Paul gave originally it. For Paul the explanation is quite simple: it is only by relying on the power of God's Spirit that one can communicate the simple message of Christ crucified as God's (saving) wisdom, and it is only by the Spirit's power (or work) that one can accept the message as wisdom. Thus, in view of the scrutiny of his role and message, Paul claims that the Spirit worked powerfully in the original proclamation and reception of that message.

---

[105] Cf. Litfin, *Theology of Proclamation*, 207-08.

2.3.3.1. In the Proclamation (1 Cor 2.1-5, 13-14)

In saying that God's Spirit is powerfully at work in the message of Christ crucified I am stating something about the nature of Paul's role in proclaiming that message. From the Jewish perspective, especially that of Second Temple Judaism, the Spirit was often described as enabling (or empowering) and speaking through God's chosen prophet (e.g. Num 23.7; 24.2; Zech 1.6; cf. also Jub 25.14; 31.12).[106] Accordingly, in this regard the role of the Spirit appears to have two important functions. First, the Spirit is the means through which the divine perspective is granted to the chosen prophet, and it is from this perspective that the prophet speaks and offers guidance or judgment. Second, the Spirit is the authentication of the message proclaimed. Thus, prophets speaking the true words or oracles of God will do so only because the Spirit comes upon and empowers them to speak the message they must proclaim (see e.g. Isa 61.1; Mic 3.8). In this way, the message has authority not because the prophet speaks it but because the Spirit authenticates what is spoken. These two functions are recognizable in Paul's reminder to the Corinthians about his apostolic sojourn and the proclamation of the gospel of Christ crucified.

I should highlight one further point as it relates not only to Paul's preaching of the cross but also the role of the Spirit in that preaching, namely the theological and historical significance of both. If the message of the cross is a message announcing the inauguration of God's kingdom, and if on the basis of 1 Cor 1.18-21 and 27-28 this message announces judgment upon the things of the world that are contrary to God, and if that judgment includes the overturning of the systems of the world and the wisdom that stands behind such systems, then it becomes clear that, for Paul, the cross of Christ is the decisive eschatological turning point in

---

[106] See Menzies (*Development*, 54), who argues that this connection appears to be made by the translators of the LXX.

history.[107] The initial confirmation for both the theological and historical significance of the message and Paul's role in proclaiming it is the role of the Spirit.

We see this by considering the Jewish understanding that the giving or presence of the Spirit for or within the people of God represented the inauguration of God's kingdom (e.g. Isa 11.2; 28.5; 42.1; 52.7; 59.21; 61.1; Joel 2.28-32).[108] By way of comparison,[109]

---

[107] Cf. Beker who sees the cross as "the *apocalyptic* turning point of history" (*Paul the Apostle: The Triumph of God in Life and Thought* [Edinburgh: T&T Clark, 1980], 205—emphasis added). Matlock more recently argued that the language of apocalyptic has not only been taken to extremes but also not consistently applied, especially in view of its basic meaning (see *Unveiling the Apocalyptic Paul: Paul's Interpreters and the Rhetoric of Criticism* [Sheffield: Sheffield Academic Press, 1996]).

[108] This argument is offered in view of Philip's observation: "There are numerous passages in the Hebrew Scriptures that are generally considered as referring to a future outpouring of the Spirit. Two strands of thought are predominant—1) the idea that in the age to come the gift of the Spirit will be bestowed upon a messianic figure (Isa 11.2; 42.1; 61.1). The post-biblical literature (*1 Enoch* 49.2-3; 61.11-12; 62.2; *Pss Sol* 17.37; 18.7; CD 2.11-13; 11QMelch 2.18; 1QSb 5.24; cf. 4QpIsa[a] 3.10-19) continue to affirm the gift of the Spirit to (a) messiah/anointed figure(s) during the end-time. 2) in the future age the community/nation will be endowed with the gift of the Spirit (Isa 28.5-6; 32.15; 44.3; 59.12; Ezek 36.23-31; 37.1-14; 39.29; Joel 3.1-5; Zech 12.10). However, references to the Spirit in Second Temple Judaism are diverse and both postulate a future anticipation (*Jub.* 1.22-23; cf. *4 Ezra* 6.26) and acknowledge the Spirit's present availability (1QS 3.6-12; 9.3-5; 1QH 8.19; 16.11b-12; Wis 1.4-7; 7.22-25; 9.17-18; Philo *Leg.* 1.31-38; *Her.* 259; *Virt.* 212-219)" (*Origins of Pauline Pneumatology*, 32-33).

[109] See J. Coppens, "'Mystery' in the Theology of Saint Paul and its Parallels at Qumran," in *Paul and Qumran: Studies in New Testament Exegesis* (ed. J. Murphy-O'Conner; London: Geoffrey Chapman, 1968), 132-58 (esp. 135-37); cf. also M. Bockmuehl, *Revelation and Mystery in Ancient Judaism and Pauline Christianity* (Grand Rapids: Eerdmans, 1997), 42-56; B.L. Gladd, *Revealing the Mysterion: The Use of Mystery in Daniel and Second Temple Judaism with its Bearing on First Corinthians* (Berlin: Walter de Gruyter, 2008), 115-23, 127-64.

the Qumran literature speaks of God as the one who establishes the mystery of his divine kingdom and reveals it to his faithful (1QS 9.18; 11.19), and the means of revelation is by God's Spirit (1QH 12.11; 13.19; cf. 1QS 4.3). If we accept that Paul's gospel was a proclamation of the in-breaking of God's eschatological kingdom, then it becomes clear why he sees the role of God's Spirit as indispensable to his apostolic mission in Corinth.

2.3.3.1.1. The Message Proclaimed (1 Cor 2.1-5)

Throughout this chapter I have stressed a distinction not only between the ways in which the Corinthians originally viewed Paul's message and their current skepticism but also between the manner in which Paul conducted his ministry and the conventions or expectations for traveling orators. Integral to this treatment has been the idea that there is a reason for the current skepticism of Paul's mission and message, one presumably based on a particular set of standards or expectations. Linked with this is the implication that there was a reason why the Corinthians originally believed and accepted Paul's mission and message, a belief and acceptance *not* based on the standards or expectations now influencing the Corinthians' skepticism. It is here in 2.1-5 that Paul explicitly underlines these observations. Specifically, it is with this passage that we find the cause for the Corinthians' original decision to see and accept the message of the cross as God's power and wisdom. Moreover, it is with this passage that we feel the weight of Paul's contrasting argument between his original apostolic mission and proclamation and the approach or methods of Sophistic orators.

To state the case bluntly: Paul argues that something other than human wisdom and eloquent speech compelled the Corinthians to understand, believe, and accept the gospel as God's wisdom. Paul supplies the content to that something else in 1 Cor 2.1-5, and he does so by way of a contrast. The contrast begins in 2.1, where

Paul emphatically states that he did not come proclaiming the message of the cross according to "superior speech or wisdom" (2.1). By the phrase, "superior speech or wisdom" we can reasonably assume that Paul is referring to the "wisdom of the world" (1.20) as a means for ascertaining the ways of God. Since the wisdom of the world deems the ways of God in the cross as foolishness, it is highly improbable that Paul would rely on such ways to proclaim the cross as wisdom. This suggests that Paul relied on other means because if he relied on the means of human wisdom, and by extension its mode of expression, he would not only fail to show the wisdom of God in the cross but also empty the cross of its inherent power. As an eschatological herald of what God has done in the cross of Christ, Paul simply cannot operate in accordance with such means; to do so would be to undermine both his mission and his message. Thus, and once again, in saying that he rejects the use of superior speech or wisdom, Paul is not employing the rhetorical device of self-deprecation in order to gain a sympathetic ear while in Corinth; he is making a logical and historical claim about his role and message that can be verified by the Corinthians' own experience.

Paul illustrates this point by stating his singular aim during his apostolic sojourn: οὐ γὰρ ἔκρινά τι εἰδέναι ἐν ὑμῖν εἰ μὴ Ἰησοῦν Χριστὸν καὶ τοῦτον ἐσταυρωμένον (2.2). This describes the essential content of his message, which is a restating of his earlier description in 1.18-20, and it is this message that was given without the aid of superior speech or (human) wisdom. Paul furthers his point by recalling the manner in which he came to the Corinthians, a manner that he describes as: ἐν ἀσθενείᾳ καὶ ἐν φόβῳ καὶ ἐν τρόμῳ πολλῷ (2.3). This descriptive phrase has been interpreted in various ways.

First, it has been suggested that Paul is referring to emotional distress as a result of his complete failure in Athens to persuade those hearing the gospel.[110] However, this sort of reading is not only speculative but also a psychologizing of the text. Second, it has been suggested that Paul's "weakness" in particular was physical (i.e. sickness or some ailment), thus causing him to be concerned with his effectiveness as a speaker—hence, "fear and great trembling."[111] This explanation would work if (and only if) Paul were concerned about conducting himself as a Sophistic orator. Alternatively, it is possible (if not more likely) that "weakness" in this context refers to something non-physical and

---

[110] E.g. Edwards, *First Epistle*, xi-xii; Dods, *First Epistle*, 12; Robertson-Plummer, *First Epistle*, 31; Grosheide, *First Epistle*, 59; S.J. Kistemaker, *Exposition of the First Epistle to the Corinthians* (Grand Rapids: Baker, 1993), 71, 72; J.L. Gonzáles, *Acts: The Gospel of the Spirit* (New York: Orbis, 2001), 203; Pascuzzi, *First and Second Corinthians*, 7; Fitzmyer, *First Corinthians*, 172. A few scholars suggest that Paul's failure in Athens was merely partial, although this is still portrayed as contributing to Paul's demeanor and style of preaching in Corinth—see e.g. Goudge, *First Epistle*, 15; J. Pathrapankal, "From Areopagus to Corinth (Acts 17:22-31; 1 Cor 2:1-5): A Study on the Transition from the Power of Knowledge to the Power of the Spirit," *MSt* 23.1 (2006): 61-80; cf. also E. Haenchen, *The Acts of the Apostles: A Commentary* (trans. B. Noble and G. Shinn; Oxford: Blackwell, 1971), 319-20; Witherington, *Conflict and Community*, 121 n.3.

For those who reject the idea of a failure in Athens as having an effect on Paul's ministry in Corinth, see e.g. Munck, *Paul and the Salvation of Mankind*, 172; Barrett, *First Epistle*, 63; Fee, *First Epistle*, 92; Lamp, *First Corinthians*, 152 n.92. Héring seems to play down the emotional consequence: "[1 Cor 1.17] reminds us that the Apostle, after his check at Athens (where he had adopted the language of philosophy, according to Acts 17), had decided to change his method in evangelizing the Corinthians: he had spoken bluntly and directly of the Cross of Christ" (*First Epistle*, 7-8).

[111] E.g. Sadler, *First and Second Epistles*, 28; A. Schweitzer, *The Mysticism of Paul the Apostle* (trans. W. Montgomery; New York: H. Holt and Company, 1931), 152-55; M. Dibelius and W.G. Kümmel, *Paul* (trans. F. Clarke; Philadelphia: Westminster Press, 1953), 42-43; M. Thrall, *The First and Second Letters of Paul to the Corinthians* (Cambridge: Cambridge University Press, 1965), 22-23; Fee, *First Epistle*, 92.

connotes something akin to an inner frailty or even a vulnerable or humble disposition. There are a number of instances, especially in the Pauline writings, where this type of meaning emerges. [112] Moreover, when φόβος and τρόμος appear together in the LXX, they function as a hendiadys illustrating the demeanor of one who is humbled by the awesome presence of God. [113] When taken together ἀσθένεια, φόβος, and τρόμος characterize the manner in which Paul proclaimed the gospel, a manner that stands in contrast to that of Sophistic orators of his day.[114] Whereas Sophistic orators would come proclaiming their superior wisdom and rhetorical abilities for expounding complex subjects, Paul claims that he came to Corinth with a simple message and gave it with humility,

---

[112] E.g. Mk 14.38 (//Mt 26.41); Rom 4.19; 5.6; 8.3, 26; 9.19; 14.1, 2; 1 Cor 1.25, 27; 8.7, 10, 11, 12; 12.22; 15.43; 2 Cor 12.10; 13.3, 4, 9; Gal 4.9; Heb 4.15; 5.2; 7.18, 28; 11.34; 1Pt 3.7.

[113] E.g. Ex 15.16; Isa 19.16; Jdt 15.2.

[114] I need to stress here that Paul's statement about himself, as it compares with the Sophistic orators of his day, applies to what he says in the letter about his visit. We cannot know if Paul stated anything (in person) about his demeanor or even if he used such a statement rhetorically to make a distinction between himself and Sophistic orators when he originally proclaimed the gospel in Corinth. As was argued earlier (see 2.2.2.3 above), we need to recognize the difference between what Paul does in writing and what he does orally, and we must remember that Paul's letters are not precise reflections of either the gospel he proclaimed or the manner in which he proclaimed it. Thus, we must be cautious in concluding that Paul used ἀσθένεια, φόβος and τρόμος as a rhetorical device in order to distance himself from Sophistic orators *while preaching in Corinth* (although cf. Witherington, *Conflict and Community*, 123-24 [cf. 46 n.139]; Collins, *First Corinthians*, 116). There is simply nothing in the text that suggests Paul needed to make such a distinction or that he in fact did so during that original visit.

reverence, and in complete reliance on God's power to work in and through that simple message.[115]

We see Paul's emphasis on relying on God's power when we consider how Paul concludes the contrast in 2.4, which began in 2.1 but was left unfinished. It is also in this passage that Paul explicitly distinguishes his proclamation from the Sophistic orators and their conventional styles or methods. More importantly, 2.4 begins to answer the question of why the Corinthians originally believed and accepted Paul's gospel message. On the basis of the preceding discussion of πνεῦμα and δύναμις being a hendiadys for God's Spirit, the twofold role that the Spirit plays in prophetic utterances, and Paul's belief that God has overturned the wisdom of the world and its ways of knowing, the only explanation for why the Corinthians originally believed and accepted Paul's simple, unpolished message is that God's Spirit was powerfully at work in that message.

As noted earlier, the "power" is not the preaching of the cross (*per se*) but the soteriological power of the cross that the preaching announces, a power made manifest not by human wisdom or eloquence but only by God's Spirit.[116] For Paul, the proof that this is the case is the Corinthians' own experience and their original acceptance and belief. In other words, they ought to know that such things were not based on human displays of wisdom or eloquence but on the powerful work of God's Spirit. Here, and following Thiselton once again,[117] we can expand the earlier

---

[115] This description of his demeanor becomes another point of reference for the Corinthians in their assessment of Paul's argument concerning his original role and message.

[116] Cf. D.L. Dabney, "*Pneumatologica Crucis*: Reclaiming *Theologica Crucis* for a Theology of the Spirit Today," *SJT* 53.4 (2000): 511-24.

[117] See in particular his conclusion: "This does not mean that argument or persuasion can play no role; it means that something more is involved that

definition of πίστις[18] so that Paul's emphasis is not simply on intellectual assent but spiritual conviction about the reasonableness of the gospel as God's saving wisdom, a conviction made possible by the powerful work of the Spirit in the proclamation of the gospel. Or as Dunn argues: "their experience was not so much of intellectual persuasion, but rather of being grasped by divine power, of being compelled with a whole-hearted conviction to accept and affirm Paul's message."[119]

2.3.3.1.2. Source of the Content Proclaimed (1 Cor 2.13-14)

In view of the remarks about the giving of the Spirit, especially as it relates to the revelation of God's wisdom, Paul in 1 Cor 2.13 argues that it is the Spirit who provides the content of what is taught. Moreover, Paul contends that it is only by the Spirit that one can discern the message of the Spirit as given by those who proclaim it; those without the Spirit fail to see and hear the message as God's wisdom (2.14). We might be tempted to read this latter point as further evidence that Paul has two different levels of instruction in mind. Accordingly, on one level Paul speaks the general words of the gospel to everyone, while on another he proclaims to the spiritual elite the Spirit-given words of the deep truths of God. However, this once again perpetuates the problem that Paul seeks to remedy, namely status-seeking on the basis of an assumed superior knowledge or spirituality.

With regard to Paul's remarks about words taught by the Spirit, we might also be tempted to see this as suggesting a type of divine instruction (or revelation) via ecstatic speech or tongue-

---

speaks to the heart as well as to the mind and creates a new reality (δύναμις θεοῦ) for the believer" (*First Epistle*, 223).

[118] See 2.3.3.1. above.

[119] Dunn, *Jesus and the Spirit*, 226-27; cf. also Lim, "'Not in Persuasive Words'," 147.

speaking. [120] However, at least three problems arise from this reading: 1) Paul's later argument on ecstatic speech or tongue-speaking, in chapters 12–14, becomes logically problematic if he is referring to such things here, 2) it does not correspond with the historical circumstances of Paul's original proclamation of the gospel in Corinth, and 3) it continues to perpetuate the issue of divisiveness among the believers in Corinth.

On the first problem, and as it was noted earlier, the context of the argument in 1 Cor 12 is post-belief whereas the context for the argument of chapter 2 is the foundation for belief, or even that which brings about belief. Moreover, even if the charismatic gift of tongues as described in chapters 12–14 is in view for 2.13-14, this means that only a select few would be able to understand Paul's Spirit-speech (cf. 1 Cor 14), which therefore leaves open the possibility of boasting by those who know what is proclaimed. To strengthen this point, we need to consider the second problem. In saying that Paul's reference in 2.13-14 deals with ecstatic speech or tongue-speaking, we are saying something about the manner in which he originally proclaimed the gospel message. However, there is nothing in the text (or other known sources) to suggest that ecstatic speech or tongue-speaking was integral to the original proclamation of the gospel, in terms of its specific articulation. To assume that it was leaves open the concern mentioned with the first problem (i.e. only a select few would benefit from the message given) and it does not alleviate the potential for boasting within the community. Hence the third problem: to say that 2.13-14 refers to

---

[120] Cf. MacDonald, who takes 1 Cor 2.13 as referring to tongue-speaking— see *The Pauline Churches: A Socio-historical Study of Institutionalization in the Pauline and Deutero-Pauline Writings* (Cambridge: Cambridge University Press, 1991), 47. It is possible, though not certain, that Schnökel allows for this when he says, "The appropriate language is pneumatic; a pneumatic message requires a pneumatic language" (*A Manual of Hermeneutics* [trans. L.M. Rosa; ed. B.W.R. Pearson; Sheffield: Sheffield Academic Press, 1998], 51).

ecstatic speech or tongue-speaking, and to admit that such things would only benefit a select few, would be to advocate either various levels of instruction or differing levels of spiritual insight, which then can become grounds for maintaining divisions.

We must therefore seek a solution that both avoids these three problems and best explains Paul's meaning in this passage. The simplest answer comes by recalling the role of a prophet and the work of God's Spirit in that role. If the Spirit of God is the one who supplies the revelatory message of God, especially God's wisdom, and if the prophet is the one who proclaims that message, and if the Spirit is the one who authenticates what is proclaimed, then in that sense the message given is not human speech attempting to disclose the wisdom of God. Instead, the prophetic message articulates the divine wisdom that God's Spirit discloses to the prophet. Therefore, what the prophet speaks will be based on the (revealed) wisdom of God, reflecting the truths of that wisdom, and in harmony with what the Spirit has revealed. Thus, Paul, as an eschatological prophet of what God has done in Christ, proclaims the wisdom of what God has done—a work that remained hidden with God throughout the ages—and the wisdom Paul proclaims is that which was given to him by God's Spirit, and the Corinthians can know the truth of what Paul proclaims because the Spirit is also at work in the reception of that message. This follows from Paul's argument that the cause for the Corinthians' belief in the gospel was not eloquent or persuasive words of human wisdom; it was the Spirit working powerfully in the message.

2.3.3.2. In the Reception (1 Cor 2.8-12, 15-16)

When Paul deals with the wisdom he professed in his preaching, he makes a categorical distinction about the kind of wisdom he has in view. The wisdom of which Paul speaks is God's wisdom, not the wisdom of the world—or the wisdom of the rulers of this age.[121] It must be stressed here that the wisdom Paul teaches refers to the gospel message he proclaimed and not some second-level teaching of divine wisdom only reserved for a select few.[122] It is true that scholars, especially those of the *religionsgeschichtliche Schule*, have read Paul's remarks about teaching wisdom to the "perfect" as referring to a select group in Corinth. Moreover, this sort of reading also finds itself in the service of those advocating influences from mystery religions or Gnostic theology, where the recipients of the secret wisdom or knowledge are made "perfect."

However, these types of readings create contradictions within Paul's argument, whereby in one place he speaks against classes of believers but here acknowledges—if not endorses—distinct levels of believers.[123] Two additional issues arise from these types of readings. First, they lack support from the text itself, for nothing in Paul's argument suggests different levels of instruction given at different times during his ministry in Corinth. Second, they relegate what seems to be the primary focus of Paul's argument to a secondary position. Specifically, Paul's words about speaking wisdom to the "perfect" are claims about ways of knowing, or right

---

[121] This distinction prohibits us from reading Paul's words in 1 Cor 2.1 as a rejection of the entire notion of wisdom.

[122] Fatehi makes the explicit connection between σοφία θεοῦ in 1 Cor 1.17 and the gospel message—see *The Spirit's Relation to the Risen Lord in Paul: An Examination of Its Christological Implications* (Tübingen: Mohr Siebeck, 2000), 180.

[123] See Theissen who argues: "The limitation to a particular circle in the community would not have been possible in the letter, since the letter was read to all in the liturgy, at which both outsiders and unbelievers could be present (1 Cor 14:16, 23ff). The announcement that 'we speak wisdom among the perfect' (1 Cor 2:6*) is meaningful only in the situation of oral discourse, where the speaker can know all the addressees and where his speech occurs only once; through being fixed in a letter it becomes potentially accessible to all" (*Psychological Aspects of Pauline Theology* [trans. J.P. Gavin; Edinburgh: T&T Clark, 1987], 347).

discernment. For the purposes of this chapter, we are concerned only with Paul's view of the Spirit's role in how believers know (or rightly discern) the gospel to be God's wisdom.

2.3.3.2.1. The Wisdom God Gives (1 Cor 2.8-12)

In 1 Cor 2.6b-7, Paul begins to explain this role by asserting that God's wisdom is a mystery, one that has remained undisclosed throughout the ages. Since this wisdom is of God and since this wisdom is an unseen (or unknown) mystery, Paul declares that the only way in which anyone other than God can know it is if God chooses to reveal it (2.11). With God's hidden wisdom being distinct from the wisdom of the world, and with God's wisdom being something that can only be known by divine revelation, Paul can readily argue the rulers of this age do not know (or understand) God's wisdom (2.6, 8). Thus, ways of knowing rooted in human wisdom will necessarily fail to ascertain God's wisdom.

Paul further stresses the inabilities of human wisdom by stating that God has already rendered them impotent (cf. 1.20-21). Thus, knowledge of God's wisdom must come through other means, in this case, God's self-revelation—a work that Paul says is only performed by God's Spirit (2.10). This is why Paul emphatically states that the πνεῦμα τὸ ἐκ τοῦ θεοῦ is the only means by which believers can know the things freely given to them by God (2.12); the πνεῦμα τοῦ κόσμου fails in this regard because the spirit of the world is not the Spirit of God, and only the Spirit of God can know the things of God (cf. 2.11). Therefore, for Paul, the proof that the Spirit was powerfully at work in the message is found in the Corinthians' original acceptance of the gospel as God's wisdom; for it is only by such a powerful work that they could come to know (or discern) the gospel as God's wisdom.

2.3.3.2.2. God's Wisdom Employed (1 Cor 2.15-16)

Paul climaxes this point by asserting that an extension of this work of the Spirit is that those who "have the mind of Christ" are able to know the "mind of the Lord [God]" (2.16), which enables them to discern the things of God (i.e. wisdom), things that are foolishness to the ψυχικὸς ἄνθρωπος (2.14). This builds on Paul's earlier claim that God's Spirit is the one who reveals the things of God, "even the depths of God" (2.10), things that Paul now says can only be discerned by ὁ πνευματικός (2.15). This type of categorical distinction in how the things of God (i.e. wisdom) are understood by opposite groups follows from the distinctions that Paul has made all along.

From the start of his argument, Paul has distinguished those who see the gospel of Christ crucified as God's wisdom from those who see it as foolishness; the former are those "being saved," the latter are those "being destroyed" (1.18). Throughout the specific argument of 1 Cor 2.6-16, Paul argues that the wisdom of the world is incapable of knowing the things of God, whereas those who have the Spirit of God are able to know the wisdom of God. The distinction between the ψυχικὸς ἄνθρωπος and ὁ πνευματικός, and the kind of discernment ascribed to each, is an emphatic way of maintaining the larger contrast. Moreover, it furthers Paul's case for why the Corinthians originally accepted his gospel as God's (saving) wisdom.

2.4. Conclusions

This chapter explored Paul's view of the Spirit's role in the proclamation of the cross and how that view compares with Greco-Roman perceptions of rhetorical skill and persuasiveness. Specifically, I examined why Paul contrasts a message proclaimed in wise, eloquent or persuasive (human) speech and one that demonstrates the power of the Spirit. First, I argued that Paul's simple message was originally given in a social context where rhetorical prowess and claims of possessing wisdom were highly prized. Here I emphasized the cultural assumptions commonly held within 1st century Corinth and how they might have played a role in how Paul's original sojourn and gospel message were received. However, it was argued, based on the textual evidence and the specific claims made by Paul, that neither Paul nor his message were originally judged according to the standards of human wisdom, specifically the standards of rhetorical skill and persuasiveness. Only after Paul departed Corinth did his role and message come under a scrutiny influenced by human wisdom. Thus, crucial for Paul's argument is that the Corinthians originally accepted his message in the manner in which he gave it. In effect, therefore, the function of the contrast in Paul's argument is to turn the criticisms back onto the Corinthians.

Secondly, I argued that Paul supplies the reason for the Corinthians' original belief and acceptance of the gospel, in spite of the simple and unpolished way in which he proclaimed it. Here I emphasized Paul's belief that by the Spirit alone, working in and through the message of the cross, were the Corinthians able to see the message of the cross as God's wisdom. As stated above, this emphasis points away from any rhetorical ability or persuasiveness on Paul's part and toward the power of the Spirit at work in the messenger and message. A key implication for Paul's argument is that it is by the Spirit, working in and through the message of the cross, that the Corinthians were then able to see that message as God's wisdom. The only reason, for Paul, why the Corinthians are skeptical of his role and message now is because they have begun to judge both according to a different set of criteria for discerning wisdom. Thus, the contrast performs two functions: 1) it speaks to the nature of Paul's original role and message in Corinth (i.e. not dependent upon superior speech or wisdom), and 2) it answers the twofold question of what defined Paul's role and message and why that message was originally received.

Throughout this chapter, I have kept in mind how Paul views (divine) wisdom and the way in which that wisdom manifests itself. He has already articulated his views in 1.17-31 and this helps us understand why Paul argues what he does in 2.1–3.4, particularly about the role of God's Spirit in the proclamation and reception of the gospel. Moreover, this framework helps to reveal why Paul makes this case about the Spirit's role where he does in the argument of the letter. Paul's simple message relied on a different view of wisdom and its means of persuasion, an approach that stands in opposition to the competing framework as defined by the wisdom of the world. In particular, Paul believes that 1) the wisdom of the world fails to ascertain the wisdom of God, and 2) the wisdom of the world, in how it defines life, ultimately fosters divisiveness and competition for places of honor.

Paul therefore cannot and does not rely on the wisdom of the world and its ways of knowing as a criterion for how to ascertain God's wisdom and how harmonious life within the community is to be obtained. In view of 1 Cor 1.18-25, Paul argues that the apostolic message—ὁ λόγος τοῦ σταυροῦ—alone is the criterion by which believers come to see and know God's wisdom, which in turn defines how the new life in Christ is to be lived by those who believe. Admittedly, this theme of Paul relying on a distinct framework supplied by the Spirit could not be explored in great detail within this chapter. The reason for this is because it represents a theme that stands behind Paul's understanding of the Spirit's role in the proclamation and reception, and therefore needs to be explored separately.

Chapter 3
THE SPIRIT'S ROLE IN MEDIATING DIVINE WISDOM

3.1. Introduction

In 1 Cor 2.9-13, Paul articulates the Spirit's role in mediating divine wisdom. Foundational to the argument is a simple truth: divine wisdom cannot be known or ascertained unless it is revealed or disclosed by the one who possesses it. For Paul this simple truth is both the problem and the solution for those in Corinth. With regard to the negative (or the problem), two related points repay brief attention. First, no amount of effort or attempts on the part of the one seeking wisdom will cause the one who possesses the desired wisdom to reveal or disclose it; to say otherwise is to misconstrue the notion of revelation. Second, and by extension, no one can legitimately advocate access to divine wisdom through personal effort or even other ways of knowing, and no one can claim knowledge of divine wisdom when such wisdom has not been revealed or disclosed.

The implication of these two points must also be recognized: those to whom divine wisdom has not been revealed or disclosed are unable to discern or judge the true nature and validity of that wisdom. For Paul this inability to discern or judge results from employing faulty criteria, whose standards of measure are limited in their capacity and diametrically opposed to what is being assessed. In the light of Paul's argument, the wisdom assessed is nothing other than the divine plan of a crucified messiah as the means for salvation, as proclaimed in the gospel, and human wisdom represents the faulty criteria that measures the gospel message of Christ and finds it wanting (or foolish). The problem, therefore, is twofold: it involves 1) the understanding of revelation and 2) the framework within which discernment operates. Thus, how can the Corinthians know that the gospel of Christ crucified does in fact express God's revealed wisdom? With this in mind, we must now consider the positive side or the solution to this problem.

While Paul asserts that divine wisdom is only revealed or disclosed by the one who possesses it and that all attempts to obtain this wisdom or even discern its validity through other means will necessarily fail, he announces that the needed revelation or disclosure has in fact occurred and that God is the one who caused it. Moreover, the implication, as Paul contends, is that in receiving this revelation of divine wisdom one also receives new criteria for discerning or judging the nature and validity of what is revealed.[1] It is within this context that Paul stresses the central role played by God's Spirit in both sides of the solution: the Spirit as God's agent for revelation, and the Spirit's involvement in ensuring right discernment for understanding the nature and purpose of God's wisdom. As will be argued below, this role of the Spirit is closely tied to Paul's apostolic preaching of the gospel, a connection that is specifically relevant for the defence of his ministry.

3.2. Critical Views about "Wisdom" in Paul's Argument

Before examining the specific argument of 2.9-13 we must consider its surrounding context (2.6-16), one that has raised a number of questions by various scholars. Many of these questions relate to the terms and content of 2.6-16, which seem to divorce the passage from the rest of Paul's argument. Accordingly, if we are to make sense of Paul's argument and also the text as it stands, then we must offer adequate responses to, as Brown describes it, the "notorious...exegetical and hermeneutical difficulties" [2] that

---

[1] Whether or not the reception of these new criteria is a direct or indirect result of the revelation will be addressed below.

[2] Brown, *Cross and Human Transformation*, 105.

generate such questions. Thus, what follows is a summary of the dilemma, specifically noting the linguistic concerns and matters of content, and a proposed solution for these specific areas.

3.2.1. Summary of the Dilemma

An apparent conflict exists between how Paul speaks of "wisdom" in 1 Cor 2.1-5 and then in 2.6-16, a conflict that Conzelmann starkly labels a contradiction. [3] The so-called contradiction is that Paul seems to reject wisdom emphatically in 2.1-5 whereas in 2.6-16 he openly promotes and/or embraces it. This dilemma remains a perennial topic of discussion for Pauline scholarship,[4] and it is one that must be addressed in order to do justice to Paul's argument, specifically as it relates to the description of his preaching ministry in Corinth.[5] This conflict, however, does not constitute the only dilemma scholars recognize in 2.6-16. There is also the sudden shift in person, and the

---

[3] Conzelmann, *1 Corinthians*, 57; cf. also R. Bultmann, "Karl Barth, *The Resurrection of the Dead*," in *Faith and Understanding I* (ed. R. W. Funk; trans. L.P. Smith; London: SCM Press, 1969), 70-72; W.O. Walker, "1 Corinthians 2.6-16: A Non-Pauline Interpolation," *JSNT* 47 (1992): 75-94.

[4] See e.g. Welborn, "On the Discord in Corinth," 104-06; Cousar, "1 Corinthians 2:1-13," 170-73; Sterling, "'Wisdom Among the Perfect,'" 367-70. Scholarship of the mid- to late-19th century seems either unaware of or unconcerned by this apparent conflict, for it is not mentioned as an interpretative problem (although cf. Hodge, *First Epistle*, 33). A few recent interpreters have also exhibited minimal concern—see e.g. Polhill, who says nothing about it ("The Wisdom of God," 331-33; cf. also V.P. Branick, "Apocalyptic Paul," *CBQ* 47.4 [1985]: 671; J.F. Smit, "Epideictic Rhetoric in Paul's First Letter to the Corinthians 1–4,'" *Bib* 84 [2003]: 192-94; D. Lioy, "Divine Wisdom versus Human Wisdom: An Exegetical-Theological Analysis of 1 Corinthians 1:10–2:16," *Cons* 8 [2009]: 51-56); Lampe refers to it but immediately dismisses it as a mistaken conclusion (see "Theological Wisdom," 127-28).

[5] Cf. Schmithals, *Theology*, 121.

uncharacteristic use of seemingly esoteric vocabulary, or at least an apparent redefinition of specific Pauline ideas or terms.

With regard to the shift in person,[6] the issue is that Paul ceases using the first person singular at 2.5, adopts the first person plural throughout 2.6-16, and finally resumes singular references at 3.1. In the light of this oscillation, and since the content of 2.6-16 is deemed unrelated (historically) to the surrounding context, Walker suggests the possibility of extracting 2.6-16 without causing any disruption to the flow of the argument from 2.1–3.4.[7] By doing so, he argues, one is left with a "smoothly connected passage (2.1-5; 3.1-4) dealing with Paul's initial visit to the Corinthians and emphasizing both his own 'weakness' (2.1-5) and the 'fleshly' nature of his hearers (3.1-4)."[8] I will address these linguistic concerns first before dealing with the issues of content.

3.2.2. Assessment of the Linguistic Features

Three points of concern about Walker's interpretation deserve close attention. First, the shift to first person plural in 2.6-16 is admittedly abrupt and this section does contain material that appears to detract from Paul's recollection of his Corinthian ministry. However, the abrupt shift in person is not unusual for Paul; in 2 Corinthians he makes a similar shift ten times in the first nine chapters alone.[9] Moreover, since scholars now generally agree that 2 Cor 1–9 constitutes a single literary unit from Paul's hand,[10]

---

[6] Cf. Willis, "'The Mind of Christ,'" 110.

[7] Walker, "1 Corinthians 2.6-16," 81-86.

[8] Walker, "1 Corinthians 2.6-16," 83.

[9] For the first person plural, see 1.3-14, 18-22; 2.14–7.2; 7.13–8.7, 16-24. For the first person singular, see 1.15-17, 1.23–2.13; 7.3-12; 8.8-15; 9.1-15.

[10] I am leaving to one side the debate over whether or not 2 Cor 1–7 and 8–9 represent two of the three stages of writing 2 Corinthians. For those arguing for a literary unity of 2 Cor 1–9 from Paul's hand (whether in stages or not), see e.g. P.E. Hughes, *Paul's Second Epistle to the Corinthians* (Grand Rapids:

and further agree that nothing in those chapters suggests an interpolation;[11] there is no reasonable ground to assume that such shifts necessarily create disruptions in the overall argument.[12] The same reasoning applies to 1 Corinthians.

Scholars agree that (at the very least) 1 Cor 1–4 represents a single logical (or rhetorical) argument, and that no textual evidence exists for an interpolation within those chapters;[13] thus, other

---

Eerdmans, 1962), xxii; J. Thompson, *The Second Letter of Paul to the Corinthians* (Austin: R.B. Sweet Co., 1970), 14-15; J.M. Scott, *2 Corinthians* (Peabody: Hendrickson, 1998), 4-5; D.E. Garland, *2 Corinthians* (Nashville: Broadman & Holman, 1999), 38-44; J. Lambrecht, *Second Corinthians* (Collegeville: Liturgical Press, 1999), 9; D.R. Hall, *The Unity of the Corinthian Correspondence* (London: T&T Clark, 2003), 113-23; Harris, *Second Epistle*, 8-51; F.G. Carver, *2 Corinthians: A Commentary in the Wesleyan Tradition* (Kansas City: Beacon Hill, 2009), 44-45.

[11] While a handful of scholars still contend that 2 Cor 6.14–7.1 represents an interpolation—e.g. M.M. Mitchell, "The Corinthian Correspondence and the Birth of Pauline Hermeneutics," in *Paul and the Corinthians: Studies on a Community in Conflict. Essays in Honor of Margaret Thrall* (eds. T.J. Burke and J.K. Elliott; Leiden: Brill, 2003), 27; M.L. Minor, *2 Corinthians* (Macon: Smyth & Helwys, 2009), 15, 131-32; cf. M. Thrall, *2 Corinthians 1–7* (London: T&T Clark, 2004), 12, 32-36—this is not the majority view (see e.g. those listed in n.10 above. Cf. also, J. Lambrecht, "The Fragment 2 Cor vi 14–vii 1: A Plea for Its Authenticity," in *Studies on 2 Corinthians* [eds. R. Bieringer and J. Lambrecht; Leuven: Leuven University Press, 1994], 531-49).

[12] Cf. Lambrecht: "No break in the narrative or argument, no change in the vocabulary or tone appears to be so great that the parts could not have stood originally, one next to the other, in a single letter" (*Second Corinthians*, 9).

[13] Walker acknowledges this fact when he states: "So far as I can ascertain, such *direct* text-critical evidence does not exist with regard to 1 Cor 2.6-16"—i.e. direct evidence that would suggest an interpolation ("1 Corinthians 2.6-16," 80—emphasis original). He also acknowledges that the *"[i]ndirect* text-critical evidence" (80—emphasis original) does not appear to support the idea of an interpolation. The two criteria he uses related to this indirect evidence are: 1) the presence of insignificant textual problems surrounding the passage in question, and/or 2) the lack of reference from post-apostolic writers to the specific passage. "The former suggests the possibility of attempts by different scribes to

solutions must be offered for why the shift in person occurs where it does in the argument. Three options are commonly given: 1) evidence of joint authorship, or collaboration with the co-senders of the text, where such individuals contribute to that portion of the argument;[14] 2) the use of an authorial "we," where Paul speaks on behalf of the co-senders, thus maintaining primary authorship;[15] or 3) emphasis on a particular point, either for the sake of establishing consistency in the apostolic witness or for marking a contrast between the apostles and their opponents.[16]

Second, as intimated above, virtually all scholars acknowledge the literary integrity of 1 Corinthians as a whole;[17] to argue otherwise is to do so on precarious grounds. Even those who advocate partition theories for the composition of the letter nevertheless recognize the integrity of the specific rhetorical

---

smooth out otherwise awkward transitions between original and interpolated materials; the latter that the passage in question was unknown to one or more early church writers (presumably because it was absent from their texts)" (ibid).

[14] See E. Verhoef, "The Senders of the Letters to the Corinthians and the Use of 'I' and 'We'," in *The Corinthian Correspondence* (ed. R. Bieringer; Leuven: Leuven University Press, 1996), 417-25.

[15] See esp. Kaiser, "A Neglected Text in Biblology Discussions: 1 Corinthians 2:6-16," *WTJ* 43.2 (1981): 311. This type of claim is often made in response to the first option, which leaves open the possibility of Paul not being the sole (or primary) author of the text. The need for such an argument appears to be for the sake of maintaining apostolic, and inspired authorship. Cf. also Fee, *First Epistle*, 101 n.13.

[16] See e.g. R.W. Funk, "Word and World in 1 Corinthians 2:6-16," in *Language, Hermeneutics and the Word of God: The Problem of Language in the New Testament and Contemporary Theology* (New York: Harper & Row, 1966), 275-305.

[17] This is primarily due to Mitchell, *Rhetoric of Reconciliation*; cf. also Dunn, *1 Corinthians*, 24-25; Collins, *First Corinthians*, xiii, 6, 10; Furnish, *Theology of the First Letter*, 12, 15-18.

units.[18] For example, Schmithals, who contends for several stages of redaction in the Corinthian correspondence, affirms an unquestioned integrity for 1 Cor 1.10–3.23.[19] Moreover, he sees no disruption in Paul's argument beginning with 2.6, although he does acknowledge a significant shift beginning with that verse, and concludes: "The contradiction can be resolved if one determines that Paul was previously speaking [in 2.1-5] of missionary preaching and the ground of faith, but now [in 2.6–3.4] he is speaking about the message to those who stand firmly on this ground, and this is indeed probably what Paul meant."[20] While Schmithals' conclusion places the emphasis on a slightly different aspect of Paul's argument than the one argued here, it nevertheless serves as an example of how to deal with the apparent conflicts in the text without arguing for an interpolation. I will return to this point of the discussion momentarily.

In the light of the second concern, I now consider the third: while seeming to digress from the remarks about his apostolic preaching, especially the role of the Spirit in that preaching, the content of 2.6-16 is in fact foundational for Paul's understanding of the importance and implications of that role.[21] Thus, I agree with Walker on the presence of historical links between 2.1-5 and 3.1-4, however I differ with regard to the specificity of those links. Paul's focus in 3.1-4 is only secondarily concerned with his initial visit; the primary issue is the Corinthians' status at the time of writing, and that issue is essentially described as spiritual immaturity. If Paul speaks positively of the Spirit's role in the initial

---

[18] This is especially the case with regard to 1 Cor 1–4. See e.g. Rylands, *Critical Analysis*, 115-16; Hurd, *Origin of 1 Corinthians*, 43-47, 68-71, 86-89, 131-142; de Boer, "1 Corinthians," 229-45.

[19] Schmithals, *Theology*, 121; cf. idem, *Gnosticism in Corinth*, 90-91, where he places the *terminus* of the passage at 4.21.

[20] Schmithals, *Theology*, 128.

[21] Cf. Bockmuehl, *Revelation and Mystery*, 158.

proclamation of the gospel (2.4-5), and if he speaks negatively about the Corinthians' current spiritual immaturity (3.1-4), then the cause for the negative remarks must be explained.

The simplest explanation is that Paul envisages a series of events where the opposite result would have occurred—i.e. that the Corinthians would not be spiritually immature but mature. If 2.6-16 is extracted from Paul's argument, as Walker suggests, then a proper understanding of how the Spirit's relationship to the gospel and how believers become spiritually mature as a result of belief in the gospel message is left unexplained. Moreover, to extract 2.6-16 from 2.1–3.4 would diminish the force of the point made in 3.1 where the Corinthians are labelled νήπιοι. Similarly, removing 2.6-16 from the argument would leave the parallelism of νήπιος and σάρκινος in 3.1 ambiguous and random. However, retaining 2.6-16 shows the negativity of 3.1 as a contrast to the expectations of 2.6, and it provides the necessary balance to the parallelism of νήπιος and τέλειος, σάρκινος and πνευματικός.[22] More importantly, with 2.6-16 remaining original to Paul's argument, the necessity of the Spirit's role in what is to occur in the life of a believer, in the light of the gospel, comes immediately to the fore.

3.2.3. Assessment of the Content Features

With regard to the differences in the content of 2.6-16, as compared with the rest of his argument, Paul seems to advocate a wisdom teaching parallel to that of the mystery religions of the ancient world. This view held considerable sway since the work of Gunkel, the rise of the *religionsgeschichtliche Schule*, and its

---

[22] Cf. G.G. Findlay, *The First Epistle of Paul to the Corinthians* (ed. W.R. Nicoll; London: Hodder & Stoughton, 1897), 777, 785-86. Sterling also briefly notes these contrasts (see "'Wisdom Among the Perfect'," 368).

application to 1 Corinthians by Bousset.[23] Accordingly, scholars focused on specific theological themes in 2.6-16, the vocabulary associated with those themes, and then compared it with similar terms and concepts in mystery religions. Specifically, much of what Paul says about hidden wisdom (or knowledge), the revelation of that wisdom only to a select few, the distinctions between spiritual and psychical people, the presence of spiritual forces or beings at work in the cosmos, and access to the divine mind through a πνεῦμα, were taken as evidence for Gnostic influences, or at least Gnostic theological motifs within 2.6-16. A few studies have exposed certain methodological and historical problems with this approach and its application to 1 Cor 2.6-16, two of which repay brief attention.

First, there is an insistence on a singular understanding or meaning of key terms or ideas. Specifically, for example, in every place where μυστήριον and τέλειος occur in Hellenistic texts, it is assumed that such terms always refer to mystery religions.[24] This assumption is faulty since such terms or ideas are not the sole property of ancient mystery religions. The notion of μυστήριον, especially as it pertains not just to God's wisdom but also its apocalyptic revelation, appears in the Jewish texts of Daniel, 1 Enoch, 3 Enoch, 2 Baruch, 4 Esdras, and the Dead Sea Scrolls.[25] Moreover, the connection between τέλειος and wisdom,

---

[23] W. Bousset, *Kyrios Christos* (Göttingen: Vandenhoeck & Ruprecht, 1913)—this connection is noted by Stuhlmacher, "The Hermeneutical Significance of 1 Cor 2:6-16," in *Tradition and Interpretation in the New Testament: Essays in Honor E. Earle Ellis for His 60th Birthday* (ed. G.F. Hawthorne; Grand Rapids: Eerdmans, 1987), 330.

[24] Cf. Wilson, "How Gnostic," 68.

[25] See Dan 2.28, 29, 47; *1 En* 49.2; 63.3; *3 En* 9.6; 38.3; 51.3; *2 Bar* 81.4; *4 Esd* 14.5; 1Q27 13.3; 4Q299 2b.5; 35.1; 73.3; 1QHab 7.13-14. Cf. also 1QS 4.6; 9.18; 11.3, 5, 19.

especially as it relates to those seeking God's wisdom, also appears in the works of Philo.[26]

Similarly, with regard to another key concept in 1 Cor 2.6-16, Kovacs persuasively argues that Gnostic or even proto-gnostic interpretations are not the only (or most adequate) means for understanding the phrase "the rulers of this age".[27] It is entirely plausible to assume awareness of Jewish apocalyptic themes or influences at work in Paul's argument in 1 Cor 2.6-16, especially in the light of his remarks concerning revealed wisdom by God's Spirit and the overturning of opposing powers. Thus, the symbolic universe of mystery religions is not the only source from which Paul could draw for the use and meaning of key terms and ideas.

Second, identifying a specific "Gnostic" group and their particular beliefs are not straightforward exercises. As Rudolph points out: "It is no exaggeration to number the problems of the genesis and the history of Gnosis among the most difficult which are encountered in research not only into Gnosis but also into the history of the religion of later antiquity."[28] Early on, as Bultmann describes, Gnosticism "first appeared and attracted the attention of scholars as a movement *within* the Christian religion, and for a long time it was regarded as a purely Christian movement, a perversion of the Christian faith into a speculative theology, the

---

[26] E.g. *Deus. Imm.* 92, where Philo speaks of "perfect happiness" that results from God providing wisdom without human effort or request. Similarly, Philo describes wisdom from God, when revealed to a person, as the "perfect way" to God; for it was the flesh that corrupted the way (cf. *Migr. Ab.* 38-42; *Deus. Imm.* 142-43).

[27] See J.L. Kovacs, "The Archons, The Spirit and the Death of Christ: Do We Need the Hypothesis of Gnostic Opponents to Explain 1 Cor 2.6-16?," in *Apocalyptic and the New Testament: Essays in Honor of J. Louis Martyn* (eds. J. Marcus and M.L. Soards; Sheffield: JSOT Press, 1989), 218-36.

[28] K. Rudolph, *Gnosis: The Nature and History of Gnosticism* (trans. and ed. R. McL. Wilson; Edinburgh: T&T Clark, 1987), 275.

'acute Hellenization of Christianity'."[29] However, if we follow van Unnik's assessment, Gnosticism represented "an exceptionally important rival to youthful Christianity" and yet "it often attached itself to Christianity so tightly,"[30] this indicates that Gnosticism developed externally to but in conjunction with Christianity.

This last view accords well with the testimony of the Church Fathers who link the origins of Gnosticism with Simon Magus, the one from whom Irenaeus claims "all sorts of heresies derive their origin."[31] Alternatively, and also bearing the support of ancient testimony, key figures in early Gnosticism were believed to be of Jewish origin,[32] which nuances the view described by Bultmann in a more precise way. In effect, by suggesting a Jewish origin one can readily infer a pre-Christian form of Gnosticism, one that easily adapts to the later theological ideas and teaching of Christianity, since these later ideas and teachings also assert a Jewish foundation.

However, there is a methodological and even a categorical problem with each of these views: each one assumes—to varying degrees—the existence of Gnosticism as a distinct ideology and Gnostics as a distinct groups of adherents with a particular set of beliefs in the ancient world and that such a group relates in some

---

[29] R. Bultmann, *Primitive Christianity in its Contemporary Setting* (trans. R.H. Fuller; London: Thames & Hudson, 1956), 162—emphasis added; cf. also Roukema, who develops the idea of Gnosticism being "a form of Hellenized Christianity," although he incorporates ideas and themes from Judaism, Christianity, and Middle Platonism—see *Gnosis and Faith in Early Christianity: An Introduction to Gnosticism* (trans. J. Bowden; Harrisburg: Trinity Press International, 1999), 105-25.

[30] W.C. van Unnik, *Newly Discovered Gnostic Writings: A Preliminary Survey of the Nag Hammadi Find* (London: SCM Press, 1960), 90.

[31] See Irenaeus, *Adv. Haer.* 1.23.2.

[32] Cf. Eusebius, *H.E.* 5.22, where he cites the testimony of Hegesippus. See also, Rudolph, *Gnosis*, 277-82—especially 177, where he mentions (albeit briefly) the testimony of the Church Fathers.

way with nascent Christianity. Part of the trouble is that, as Williams points out,[33] "[t]here is no true consensus even among specialists in the religions of the Greco-Roman world on a definition of the category 'gnosticism,' even though there is no reason why categories as such should be difficult to define."[34] Williams goes on to show that while certain traits or "elements" can be identified as "gnostic," none of these are exclusively Gnostic. We must allow for the possibility that many of these traits or elements have roots in and grow out of existing Greco-Roman philosophical traditions—e.g. Platonism, Neopythagoreanism.

However, Williams' calling into question the very notion of "Gnosticism" as a distinct category has not yet produced a new consensus on how to describe succinctly the mix of views such a category ostensibly represented. If, with those prior to the work of Williams, we continue to use the dubious category, then we might reasonably conclude with Wilson, for example, that it makes better sense of the evidence to say Gnosticism, as a distinctive ideology, developed its theological themes and vocabulary on a foundation of early Christian belief instead of the reverse.[35] As is frequently

---

[33] See M.A. Williams, *Rethinking "Gnosticism": An Argument for Dismantling a Dubious Category* (Princeton: Princeton University Press, 1996), 3-6, 26-31.

[34] *Ibid.*, 4.

[35] "In point of fact, Gnosticism is fundamentally syncretistic, welding into a new synthesis elements from diverse cultures. It would be more correct to recognize the various 'spheres of influences' mentioned as the *ultimate* source of particular ideas, and proceed to the attempt to trace the channels by which they passed into the developed Gnostic systems" (R. McL. Wilson, *Gnosis and the New Testament* [Oxford: Basil Blackwell, 1968], 3-4). This understanding has roots in ancient views of gnostic ideas and teachings. As Perkins argues: "On the one hand, second-century writers, both gnostic and Christian, were convinced that the fundamental structures of gnostic speculation and cult arose outside Christianity. On the other hand, identifiable gnostic sects do not appear

argued on this view, there is no conclusive historical data for placing Gnostics as a definable group or Gnosticism as a set of influential theological ideas, either prior to or contemporaneous with Paul's apostolic ministry, especially in Corinth.[36]

If, however, we take Williams' discussion seriously, one consequence must be to consider alternatives to "Gnostic" or "gnostic" when attempting to identify the sources of Paul's own thoughts and especially the opponents in Corinth or the ideas that he repudiates.[37] Klutz, following Williams' observations,[38] has suggested a group of social elite (i.e. "the Strong"), whose identity is shaped by perceptions of and allegiance to wisdom or knowledge[39] and who more readily align themselves with civic structures of the Greco-Roman world rather than those of the church.[40] In my own discussion I shall decline the use of the label "gnostic" and take Paul's remarks concerning divine wisdom as a sharp antithesis to philosophical notions of wisdom that were commonly espoused by various philosophical groups of his day.

---

prior to the emergence of Christianity" (*Gnosticism and the New Testament* [Minneapolis: Fortress, 1993], 10).

[36] Thus, any "gnostic" features in 2.6-16 are merely incipient details and themes that develop later and do so in the wake of Christianity's spread throughout the Empire. See esp. Wilson, who notes: "it is not the separate elements in themselves which are Gnostic, but the total synthesis, the system, in which they are combined" (*Gnosis and the New Testament*, 4-5); cf. also Wilson, "How Gnostic," 65-74.

[37] Cf. Klutz, who took Williams' argument and implications and applied them to the social and historical context of Paul's letter to the Corinthians (see "Re-Reading 1 Corinthians after *Rethinking 'Gnosticism*,'" *JSNT* 26.2 [2003]: 193-216 [esp. 206-14]).

[38] Cf. Williams, *Rethinking*, 51-53; Klutz, "Re-Reading 1 Corinthians," 203.

[39] See Klutz, "Re-Reading 1 Corinthians," 206-10.

[40] See *ibid.*, 211-14 (esp. 213-14).

3.2.4. Proposed Solution to the Dilemma

If we hold to a unified argument for at least 2.1-16, how then do we account for the sudden shift in language and the apparent difference in content between 2.1-5 and 2.6-16? Moreover, what options are available to us if we argue against either Gnostic influence in Corinth or theological motifs found in the mystery religions from the ancient world? One option is to see Paul adopting the terminology of the Corinthians' view of wisdom and spirituality, redefining it, and then applying it back to the circumstances to which he writes. This option accounts for the relatively unique vocabulary and conceptual data found in 2.6-16 as compared with the rest of Paul's argument, which in turn keeps the content of 2.6-16 authentically Pauline (*contra* Walker). This has been a leading method for commentators examining Paul's argument in this passage.[41]

Another option is to read Paul's argument against the backdrop of Jewish apocalypticism and wisdom traditions. Like the first option, this keeps the content of 2.6-16 authentically Pauline yet it differs with regard to the source of that content. Here Paul is not so much appropriating ideas or concepts that are otherwise foreign to his symbolic universe; instead, Paul draws from a stream of tradition that is longstanding and intrinsic to his Jewish heritage. We see the basic features of this approach outlined in Schoeps' work on Pauline theology in general[42] and also in Lang's remarks on 2.6-16 in particular.[43] By reading the text in this way, according to Lang, one is able to see a theory of wisdom that is pneumatic in form and content, and to understand that the bestowal of this

---

[41] See e.g. Pearson, *Pneumatikos-Psychikos*, 27; J. Koenig, "From Mystery to Ministry: Paul as Interpreter of Charismatic Gifts," *USQR* 33.3/4 (1978): 168; Horsley, *1 Corinthians*, 56-57; Collins, *First Corinthians*, 124.

[42] Schoeps, *Paul*, 13-50.

[43] See Lang, *Die Briefe an die Korinther*, 38-48.

wisdom indicates the beginning of God's eternal kingdom in the present world.

Maintaining this balance between Jewish apocalypticism and wisdom traditions is not only crucial for interpreting Paul's meaning but also necessary in the light of the apparent imbalance in recent scholarship. This imbalance tends to result from improper definitions and methodological applications of the particular concepts. Matlock has alerted us to this tendency and articulated some of the problems it creates with apocalyptic readings of Paul's theology.[44] Moreover, the imbalance comes from prioritizing one approach over the other, or at least the value of one is subsumed under the other.

For example, Beker argues: "only a consistent apocalyptic interpretation of Paul's thought is able to demonstrate its fundamental coherence"[45] and "that the coherence of the gospel is constituted by statements that have been shaped by apocalyptic thought and, consequently, cannot be separated from their ultimate goal, the imminent apocalyptic triumph of God."[46] This view then becomes the way in which Paul is seen articulating the message of the gospel—both in terms of content and form.[47]

---

[44] See Matlock, *Unveiling the Apocalyptic Paul*, especially chapter 4.

[45] Beker, *Paul the Apostle*, 143.

[46] J.C. Beker, *The Triumph of God: The Essence of Paul's Thought* (Minneapolis: Fortress, 1990), 20.

[47] Beker stresses these two points when he argues: "1. The entire center of Paul's gospel is his conviction that Christ's death and resurrection have opened up a new future for the world. This future will reach its climax when the reign and triumph of God are made manifest and the whole created order attains its wonderful perfection according to God's promises to Israel. 2. The apocalyptic framework of the gospel also corresponds to the manner in which Paul proclaims it. The gospel concerning the future reign of God is brought to expression in such a way that, analogous to the incarnation of God in Christ, it embodies itself in the concrete and varied circumstances of human life. In this way Paul enables his churches to discern already in the present time signs of

While apocalyptic themes can certainly be found, the Jewish wisdom traditions, as we will see, appear to have the strongest relevance for tracing Paul's thought in general and his argument in 1 Corinthians in particular. However, these wisdom traditions have not been explored to their fullest extent, especially as they relate to 1 Corinthians. There is much within these traditions that support ideas of divine wisdom being given to individuals, wisdom being a means for understanding the will or ways of God, wisdom providing knowledge within the individual, wisdom being the means by which a person knows what is true and good, and, specifically relevant for this chapter, wisdom serving as the framework for knowing how life is to be lived in accordance with the will or ways of God. All of these can be explored without relying on assumptions that divorce Paul from his Jewish heritage and without the need to cast his thought and expression in the light of a later divergent theological system. This brings me to a final option for examining Paul's argument in 2.6-16, an option that was elaborated by Stuhlmacher[48] but has received scant attention by virtually all commentators since.

By seeing the specific argument of 1 Cor 2.6-16 within the larger logical framework of 1 Cor 1–4, Stuhlmacher reads 2.6-16 as an epistemological explanation for the theological assertions of 1.18-25. [49] For Stuhlmacher, Paul in 2.6-16 explains how the Corinthians are able to know that what he professes in 1.18-25 is in fact true or that it indeed reflects the wisdom of God. While other

---

God's future glory. Moreover, Paul's churches are empowered by God to participate in redemptive praxis in the world, which aims at preparing the whole creation for its future glory. Paul borrows certain components of his apocalyptic gospel from the Jewish apocalyptic thought world, but modifies them because of his encounter with the exalted Christ and through the influence of Christian tradition" (*ibid.*, 20).

[48] Stuhlmacher, "Hermeneutical Significance," 328-47.

[49] *Ibid.*, 332.

analyses of Paul's argument tend to prioritize the theological over the epistemological (or vice versa) with the unfortunate result of diminishing any possible continuity or balance between them, Stuhlmacher's approach not only explains the two units of the argument on their own terms but also reveals the inextricable links between them.

This approach also moves the discussion from abstractions to practical applications. Accordingly, while 2.6-16 represents an epistemological explanation for the theological claims of 1.18-25, it is a theory of knowledge requiring real-life changes that are necessitated by what is known to be true. In this case, the Corinthians are to recognize the wise salvific plan of God as displayed in the cross of Christ, and they are to live in accordance with that wisdom made known by the power of God's Spirit. Accordingly, this approach remains sensitive to the Jewish wisdom traditions that promote a balance between theory and praxis, where the life lived reflects the ideas believed.

3.3. Wisdom and Paul's Argument

To understand Paul's view of the Spirit's role in mediating divine wisdom, we must begin where he does: with the seemingly disconnected citation in 1 Cor 2.9. The apparent disconnection is largely due to the specific content of 2.9 and the lack of any reference to the Spirit. However, after considering the function of this passage its essential relationship with Paul's wider view of the Spirit as seen in 2.1–3.4 in general and 2.6-16 in particular comes to the fore. [50] However, before examining the function and

---

[50] Brown views 1 Cor 2.9-10a as foundational for understanding the larger argument of 2.6-16: "The analysis of 2:6-16 will follow the tripartite structure of the passage by focusing on the major themes of each section. I. *Sophia tou Theou* vs. *Sophia tou Aiōnos Toutou* 2:6-8 (Wisdom of God versus Wisdom of This Age). <<Apocalyptic Signal 2:9-10a>> II. *Pneuma tou Theou* versus *Pneuma tou Kosmou* 2:10b-14 (Spirit of God versus Spirit of the World). III.

relationship, I must address the dilemma concerning the source of the quotation in 2.9.

3.3.1. Source of Paul's Quotation

The prefatory formula, καθὼς γέγραπται is Paul's usual way of introducing a Scriptural quotation into his argument,[51] although the formula here in 2.9 includes the unusual initial emphatic conjunction ἀλλά.[52] On the one hand, commentators agree that Paul quotes something from Jewish literature,[53] and he does so because he believes that the source carries authority. However, on the other hand, commentators disagree on the precise text(s) or passage(s) that Paul quotes, although this assumes that he is in fact quoting faithfully from the source(s),[54] which is itself another dilemma. The common hypothesis is that Paul quotes loosely from Isa 64.4 and then from 65.17.[55] The reason for suggesting a "loose"

Nous tou Christou 2:15-16 (Mind of Christ). By following the contours of this section, as it builds from the familiar antithesis at the foundation to the unfamiliar term *nous tou Christou*, we discover the structure of the cognitive transformation the text requires of the reader. Within this structure, I will argue, vv 9-10a function to signal the crucial transition without which the whole text remains obscure" (*Cross and Human Transformation*, 110-11).

[51] See Rom 1.17; 2.24; 3.4, 10; 4.17; 8.36; 9.13, 33; 10.15; 11.8, 26; 15.9; 2 Cor 8.15; 9.9. On other occasions, Paul employs a slightly different formula, γέγραπται γάρ—see Rom 12.19; 14.11; 1 Cor 1.19; 3.19; Gal 3.10; 4.22, 27; cf. 1 Cor 9.9.

[52] Only in two other locations does Paul begin a quotation with the emphatic phrase, ἀλλὰ καθὼς γέγραπται: Rom 15.3, 21.

[53] "Die typische Zitationsformel schließt eine bloße Anspielung aus" (Schrage, *Der erste Brief*, 1.245).

[54] See W.H. Mare and M.J. Harris, *1, 2 Corinthians: The Expositor's Bible Commentary with the New International Version* (Grand Rapids: Zondervan, 1995), 29.

[55] See e.g. Grosheide, *First Epistle*, 66; Morris, *First Epistle*, 55-56; Kistemaker, *Exposition*, 84-85; Witherington, *Conflict and Community*, 127; Barclay, "1 Corinthians," 1113; cf. also Collins, *First Corinthians*, 131-32;

quotation of Isa 64.4 is that the stronger connections between that text and 1 Cor 2.9 are conceptual rather than linguistic. Hence, Ciampa and Rosner argue: "The loose form of the citation precludes any discussion of textual differences."[56] The reason for using Isa 65.17 with 64.4 is that the specific phrase, "not entering into the human heart" in 1 Cor 2.9 appears neither in the MT nor the LXX of Isa 64.4, yet it does appear in the LXX of Isa 65.17. While this joining of texts is likely, there are at least three specific details worth considering before forming any solid conclusions.[57]

First, the key phrase "not entering into the human heart" not only comprises a small portion of the whole Isaiah passage, specifically it is the final remark, but also reveals an adaptation to the phrase. With regard to the whole passage, emphasizing what Paul ostensibly cites, the MT of Isa 65.17 reads: "For behold, I create new heavens and new earth and the former things will neither be remembered nor *come into mind* [ולא תעלינה על־לב],", which the LXX renders: "For there shall be the new heaven and the new earth and they shall neither remember the former things nor shall they *come up upon their heart* [ἐπέλθῃ αὐτῶν ἐπὶ τὴν καρδίαν]." Accordingly, Paul would be employing Isa 65.17 for the sake of borrowing an otherwise incidental phrase for his quotation. Moreover, the Isaiah phrase is about forgetting and not remembering the things of old; Paul's emphasis is on the things of God not being known categorically. With regard to the adaptation, Paul's version reads: ἐπὶ καρδίαν ἀνθρώπου, which adds a specificity lacking in both the MT and the LXX of Isa 65.17—still assuming this to be his source. One way to respond to this is to say

---

Thiselton, *First Epistle*, 251-52; cf. also Conzelmann, *1 Corinthians*, 64; Fee, *First Epistle*, 108-09; R.E. Ciampa and B.S. Rosner, *The First Letter to the Corinthians* (Grand Rapids: Eerdmans, 2010), 108.

[56] Ciampa-Rosner, *First Letter*, 108 n.30.

[57] Cf. Thiselton, *First Epistle*, 250-51; Ciampa-Rosner, *First Letter*, 108-09.

that Paul quotes this text just as loosely as he quotes Isa 64.4. It is also possible that the quotation is more of what Hays terms, "an echo",[58] whereby Paul allows or even desires the conceptual or rhetorical resonances of both Isaiah passages to be heard in his reapplication of those texts.[59]

Second, and this might constitute another adaptation, the difference in verb tense between the Isa 65.17 passages and 1 Cor 2.9 cannot be ignored: the former is future while the latter is aorist. We could say that Paul supplies a theological interpretation or application of the Isaiah passage for his argument. Since the Isaiah passage speaks of a coming new age when Yahweh makes all things new, and since Paul believes that expected new age has been inaugurated in Christ, Isaiah's future hope is therefore a past event from the perspective of Paul. Moreover, since the establishment of a new age and thus a new creation are parts of the divine plan for the salvation of all things, and since Paul believes that this plan has remained a mystery (i.e. hidden) until the advent of Christ, its inability to be perceived by human wisdom suits Paul's argument quite well. This agreement finds additional support if we assume that Paul joins Isa 65.17 with 64.4, the latter dealing with divine ways not previously known. The trouble here is that we cannot be sure if Paul combined both texts in this way to make this precise connection. We can only speculate. Moreover, we cannot be sure that Paul only had these passages from Isaiah in mind; it is possible that he also drew from other sources (e.g. Isa 52.15 or Jer 3.16).

Finally, the concluding phrase in Paul's quotation (ἃ ἡτοίμασεν ὁ θεὸς τοῖς ἀγαπῶσιν αὐτόν) brings us back to the

---

[58] For what Hays means by "echoes" and how this might shape our reading of Paul's letters, see *Echoes of Scripture in the Letters of Paul* (New Haven: Yale University Press, 1989), 1-33.

[59] This obviously assumes an above-average awareness or knowledge of the Hebrew Scriptures by the Corinthians believers—an assumption that Hays does not explain or support.

dilemma of source, for this specific phrase appears nowhere else in Jewish literature.[60] Moreover, we can be sure that Paul is not adapting an Isaiah passage to suit his argument, for what he says in 1 Cor 2.9 clearly departs from Isa 64.4c. Thus, we must look elsewhere to find a likely source. The closest parallel comes from the Second Temple Jewish text, Sirach, which reads: καὶ ἐχορήγησεν αὐτὴν τοῖς ἀγαπῶσιν αὐτόν (1.10). Two similarities between this passage and the one cited in 1 Cor 2.9 are worth noting: 1) the subject of the action in both cases is God, and 2) the indirect object of the action are τοῖς ἀγαπῶσιν αὐτόν.

A third similarity exists, but it is one that must be drawn from the context of both passages. In Sir 1.10 the direct object is (lady?) wisdom, referred to in this passage with the personal pronoun, αὐτή; in 1 Cor 2.9, the direct object is the salvific plan of God, vaguely referred to in this passage with the definite relative pronoun, ἅ. As will be stressed below, Paul's argument reveals that the cross of Christ is the enactment of God's wisdom as the means of salvation, and only those who love God can know such things. However this third similarity signals a key difference between the two texts: Sirach appears to operate on an assumed hypostatic view of wisdom, whereas Paul simply ignores such a view here.[61]

---

[60] Although something close to this appears in Deut 7.9; Neh 1.5; Ps 97.10.

[61] If anything, we might say Paul redefines the hypostatic view of lady wisdom into a wisdom Christology, although Fee has offered a cogent case against such a suggestion—see *Pauline Christology: An Exegetical-Theological Study* (Peabody: Hendrickson, 2007), 594-630; cf. also A. van Roon, "The Relation Between Christ and the Wisdom of God According to Paul," *NovT* 16.3 (1974): 207-39. The earlier assessment of Whiteley bears repeating: "When St. Paul speaks of Christ in terms of Wisdom his intention is not to identify Him with an hypostatization of Wisdom, but to ascribe to Him the function of being God's agent in creation, revelation and redemption. In fact, the 'Wisdom Christology' of St. Paul may be summed up in these words: What Wisdom meant to the Jews was part of what Jesus Christ meant for St. Paul" (*The Theology of St. Paul* [Oxford: Basil Blackwell, 1964], 112).

However, it must be said that this difference would not necessarily prevent Paul from using Sir 1.10 as his source, especially if we maintain the earlier assumption about loose quotations.

In the light of these difficulties, various solutions to these problems have been given. One suggestion is that Paul quotes the relevant material from memory and does so quite badly,[62] which would then account for the differences in style and content or adaptations between the original and his use of them. Schrage rejects this view for at least Isa 52.15, since Paul quotes the same passage in Rom 15.21 and does so with great precision; thus, as Schrage intimates, it would be odd for Paul to remember the passage accurately in one letter (i.e. Rom 15.21) while citing it wrongly in another (i.e. 1 Cor 2.9).[63] This oddity would be all the more surprising given the close span of time within which 1 Corinthians and Romans were composed.

Another proposed solution is that Paul draws from sources outside of the Hebrew Scriptures. In fact, both Origen and Ambrosiaster contend that Paul's quotation in 1 Cor 2.9 comes from the *Apocalypse of Elijah*.[64] However, as Fitzmyer points out, the *Apocalypse of Elijah* not only represents a later Christian text but also contains no statements resembling what we see in Paul's quotation.[65] Fitzmyer also mentions a number of other assumed

---

[62] "But since it is only passages from the *canonical* Scriptures that are ever cited by Paul with καθὼς γέγρ., we must at the same time assume that he *intended* to do so here also, but *by some confusion of memory took the apocryphal saying for a canonical passage possibly from the prophecies*, to which the passage of kindred sound in Isaiah might easily give occasion" (Meyer, *Critical and Exegetical*, 65-66—emphasis original). Cf. also Barrett, *First Epistle*, 73.

[63] See Schrage, *Der erste Brief*, 1.245.

[64] Origen, *Comm. Matt.* 27.9; Ambrosiaster, *Ad Cor Prim* 2.9.

[65] Fitzmyer, *First Corinthians*, 178.

sources from which Paul could mine for his quotation;[66] however, each of these texts post-date Paul's life and therefore cannot be considered as viable source material.

A final suggestion is that Paul quotes from a source no longer extant,[67] or simply borrows from a Jewish stream of tradition known in his day. Evidence for this comes from a similar quotation found in the *Gospel of Thomas* and Pseudo-Philo. In *Thomas* the quote reads: "I shall give you what no eye has seen and what no ear has heard and what no hand has touched and what has never occurred to the human mind" (17). While this text most plausibly dates to the 2nd century CE, the tradition it assumes places the substance and terminology of the saying within the time of Jesus, thus making it pre-existing source material for Paul's usage.[68]

In Pseudo-Philo it reads: "What eye has not seen and ear has not heard and has not surged in a human heart" (*LAB* 26.13).[69] This represents the closest parallel to what we find in 1 Cor 2.9. However, as Fitzmyer demonstrates, *LAB* post-dates Paul and "is, practically speaking, unaware of Christianity and specifically of the Pauline letters,"[70] thus making it difficult to prove literary dependence between them.[71] At best all we can suggest in this

---

[66] The alternatives mentioned include: *Ascen. Isa.* 11.34; *1 Clem* 34.8; *Gos. Thom* 17; (Eth) *Apoc. Ezra*; (Syr) *Apoc. Dan.*; *Apoc. Ps-Hipp.*; *Apoc. Pet.*; (Arab.) *Gos. Ps-Jn.*; (Eth) *Gos. Mary*; *Ep. Ps-Titus* (see Fitzmyer, *First Corinthians*, 178).

[67] Hays, *First Corinthians*, 44-45.

[68] On the other hand, it is equally plausible that *Thomas* borrows the wording from Paul yet understands its meaning as originating from Jesus. This suggestion came from Klutz during a personal conversation at the British New Testament Conference in Nottingham in 2011.

[69] Translation from Fitzmyer, *First Corinthians*, 179.

[70] *Ibid.*, 179.

[71] Although Reinmuth appears to argue the opposite—see "LAB 40,4 und die Krise der Weisheit im 1 Korintherbrief: Ein Beitrag zu den hermeneutischen Voraussetzungen der paulinischen Argumentation," in *The Corinthian*

regard is that both draw from an unknown source or tradition. This, however, leaves open the question of how we handle the prefatory formula to the quotation.

To follow the conclusion of Stanley, we could say that "[i]n view of the difficulty of determining what text [or source] Paul had in mind in adducing this quotation, it would be presumptuous to offer any analysis of the way Paul handles the wording of his *Vorlage* in 1 Cor 2.9."[72] Or, as dissatisfying as it seems, we might have to admit ignorance in this regard and allow the source(s) to remain a mystery and trust that Paul believed they possessed authority—at least in what they affirm. Alternatively, we could say Paul relies not so much on what the explicit text says but its logical and theological relevance. This brings me to the discussion of the quotation's function.

3.3.2. Function of Paul's Quotation

One reason why the emphasis might fall not on a specific source but on the relevance of the claim is the kinds of proposed sources and their theological tenor. All of the proposed sources for Paul's quotation share to varying degrees an apocalyptic view of the world and God's future dealings with creation. Moreover, in each of the proposed sources divine wisdom plays a role not only in how these apocalyptic events unfold but also how they are understood. Momentarily leaving to one side the question of the initial and ambiguous pronoun ἃ and its antecedent, we must

---

Correspondence (ed. R. Bieringer; Leuven: Leuven University Press, 1996), 471-78. Reinmuth explores the possibility of an argumentative approach that relies on yet reshapes narrative elements to reinforce a theological truth. This approach, for Reinmuth, can be found in *LAB* and Paul's letters—specifically 1 Corinthians—and the similarities suggest some awareness between the two.

[72] C.D. Stanley, *Paul and the Language of Scripture: Citation and Technique in the Pauline Epistles and Contemporary Literature* (Cambridge: Cambridge University Press, 1992), 189.

consider Paul's vague reference to things unseen, unheard, and unattained.

The specific phraseology of eyes not seeing nor ears hearing is reminiscent of OT prophetic announcements, specifically the announcements concerning those ignorant of the ways in which God sovereignly operates over creation and shapes the events of history in accordance with the divine will (cf. Isa 6.9-10; Jer 5.21; Ezek 12.2).[73] Conversely, the language of eyes seeing and ears hearing also has OT parallels where the emphasis is on those who know or shall know the ways or will of God (cf. Job 42.5; Isa 32.3; 43.8; 64.4). Relevant for my purposes is how the respective groups are defined: the ignorant are those who have rebelled against God and act contrary to the divine will, while the ones who possess knowledge are faithful to God and live according to the divine will.

If we understand the object of what eyes see and ears hear as the ways or will of God, then we can begin to make sense of the significance of such things (not) entering the human heart (i.e. ἐπὶ καρδίαν ἀνθρώπου οὐκ ἀνέβη). At least within Judaism the heart served as the seat for wisdom,[74] specifically the place where God's gift of wisdom is received.[75] Equipped with this wisdom, the heart becomes the source from which a person derives his or her

---

[73] Greenberg's remarks are worth noting: "In those passages [i.e. Is 6.9 and Jer 5.21], however, it is the stupidity and mindlessness of the people that is denounced . . ., while here [in Ezek 12.2] it is their willfulness. Having eyes 'to see' (that can see) and ears 'to hear' (that can hear) they have refused to use them, 'for they are a rebellious house' " (*Ezekiel 1–20: A New Translation with Introduction and Commentary* [Garden City: Doubleday, 1983], 208-09).

[74] See e.g. Job 9.4; 37.24; Prov 10.8; 16.21, 23; 18.15; Eccl 8.5. For a fuller examination of this theme in both Jewish and Egyptian wisdom texts, see N. Shupak, *Where Can Wisdom Be Found? The Sage's Language in the Bible and in Ancient Egyptian Literature* (Friborg: University Press, 1993), 297-311.

[75] See e.g. 1 Kgs 3.12; Eccl 1.13, 16, 17; 2.3; Sir 6.37.

understanding of life and how to live in harmony with the wisdom of God.[76]

Alternatively, those who refuse to allow such wisdom to govern their lives or receive such wisdom will not be able to define life wisely or live in harmony with the wisdom of God. Specifically, the way of life espoused by this latter group is portrayed not only as opposed to the ways of God[77] but also as a path that leads to darkness or death.[78] In broader terms, defining life apart from or in contradistinction to the wisdom of God is depicted as the way of folly or foolishness,[79] and it is understood to be the sharp antithesis to the way of righteousness—i.e. life lived according to God's wisdom. It is therefore not uncommon in Jewish wisdom texts to find a marked dualism between the righteous (wise) and the wicked (fools),[80] a theme that has relevance specifically for 1 Cor 2.9 and the wider argument of 1 Cor 1.14–3.4.

---

[76] This theme is a particular emphasis within Jewish wisdom literature, one that attempts to inculcate a specific means for defining and interpreting reality, or establish a particular worldview, which then determines how Israel was to live. Cf. L.H. Schiffmann, *From Text to Tradition: A History of Second Temple & Rabbinic Judaism* (New York: KTAV Publishing, 1991), 32; J.L. Crenshaw, *Old Testament Wisdom: An Introduction* (Louisville: Westminster John Knox, 1998), 10.

[77] See e.g. Pss 50.10; 119.155; Prov 28.4.

[78] For "darkness" see e.g. Job 10.22; 23.17; Pss 10.10-14; 11.2; 35.6; Prov 2.13; 20.20; Eccl 2.14; 6.4. For "death" see e.g. Pss 6.5; 7.13; 49.14, 17; 55.15; 107.18; Prov 2.18; 5.5; 7.27; 14.12.

[79] See e.g. Pss 14.1 (//53.1); 49.12-14; 74.22; 93.6; 94.8; Prov 1.7; 10.8, 14, 21; 12.15, 23; 13.20; 14.16, 24; 15.2, 5, 7, 14, 20; 16.22; 18.2; 19.29; 24.7.

[80] See e.g. Job 3.17; 9.22; Pss 1; 7.9; 11.5-7; 31.17; 32.10; 34.21; 37.10-11, 16, 21, 28, 39-40; 58.3-11; 68.2-3; 75.8-10; 82; 91.7, 12; 112.6-10; Prov 2.21-22; 3.33; 4.18-19; 21.12, 18, 29; 24.16; 25.26; 28.12, 28; 29.2, 7, 16; Eccl 7.15; 8.14. Cf. esp. Prov 10.1–18.24.

We begin to see traces of this dualism when we consider the final clause of Paul's quotation: ἃ ἡτοίμασεν ὁ θεὸς τοῖς ἀγαπῶσιν αὐτόν (2.9c). On one side there are those who love God and receive from God because of that love, while, on the other side, by implication there are those who do not receive because they do not love God. This would seem to create a natural cause-and-effect relationship between the ideas of receiving from and loving God. However, what is the object received and is it contingent upon one's love for God? This brings me to the issue of the initial, ambiguous relative pronoun ἅ. Part of the concern is identifying the most natural antecedent for the pronoun, for which scholars have suggested various possibilities. For example, Morris says that it refers to "the wonderful things that God has made ready for those who love him"[81]—a reading that appears to combine the essence of both 2.9c and 2.12-13. This suggestion, however, does very little to explain the referent in a precise way; it merely offers a broad idea.

Ostensibly trying to avoid generalities, Schrage links ἅ with either the specific concept of "glory" in 2.7 or the basic idea of the gift of salvation for those who believe.[82] However glory and the gift of salvation are each singular ideas whereas the pronoun in 2.9 is plural,[83] a dilemma that Morris' reading avoided with the gloss, "wonderful things." Moreover, the precision of Schrage's reading becomes difficult to sustain when the rest of Paul's argument is considered—i.e. he is concerned with more than the notion of

---

[81] Morris, *First Epistle*, 56—emphasis removed.

[82] Schrage, *Der erste Brief*, 1.256.

[83] Scholars advocating this view tend to offer no explanation for the dilemma—see e.g. Grosheide, *First Epistle*, 66-67; G. Deluz, *A Companion to 1 Corinthians* (ed. and trans. G.E. Watt; London: Darton, Longman & Todd, 1963), 28; Kistemaker, *Exposition*, 85; Mare-Harris, *1, 2 Corinthians*, 28; Keener, *1–2 Corinthians*, 38-39; M.L. Soards, *1 Corinthians* (Peabody: Hendrickson, 1999), 59-60; Schnabel, *Der erste Brief*, 169-70.

"glory" and the gift of salvation. For Paul the concern deals with *how* that glory is revealed and obtained and what it means for those who receive it—i.e. those who are being saved. With this wider emphasis in view, Grosheide and others connect the relative pronoun with "the wisdom of God in Christ which the world did not acknowledge."[84] While this reading corresponds with the focus of Paul's argument in a more consistent way, it does not avoid the dilemma of a plural pronoun referring to a singular idea.

However, Fee's comments in this regard are worth noting, for they appear to address this dilemma in a way that is both fair to the syntax and consistent with the argument.[85] Specifically, according to Fee, the quotation of 2.9 is divided into four lines:

(1) ἃ ὀφθαλμὸς οὐκ εἶδεν

   (2) καὶ οὖς οὐκ ἤκουσεν

   (3) καὶ ἐπὶ καρδίαν ἀνθρώπου οὐκ ἀνέβη

(4) ἃ ἡτοίμασεν ὁ θεὸς τοῖς ἀγαπῶσιν αὐτόν

Fee argues that the relative pronoun in line 4 refers back to the implied—albeit ambiguous—objects in lines 1-3, thus making them the objects of the main verb in line 4 (i.e. things which God has prepared). Admittedly, this reading settles the use of the plural in line 4, yet it does not account for the plural pronoun use in line 1. One option would be to consider the meaning of the whole quotation, noting the particular emphasis of line 4, in the light of Paul's surrounding argument. Specifically, Paul in 2.6-8 stresses

---

[84] Grosheide, *First Epistle*, 66-67. A small number of commentators say virtually nothing about the antecedent—see e.g. Barrett, *First Epistle*, 73; Lietzmann, *An die Korinther*, 13; Ruef, *First Letter*, 19; Witherington, *Conflict and Community*, 127; Collins, *First Corinthians*, 132. Conzelmann suggests that the entire structure of the passage makes it impossible to know anything for certain—Conzelmann, *1 Corinthians*, 64.

[85] Fee, *First Epistle*, 107-08.

what he does speak, and that the substance of that message is God's wisdom, wisdom which is hidden in mystery, the mystery of salvation via a crucifixion, and how this wise mystery remained unknown to the rulers of this age.

All of this, therefore, collectively forms the substance of the gospel message, thus representing the "things" which God has prepared and revealed "for those who love him." Moreover, the notion of some receiving God's wisdom and others not reflects a similar idea found in 1.18, where some judge the word of the cross to be foolishness while others know it to be God's power, and it is the latter who are being saved while the former are being destroyed. This then ties in with 2.1-5 where the Corinthians' faith is rooted in the power of God, in the cross of Christ, made known to them through Paul's apostolic preaching of Christ crucified. It is precisely this preaching, especially its content, that receives the derogatory label, "foolishness"; yet it is precisely this foolishness that Paul proclaims to be God's wisdom.

With regard to the implied recipients of 2.9, this object of discussion (i.e. God's wisdom) necessarily applies to both those who receive and those who do not know, and the distinction relates to how this wisdom is understood by both parties. As intimated above, in 2.6-7 Paul emphasizes the otherness of this wisdom with regard to its origin or source, and he does so in two forms: a negative and a positive. As a negative, Paul specifically states that the wisdom he declares is not derived from "the rulers of this age" (2.6), nor is it a wisdom that the rulers of this age would proclaim. As a positive, he declares it to be wisdom from God (2.7). Moreover by stressing the mysteriousness and hiddenness of God's wisdom (2.7), Paul not only further separates it from the wisdom of "the rulers of this age" but also intimates why they are ignorant of it—i.e. it is not theirs. Moreover, it is beyond the reach of *any* human.

For Paul, proof that the rulers of this age are ignorant of God's mysterious and hidden wisdom is the very act of them crucifying Christ (see 2.8);[86] or as Grosheide puts it: "[t]o condemn Him to the ignominy of a cross is evidence of unbelief and of not acknowledging the wisdom of God who revealed Himself in Christ's glory."[87] This corresponds with Paul's earlier claims in 1.18-25 where he notes the divergent views concerning the message of the cross. As noted before, in 1.18 Paul distinguishes between those who see the message of the cross as folly and those who see it as God's power. Moreover, Paul stresses the idea that the former are being destroyed (1.18a) while the latter are being saved (1.18b). This corresponds with the earlier OT portrayals of the wicked fools rejecting God's wisdom, thus bringing about darkness or death, and the righteous wise receiving God's wisdom, thus bringing about life or salvation. The antithesis of 1.18-25 appears to be carried over to Paul's remarks in 2.9, where he emphasizes the contrast between those who fail to see, hear, and receive God's wisdom with those who receive what is prepared for them.

However, when we come to 2.9 and recognize its object as God's wisdom, and when we consider this in the light of Paul's remarks in 2.7-8, we seem to encounter a dilemma for which there is no solution. If God's wisdom is hidden, mysterious, and reserved only for a select few, and if human wisdom is incapable of locating and plumbing the depths of this wisdom, how then can the specific group in 2.9 come to know or obtain that which has been prepared for them? Part of the solution is implied in the statement, ἃ ἡτοίμασεν ὁ θεὸς τοῖς ἀγαπῶσιν αὐτόν, while the remainder of the solution is emphatically given in 2.10a. With regard to the implied solution, the idea of something prepared

---

[86] A further discussion of this passage will be given below.

[87] Grosheide, *First Epistle*, 66.

suggests the potential for bestowal and receipt, which further suggest active and passive participants in the transaction. Here in 2.9c the participants are loosely described: God is the active agent in preparing "the things," and those who love God are the passive recipients of what God prepared.[88] All that remains is for the transaction to occur, which Paul announces in 2.10-13 as having taken place.

Before considering that announcement, we should briefly note the qualifier "those who love" God, which alters the usual expectation for how one obtains divine wisdom. The usual expectation would be knowledge, whereby God blesses those who strive to know the things of God by granting them access to the unseen riches of divine wisdom. Thus, Paul's readers would have expected, "those who *know* God." However, this suggests a sufficient ability within the human mind to achieve such things, yet it is precisely this notion that Paul repudiates. This follows from a comparison of what Paul says and a similar theme expressed in Jer 5, where the prophet announces God's judgment on the people for their "rebellious heart" (5.23). Specifically, Jeremiah calls them a "foolish and heartless people" (5.21a), those "who have eyes but do not see; who have ears but do not hear" (5.21b-c).

As Fretheim observes, "[t]he problem is not one of ignorance, however, as if to say that with a little more knowledge, the issue could be resolved. The language is relational; the issue is that they do not know the LORD, which leads to a foolish life of evil rather than good."[89] Similarly for Paul, the solution is not knowledge, since no amount or exercise of knowledge will ever be adequate for obtaining access to God's hidden wisdom. Moreover, Paul has already stressed this reality and the fact that God has rendered the

---

[88] The phrase, "passive recipients" simply refers to the fact that they do not initiate the transaction.

[89] T.E. Fretheim, *Jeremiah* (Macon: Smyth & Helwys, 2002), 114.

power of human wisdom impotent, thus making it incapable of achieving what it desires. For Paul, the solution is relational: it is love for God. This prepares the way for what Paul says in 2.10-13, where he explicitly states how those who love God come to know God's wisdom.

3.3.3. God's Wisdom and the Mediation of the Spirit

Specifically in 1 Cor 2.10-13 Paul expresses his understanding of the agency of the Spirit in revealing the hidden, divine wisdom to believers. This expression can be divided into four parts, each of which will be examined below in order to draw out their individual significance and their collective relevance for the rest of Paul's argument.

3.3.3.1. Agency of the Spirit

First, in 2.10a Paul asserts the simple reality concerning the agency of the Spirit in revealing divine wisdom. In the light of the discussion above, since we can be confident that the object of revelation is God's wisdom, we can now begin to see how the quotation in 2.9 functions in Paul's argument. While it is certainly possible to view the quotation as support for or a conclusion to the claims of 2.6-8, or even to see it as a supporting hinge on which the logical transition between 2.6-8 and 2.10-16 swings, it is more likely that Paul's focus is not on the external details of the quotation but rests squarely on the internal logic of what is quoted.

Thus, agreeing with Lamp, the quotation supplied "appears to be more focused on illustrating Paul's point rather than proving it from Scripture."[90] Accordingly, and as the quotation suggests, the things of God are completely inaccessible to humans and human wisdom. The only way in which the inaccessible things of God become accessible is by God's initiative; no amount of human

---

[90] Lamp, *First Corinthians*, 165-66.

effort or wise attempts will alter this reality.[91] However, with the emphatic conjunction δέ in 2.10,[92] Paul announces that such inaccessibility no longer exists because God has made wisdom accessible by the Spirit.[93] This brings me to the second part of Paul's understanding of the Spirit's role in mediating wisdom.

3.3.3.2. Necessity of the Agency

In 1 Cor 2.10b-11 Paul explains why the Spirit must be the agent of revelation.[94] Admittedly, Paul's remarks here are more or less tangential to his primary claim about the Spirit's necessary role in revealing divine wisdom; however the tangent is ultimately germane to the argument of 2.9-13. Paul begins his explanation

---

[91] Cf. Tillich: "the human spirit is unable to compel the divine Spirit to enter the human spirit. The attempt to do so belongs directly to the ambiguities of religion and indirectly to the ambiguities of culture and morality. If religious devotion, moral obedience, or scientific honesty could compel the divine Spirit to 'descend' to us, the Spirit which 'descended' would be the human spirit in a religious disguise" (*Systematic Theology* [Digwell Place: James Nisbet & Co., 1964], 3.119-20).

[92] "The loose use of the connective δέ (‭א‬, A, C, D, G, P, Ψ, 33, 81, 614, *Byz al*) is entirely in Paul's manner, whereas γάρ, though strongly supported by $\mathfrak{P}^{46}$, B, 1739, Clement, *al*, has the appearance of being an improvement introduced by copyists" (Metzger, *Textual Commentary*, 481).

[93] A small number of manuscripts support the inclusion of the personal pronoun αὐτός following διὰ τοῦ πνεύματος (‭א‬², D, F, G, Ψ, *Byz*, latt, syr, sa^ms, bo^ms, Epiphanius, Speculum), presumably to supply (theological) clarity for the nature of the Spirit in relation to God. However, the absence of αὐτός in other key manuscripts ($\mathfrak{P}^{46}$, ‭א‬*, A, B, C, 630, 1739, 1881, *pc*, sa, bo, Clement) supports the omission as being original. As Thiselton argues: "Had the word *his* been original, it is difficult to understand both its lack of early support and why it should have been omitted" (*First Epistle*, 255; cf. also Collins, *First Corinthians*, 132).

[94] This follows Collins' observation: "Paul uses an explanatory *gar* to explain why it is that the Spirit of God is the one who has revealed the mystery and divine wisdom" (*First Corinthians*, 132-33).

with a brief statement about what the Spirit is able to do (i.e. τὸ πνεῦμα πάντα ἐραυνᾷ [2.10b]), and the extent to which this occurs (i.e. καὶ τὰ βάθη τοῦ θεοῦ [2.10c]).[95] This type of claim has a bearing not only on Paul's understanding of the Spirit as a revelatory agent (2.10a) but also the nature and scope of what is revealed. Thus, if this Spirit is able to search all things, and if the extent of "all things" includes knowing the depths of God,[96] then at the very least we can safely assume that this Spirit possesses an ability or capacity to know things only God can know, which further suggests that this Spirit shares a unique (or privileged) relationship with God. Moreover, if this unique relationship and ability or capacity to know are admitted, then we can further assume that the Spirit as a chosen revelatory agent would act in accordance with that relationship and disclose only that which is consistent with God's wisdom.

Then, in 1 Cor 2.11 Paul goes on to explain why the Spirit must be the chosen agent of revelation,[97] and he does so in a particular way. A number of scholars have argued that Paul employs a logical (or rhetorical) device known as the "like by like" principle.[98] According to Gärtner, this principle appears in four strands of tradition: the Stoics, Hermetic writings, Gnostics, and Philo.[99] Gärtner contends that the principle was often employed by Greek thinkers in order "to understand the world and man, the

---

[95] "To these depths of God the plan of salvation in Christ Jesus also belongs as Rom 11.33 bears out" (Grosheide, *First Epistle*, 68).

[96] Cf. Dan 2.22; *2 Bar* 14.8-9; Wis 7.22-30; 9.9-18.

[97] For similar arguments, see Grosheide, *First Epistle*, 69; Fee, *First Epistle*, 111-12; Mare-Harris, *1, 2 Corinthians*, 30; Collins, *First Corinthians*, 133.

[98] E.g. B.E. Gärtner, "The Pauline and Johannine Idea of 'to Know God' Against the Hellenistic Background," *NTS* 14.2 (1968): 209-31; Conzelmann, *1 Corinthians*, 66; Fee, *First Epistle*, 111-12; Witherington, *Conflict and Community*, 127-28; Fitzmyer, *First Corinthians*, 180.

[99] Gärtner, "Pauline and Johannine," 209.

rules governing the world and man's ethical actions" and even "how man can be capable of knowing God."[100] However, Gärtner's thesis fails to persuade for two reasons.

First, the principle in these traditions applies more to how humans can come to know as God knows and therefore think or reason like God.[101] Such an emphasis is quite separate from Paul's argument. Secondly, and more foundational, the traditions in question, with the possible exception of Philo,[102] present the path of knowing as bottom-up, from humanity to God, which is also contrary to Paul's argument. Other scholars are more inclined to sees Paul's remarks as nothing more than simple analogy,[103] one that not only remains consistent with Paul's thought but also does not require a complex device for whose existence there is little evidence. This alternative is the one adopted here.

The simple analogy, therefore, is that only the spirit of a person can know the (innermost) things of that person. The only way in which those innermost things can be known by others is if the one who possesses them decides to reveal them. Until such a decision or time, the innermost things of that individual remain hidden. Similarly, for Paul's argument, only the Spirit of God can know the (innermost) things of God—or, in this case, "the depths of

---

[100] *Ibid.*, 210.

[101] Specifically, humans—by their own efforts and/or wisdom—seek to know and reason like the divine, thus making them more or less equal with the divine. Where Gärtner's thesis fails is in both the comparison and anticipated results of the "like by like" principle he surveys. For him, humans are able to think or reason *like* the divine whereas for Paul it is impossible for a human to know the thoughts of God because humans are *unlike* God. Davis stresses a similar point—see *Wisdom and Spirit*, 111.

[102] Gärtner does acknowledge that the Philo tradition presents the human mind (νοῦς) as incapable of knowing God even though the former has an essential connection with the latter via the πνεῦμα—see "Pauline and Johannine," 213-15.

[103] See e.g. Thiselton, *First Epistle*, 258-59.

God." Before dealing with what Paul is saying, we must be clear about what he is not advocating with this analogy.

First, a small number of scholars have suggested that Paul's meaning in 2.11 points to an awareness of a subconscious or *ego* within the human being, and that this is what he refers to with the term, πνεῦμα.[104] Second, others have taken Paul's use of πνεῦμα as being synonymous with the human mind, which represents a broader category than a subconscious or *ego*.[105] While this latter interpretation aligns better with ancient anthropological views, such views do not appear to be Paul's primary concern in this text.[106] Paul's focus is the inherent logic of the analogy itself—i.e. the innermost things of a person or even a divine being cannot be known unless that person or divine being discloses them. We can be confident of such a focus given that Paul's argument is dealing with the very nature and act of revelation, specifically the depths of God being revealed τοῖς ἀγαπῶσιν αὐτόν.

3.3.3.3. Nature of the Agent

In 2.12, Paul offers a word of assurance concerning the nature of the Spirit as God's agent of revelation. It is also at this point that Paul resumes his initial claim in 2.10a, which was broken off momentarily by the explanation of 2.10b-11. Paul immediately presents a categorical distinction, one that involves the "spirit of the world" and "the Spirit from God." I will return to the question of what Paul means by these phrases later; for now it is important only to recognize the nature of the distinction and its essential function for Paul's argument. With regard to the nature of the

---

[104] See Grosheide, *First Epistle*, 69; Barrett, *First Epistle*, 74.

[105] See e.g. Ruef, *First Letter*, 19; Conzelmann, *1 Corinthians*, 66.

[106] See e.g. Fee, *First Epistle*, 112; Mare-Harris, *1, 2 Corinthians*, 30; Witherington, *Conflict and Community*, 128.

distinction, Paul is quite clear: the one is not the other.[107] In the light of what Paul has said about the wisdom of this age and how that wisdom represents a particular way of knowing, one incapable of ascertaining God's wisdom, and since only God's Spirit has access to and is the revealer of God's wisdom, it makes sense for Paul to categorize the wisdom of this age as "the spirit of the world."

This brings me to the functional aspect of the distinction, which is to assure the Corinthians that they have not received a spirit that is unable to know God's wisdom; instead they have received the one who is able to know the wisdom of God—or even the depths of God. The result of this, as Paul goes on to say in 2.12b, is that the Corinthian believers can know the things freely given to them by God. The ambiguous τά appears to have two likely referents.

Immediately, and grammatically, it relates to what Paul states in 2.13-14a, an argument I will return to shortly. However, "things" also seems to relate back to Paul's claims in 2.9—i.e. the things unseen, unheard, and divinely prepared. The obvious implication would be if the Corinthians received "the spirit of the world" they would be those who do not see, do not hear, and do not partake of what is prepared. Yet because the Corinthians have received "the Spirit of God" they are able to see, hear, and partake of the things of God, for it is only by this Spirit that such things can be revealed, known, and even experienced. This follows from the earlier point about the nature of the Spirit described in 2.10b and the content of what is revealed as noted in 2.9.

---

[107] In saying, "the nature of the distinction," I am referring to both the concept and the ontology of "spirit". The recent work of Rabens emphasizes the need for clarity on this distinction, particularly the idea of God's Spirit as material or physical substance and whether or not Paul actually thought in or used such terms—see *Holy Spirit and Ethics*, 13-15, 17-19, 25-29.

3.3.3.4. Apostolic Preaching and the Agency of Spirit-Revelation

In 2.13, Paul anchors the substance of his message to the revelation of the Spirit, which brings me back to the question of the immediate referent for τά in 2.12b. Particularly relevant here is the connection between what believers know as a result of receiving God's Spirit and the things which Paul teaches, [108] specifically the things ἐν διδακτοῖς πνεύματος and the things only discerned by the Spirit. Moreover, we must recognize the links between what is known and what is received and how the Spirit plays a role in the entire process. To begin in reverse, in 2.12 Paul states that "we have received...the Spirit from God," which establishes the necessary condition for him to say, "we know the things freely given to us"; and it is precisely these things that Paul says, "we speak".

In keeping with the reception of God's Spirit, and the revelation of the things of God as a result, Paul qualifies the nature of his speaking in negative and positive terms. Negatively, he affirms that his speaking was οὐκ ἐν διδακτοῖς λόγος ἀνθρωπίνης σοφίας, an affirmation that reflects his earlier claims in 2.4 (cf. also 1.17), and positively he asserts that his speaking was ἐν διδακτοῖς πνεύματος, which also bears connections with 2.4. What exactly is Paul saying with this contrast, specifically the notion of the Spirit teaching, and how does it affect his overall argument?

Since 2.13 is the third time Paul uses λαλέω to describe his teaching or instruction (cf. 2.6a, 7a), and since the object of the initial λαλέω is "wisdom," and since Paul identifies the recipients of this wisdom as οἱ τέλειοι, one might be tempted to read Paul's remarks in 2.13 as evidence of a deeper level of instruction vis-à-vis the more basic teaching of the *kerygma* in 2.1-5. Accordingly,

---

[108] I will return later to the dilemma of the plural, λαλοῦμεν in this passage and who are the most likely referents.

that which he proclaims in general for the initial gospel message represents the basic *kerygma*, whereas the Spirit-teaching of divine wisdom is reserved only for the spiritual elite. However, as noted earlier,[109] this type of reading perpetuates that which Paul seeks to correct—i.e. status-seeking on the basis of an assumed superior knowledge or spirituality. Moreover, as Willis argues: it is

> most unlikely that having opposed divisiveness on the basis of the *Corinthians'* wisdom, Paul would sponsor a similar division with *his own* teaching. Would not this encourage the Pauline faction? It would seem most awkward in the midst of an argument against divisiveness that Paul would endorse any bi-level divisions of believers![110]

Thus, we must consider alternative ways for understanding Paul's meaning in this passage. One alternative, in the light of the revelation idea, is that Paul refers to a kind of wisdom instruction via ecstatic speech, particularly tongue-speaking.[111] Such a reading would be possible in the light of the immediate connection between the relative pronoun in 2.13 and its antecedent, τὰ χαρισθέντα in 2.12b, which would also appear to relate to Paul's earlier remarks in 1.7 where the cognate, χάρισμα is used. This reading appears to garner additional support by virtue of the connection between these gracious gifts and what is spoken to the πνευματικός. Moreover, as Horsley points out, in chapters 12-14 "the *pneumatika* are clearly the special spiritual gifts such as

---

[109] See 2.3.3.1.1. above.

[110] Willis, "'The Mind of Christ'," 120-21—emphasis original; cf. Collins, *First Corinthians*, 128.

[111] Cf. Koenig, "From Mystery to Ministry," 170, 172; D. Nichols, "The Problem of Two-Level Christianity at Corinth," *Pneuma* 11.2 (1989): 107-08.

glossolalia and ecstatic prophecy, and *pneumatikos* refers to the special standing of one who enjoys such spiritual gifts."[112]

However, this alternative creates historical problems with regard to Paul's initial proclamation, which is a major focus of 1 Cor 2.1–3.4. The implications of and most plausible inferences drawn from Paul's statement in 1 Cor 2.1-5 are that he spoke not only in simple speech but also speech that was intelligible or recognizable.[113] The only way this could be avoided is if one presupposes varying levels of instruction, where the initial proclamation was given in simple, intelligible, or recognizable speech whereas the deeper instruction involved a message given in ecstatic speech or tongue-speaking.[114] Even if these problems and conjectured solutions were set aside, the fundamental dilemma remains: a two-tiered body of believers is created, and Paul is explicitly arguing against a divided body.

A more plausible solution would be to re-examine the specific contrast that Paul establishes and then recognize the function of the phrase πνευματικοῖς πνευματικὰ συγκρίνοντες with regard to that contrast. First, the controlling verb of 2.13 is λαλέω, and in the light of the preceding discussion we can be sure that the initial relative pronoun of 2.13 refers to all the things God graciously gives, which would certainly include wisdom, thus making such things the object of λαλέω. The contrast is established by the

---

[112] Horsley, "Pneumatikos vs. Psychikos," 270.

[113] Scott, summarising Gooch, argues "that the Spirit's revelation retains a cognitive content ('wisdom' in 2:6, 7) which can be expressed by human language (2:7, 13), and that the 'words taught by the Spirit' are 'words serving interpretation (v. 13) and investigation (v. 14) rather than expressing nonrational ecstasy' " (*Implicit Epistemology*, 45 n.124—quotes from Gooch, *Partial Knowledge*, 37).

[114] Instruction via ecstatic speech or tongue-speaking presupposes a group able to understand what is articulated, which then leaves open the possibility of boasting of superiority—or at least special privilege—by that group.

emphatic comparative conjunction formula, οὐκ...ἀλλά, and the specificity of the contrast deals with a distinction between modes of speaking wisdom.

On both sides of the contrast lies the prepositional phrase, ἐν διδακτοῖς, which not only qualifies the aspect of speaking but also suggests ways of instruction or knowing. It appears to be this latter nuance that is in view, for Paul distinguishes instruction given through "human words of wisdom" from instruction given through "[the] Spirit." This distinction has a ready parallel in 2.4, where Paul emphatically states that he did not rely on wise, persuasive speech[115] but on the demonstration of the power of the Spirit in what he asserts was an unpolished message. Thus, Paul's contrast in 2.13 is best seen not only as a continuation or re-emphasis of the contrast in 2.4 but also of the one pervading the entire argument—i.e. human wisdom and its ways of knowing versus God's wisdom and ways of knowing.

Second, the phrase, πνευματικοῖς πνευματικὰ συγκρίν-οντες plays an important role in emphasizing Paul's argument about the distinct ways of knowing. However, this phrase is one of the more troubling aspects of this text, in terms of its translation and interpretation. To begin with, the meaning of συγκρίνω remains a point of dispute among scholars: Grosheide favors the idea of comparing or judging,[116] the former being parallel to Paul's use of συγκρίνω in 2 Cor 10.12;[117] Barrett extends the range to

---

[115] The textual variant, πειθοῖς ἀνθρωπίνης σοφίας λόγοις in 2.4 suggests that scribes were aware of this thematic parallel.

[116] Grosheide, *First Epistle*, 72. Admittedly, Grosheide allows for "combining" but dismisses it. Morris, however, finds "combining" to be the more plausible reading—see *First Epistle*, 58.

[117] Fee (*First Epistle*, 115) recognizes this parallel but says the idea of comparing "does not seem appropriate here" in 1 Cor 2.13, yet he does not provide any explanation for his conclusion.

include interpreting, composing, or combining; [118] and Fee advocates the inclusion of discerning, "in the sense of being able to make appropriate 'judgments' about what God is doing in the world."[119] While these definitions contribute to our understanding of the term and its usage, they seem to operate within the same semantic range, sharing various degrees of overlap.

In each case, the proposed definitions stress the idea of examining two or more things together and recognizing, in a rational way, their harmony or interrelatedness. We should at least be aware of this fluidity before making decisions about its exact meaning in 2.13. The other difficulty with the phrase is the repeated use of πνευματικός, albeit in different cases, and what precisely Paul means by each (or both). Moreover, the ambiguity in the term's gender allows it to be used as either masculine or neuter, a distinction that affects how one interprets Paul's claim. Fitzmyer offers a helpful summary of the four leading options for how to deal with this phrase,[120] each taking into consideration the gender of πνευματικός and the meaning and use of συγκρίνω.

First, it is possible to read both πνευματικοῖς and πνευματικά as neuter in gender, thus interpreted as "spiritual things," and to translate the verb συγκρίνω as "compare," similar to what appears in 2 Cor 10.12. The resultant phrase would then be rendered: "comparing spiritual realities with spiritual realities." Fitzmyer rightly points out that "since the [participle] *Synkrinontes* modifies the subject of *laloumen*, it is not a question of receiving *pneumatika*, but of proclaiming them."[121] Second, it is possible to

---

[118] Barrett, *First Epistle*, 76. Morris soundly rejects "interpreting" (see *First Epistle*, 58; *contra* Fee, *First Epistle*, 115, although he opts for "explaining"); Kistemaker, *Exposition*, 89; Witherington, *Conflict and Community*, 128; Collins, *First Corinthians*, 135; Fitzmyer, *First Corinthians*, 182.

[119] Fee, *First Epistle*, 117.

[120] See Fitzmyer, *First Corinthians*, 181-82.

[121] See *ibid.*, 182.

read πνευματικά as neuter on its own, πνευματικοῖς as masculine and modifying "words" in 2.13a, and translate συγκρίνοντες as "interpreting," similar to what appears in Gen 40.8, 16, 22; 41.12; Jdg 7.15; Dan 5.7 (LXX). The phrase would then be read as: "interpreting spiritual realities in spiritual terms." While this is the option that Fitzmyer prefers, the others must still be considered.

Third, it is possible to maintain a neuter reading for πνευματικά and a translation of "interpreting" for συγκρίνοντες, yet take πνευματικοῖς as a masculine substantive, which then results in the reading: "interpreting spiritual realities for spiritual people." Fitzmyer objects to this option for one surprising reason: "[it] anticipates the antithesis of vv. 14-15." [122] However, this anticipation appears to be precisely what is happening within Paul's argument, thus making this option more likely. The final possibility returns to the decision of reading both πνευματικά and πνευματινοῖς as neuter, yet translate συγκρίνοντες as "combining" or "fitting together." The resultant phrase is then rendered: "fitting spiritual things to spiritual expression." Fitzmyer offers no explanation for why this option could not be viable or why it should be rejected.

However, it appears as though the whole endeavour seeks to understand the phrase in isolation. Lang offers an approach that examines the components of the phrase in turn and then applies the whole statement back to the argument, an approach that requires several vital steps.[123] First, both uses of πνευματικός are read as neuter in gender, although a gloss for this usage will be withheld for now. Second, one must take into consideration that the first πνευματικός is in the dative case while the second is in the accusative. Third, one must not only allow συγκρίνω to operate

---

[122] See *ibid.*, 182.

[123] Lang argues along similar lines in *Die Briefe an die Korinther*, 45-46.

(initially) within its immediate context, thus recognizing its syntactical relationship to the two uses of πνευματικός, but also rely on the general (albeit fluid) definition of συγκρίνω as stated above. Thus, the act of examining two or more things together and recognizing, in a rational way, their harmony or interrelatedness applies to the two uses of πνευματικός—one being the object and the other being the means. From this the reader can supply appropriate glosses for the two terms: for the dative use, "spiritual means"; for the accusative, "spiritual things." Accordingly, the phrase could be rendered, "defining spiritual things by spiritual means." Finally, the entire phrase is seen as qualifying Paul's primary remarks in 2.13—i.e. it explains what it means to speak in words taught by the Spirit by specifying how those words are received and comprehended.

Since the object of the message is God's wisdom, which suggests the content of the message is spiritual in nature and origin, and since that wisdom can only be revealed by God's Spirit, which makes knowledge of that wisdom dependent upon the agency of the Spirit, then as Lang argues, "[t]he nature and manner of speech should correspond to the origin of knowledge. The wisdom of God can only be made known by the Spirit of God, according to the rule that like is known by like." [124] This correspondence is precisely what Paul is stressing with regard to his spoken message in Corinth.

However, this correspondence has another facet that cannot be overlooked: the criterion by which Paul speaks the message of God's wisdom is the same criterion by which that message is to be understood and judged.[125] Thus, just as Paul relies on the powerful work of the Spirit to reveal God's wisdom in a message not relying on rhetorical flair, the Corinthians must rely on the same Spirit for

---

[124] *Ibid.*, 45.
[125] See Conzelmann, *1 Corinthians*, 67.

a correct understanding and acquisition of that wisdom even when delivered through an unpolished message. However, the substance of Paul's argument suggests that the Corinthians are now interpreting or judging his original message according to a criterion that is not "spiritual" (or Spirit-given). They appear to be judging the message through human wisdom; they are employing a human criterion to interpret spiritual content, a strategy that ultimately fails because like is not interpreting by like.

Paul then explains what he asserts in 2.13 with another contrast in 2.14-15, this time pitting the "natural person" (ψυχινός) against the "spiritual person" (πνευματικός).[126] Scholars remain divided over how to address this terminology. Some maintain that the explicit terms and the specific distinction provide further evidence for a Gnostic or proto-Gnostic influence on Pauline thought, where the "natural" person is the one not illuminated by the secret γνῶσις while the "spiritual" person is.[127] As a result, it is only the "spiritual" person who has access to the secret knowledge or wisdom imparted by God—presumably through Paul's additional, selective, or exclusive post-gospel teaching—while the "natural" person remains ignorant of such things. While avoiding the idea of a Gnostic or proto-Gnostic influence, yet wanting to explain the apparent uniqueness of Paul's description, others have argued that he merely adopts the language or terms used within Corinth, which might have been influenced by Gnostic or proto-Gnostic teaching.[128] Thus, Paul is once again portrayed as taking on the

---

[126] I will deal with Paul's reference to the "spiritual person" later in this chapter.

[127] See e.g. Wilckens, *Weisheit und Torheit*, 70-80; Schmithals, *Gnosticism in Corinth*, 229. Cf. also Bultmann, *Theology*, 165-66, 174; Jewett, *Paul's Anthropological Terms*, 121-23; G. Strecker, *Theology of the New Testament* (trans. F.W. Horn; Louisville: Westminster John Knox, 2000), 62.

[128] See e.g. Winter, *Pneumatiker und Psychiker in Korinth*, 231-32.

ideas of his opponents, subverting, and then redefining those ideas for his argument.[129]

However, neither of these explanations is necessary, especially the Gnostic or proto-Gnostic reading, for understanding Paul's meaning or determining the source of his ideas.[130] Moreover, both readings presuppose an internal dichotomy where there are "natural" and "spiritual" believers. This not only perpetuates the faulty assumption of a tiered body of believers in Corinth, it also overlooks the clear distinction and the force of that distinction in Paul's argument, not just in 2.14-15 but also 2.1–3.4. Paul's explicit claims about the "natural person" are directed toward non-believers, not a particular (non-illumined) group of believers. Evidence for this initially comes from the fact that the ψυχικὸς ἄνθρωπος οὐ δέχεται τὰ τοῦ πνεύματος τοῦ θεοῦ· μωρία γὰρ αὐτῷ ἐστιν καὶ οὐ δύναται γνῶναι, ὅτι πνευματικῶς ἀνακρίνεται (2.14).

This echoes Paul's earlier claims about the rulers of this age not knowing God's wisdom, and their ignorance was primarily due to their not having (or receiving) the revelation of God's Spirit, whereas believers do know God's wisdom and that knowledge is explicitly tied to having (or receiving) the Spirit's revelation. Moreover, the charge of foolishness laid against God's wisdom characterises those who are being destroyed, while those who

---

[129] Cf. Pearson, *Pneumatikos-Psychikos*, 27, 34-40; Davis, *Wisdom and Spirit*, 99, 114-17, 125-26; Horsley, *1 Corinthians*, 61-62. Litfin is skeptical of this approach—see *Theology of Proclamation*, 214 n.2.

[130] As Scott reminds us: "Paul frequently describes believers as possessing the Spirit, and in Gal 6:1 he designates the Galatian believers as οἱ πνευματικοί. While the adjective ψυχικός is used by Paul only in 1 Cor, the opposition between those with the Spirit and those without it is hardly uncharacteristic of Paul, and the adjective ψυχικός would not have been recognized in the first century as technical vocabulary" (*Implicit Epistemology*, 37 n.92).

know it to be God's power are characterized as those being saved. Thus, Paul's distinction here in 2.14 is consistent with the one he makes throughout—i.e. those who belong to God and those who do not. It is therefore not appropriate to see his remarks about the "natural person" as referring to a type of lower-level believer.

3.4. Spirit, Wisdom and Gospel in Corinth

Earlier it was argued that the *object* of revelation in 1 Cor 2.9-13 is God's wisdom and that God's Spirit is the necessary agent for mediating this wisdom. I now turn my attention to the question of what precisely is revealed, or: what is the *content* of that revelation? My concern here is not only identifying the content and the Spirit's role in disclosing that content but also its relationship to Paul's ministry in Corinth and the problems that arise following his departure. Therefore I must examine the elements of Paul's argument in 2.6-16 in the light of the larger argument of 2.1–3.4.

3.4.1. Gospel Proclaimed as God's Wisdom

After describing the manner in which he proclaimed the gospel of Christ crucified (2.1-5), specifically that he did not depend on assumed superior (human) speech or wisdom, Paul goes on to announce the wisdom he does proclaim (2.6-16) and how that wisdom is meant to shape the Corinthians' thinking and behavior (cf. 3.1-4). As already noted, Paul's announcement of proclaiming a wisdom message in 2.6-16 appears to conflict with his rejection of wisdom in 2.1-5, thus leading some scholars to see a contradiction.[131] However the apparent contradiction persists only if one fails to interpret the "wisdom" of 2.1-5 as distinct from the "wisdom" of 2.6-16. One part of the distinction pertains to Paul's remarks about the two wisdoms, especially his specific focus in

---

[131]Again, see Bultmann, "Karl Barth," 70-72; Conzelmann, *1 Corinthians*, 57; Walker, "1 Corinthians 2.6-16," 75-94.

those remarks. On a basic level, the "wisdom" of 2.1-5 is concerned with the form or expression whereas the "wisdom" of 2.6-16 deals with the content or substance.

More substantially, as argued in the previous chapter, Paul's rejection of wisdom (and wise speech) in 2.1-5 is not a wholesale rejection of wisdom; instead, he rejects a particular kind or form of wisdom, one he deems incapable of revealing the mystery of God as displayed in the cross of Christ. Naturally, this rejection of a particular form does not entail the discontinuation or discrediting of the notion of wisdom, especially divine wisdom. The rejection simply asserts that a particular approach or form is unable to ascertain that divine wisdom.

Therefore, Paul's rejection of (or his refusal to employ) human wisdom to proclaim the gospel of Christ crucified does not imply that his gospel is necessarily unwise or devoid of wisdom. The way Paul continues his argument in 2.6, with the emphatic conjunction δέ, stresses this very point: while he rejects human wisdom and wise speech as a means for knowing divine wisdom, he does speak a message that is in fact wisdom. When one views things in this way, especially the distinction made between 2.1-5 and 2.6-16, two things become clear. First, Paul is neither diverting from his earlier claims nor contradicting himself; he is elaborating on a distinction that has been at work since 1.18, especially as it relates to his apostolic mission and preaching. Second, in recognizing that what Paul rejects in 2.1-5 is a particular *form* for proclaiming the gospel, one sees that the central focus of his argument has not changed; he is still concerned with the content or nature of the gospel message and how that message is being interpreted by the Corinthians.

Specifically, Paul continues to stress the distinctive and incompatible ways in which people can know God's wisdom and that only one of these ways is effectual. When we take these points together, we are led to the conclusion that the wisdom of which

Paul speaks in 2.6-16 is another way of referring to the gospel message he proclaims in 2.1-5. Specifically, as Schnabel argues: "In V. 6-16 erläutert Paulus die Verkündigung und die Erkenntnis des gekreuzigten Messias als rettende Weisheit Gottes." [132] However, before we examine how the gospel is God's wisdom and the relationship of the Spirit with that wisdom, we must address two hermeneutical concerns.

3.4.1.1. Identifying the "Speaker(s)" of the Gospel

The first deals with the shift from the first-person singular in 2.1-5 to the first-person plural in 2.6-16. As noted above, scholarly opinion about this shift essentially falls into three categories: 1) those viewing the shift as evidence of joint authorship, or collaboration with the co-senders of the letter, where such individuals contribute to that portion of the argument; 2) those arguing for the use of an authorial "we," where Paul speaks on behalf of the co-senders, thus maintaining primary authorship; or 3) those interpreting the shift as emphasizing a particular point, either for the sake of establishing consistency in the apostolic witness or for marking a contrast between themselves and their opponents. With regard to the last, it is possible that Paul is

---

[132] Schnabel, *Der erste Brief*, 163. Prior to this, Schnabel highlights a number of textual features that suggest the unity of 2.1-16: "Der Abschnitt 2,6-16 is mit 2,1-5 eng verbunden: 1. In V. 1 bezeichnet Paulus seine Verkündigung mit der ungewöhnlichen Formulierung τὸ μυστήριον τοῦ θεοῦ, die er in V. 7 aufgreift, wo er seine Predigttätigkeit mit der Wendung θεοῦ σοφίαν ἐν μυστήριῳ beschreibt. 2. In V 4 verwendet Paulus (zum ersten Mal in 1Kor) die Vokabel πνεῦμα, die in V. 10 aufgegriffen wird und sodann in dem gesamten Abschnitt eine wichtige Rolle spielt (V. 11.12.13.14). 3. Die antithetische Aussage von V. 4 hat in V. 13 eine deutliche Parallele: ὁ λόγος μου καὶ το κήρυγμά μου (V. 4a) entspricht ἃ καὶ λαλοῦμεν (V. 13a), οὐκ ἐν πειθοῖ σοφίας (V. 4b) entspricht οὐκ ἐν διδακτοῖς ἀνθρωπίνης σοφίας (V. 13a [*sic*]) und ἀλλ' ἐν ἀποδείξει πνεύματος καὶ δυνάμεως (V. 4c) entspricht ἀλλ' ἐν διδακτοῖς πνεύματος (V. 13c)" (ibid).

contrasting himself (and ostensibly those carrying out the apostolic message) with those who either proclaim a different gospel or rely on a form and style of wisdom different from his own. Functionally, this interpretation speaks to the content of Paul's remarks and the overall scope of his argument. However, this interpretation fails to identify specifically who are included in the "we" and why the shift occurs.

With regard to the first two options, they share a similarity in that those collectively referred to as "we" are the ones involved in the composition of the letter. Unlike the third option, these two seek to identify those who make up the "we." However, while this identification could be established by the implication of Paul's argument, it does not fit the immediate aims or purpose of his argument or explain why he must present the case he does. Accordingly, Sosthenes (the stated co-sender of the letter in 1.1) and his role in Paul's apostolic mission and message are not matters of dispute in the letter, nor is his name listed among those around whom the Corinthians are rallying. Thus, to include Sosthenes in the "we" portion of Paul's argument would seem rather curious or even unexpected for the Corinthians. This leaves us with the third option, which offers us a way into dealing with Paul's argument in an appropriate manner.

Earlier it was argued that the shift in "person" in 2.1-16 is not inexplicable in Paul's letters in general and the same could be said for 1 Corinthians in particular. From 1.4-17 Paul speaks primarily in the first-person singular; with 1.18 he shifts to the first-person plural and maintains it until 1.31.[133] Then in 2.1-5 he reverts to the first-person singular only to adopt the first-person plural for 2.6-16 before returning once again to the first-person singular from 3.1 onward. The point of interest is that the shift to the plural occurs

---

[133] This claim about this particular rhetorical unit is excluding the first-person singular used in 1.31, for that usage simply follows the quotation cited.

when Paul speaks about the preaching of the gospel in general (1.23; 2.6, 7; cf. 2.13), and he employs the singular when he defends his particular expression of it (1.17; 2.1-4; 3.1-4). The need for a defense suggests criticisms laid against Paul's style or form of preaching, criticisms based partly on preconceived notions of public speaking and possibly comparisons between Paul's style and another's. Can we know anything about the possibility of a "rival" preacher in Corinth, one whose style or form is ostensibly appealing to or in harmony with the usual expectations?

From Acts we see Paul originally teaching on his own (Acts 18.4), even though he was presumably accompanied by Aquila and Priscilla (18.1-3), and even after the arrival of Timothy and Silas (see 18.5-7). The narrative of Acts supplies no information about preachers other than Paul in Corinth during his sojourn,[134] nor are there any suggestions that Aquila, Priscilla, Timothy, or Silas took part in the original proclamation of the gospel. The only other reference to someone coming to Corinth is the passing mention of Apollos in Acts 19.1. If we accept the description of Apollos as ἀνὴρ λόγιος...δυνατὸς ὢν ἐν ταῖς γραφαῖς (Acts 18.24c, e), and if we accept the argument that Paul's proclamation, following his departure, is being measured according to the criterion of wise, persuasive (human) speech, then we might assume that Paul's

---

[134] However cf. Voigt: "Ist auch Petrus in Korinth gewesen? Unmöglich ist es nicht, unternimmt doch auch er Missionsreisen (9.4f). Zwar besteht seit dem Apostelkonzil die Abmachung, daß die Jerusalemer 'Säulen' unter den Juden predigen sollen, während Paulus der Heidenapostel ist (Gal 2,9); aber wir finden Petrus auch in Antiochien (Gal 2,11), und der 1.Petr (wie immer man die literarische Echtheitsfrage beantworten mag) kennt Beziehungen zu Gemeinden in Pontus, Galatien, Kappadozien, der Provinz Asien und Bithynien. Schon möglich, daß Petrus auch in Korinth gewesen ist. Judenchristen in Korinth mögen in ihm 'ihren' Mann und den vollgültigen 'Apostel' gesehen haben, wogegen die apostolische Vollmacht des Paulus bestritten ist" (*Gemeinsam*, 19).

mission and message are being viewed as in some way distinct from or even subordinate to that of Apollos.[135]

Thus, Paul at least seeks to show the Corinthians that he and Apollos are not to be pitted against each other because they are both speaking God's wisdom.[136] However, it might be better to see the focus of Paul's argument as an attempt to reorient the way in which the Corinthians are judging the gospel message in general. If this is the case, then we could broaden the boundaries of what Paul means by "we," where he is referring to the apostolic witness (see 2,6a, 7a, 13; cf. also 3.1-4; 4.1, 6, 9; 9.1-12; 15.11). However, we must be careful not to apply this plurality too rigidly, for there are occasions when Paul has in mind more than himself and the apostolic witness; in these other cases, he seems to be speaking of all believers (see 2.7b, 10, 12, 16).

3.4.1.2. Identifying the Recipients of the Gospel

The second concern deals with identifying the stated recipients in 1 Cor 2.6: οἱ τέλειοι. By following the approach of the *religionsgeschichtliche Schule* it is possible to read οἱ τέλειοι as referring to a select group of believers who receive deeper levels of instruction, where the content of this instruction is a secret wisdom or knowledge. This further instruction thus refers to that which is given only to this select group and that which is ostensibly given beyond the initial proclamation. Moreover, this reading also finds itself in the service of those advocating influence from mystery religions or Gnostic theology, where the recipients of the secret wisdom or knowledge are made "perfect" or "complete" as a result of the additional teaching. However, as I argued earlier, these types of interpretations create contradictions within Paul's argument, whereby in one place he speaks against classes or levels of

---

[135] Cf. Litfin, *Theology of Proclamation*, 253.

[136] See Voigt, *Gemeinsam*, 19.

believers yet here acknowledges—if not praises or advocates—varying levels. These interpretations also create historical problems for scholars attempting to reconstruct the circumstances and proceedings of Paul's original visit to Corinth.

The historical problems created stem from the fact that nothing in the text suggests differing levels or times of instruction given during Paul's ministry in Corinth; such suggestions can only be assumed for the sake of the argument advanced—i.e. Paul *is* referring to varying levels of instruction, one for the initial proclamation and another for a select few. Moreover, the logic of Paul's argument stresses both the manner in which he proclaimed the gospel and the manner in which it was received or understood, a stress that has as its primary reference the original proclamation of the gospel; nothing in Paul's argument suggests an additional period of second-level instruction.

Therefore, since it is not likely that Paul is thinking of a select group of believers who receive deeper, secret teaching—to do so would undermine his plea for unity; and since it is equally unlikely for Paul to be thinking of an additional time of instruction for a select group—to argue otherwise is to go beyond the textual evidence; we must seek a more reasonable explanation for Paul's use of οἱ τελείοι and his purpose for employing this description at this stage in the argument. To ascertain this purpose, we must examine two related details.

First, it is possible to read τέλειος as "perfect" in the sense of having complete knowledge via divine wisdom. Thus, τελείοι refers to those who have been given God's wisdom and it is only by such blessing that they can consider themselves perfect or complete in mind and soul. This interpretation still applies to the situation in Corinth, where status-seeking on the basis of perfected knowledge and spirituality emerge prior to Paul's writing. Accordingly, Paul could be seen as using τέλειος in 2.6-16 in a subversive manner—i.e. he adopts the terminology of the Corinthians, empties its meaning or interpretation, fills it with his own (corrected?) meaning or interpretation, and throws it back to them. However, before following this reading we must take into consideration the argument beyond 2.6-16, specifically Paul's remarks in 3.1-4.

In this larger context we find what appears to be an explicit contrast between τέλειος in 2.6-16 and νήπιος in 3.1-4. Initially, in the light of this awareness, we can assume that Paul's argument focuses more on the question of maturity in knowledge rather than the existence of knowledge within the believer. Accordingly, τέλειος could be read as "mature" or "fully developed," a reading not incongruent with the theological results of receiving divine wisdom. As Sterling points out, Philo often speaks of the truly wise individual as one who is mature or whose mind (νοῦς) is fully developed; and, in keeping with his commitment to the Platonic notion of ideas and forms, Philo sees τέλειος as referring to the person who has developed into the ideal, whereas νήπιος represents the person who is still in formation.[137] This contrast between τέλειος and νήπιος and its significance can be an appropriate framework for understanding Paul's argument, which bears striking similarities to that of Philo. This brings me to the second point.

If this contrast and definition of terms apply to Paul's argument, then we can assume that he envisages an expectation of what a believer truly is: one to whom God's wisdom has been given, and one who is able to see, know, and even rightly discern God's wisdom in the cross of Christ. As discussed already, this ability to see, know, and discern results from the Spirit's role not

---

[137] *Post.* 152; *Agr.* 9; *Sobr.* 9; *Migr. Ab.* 46; *Congr.* 154; *Somn.* 2.10; cf. *Spec.* 2.32; 3.119; *Hypoth.* 8.11.3—all noted in Sterling, "'Wisdom Among the Perfect'," 373.

only in mediating the kind of wisdom of which Paul speaks but also in providing the framework within which that wisdom can be ascertained. With this expectation in mind, Paul not only argues for what should be the case for believers but also uses this expectation as a point of comparison for the Corinthians at present. Thus, in one sense τελειοι applies to the believers in Corinth yet in another sense it does not. With regard to the affirmative, we know that Paul is using τελειοι as a descriptor for the Corinthians, and we know this by noticing how he refers to the believers and the context in which he does so.[138]

On the two previous occasions when Paul speaks of God's wisdom and its relationship to a particular group, specifically the believers in Corinth, he employs a dative construct to stress the connection: αὐτοῖς τοῖς κλητοῖς...θεοῦ σοφίαν (1.24); ἡμῖν...σοφία ἀπὸ θεοῦ (1.30). In the first instance, the implication is believers; in the second, Paul explicitly says, "us," which most naturally refers to believers in Corinth—Paul included. A similar pattern emerges in 2.6, where Paul states: σοφίαν...τοῖς τελείοις. While the genitive use of θεός is lacking in this instance, it can be safely assumed in view of Paul's argument, especially in the light of what he embraces (see 2.7). Moreover, when we consider Paul's remarks in 2.10 (ἡμῖν δὲ ἀπεκάλυψεν ὁ θεὸς διὰ τοῦ πνεύματος) and take the unstated object as God's wisdom, we see that Paul not only has in mind believers (2.6) but also himself (2.10). Therefore, by comparing the way Paul uses τελειοι with how he uses other identifying terms throughout his argument, we find that τελειοι is simply another way of referring to those who believe the gospel.

However, with regard to the negative (i.e. that τελειοι does not apply to the Corinthians), Paul uses this idealised state against the Corinthians in order to further his case that they are not at

---

[138] This follows Litfin, *Theology of Proclamation*, 213-14.

present interpreting God's wisdom by God's wisdom. If we follow the assumption that Paul's message is being critiqued through the lens of human wisdom and that lens causes the Corinthians to see his message as foolishness, then they distinguish themselves from the one who is fully developed by God's wisdom and the one who operates according to what God's Spirit reveals. Paul emphasizes this dilemma in 2.14-15, where he defines (or distinguishes) two types of interpreters: ψυχικός and πνευματικός, which, as argued earlier, is an expansion of Paul's claim in 2.13.

In terms of comparison, therefore, Paul is suggesting that those critical of his message are interpreting it as ψυχικοί, whereas they should be interpreting it as πνευματικοί. This also applies to a vital (albeit implicit) feature of Paul's larger case: the Corinthians originally accepted Paul's message as God's wisdom in the manner in which he proclaimed it, whereas now they are asserting it to be foolishness. In terms of this implied contrast applying to Paul's argument: while the Corinthians began as and still should be τελειοι (2.6-16), at present they are not τελειοι but are in fact νήπιοι (3.1-4). It is to this idea of originally accepting the message as God's wisdom that I now turn.

3.4.1.3. Identifying the Gospel as Wisdom

When Paul defines the content of the apostolic witness, he begins with a general description, which is cast in positive and negative terms, before clarifying his meaning with a specific claim. With regard to the general description, he states positively that "we speak wisdom" (2.6a) but, negatively, this wisdom originates "neither from this age nor the rulers of this age" (2.6b). Implicit in this negative remark are two related points, both of which have been stressed already. First, in asserting that the wisdom they speak does not come from this age or its rulers Paul appears to be re-emphasizing his earlier claims in 2.1 and 2.4, which were also restatements of his remarks in 1.18-21. If this connection exists, then we can begin to understand Paul's negative remarks about wisdom here in 2.6b—i.e. he does not speak of (or from) a wisdom that is both incapable of knowing God's wisdom and supplanted by God's wisdom. Thus, in this first instance, Paul is claiming that the wisdom proclaimed does not have the appearance of wisdom, if judged according to the standards of worldly wisdom.

The second implication deals with the substance or content of the wisdom as proclaimed in the apostolic witness. Thus, by stressing in a negative way that their wisdom is not from this age, the apostles are emphasizing the substantial difference between their message and a message proclaimed by the wise of this age. To say it differently: the message of the apostolic proclamation is wisdom, although it is one that the wise of this age deem foolishness according to the standards of worldly wisdom. This distinction was made in 1.18-25,[139] where those being destroyed judge the gospel (i.e. ὁ λόγος τοῦ σταυροῦ) to be foolishness, and where the wisdom of this world could not—ostensibly by its own merits or abilities—know the wisdom of God.

The idea of being destroyed resurfaces with Paul's claim in 2.6b when he further defines the wisdom and rulers of this age; he defines them as those passing away or being abolished. Moreover, the idea of incapability will emerge again when Paul elaborates on this point in 2.8. The obvious inference is that Paul would not rely on something touted to be the means for ascertaining divine wisdom when such means are not only under God's curse (cf. 1.20d) but also impotent for truly knowing God's wisdom.

After offering a general description, cast in both positive and negative terms, Paul proceeds to clarify his meaning in a specific way. He emphatically states that the apostolic witness speaks

---

[139] A similar distinction that further supports our argument that the gospel message is wisdom, as presented here in 2.6-16.

God's wisdom, one that has been hidden in mystery before the ages (or prior to creation). By defining this wisdom as God's wisdom Paul emphasizes its otherness in terms of source, content and, by implication, its potential for being known. Moreover, in emphasizing this threefold otherness Paul further stresses the complete separation between God's wisdom and human wisdom, a separation that has run like a thread through the main portion of his argument. For Paul, the source of the wisdom proclaimed is from God, not this world or its self-professed wise; the content is determined and filled according to God, not human wisdom; and its potential for being known is actualised only through God's decision, not persuaded or coerced by human means or cleverness.

Furthermore, Paul intensifies the separation by defining God's wisdom as hidden in mystery, which not only carries significance for his immediate claim but also the wider theological truths of his argument. The immediate significance pertains to the unobtainable or unknowable nature of God's wisdom, not just for the self-professed wise but also for all people. The wider significance relates to the eschatological nature and reality of God's wisdom being revealed in the world through the Christ-event.[140] We can see that this coincides with Paul's understanding of the Spirit's role in revealing God's wisdom, especially in the gospel of Christ crucified, and how those who accept this revelation are constituted as the people of God.

Thus, Paul can affirm that God's wisdom, which hitherto remained hidden in mystery, was προώρισεν...πρὸ τῶν αἰώνων εἰς δόξαν ἡμῶν (2.7b). The "our" of this claim most naturally refers to those who already accepted the gospel of Christ crucified and know it to be God's wisdom. This accords well with Paul's earlier claim that the word of the cross is "foolishness to those who

---

[140] Scroggs argues, "this motif is common to wisdom-apocalyptic theology" ("Paul: ΣΟΦΟΣ and ΠΝΕΥΜΑΤΙΚΟΣ," *NTS* 14 [1967]: 41).

are perishing" but "God's power to us who are being saved" (1.18), with God's power being the means of that salvation process. Moreover, the Corinthians placed their "faith" in that power and not in human wisdom (2.5), which views that power as weakness.

3.4.2. Gospel Rejected as God's Wisdom

This brings me to the opponents of the gospel as God's wisdom, a group already alluded to in Paul's argument. Here I am concerned with their identity in general and the reason for their rejection of the gospel in particular. As will be argued below, this portion of Paul's argument simply functions as a contrast for the larger purpose of affirming the validity of the Corinthians' original acceptance of and faith in the gospel that Paul proclaimed.

3.4.2.1. Identifying those Rejecting the Gospel as Wisdom

Considerable debate surrounds the identity of those whom Paul categorizes as "rulers of this age" (2.6b, 8a). First, in view of the apocalyptic tenor of Paul's argument, it is certainly possible to understand this phrase as referring to (evil) spiritual forces or beings at work in the cosmos.[141] Such an understanding would not be foreign either to Paul's theological heritage or that of the Corinthians; both allowed for the possibility of such forces or beings at work in creation—albeit in an unseen way.

---

[141] For those promoting this view, see e.g. Wilckens, *Weisheit und Torheit*, 60-64; Barrett, *First Epistle*, 70-72; Conzelmann, *1 Corinthians*, 61; C.E. Arnold, *Powers of Darkness: Principalities & Powers in Paul's Letters* (Downers Grove: InterVarsity, 1992), 101-04. Finney criticizes those who hold this view by saying they "have missed seeing the political basis and thrust of Paul's own gospel" ("Conflict in Corinth: The Appropriateness of Honour-Shame as the Primary Social Context," [Ph.D. diss.; University of St Andrews, 2004], 113 n.1).

On the other hand, it is equally possible to understand "rulers of this age" as referring to human leaders or authorities.[142] This view accounts for the explicit accusation in 2.8 about such rulers crucifying Christ, and does so without creating further historical or hermeneutical difficulties—e.g. how can spiritual forces literally crucify Christ, and how can such forces be blamed when the passage clearly shows the crucifixion to be the work of human decision and action? However, this view has been criticized because its relevance only applies to ancient notions of the cosmos, where spiritual forces or beings are inherent to the conceptual fabric of an age steeped in mythological traditions.[143] Now (i.e. in the present) such forces or beings are understood as representing evil ideas or deeds inherent to humanity, or they are mere descriptions of abstract concepts.[144]

However, an alternate view is often suggested that appears to synthesize the first two. Here the "rulers of this age" refers to spiritual forces or beings that influence or use human authorities to carry out their desires or schemes.[145] Like the first view, this one

---

[142] For those promoting this view, see e.g. Robertson-Plummer, *First Epistle*, 36; G. Miller, "ἀρχόντων τοῦ αἰῶνος τούτου—A New Look at 1 Corinthians 2.6-8," *JBL* 91.4 (1972): 526-28; Carr, "The Rulers of this Age," 20-35; Fee, *First Epistle*, 103; Hays, *First Corinthians*, 44; Garland, *1 Corinthians*, 93; Keener, *1–2 Corinthians*, 38.

[143] Admittedly, this is not a criticism if one is attempting to understand Paul in his own context.

[144] In response to this criticism, Thiselton argues: "Paul stands closer to Jewish apocalyptic than to Western individualism from Descartes to the late twentieth century. Humankind is more than a collection of individual entities or agents, but a corporeity within which evil and evil forces become endemic and structural" (*First Epistle*, 238).

[145] For those promoting this view, see e.g. O. Cullmann, *Christ and Time: The Primitive Christian Conception of Time and History* (trans. F.V. Filson; London: SCM Press, 1951), 190-95; G.B. Caird, *Principalities and Powers: A*

was not without precedent in the ancient world and could therefore be a plausible explanation for both Paul and the Corinthians. Cullmann argues this, at least for Paul, on the basis that the "abundantly attested late Jewish belief that all peoples are ruled through angels is present particularly in the Book of Daniel, in the Wisdom of Jesus, Son of Sirach, and in the Book of Enoch, and it can be shown to be present also in the Talmud and Midrash."[146]

Moreover this view is able to avoid the historical and hermeneutical dilemma noted above by revealing the guilty parties involved in the crucifixion as both spiritual beings and human authorities. As Caird argues: "Behind Pilate, Herod, and Caiaphas, behind the Roman state and the Jewish religion of which these men were the earthly representatives, Paul discerned the existence of angelic rulers who shared with their human agents the responsibility for the crucifixion."[147] This would certainly maintain the intensity of Paul's remarks concerning divine judgment on those who reject God's wisdom and salvation in Christ: God's judgment is not bestowed upon either spiritual powers or human authorities but upon both. A central problem with the assessments of Cullman and Caird, however, is that they misread (or misapply) the ancient texts used to support their views. Specifically, as Lincoln points out, in the Jewish texts "the powers are *behind* the state" or nations; the texts do not say the state or nation *and* the human rulers within them are the powers.[148]

Study in Pauline Theology (Oxford: Clarendon, 1956), 15-22; Scroggs, "ΣΟΦΟΣ and ΠΝΕΥΜΑΤΙΚΟΣ," 41-44; Perkins, *First Corinthians*, 59.

[146] Cullmann, *Christ and Time*, 193; cf. also Caird, *Principalities and Powers*, 5-8.

[147] Caird, *Principalities and Powers*, 17.

[148] See A.T. Lincoln, "Liberation from the Powers: Supernatural Spirits or Societal Structures?," in *The Bible and Human Society: Essays in Honor of John Rogerson* (eds. M.D. Carroll R., D.J.A. Clines and P.R. Davies; Sheffield: Sheffield Academic, 1995), 339-40, 341-42. Quote from 342.

While all three options have their individual merits, they all seem to operate on the assumption that Paul is concerned with identifying the "rulers" in an explicit way. For example Carr suggests a distinction between the use of the singular and the plural forms of ἄρχων, where the singular always refers to spiritual beings and the plural always speaks of human authorities, specifically political leaders.[149] Thus, because Paul uses the plural in 2.6b and 2.8a he must be thinking of the political rulers responsible for the death of Jesus, namely Herod and Pilate.[150] However, such an identification does not appear to be Paul's concern or even the point of his argument.

It is entirely possible that Paul uses "rulers of this age" ambiguously and thus as applicable to either spiritual forces or human authorities (or both), and an explicit identification is not necessary for Paul's argument.[151] Thus, the phrase might serve as a reference for anything or anyone opposed to God's wisdom. Moreover, this has ties with Paul's earlier argument about the unexpected reversal of how wisdom is known and to whom it is given (cf. 1.18-20, 26-28). God's wisdom is not given to and made known by the elite of the world with superior wisdom and speech; it is given to those who are weak and lowly, and it is made known by those who humbly proclaim its simplicity by the power of the Spirit (cf. 2.1-5).

3.4.2.2. Cause for Rejection

Whether we identify the opponents of the gospel as spiritual beings or human authorities (or both), the cause of their rejection

---

[149] See Carr, "The Rulers of this Age," 23-24.

[150] Schnabel (*Der erste Brief*, 166, 168) sees Caiaphas and Pilate as the rulers in question.

[151] Admittedly, the phrase "rulers of this age" in 1.20 suggests human rulers or authorities, which might serve as a ready parallel for Paul's usage of the phrase here in 2.6b and 2.8a.

remains the same: they neither have God's Spirit nor rely on that Spirit to reveal God's hidden wisdom. Admittedly, while this cause is not explicitly stated in 2.6-16, Paul provides logical clues that lead to this conclusion. A key passage in this regard is 2.7-8 where Paul specifically states the wisdom of the gospel and how this gospel was not judged wise by the rulers of this age. We know that God's wisdom (2.7a) is the focus of the passage because it remains the focus throughout the argument. With the possible exception of the explanatory clause of 2.8b-c, God's wisdom is the object—whether stated or unstated—of all the verbal ideas. God's wisdom is what the apostles *speak* (2.7a), it is that which *remained hidden* in a mystery (2.7a), it is that which God *predestined* before the ages (2.7b) and it is that which *remained unknown* by the rulers of this age (2.8a). Setting aside the explanatory argument of 2.8b for a moment, we need to consider the implications of these claims.

First, and beginning with the last component, the emphasis on the ignorance of the rulers continues the theme of human wisdom's impotence in knowing God's wisdom. Thus, we are here reminded of the earlier discussion on the source, content and disclosure of God's wisdom, and the argument that no amount of human effort or ability can ascertain that wisdom. Moreover, the verbal aspect of this ignorance suggests a perpetual state, which further confirms the incapacity of human wisdom to ever know God's wisdom by its own means.

Second, and continuing in reverse, the wisdom of God and its revelation were predestined, not only for a particular time (cf. Gal 4.4) but also a particular people (cf. 1 Cor 2.9c-10a). This additionally affirms the idea of no amount of human effort or ability ascertaining God's wisdom, and the argument of disclosure being the sole decision of the one who possesses that wisdom. If God predestines wisdom and its revelation, then God also determines when and how it will occur and be made known.

Third, until that time wisdom was kept secret; however, and this brings me to the fourth point, the wisdom of God has emerged from its hidden, secret state through the preaching of the gospel and the powerful work of God's Spirit. With regard to Paul's own ministry, as argued in the previous chapter, this preaching took on the *form* of a simple proclamation and its *content* focused primarily on Christ crucified as God's wise means of salvation. It appears to be precisely this form and content that the rulers of this age would deem foolish and therefore reject.[152]

However, for Paul this rejection of the gospel message as wisdom represents a milder form of a more intense and even grotesque rejection: Christ as God's wise means of salvation (cf. 1.30). This brings me to the statement of 2.8b. This passage, in relation to what precedes, functions as an explanation or logical consequence of the initial claim of 2.8a. Paul stresses the intensity of his argument via a second-class condition, where he assumes the protasis to be false and the outcome in the apodosis is contingent upon the reality of the protasis. Thus, Paul's argument could be restated as: εἰ ἔγνωσαν (which they did not), ἄν ἐσταύρωσαν οὐκ τὸν κύριον τῆς δόξης (which they did). The contingency in question is the possession of knowledge, specifically knowledge of who Christ is and the mission he came to fulfill.

However, since the rulers lacked this necessary knowledge, they failed to recognize the identity of Jesus as God's true messiah and therefore executed him, but not simply because of a failure to recognize Jesus' identity and how God's wisdom could be manifest in and through the person and mission of Jesus.[153] Thus,

---

[152] Cf. again Schrage, *Der erste Brief*, 1.231.

[153] Specifically, they failed to see Jesus as "the Lord of glory"—a phrase that appears only here, Jas 2.1, and, as Lang mentions, *1 En* 22.14 (cf. 63.2) where the phrase is a "predicate for God" (Lang, *Die Briefe an die Korinther*, 44; cf. also Thiselton [*First Epistle*, 246], who adds *1 En* 25.3, 7; 27.3, 4 [cf. 66.2]; and Fitzmyer [*First Corinthians*, 177], who adds *1 En* 27.5; 36.4; 40.3).

we can initially say: just as the rulers were unable to know or discern the revelation of God's wise plan in the cross of Jesus, the rulers were also unable to know or discern God's wisdom in the proclamation of the cross.[154] We can be sure that knowledge is the focus of the argument at this point because Paul's remarks in 2.9-12 have knowledge as the central theme, specifically knowledge that God's wisdom has been revealed and that the revelation is mediated by God's Spirit.

3.4.3. Gospel Known to be God's Wisdom

As stressed already, the Corinthians know the message originally proclaimed to them to be God's wisdom, and the way in which they know this is by the mediating role of God's Spirit. Throughout Paul's argument the emphasis has fallen on this role, specifically its necessity and its exclusivity. The analogy of 2.11 provides the basic framework for understanding the necessity of the Spirit's role, which also underlies Paul's remarks in 2.8-9 and 2.13-14, while 2.12 secures Paul's views on the exclusivity of that role, which also underlies his contrasting claims in 2.4, 6-7, and 15. It is to this latter quality of the Spirit's role that I now turn, for it represents a defining characteristic of Paul's larger argument. Specifically, it functions as his assessment of why the Corinthians originally believed his message but are now questioning its authenticity, or at least its description as God's wisdom.

---

[154] This follows Lang's argument: "In den Versen 8 und 9 argumentiert Paulus für seine Aussage, dass die Vertreter der Weisheit dieser Welt die im Kreuz Jesu offenbarte Weisheit Gottes nicht erkannt haben, mit einen doppelten Hinweis: auf das geschichtliche Ereignis der Kreuzigung Jesu und auf ein Wort der Schrift" (*Die Briefe an die Korinther*, 43).

3.4.3.1. Competing Spirits of Knowledge

In 2.12 Paul definitively states, ἡμεῖς δὲ οὐ τὸ πνεῦμα τοῦ κόσμου ἐλάβομεν ἀλλὰ τὸ πνεῦμα τὸ ἐκ τοῦ θεοῦ, ἵνα εἰδῶμεν τὰ ὑπὸ τοῦ θεοῦ χαρισθέντα ἡμῖν. A perennial question in this regard is what Paul means by τὸ πνεῦμα τοῦ κόσμου, since it is not a phrase used by him elsewhere nor is it one that he clearly defines in this passage. The closest we come to a parallel usage is found in 2 Cor 11.4, where he speaks of the regrettable possibility of receiving "another spirit" (πνεῦμα ἕτερον). However this reference is nearly as vague in meaning as our 2.12 passage. Since the phrase appears nowhere else in the NT or the LXX[155] a possible source is provided by similar ideas or concepts found in the Hellenistic world, specifically elements of Stoic philosophy.[156]

Stoic philosophy argues for an essential, if not elemental connectivity between all of creation and the (impersonal) divine. The Stoics expressed this connectivity not only with their materialistic view of the cosmos,[157] which included a physical understanding of the divine, the mind and the soul,[158] but also with their idea that fire constituted the foundational element for creation.[159] With fire being the foundational element, it was understood to be the reason (i.e. λόγος) or cause for creation, thus

---

[155] See Collins, *First Corinthians*, 134.

[156] Cf. D.B. Martin, *The Corinthian Body* (New Haven: Yale University Press, 1999), 9-15; Thiselton, *First Epistle*, 260-61.

[157] See R. Scott, *The Pauline Epistles: A Critical Study* (Edinburgh: T&T Clark, 1909), 58.

[158] See E. Zeller, *Outlines of the History of Greek Philosophy* (trans. L.R. Palmer; rev. W. Nestle; New York: Meridian, 1955), 233-34; cf. also J. Sellars, *Stoicism* (Durham: Acumen, 2010), 106.

[159] See F.C. Copleston, *History of Philosophy* (London: Search Press, 1946), 1.387-88. Diogenes notes that the Stoics espoused a harmonious view of fire and the other elements—i.e. air, water, and earth (see *Zeno*, 70).

giving it divine status.[160] Accordingly, the ideas of fire and λόγος were interchangeable for what the Stoics classified as "god."

From this the Stoics assumed that if the divine λόγος (or fire) was elemental to all creation, then all living beings were intimately linked with the divine, which gave way to the idea of a "divine spark" within the human soul.[161] Moreover, the Stoics believed that a cosmic πνεῦμα facilitated the connectivity between creation and the divine λόγος,[162] and it was this πνεῦμα that allowed humanity to know the ways of the divine as displayed in the order of the cosmos. However, it was the responsibility of the individual to recognize this reality, by awaking the divine spark within, and all the knowledge gained to bring that person to a point where he or she ultimately merges into the divine, thus making him or her just as impersonal as the divine they seek.[163]

Such cosmology is diametrically opposed to the theological tradition out of which Paul forms his argument. For Paul there is a categorical distinction between God, creation, and humanity; and while God is portrayed as the one responsible for creating the cosmos and humanity, there are no elemental links between them. Specifically, there is no πνεῦμα that (materially) unites all things and ensures order to the cosmos. At the very least, we would seem to have an adequate conceptual candidate for Paul's polemic in 2.12.

While a Stoic cosmology, especially its views on πνεῦμα, might explain the conceptual context for Paul's argument, we cannot be sure that this context applies specifically to the Corinthians' understanding of creation or even acquiring wisdom. Moreover, such a reading appears to require more than the text can

---

[160] Cf. Diogenes Laertius, 44b; Aetius, 46a.

[161] E.g. Seneca, *Epis.* 41.2; 92.30; Epictetus, *Diss.* 1.14.13-15; 2.8.11-13.

[162] See Cicero, *Nat. Gods* 2.19, 24.

[163] Cf. Marcus Aurelius, *Med.* 4.21; Dio Cassius, *Rome* 52.4.3.

provide. It seems more reasonable to take what Paul says in 2.12 as another contrast between human wisdom and God's wisdom. Paul simply classifies the wisdom of this age (or human wisdom) as τὸ πνεῦμα τοῦ κόσμου for the sake of contrasting it with τὸ πνεῦμα τὸ ἐκ τοῦ θεοῦ.[164]

This fits with Paul's previous remarks about the Spirit of God being the only means by which the wisdom of God can be known; the wisdom of this age is incapable or powerless to obtain access to God's wisdom. Specifically, the contrast in 2.12 follows directly from the truth established in the analogy in 2.11. Moreover, the idea of mediation by God's Spirit vis-à-vis the spirit of the world not only sets the condition for the purpose clause of 2.12b, which relates back to the implication of 2.9-10, it also prepares the way for Paul's contrast in 2.13, and even 2.14-15.

As argued earlier, since the contrast of 2.13 deals first of all with two forms of speech, only one of which is able to reveal God's wisdom, and secondly with how the message spoken is understood to be God's wisdom, Paul's argument in 2.12 exclusively and succinctly defines the only means by which God's wisdom can be known: God's Spirit. However, when we take the wider argument into consideration, we find further support for such an exclusive claim (see 2.4, 6-7, 15). Collectively Paul's argument in these verses shows that without the Spirit's mediating role, the cross of Christ as God's wise plan of salvation would remain unknown (or undisclosed), and no amount of human effort, ability, or wisdom could obtain access to that which is hidden in mystery.

---

[164] Cf. Fee, *First Epistle*, 112-13; Thiselton, *First Epistle*, 261-63; Fitzmyer, *First Corinthians*, 181. However, Davis critically says "the strength of this view lies precisely in the lack of a more convincing reason as to why Paul might choose to coin the phrase" (*Wisdom and Spirit*, 110).

3.4.3.2. Spiritual Knowledge, Spiritual Discernment

In 2.15-16 Paul applies this discussion on knowing God's wisdom through the mediating role of the Spirit to the defense of his apostolic ministry. I conclude this on the basis of two features in the argument.

First, it is within the immediate context of 2.14-15 that Paul articulates not only the Spirit's necessary role in revealing God's wisdom through his and Apollos' teaching but also the Spirit's role in enabling the Corinthians to see the gospel-teaching as God's wisdom. Since the focus of Paul's argument is an attempt to reorient the way in which the Corinthians are judging the gospel message in general, and since Paul's aim is to show the Corinthians that they originally accepted and believed his initial proclamation as God's wisdom—something made possible only by the Spirit, it is crucial for Paul here to stress the Spirit's role in the proclamation and acceptance.

Second, it is precisely with the contrast of 2.14-15 that Paul isolates the two ways in which God's wisdom is judged: the "natural" way is effectively Spirit-less and therefore unable to discern correctly God's wisdom in the gospel message, while the "spiritual" way is guided by the Spirit so that the things of God can be discerned.

When we come to the details of Paul's argument in 2.15-16, we find Paul not only implicitly indicting the Corinthians for their false judgment of his message but also employing his own criteria as he critiques their false judgment. The claim, ὁ δὲ πνευματικὸς ἀνακρίνει [τὰ] πάντα shares the expectations in Paul's views on τέλειος. Thus, in keeping with my earlier argument, πνευμα-τικός should not be read as a reference to an elite believer or one who has received additional, secret instruction from either Paul or Apollos. Instead, πνευματικός while functioning as a synonym for τέλειος, represents another way for Paul to describe a believer—i.e. one who has accepted the gospel of Christ crucified (2.4-5) and received God's Spirit (2.10, 12).

However, there is another layer to Paul's use of πνευματικός that we must recognize. The idea of "examining everything" calls to mind Paul's assertion in 2.10b, where the Spirit of God "searches all things, even the depths of God." Ideally, the πνευματικός would employ the Spirit-given criterion to assess the merits of any and all messages purported to be God's wisdom (cf. 2.14c). As a corollary, the πνευματικός would be able to utilize the same criterion to discern (or recognize) when a message claims to be God's wisdom but ultimately arises from human wisdom.

The same, however, is not true for discerning God's wisdom and the messenger of such wisdom by using criteria inherent to the ψυχικός, hence αὐτὸς δὲ ὑπ' οὐδενὸς ἀνακρίνεται (2.15b). It is in the light of this ideal state that Paul implicitly indicts the Corinthians and employs his own criteria to do so. Thus, the Corinthians are relying on "natural" criteria to assess the merits of his gospel as God's wisdom.

As a result, they are judging it to be foolishness and by extension they are accusing Paul of being unwise, or one not endowed with divine wisdom. Following Paul's logic, this twofold assessment is rendered invalid because it relies on faulty (or powerless) criteria.[165]

However, if the Corinthians employed the Spirit-given criteria and examined both Paul and Apollos' message, they would have discerned God's wisdom in the content of both, despite the differences in form. Paul is able to make this implicit accusation because he certainly views himself as a πνευματικός, thus allowing him to "examine all things"—e.g. the criteria by which

---

[165] This might relate to Paul's lack of concern about being judged by the Corinthians (cf. 1 Cor 4.3).

the Corinthians are judging him—and expose it for what it really is.

3.5. Conclusions

This chapter examined in detail Paul's understanding and teaching on the Spirit's role in mediating divine wisdom. I proceeded with one central theme in mind: divine wisdom cannot be known or ascertained unless it is revealed or disclosed by the one who possesses it. This theme was characterized as both the problem and the solution for those in Corinth. The problem relates to the reality that no amount of human effort or wisdom would be able to obtain access to God's wisdom. The solution relates to the fact that God has revealed wisdom, and Paul contends that that the means by which this occurred was the mediating agency of God's Spirit.

Implicit to this analysis was the added problem that the Corinthians, following Paul's departure, began to assess the merits of his proclamation as God's wisdom, and the criterion of their assessment was that which arises from human wisdom. Thus, just as the initial solution to the initial problem was God's Spirit, Paul argues a finely constructed case for the Corinthians' need to rely on God's Spirit once again to settle the new problem. My primary goal here was to establish Paul's understanding of the Spirit's exclusive role in not only mediating God's wisdom but also establishing a criterion for discerning that wisdom and its expression.

I also stressed the fact that Paul used this understanding to indict the Corinthians for judging his message according to faulty criteria; he also employed this understanding to critique the Corinthians' assessment of his proclamation. It was argued that this faulty assessment stands as a crucial problem that requires Paul's immediate response. The extent of this problem will become the focus of the next chapter, where I will discuss the role of the Spirit in establishing and maintaining communal discernment.

Chapter 4
THE SPIRIT'S ROLE IN ESTABLISHING
RIGHT DISCERNMENT

4.1. Introduction

Following the logical climax of 1 Cor 2.10-13, Paul in 2.14-15 distinguishes two modes of discernment as they relate to one's capacity for knowing God's wisdom. As should be clear from his previous remarks, Paul is keen to prioritize one mode as the most appropriate (or the only) means for discerning God's wisdom and to reject the assumed value and effectiveness of the other mode. To contextualize this reading, I will begin this chapter with a brief summary of Paul's thought up to 2.14-15. After this summary, I will examine the details and implications of Paul's distinction between the two modes of discernment. Specifically I will consider Paul's view of the Spirit's role in discernment, how that role manifests itself in the life of the believing community, and how this Spirit-given discernment is the only mode appropriate for "spiritual" people.

Moreover, I will stress the ways in which Paul relies on Spirit-given discernment as he critiques the present dilemma in Corinth (cf. 3.1-4), especially as it relates to the manner in which the Corinthians are currently assessing his apostolic mission and message. One key implication follows from this argument: while the Corinthians exercised spiritual, communal discernment in the original acceptance of both the gospel as God's wisdom and Paul as an apostolic witness, the present situation suggests, by seeing the gospel as foolishness and Paul as an inadequate or unskilled witness, they are now exercising a form of discernment guided by human wisdom. Thus, Paul must persuade the Corinthians, as a unified community, to rely again solely on God's wisdom and to be guided by the discernment of God's Spirit.

4.2. Reconsidering the Progression of Thought

Before examining Paul's distinction between the two modes of discernment, it will be helpful to reconsider briefly at least three salient details of his argument leading up to 1 Cor 2.14-15. First, implicitly since 1.18 but explicitly in 2.6-16, Paul polarizes two types of wisdom (or ways of knowing) and only one is to characterize the community of believers. On the one hand there is the wisdom of this age (or of this world), while on the other there is God's wisdom, and confusing the one with the other (or even attempting to blend or synthesize the two) is for Paul unacceptable. It is unacceptable not just because God has rendered the wisdom of the world foolish (1.20) but also because, even if God did not render it foolish, the wisdom of the world is incapable of ever ascertaining God's wisdom (cf. 2.9, 11, 14). It is unacceptable (even foolish) to employ what will ultimately fail in its efforts to achieve. For Paul one example of this incapability can be found in the decision of the rulers of this age to crucify Christ—i.e. had they known, they would not have done it (see 2.8). A broader example, and one related specifically to the Corinthian context, would be the faulty assessment of the gospel message, an assessment that sees the message of Christ crucified as foolishness (1.18, 23).

Second, and related to the first, Paul articulates the differences in how the respective types of wisdom are expressed and even the means by which wisdom is judged. For those relying on the wisdom of this age (or this world), wisdom is manifest through eloquent or persuasive speech (cf. 2.1, 4); thus the one who speaks accordingly is deemed wise, or is seen as possessing wisdom. In terms of function it is the polished, rhetorical form and eloquence of delivery that bring about the persuasiveness or believability of the speech (cf. 2.4). For those relying on God's wisdom, however, the proof or conviction concerning the validity of the message comes from the demonstrable power of the Spirit; thus, those who speak God's wisdom are deemed wise not because they adhere to particular forms or patterns of speech but because the content reflects God's revealed wisdom and relies on God's means of persuasion (2.4-5), which in this case is the Spirit at work in the message.

Finally, and linked with the previous two aspects of his argument, Paul emphasizes the distinction between the types of wisdom by differentiating their respective forms of revelation and, by extension, their ways of knowing (or discernment). For the wisdom of this age, wisdom is revealed and learned via the teaching (or instruction) of the sages (cf. 1.20). These sages often profess to know the ways of the divine and claim the ability to teach others also how to know the divine and thus obtain wisdom. Proof for such claims, and that wisdom has been revealed, comes in the form of things more or less tangible or experiential—i.e. either a miraculous sign or a polished, eloquent speech. In this case the sage possesses the authority and power of the divine to perform mighty tasks, or the gods and/or goddesses have blessed the sage with the ability to speak eloquently. Thus, the link between the sage's teaching and the evidence of his or her assumed wisdom becomes the criterion for determining the validity of others who claim to be wise or profess wisdom, especially divine wisdom. However, for Paul, neither miraculous signs or abilities nor polished or eloquent speeches are necessary proofs for one's claim of wisdom,[1] nor are such things appropriate criteria for judging claims of wisdom. Moreover, Paul rejects the notion that divine

---

[1] Cf. Garland who plainly states: "If the message does not come with authenticating signs or sophisticated wisdom (1:22), it whizzes right by those dependent only on natural faculties" (*1 Corinthians*, 101).

wisdom can be ascertained and even taught via human effort and understanding; instead, for Paul divine wisdom can only be known if God chooses to reveal it. Furthermore when this wisdom is revealed, it brings with it a new criterion for judging (or discerning) all other messages and, by extension, messengers who profess wisdom or claim to be wise.

When we come to the climactic statement in 2.10-13, we find Paul addressing these themes and distinctly separating the two types of wisdom and their respective means of expression. We see this primarily with the ἐλάβομεν, εἰδῶμεν, and λαλοῦμεν verbal sequence in 2.12-13,[2] which carries with it an explicit and implicit polemic. In terms of reception, Paul asserts that the believers have received God's Spirit and not the spirit of the world. The focus here is explicitly on the *means* of revelation and implicitly on the appropriateness of one over the other. With regard to knowledge, Paul briefly highlights the "things graciously given by God" to believers, which in this instance refers to salvation in Christ crucified and how this means of salvation is a necessary component within God's wise plan. Accordingly, believers now know the things of God because of the Spirit's mediating role, while the rulers of this age do not know because they do not have God's Spirit. Thus, the focus here is explicitly on *what* is revealed and implicitly on why the message revealed is wise instead of foolishness. Finally, in terms of speech, Paul reminds the Corinthians not only of his manner of speech but also its content and how both depended on the Spirit's powerful work. The focus here, therefore, is explicitly on the *manner* of proclaiming the revelation (i.e. "in words not taught by human wisdom") and implicitly on the adequacy of one way over the other. When taken together, the verbal sequence in 2.12-13 is the foundation upon which Paul builds his argument for how believers form right

---

[2] See Davis, *Wisdom and Spirit*, 107.

conclusions concerning the things of God—specifically the message of salvation and those who proclaim it.

4.3. Paul's Two Modes of Discernment

This brings us to the two modes of discernment briefly noted in 1 Cor 2.14-15, which will here be categorized as, "discernment of the 'natural' person" and "discernment of the 'spiritual' person." Admittedly, Paul's specific remarks in 2.14-15 about these two are neither exhaustive nor elucidating in themselves; he simply makes his point and then carries on with the rest of the argument. However, as we have just seen, the claims of 2.14-16 follow from all that Paul argued previously, especially the distinctions between types of wisdom and their respective ways of knowing. Thus, we can allow Paul's previous claims to inform and guide our discussion. However, before proceeding we must address the question of the categorical terminology Paul uses in his argument. Here we will briefly survey the three main views found among scholars before emphasizing a fourth possible solution.

4.3.1. Origin, Meaning and Use of ψυχινός and πνευματικός

As noted in the previous chapter,[3] while there is general agreement that Paul uses ψυχικός as a categorical term, distinct from πνευματικός, scholars remain divided on what Paul means by the term. Specifically there is the question of origins, where some view the terminology as coming from the Corinthian enthusiasts.[4] Accordingly, the terminology does not originate with Paul. Those advocating this view therefore see Paul appropriating the terms, emptying them of their original meaning, and refilling

---

[3] See the conclusion of 3.3.3.4 above.

[4] See e.g. Pearson, *Pneumatikos-Psychikos*; idem, *Gnosticism, Judaism, and Egyptian Christianity* (Minneapolis: Fortress, 1990); Horsley, "Pneumatikos vs. Psychikos," 269-88; Davis, *Wisdom and Spirit*, 114-25.

them with his own before applying them back to the enthusiasts—albeit in a critical fashion.[5] The assumption that Paul borrows the language or terminology is usually based on the observation "that ψυχικός is found only in 1 Corinthians, and by the fact that πνευματικός, though it occurs elsewhere in Paul's epistles, is found no less than fifteen times in 1 Corinthians."[6] If it is true that the terminology comes from the enthusiasts in Corinth, and if Paul does in fact appropriate and redefine the terms for his purposes, then we need to ask: how did the enthusiasts define them, and from where (if applicable) did such terms emerge? On both counts, two views are generally presented with a third functioning as a type of synthesis of the first two.[7]

---

[5] So Pearson: "It has been determined that Paul, in 1 Corinthians 2.1-16, has skilfully used the language of his opponents, and has turned it back against them by interpreting their language in an apocalyptic fashion" (*Pneumatikos-Psychikos*, 41; cf. idem, "Philo, Gnosis and the New Testament," in *New Testament and Gnosis* [eds. A.H.B. Logan and A.J.M. Wedderburn; London: T&T Clark, 2004], 75). Or as Bünker excitedly puts it: "er stellt ihre eigenen Anschauungen in den Dienst seiner Sache (2,6-16): Die Protagonisten der Parteien werden mit ihren eigenen Waffen geschlagen" (*Briefformular*, 56). See also Wilckens, *Weisheit und Torheit*, 71; *contra* Conzelmann, *1 Corinthians*, 14, 32, 35.

[6] Davis, *Wisdom and Spirit*, 116 (cf. also Dunn, *Unity and Diversity*, 299). Davis' argument with regard to ψυχικός holds true only if he is referring to the Pauline corpus, for 1 Corinthians is the only Pauline letter that contains this term. If however Davis is referring the entire NT, then his argument is mistaken for the term appears in Jas 3.15 and Jude 19. A more pressing concern is that the logic of Davis' argument would have to say tongues and prophecy are Corinthian categories since they are more prevelant in 1 Corinthians than any other Pauline letter. Davis seems to overlook the possibility that the terminology is prevalent because the issue is especially problematic in Corinth.

[7] Here I am following the categories found in Davis, *Wisdom and Spirit*, 114-25.

4.3.1.1. Gnosticism[8]

On the one hand, some view the origin and meaning of the terms in the light of Gnosticism.[9] Here Paul's distinction between ψυχικός and πνευματικός is said to reflect the Gnostic idea that ψυχικός refers to the person not illumined by divine wisdom (or more specifically, γνῶσις) and πνευματικός refers to the one who is. This would seem to parallel Paul's earlier remarks about those having the πνεῦμα as those having access to the divine, with the implication that those without the πνεῦμα remain ignorant of such things. Moreover, those advocating this reading appear to have additional support from extant Gnostic texts that occasionally contrast ψυχικός and πνευματικός in a similar way.[10] Thus it seems we have a possible source for the enthusiasts' terminology and meaning, which could suggest we have a likely object for Paul's polemic—i.e. Gnostic views of spirituality. As Pagels argues:

> This passage commands great attention from gnostic theologians. Here, they claim, Paul clearly distinguishes the *psychic* from the *pneumatic* nature. He declares that the

---

[8] I am assuming my earlier discussion on 3.2.3 about the problems with this category and am employing the terminology here simply to interact with those who have made it the primary explanation for Paul's use of the two terms under investigation.

[9] See e.g. Wilckens, *Weisheit und Torheit*; Schmithals, *Gnosticism in Corinth*. Jewett offers a modified version of the Gnostic hypothesis—see *Paul's Anthropological Terms: A Study of Their Use in Conflict Settings* (Leiden: Brill, 1971), 23-40 (esp. 36-40). In particular, Jewett argues: "the main opponents of Paul within the Corinthian congregation itself were radical enthusiasts who can be termed Gnostics because of their belief in salvation through σοφία/γνῶσις and because of their consistently dualistic world view" (*ibid.*, 40).

[10] Scroggs' response to the ostensible parallels between Paul's language and that of the Gnostics is worth noting: "Paul never uses the noun ψυχή in a negative sense as do the gnostics" ("ΣΟΦΟΣ and ΠΝΕΥΜΑΤΙΚΟΣ," 52).

demiurge, being psychic, "does not comprehend the things of the spirit," since "being psychic, knew neither his Mother, who was pneumatic, nor her seeds, nor the aions of the pleroma"; he was "foolish, and lacked understanding, imagining that he himself made the cosmos. But he was ignorant that Sophia, the Mother, the Ogdoad, was really the cause of his activity.["] Those who, like the demiurge, are psychic have received only the "spirit of the cosmos" (2:12) and consequently lack understanding of pneumatic realities.[11]

However, Barclay criticizes this type of approach as "misguided in its attempts to trace the 'roots' of language in Greek 'mysticism' or 'Gnosticism': it relied on later texts which were themselves influenced by Christianity, or it grossly exaggerated the significance of only vaguely parallel patterns of vocabulary."[12] Moreover, while acknowledging the possibility that Paul adopts the language of the enthusiasts in Corinth in order to subvert their theological positions, Barclay remains cautious to accept such conclusions. Specifically, "much depends here on a subtle 'mirror reading' which presumes Paul's unusual vocabulary is explicable *only if* it is derived from the Corinthians' usage; and we know too little about the Corinthians to go much beyond speculation in these matters."[13]

---

[11] E.H. Pagels, *The Gnostic Paul: Gnostic Exegesis of the Pauline Letters* (Philadelphia: Fortress, 1975), 59.

[12] J.M.G. Barclay, "Πνευματικός in the Social Dialect of Pauline Christianity," in *The Holy Spirit and Christian Origins: Essays in Honor of James D.G. Dunn* (eds. G.N. Stanton, B.W. Longenecker and S.C. Barton; Grand Rapids: Eerdmans, 2004), 160; cf. Adams, *Constructing the World*, 94.

[13] Barclay, "Πνευματικός in the Social Dialect," 162—emphasis added.

4.3.1.2. Hellenistic Judaism

Others trace the origin and meaning to Hellenistic Judaism, specifically the parallels with Philo of Alexandria.[14] On this view, explicit attention is drawn first to Philo's commentary on the creation account, in which he interprets humanity as divided into two parts: a mortal body (lower nature) and an immortal spirit (higher nature). Furthermore, and to use Philo's dualistic language, the πνεῦμα not only refers to the higher nature of a person but also its source of life, while the ψυχή refers to the lower nature, one empowered or sustained by blood—just as in all creatures. While Philo sees both natures as divinely given at birth, only the πνεῦμα is able to attain the goal for which humanity was created, and that is the true knowledge of God. As Pearson explicitly states:

> This ability does not belong to man's natural soul (*psyche*) but is given him by God in creation by virtue of the divine spirit breathed into man. Thus man's higher soul, his "mind" [νοῦς] or "spirit" [πνεῦμα] enables him to rise above the level of his earthly and sense-perceptive soul and to receive impressions from the heavenly sphere.[15]

---

[14] See e.g. Pearson, *Pneumatikos-Psychikos*, 11-12, 17-21.

[15] Pearson, *Pneumatikos-Psychikos*, 54. As Logan describes it: "the Demiurge breathes into the man's face so that he becomes psychic, but a Golem whom the powers cannot raise because of their weakness, even as, despite their persistence, they cannot trap the image which had appeared to them because of their ignorance of its power. And it is only after the Spirit sees the psychic man on the earth, comes forth from the adamantine (*adamantinos*) earth, descends and settles in him that man becomes a living soul (*psychê*, cf. Gen 2:7) and is named Adam since he was found moving on the ground" (*Gnostic Truth and Christian Heresy: A Study in the History of Gnosticism* [London: Continuum, 1996], 188).

Functionally, Pearson's reading of the πνευματικός-ψυχικός distinction, in relating or even defining spiritual status, parallels the line of reasoning of those who favor a Gnostic reading.[16] However, and responding to the entire theory, Horsley raises three objections to Pearson's hypothesis, especially the distinctions, the grounds on which they are made, and the assumed results that follow from them.[17]

First, the specific categorical distinction between πνευματικός and ψυχικός cannot be found either in Philo or other Hellenistic Jewish texts. While ψυχικός appears in Philo several times and πνευματικός even less, in neither case do the terms bear the meaning or engage with each other in the way Pearson suggests. Second, neither Philo nor the specific text, Wisdom of Solomon, articulates an anthropological dualism of soul and spirit, where the two are contrasted and one is of lesser value than the other. Moreover, nothing in Philo or Wisdom suggests that the terms function as descriptions for spiritual status—i.e. ψυχή referring to a lower level and πνεῦμα referring to a higher one. For Horsley, it is difficult to account for Pearson's emphatic adjectival use of such terms as representing contrasting forms of existence when the use and meaning of the terms in Philo and Wisdom do not support such an emphasis. Finally, the literary testimony of the time does not reveal "among Hellenistic Jews a preference for the term 'spirit' (πνεῦμα) instead of 'mind' (νοῦς) for the higher, rational part of the soul. Actually the terms 'soul' (ψυχή), 'spirit' (πνεῦμα), 'mind' (νοῦς or διάνοια), 'rational soul' (λογική

---

[16] Cf. C. Mihaila, *The Paul-Apollos Relationship and Paul's Stance Toward Greco-Roman Rhetoric: An Exegetical and Socio-historical Study of 1 Corinthians 1–4* (London: T&T Clark, 2009), 75.

[17] Horsley, "Pneumatikos vs. Psychikos," 271-73. In a later work Pearson acknowledges these criticisms and accepts the validity of the first and third (see "Philo, Gnosis and the New Testament," 75-76), yet remains convinced about the legitimacy of the second.

ψυχή), etc. are largely parallel or interchangeable in Philo and Wisdom."[18] Moreover, Philo's treatment does not focus primarily on divisions of spirituality; instead his claims reflect more of the Platonic dualism of a mortal body vs. an immortal soul.[19] When applied to 1 Corinthians, as Lee points out: "In 1 Cor 2.12-15 and 15.44-46...Paul argues on the basis of the antithetical juxtaposition of ψυχικός and πνευματικός, not on the Platonic dualism of σῶμα and ψυχή."[20]

4.3.1.3. Hellenistic Jewish "Gnosis"

As a type of synthesis between the first two views, Horsley suggests a broader and more thematic reading of both Gnosticism and Hellenistic Judaism, especially Philo.[21] Explicitly, Horsley emphasizes the soteriological distinctions between πνευματικός and ψυχικός, rather than the anthropological, and then compares these distinctions with what we see in Paul (cf. 1 Cor 2.14-15; 15.44-46). Admittedly, given the lack of πνευματικός-ψυχικός

---

[18] Horsley, "Pneumatikos vs. Psychikos," 271-72.

[19] Both Wolfson and Goodenough argue for a relationship between Philo and Platonic philosophy—as noted by D. Runia, *Philo of Alexandria and the Timaeus of Plato* (Leiden: Brill, 1986), 10. Russell nuances things slightly different: "The philosopher Philo, who was a contemporary of Christ, is the best illustration of Greek influence on the Jews in the sphere of thought. While orthodox in religion, Philo is, in philosophy, primarily a Platonist; other important influences are those of the Stoics and Neo-pythagoreans" (*History of Western Philosophy* [London: Routledge, 2004], 303; cf. Schenck, who argues for similar influences [*A Brief Guide to Philo* (Louisville: Westminster John Knox, 2005), 3, 38-40, 56-64]).

[20] S.M. Lee, *The Cosmic Drama of Salvation: A Study of Paul's Undisputed Writings from Anthropological and Cosmological Perspectives* (Tübingen: Mohr Siebeck, 2010), 37 n.126.

[21] Cf. Horsley, "Pneumatikos vs. Psychikos," 269-88; idem, "Wisdom of Word and Words of Wisdom in Corinth," *CBQ* 39.2 (1977): 224-39; idem, "Gnosis in Corinth," 32-51.

language in Philo specifically, before understanding how such terminology was used in Corinth one must determine how such language compares with what Philo does say. Here, Horsley offers a ready parallel: πνευματικός refers to the "heavenly" person and ψυχικός refers to the "earthly"—the one being immortal or incorruptible, the other mortal or corruptible (cf. *Leg.* 1.31). After examining a number of key texts, Horsley argues: "it is clear that the heavenly *anthrōpos* and the earthly *anthrōpos*, the two types of humanity, are paradigms, based in creation texts, of different levels of religious endowment or status in the Hellenistic Jewish tradition represented by Philo."[22] This two-tier reading of humanity appears to have additional support from the comparable analogies of τέλειος vs. νήπιος and γαλά vs. βρῶμα, where those who are νήπιοι and receive γαλά comprise the lower tier (or lesser endowment) while those who are τελειοί and receive βρῶμα comprise the higher tier (or greater endowment). The element that distinguishes the two halves is the possession of σοφία: "For it is through the possession of *sophia* that the soul attains exalted status as perfect, nobly-born, rich, king, immortal, heavenly."[23]

However, Horsley's approach is not without its difficulties, two of which repay brief attention. First, Horsley's theory operates on the assumption of a one-to-one relationship between πνευματικός-ψυχικός language and immortal-mortal concepts; without this assumption, the theory does not work. Since the πνευματικός-ψυχικός language does not exist in the context of Philo's explanation of Gen 2.7 yet the immortal-mortal concepts do, and since Horsley assumes a parallelism between the two, he can readily transfer the nuances of the immortal-mortal concepts in Philo to the πνευματικός-ψυχικός language in 1 Corinthians, thus offering an ostensibly better understanding of the theology of

---

[22] Horsley, "Pneumatikos vs. Psychikos," 279-80.

[23] *Ibid.*, 285.

Paul's opponents in Corinth. However, as Mihaila points out, such a reading must assume that a "Philonic theology is present in Corinth,"[24] presumably introduced via the teaching of Apollos, a native of Alexandria. Thus, since Philo of Alexandria's theology exemplifies a workable synthesis of Judaism and Hellenistic thought, and since Apollos hails from Alexandria as an eloquent man, powerful in the Scriptures, then, according to Horsley, it makes sense to assume that Apollos was familiar with (or at least aware of) Philo's theology, was influenced by it, and carried it with him during his brief stay in Corinth.[25] However, this brings us to the second difficulty. The confident historical reconstruction of the Corinthians' situation, specifically their theological perspective or influence, is based upon Horsley's speculative assumptions about that situation.[26]

---

[24] Mihaila, *Paul-Apollos Relationship*, 77.

[25] Specifically, Horsley contends: "In the person of Apollos there is even a possible historical link between the Hellenistic Jewish tradition represented by Philo and the Corinthian situation, although such a direct link is hardly necessary for the analogy to be valid and helpful, given the general mobility of people, ideas, and religious cults in the Hellenistic-Roman world" ("Wisdom of Word," 231). Cf. Witherington, *Conflict and Community*, 130. Liftin, however, rejects this line of reasoning—see *Theology of Proclamation*, 231-32, 240.

[26] See again Barclay's earlier remarks: "we know too little about the Corinthians to go much beyond speculation in these matters" ("Πνευματικός in the Social Dialect," 162).

A fourth, and equally speculative theory is the one put forth by Ellis (see, *Prophecy and Hermeneutic in Early Christianity: New Testament Essays* [Grand Rapids: Eerdmans, 1978], xiii-xvii, 21-44). Here Ellis contends that the pneumatics in Corinth, who are also Paul's opponents, were initially Paul's traveling companions and fellow-workers in his apostolic mission (see 30, 38). Thus, the pneumatics were neither gnostic teachers nor Judaizing missionaries operating in direct antithesis to Paul's ministry. Instead, they were Jewish-Christians who originally supported the apostolic mission but then abused their special gifting of divine revelation and prophecy (via inspired, ecstatic speech— cf. 22, 27, 66), an abuse that subsequently affected their teaching on spirituality

4.3.1.4. A Simple Contrast

How then can we address Paul's language in 1 Cor 2.14-15, specifically the distinction between πνευματικός and ψυχικός? The simplest approach would be to see Paul employing these terms in a rather basic way, relying on their general lexical or etymological nuances. [27] Thus, for Paul the adjective ψυχικός merely refers to the physical nature or substance of a human being. Even if we assumed Gnostic or proto-Gnostic influences in Corinth, this basic meaning would not be unacceptable. As Logan shows, key gnostic texts describe the nature of the psychic person in substantive or material terms—i.e. "bone, sinew, flesh, marrow, blood, skin and hair." [28] Moreover, a distinction is maintained between the creation of a psychic person and that person having soul. Speaking of the Gnostic text, *On the Origin of the World*, Logan states it this way: "Man thus formed is described as becoming psychic (*psychikos*), although the text stoutly denies that he yet has a soul." [29]

Conversely, for Paul the adjective πνευματικός refers to one who is filled with or is characterized by God's Spirit—i.e. he or she is a Spirit-person or is spiritual. Here we should recognize a key point of overlap between the terms, yet also note their distinction. With regard to overlap, for one to be πνευματικός he

---

and ethics. For Paul this abuse can be described as stemming from a faulty notion of wisdom. Moreover, since they were originally a part of Paul's mission, and thus aware of the nature and meaning of the gospel message, "[t]hey provoke a strong response from the Apostle, who sees in their ethics and in their teaching a departure from the rule of Scripture and from the Christocentric model for Christian maturity. They have put their faith in human wisdom and, failing to recognize their gifts as a manifestation of grace, they have become boastful" (xiv).

[27] This is not to suggest that scholars (especially those just mentioned) are either unaware of this approach or ignoring it all together.

[28] Logan, *Gnostic Truth*, 189.

[29] *Ibid.*, 190.

or she must first be ψυχικός in the general sense (i.e. a physical creature); Paul does not envision "spiritual people" as disembodied entities.[30] However, and with regard to the distinction, Paul does allow for the possibility of a person being ψυχικός without being πνευματικός. This type of nuance is more theological than anthropological. In terms of Jewish anthropology, it would be impossible for a "natural" person to exist without a soul or God's life-giving breath;[31] yet theologically it is possible for a "natural" person to live physically without God's Spirit, which both facilitates prophetic insight and speech and engenders a life harmonious to the ways (or wisdom) of God (Ezek 36.26-28; cf. Jer 31.31-34). In the light of the broader distinction, two implications follow: 1) ψυχικοί are not πνευματικοί by the simple fact that they lack God's Spirit, and 2) from a soteriological perspective, ψυχικοί (i.e. those without the Spirit) represent those who are being destroyed, while πνευματικοί (i.e. those with the Spirit) represent those being saved.

---

[30] Paul's remarks in 1 Cor 15.35-54b equally do not support the idea of disembodied spirits. As Finney argues: "Paul claims that the true *pneumatikos*, the true person of the spirit, is one who will have the transformed resurrection body. But he also makes clear (vv. 45-49) that the terms ψυχή and πνεῦμα are not simply descriptive categories for the 'essence' or composition of the body. Rather, they serve to demarcate the first body in terms of its 'earthly' characteristics, which are suitable for the present age upon the earth; and the second body, the *pneumatic* body, in terms of its supernatural characteristics which will be suitable for the future heavenly age. As v. 45 goes on to explain, the supernatural dimension comes from the body's transformation by Christ himself, who, through his own resurrection, became 'a life-giving Spirit.' Here, Fee succinctly observes that, 'The transformed body is not composed of "spirit," it is a *body* adapted to the eschatological existence that is under the ultimate domination of the Spirit' " (*Honour and Conflict in the Ancient World: 1 Corinthians in its Greco-Roman Social Setting* [London: Bloomsbury T&T Clark, 2012], 216).

[31] Cf. Gen 2.7; Job 12.10; Isa 42.5. When this breath or life-giving spirit is withdrawn, the person dies (see Job 34.14; Ps 104.29-30).

We may expand this distinction one step further. Since the ψυχικοί are not πνευματικοί, and since Paul equates πνευματικοί with the τελειοί,[32] we can safely conclude that the ψυχικοί are not τελειοί. This follows from the assumption that the τελειοί are those who receive the Spirit of God, which therefore constitutes them as πνευματικοί, while the ψυχικοί lack God's Spirit, and Paul could not conceive of someone being πνευματικός without God's Spirit. Given the tenor of Paul's remarks in 2.14-15 in particular and 1.18–3.4 in general, it would seem as though he is emphasizing the basic distinction noted above—i.e. ψυχικός refers to one without God's Spirit, while πνευματικός refers to one with God's Spirit. This simple contrast becomes vital when we consider the details of Paul's argument and their relationship to the themes of having or receiving God's Spirit and the ability to know or discern the things of God (i.e. divine wisdom), especially those things related to salvation. It is from the basic distinction between ψυχικός and πνευματικός that Paul contrasts the two modes or ways of knowing (or modes of discernment).

4.3.2. Discernment of the "Natural" Person

Before examining the details of this, two initial and related observations must be recognized. First, and by comparison, what Paul says about the "natural" person in 1 Cor 2.14 is noticeably longer and more detailed than his comments about the "spiritual" person in 2.15. Moreover, Paul's remarks about "spiritual" people appear to be unrelated or unconnected to what he says about "natural" people in 2.14. Thus, if we understand Paul as creating a contrast between the two, then the relationship is not readily seen.

---

[32] See e.g. R. Schnackenburg, "Christian Adulthood According to the Apostle Paul," *CBQ* 25.3 (1963): 357, 359; *contra* Scroggs, "ΣΟΦΟΣ and ΠΝΕΥΜΑΤΙΚΟΣ," 47 n.5.

Specifically, the focus in 2.14 is on the "natural" person's refusal to accept the things of God's Spirit and that person's decision to view such things as folly.[33] This refusal is based on his or her inability to know because he or she does not measure them according to the Spirit. However, the focus in 2.15 is on the "spiritual" person's ability to judge or discern all things while at the same time remaining immune from the judgment or assessment of others.[34]

A likely solution for the apparent disjointedness comes from considering the second observation: while contrasting the "natural" with the "spiritual" person in general, Paul also contrasts the particular ways of knowing with how such ways manifest themselves. Accordingly, we see Paul working with clear recognizable opposites: "natural" vs. "spiritual" and inability vs. ability to discern the things of the Spirit. Moreover, we see Paul—albeit implicitly—furthering his overall case: the "natural" person sees the message of Christ crucified and its proclaimer as foolish, whereas the "spiritual" person sees the message and messenger as wise. With this basic idea in mind, we now turn our attention first to the categories themselves and then to Paul's treatment of the two modes of discernment.

---

[33] As Robertson-Plummer helpfully point out, οὐ δέχεται does not refer to an inability; it refers instead to a posture of resistance, or non-acceptance (see *First Epistle*, 49).

[34] While the focus of his remarks is more specific than mine, Dunn's observation in this regard is worth noting: "*Pneumatika* (spiritual things/gifts) should be subjected to scrutiny and evaluated, but not *pneumatikoi* (spiritual people). The charisma of evaluating does not include the passing of opinions about this or that man's worth or status; it is confined to the investigation and evaluation of particular charismata on the occasion of their manifestation" (*Jesus and the Spirit*, 235).

4.3.2.1. Definition of the Category (ψυχικός ἄνθρωπος)

Paul appears to define "natural" discernment negatively. Specifically Paul identifies it as not spiritual or not of the Spirit. (Admittedly, this is based on the details and conclusions drawn from the other half of the definition.) Moreover, Paul states that the "natural" person does not receive or accept the things of the Spirit of God (2.14a). The specificity of the giver relates back to Paul's remarks in 2.12, where he distinguished τὸ πνεῦμα τοῦ κόσμου from τὸ πνεῦμα τὸ ἐκ τοῦ θεοῦ. Thus we can say that Paul associates the "natural" person with those who have not received τὸ πνεῦμα τὸ ἐκ τοῦ θεοῦ,[35] which then explains why such people do not receive the things of the Spirit, why they see these things as foolishness, and why they are unable to know otherwise (μωρία γάρ αὐτῷ ἐστιν καὶ οὐ δύναται γνῶσαι). As with the specificity of the giver, the connection between having or receiving τὸ πνεῦμα τὸ ἐκ τοῦ θεοῦ and the ability to know the things of God's Spirit relates to the resultant clause in 2.12: ἵνα εἰδῶμεν τὰ ὑπὸ τοῦ θεοῦ χαρισθέντα ἡμῖν.

Therefore if knowing the things of God is contingent upon having the Spirit of God (cf. 2.11), and if the "natural" person has not received God's Spirit, then it follows that they cannot (or are unable to) know the things of God revealed by the Spirit. Yet more is involved than a divinely-given capacity or ability to know; for Paul the knowledge given by the Spirit carries with it a framework for *how* to know (or discern) the things of God. Thus, the "natural" person not only fails to receive the things of God's Spirit but he or she lacks the ability to understand or know the things of God ὅτι πνευματικῶς ἀνακρίνεται (2.14c). As Litfin observes: since the things of God can only be spiritually discerned, and since it is only

---

[35] Cf. J.–M. Sevrin, "La gnose à Corinthe. Questions de méthode et obversvations sur 1 Co 1,17–3,3," in *The Corinthian Correspondence* (ed. R. Bieringer; Leuven: Leuven University Press, 1996), 135.

God's Spirit who reveals the wisdom of Christ crucified, and since the "natural" person does not have God's Spirit, which therefore implies he or she must discern the message of Christ crucified by other means, "it is not surprising that such a [person] should find the form and content of Paul's preaching foolish," since "foolish" is the conclusion formed when the message is measured via human wisdom.[36] This reinforces my earlier point about the identification or nature of this form of discernment—i.e. it is not spiritual; it is merely human.[37]

4.3.2.2. Basic Characteristics

When we see this discernment in the light of Paul's earlier remarks about human wisdom (1.18–2.13), a few important conclusions follow. First, "natural" discernment is rooted in the categories of human wisdom and that wisdom's criteria for examining the teachings of others, especially those purporting to be wise. This stresses the source and manner of knowing, a stress that helps Paul distinguish it from the mode of discernment he advocates. Second, "natural" discernment is exercised through the efforts of the individual and that person's ability not only to reason on his or her own but also to assess the merits of another's teaching. This stresses the dependence upon the particular source and manner of knowing, which in this case is human wisdom. Third, "natural" discernment supports individualistic or even self-interested perspectives. This stresses the motivation for either asserting one's views or judging the merits of another's, which

---

[36] Cf. Litfin, *Theology of Proclamation*, 220.

[37] We can add here Paul's claim in 2.13 with regard to how the things of God are taught not in accordance with wise human speech but in accordance with the Spirit, or πνευματικοῖς πνευματικὰ συγκρίνοντες. To teach the things of God by means of wise human speech would be attempting to discern spiritual things by human means, yet Paul has already rejected this approach as not only illogical but also completely incapable of achieving its goal.

often results in self-praise or boasting.[38] Finally, such efforts and abilities are ultimately limited in scope and effect. This follows from two key points in Paul's argument: 1) God has rendered human wisdom impotent in being able to know true (divine) wisdom (1.19-20), and 2) only through divine self-disclosure can God's wisdom be known (2.9-11); human wisdom and effort on their own cannot know what has not been revealed. None of these features, either individually or collectively, represent the type of discernment that Paul has in mind for those who believe.

4.3.3. Discernment of the "Spiritual" Person

We come now to the second part of Paul's contrast, which he describes as the discernment exercised by the "spiritual" person. Given the paucity of explicit details in 1 Cor 2.15 regarding this mode of discernment, we will need to consider the implications of what Paul says elsewhere in his argument about the Spirit's role in relation to divine wisdom and the believer. Here we will follow a similar line of inquiry as we did with the topic of "natural" discernment.

4.3.3.1. Definition of the Category (ὁ πνευματικός)

As noted earlier, what Paul says about discernment of the "spiritual" person is noticeably shorter than his remarks about discernment of the "natural" person. Moreover, we referred to the apparent imbalance of the contrast in the sense that Paul's comments about the "spiritual" person do not necessarily respond to or appear in a similar form as the remarks about the "natural" person. Instead, Paul issues two related claims and then presses on with his argument. However, when we consider the claims he does make—albeit briefly—we see not only a clear distinction between

---

[38] Cf. esp. Finney, "Conflict in Corinth," 44-45, 84-87, 114-19; Donahoe, "From Self-Praise to Self-Boasting," 79-84.

the two modes of discernment but also a vital clue for where Paul is taking the argument. Specifically, in the short remarks of 2.15 Paul prepares the Corinthians for the next stage of his argument, one that is in itself an example of the discernment he advocates. However, before we examine that next stage and what he is doing with it, we need to consider the two related claims about "spiritual" discernment.

First, Paul emphatically asserts, ὁ δὲ πνευματικός ἀνακρίνει πάντα (2.15a).[39] The use of ἀνακρίνω and πνευματικός links this statement with what Paul said in the previous clause (i.e. ὅτι πνευματικῶς ἀνακρίνεται [2.14d]). The link is important not only for identification purposes but also for articulating what the "spiritual" person is able to do. It was noted above that the "natural" person cannot be πνευματικός simply because he or she lacks the Spirit. Moreover, it was argued that this lack of the Spirit explains the "natural" person's inability to discern the things of God's Spirit, for it is only by God's Spirit that such things are made known and understood. Conversely, since the "spiritual" person (by definition) has God's Spirit, and since it is only by God's Spirit that such things are made known and understood, he or she is able to discern the things of God. This ability follows from what Paul says negatively about the "natural" person in 2.14. Thus, through "spiritual" discernment one has the ability to know (reversing 2.14c), and the object of what is known is discerned to be wise (reversing 2.14b), and it is known to be wise because the believers have received God's Spirit who is the agent of divine revelation (reversing 2.14a).

---

[39] 𝔓⁴⁶, A, C, and D* include τά before πάντα whereas ℵ, B, and D² lack the article. The inclusion is explained as a way for clearly identifying πάντα as a neuter plural rather than a masculine singular accusative (see Thiselton, *First Epistle*, 271).

This connection of ideas becomes clearer when we recognize the links between πάντα here in 2.15 and its use in 2.10. Since the Spirit πάντα ἐραυνᾷ, καὶ τὰ βάθη τοῦ θεοῦ (2.10b), and in the light of Paul's claim that ἐλάβομεν...τὸ πνεῦμα τὸ ἐκ τοῦ θεοῦ (2.12a), it would not be too much to assume that God's Spirit is able to assist the πνευματικός in discerning πάντα (2.15). While Fitzmyer rightly points out that the scope of πάντα in this context refers "not only [to the] affairs of this world or age, but also 'what comes from God's Spirit,' and the 'gifts bestowed on us by God' (v 12),"[40] there is an additional and more immediate connection to be recognized. Specifically, Paul appears to have in mind the proclamation of the gospel of Christ crucified as God's wisdom, a wisdom revealed by the Spirit and a proclamation that relies on the Spirit's powerful work in the both the preacher and audience. We can assume Paul has this focus in mind, given the likelihood that he is confronting those who interpret both the message and messenger as foolish.[41] We can further assume that Paul wants the Corinthians to see the assessment of message and messenger as essential for judging other "inspired" teachers and their claims to divine wisdom, or that their inspired messages correspond with the gospel of Christ crucified. Thus, if one claims divine wisdom or inspired speech and yet the substance of the message does not correspond with how God's revelation occurs, that person, in spite of their claims, cannot be considered a true witness (cf. Gal 1.6-9).

Paul contends, in the second and related claim about the "spiritual" person that, αὐτὸς δὲ ὑπ' οὐδενὸς ἀνακρίνεται (2.15b). While the claim as a whole is worthy of attention, we must first address a seemingly minor detail: the shift from the active to passive use of ἀνακρίνω. In the previous clause, Paul describes the πνευματικός as the one exercising discernment; however, here,

---

[40] Fitzmyer, *First Corinthians*, 184.
[41] Cf. Pickett, *Cross in Corinth*, 62-66, 68-69, 71-74.

the πνευματικός is the recipient or object of discernment. As the remainder of the clause suggests, the one judging or critiquing the πνευματικός can ostensibly be either a fellow believer or a non-believer. Given the emphatic negativity of the claim it would appear that Paul advocates absolute immunity for the πνευματικός when being judged. If we assume that Paul's opponents in Corinth are claiming superior status as a result of inflated views of spirituality, then this promise of immunity would seem to be counterproductive for Paul's case against these spiritual elite.[42] Moreover, if this immunity does in fact exist in this way, then Paul has no ground or support for repudiating the claims of the elite; by his own definition they would be exempt. However, as 1 Cor 14.29 suggests, the claims (or even inspired words) of the πνευματικός (or προφήτης, in 14.29) are certainly open to critique and should be measured by spiritual standards (i.e. πνευματικοῖς πνευματικὰ συγκρίνοντες [2.13b]). The immunity would therefore seem to apply to one's status as πνευματικός but not to the manifestations of that status (e.g. πνεύματικα, χαρίσμα).[43] However, we could say the status and manifestations are immune to the criticisms of those who judge both according to the standards of human wisdom. Given the explicit contrast between ψυχικός and πνευματικός in 2.14-15, and the wider context of the argument, this latter immunity seems to be Paul's primary claim.

4.3.3.2. Basic Characteristics

When we see this discernment in the light of Paul's earlier remarks about divine wisdom (esp. 1.18–2.13), a few important conclusions follow. First, "spiritual" discernment is rooted in the

---

[42] This tension in the text is an underlying reason why Thiselton views 2.15 as a quotation of the elite in Corinth (see *First Epistle*, 272-74).

[43] See again Dunn, *Jesus and the Spirit*, 235.

categories of divine wisdom and that wisdom's criteria for examining the teachings of others, especially those purporting to be wise. This stresses the source and manner of knowing, a stress that helps Paul maintain the separation between this form and "natural" discernment. Second, "spiritual" discernment is exercised through the Spirit's work and the Spirit's ability to know and reveal the depths of God. This stresses the dependence upon the particular source and manner of knowing, which in this case is God's wisdom. Third, "spiritual" discernment is not limited in its ability or scope. This follows from two key points in Paul's argument: 1) God has given the Spirit to those who believe, a Spirit who knows all things, even the depths of God (2.10-11), and 2) because of divine self-disclosure, God's wisdom can be known and this wisdom forms the basis upon which all other wisdom-teachings are judged (2.15). Finally, "spiritual" discernment benefits the community, especially when the community collectively relies on Spirit-given insight or guidance. For Paul, while on the verge of being circular, it is this collective exercise of discernment for the benefit of the whole—and not the exaltation of an individual—that characterises the whole body as πνευματικός.

4.3.4. Condition(s) for Right Discernment

We must now consider the conclusion of Paul's argument in 1 Cor 2.6-16, not only as it relates to the issue of discernment but also the larger topic of receiving and accepting God's wisdom via the Spirit. Specifically, we seek to understand what justifies right discernment (i.e. whether there are basic conditions or criteria) and how Paul goes about supporting that case. We will address this in reverse by first focusing on the scriptural quotation in 2.16, which seems to function as his support, and then examine the relationship between the substance of that quotation and Paul's preceding remarks on spiritual discernment.

4.3.4.1. Paul's Appeal to Scripture

The argument of 2.6-16 ends with a scriptural quotation, one presumably employed to validate its preceding claims.[44] Similar to the quotation in 2.9, Paul's usage here in 2.16 repays attention. Commentators maintain that Paul's source is Isa 40.13 and that he follows the LXX rather than the MT.[45] When we consider the respective contents of the sources, Paul's use of the LXX might come as a surprise. Part of this stems from the fact that the MT provides textual (if not linguistic) support for the idea of how one knows via the Spirit—a crucial feature to Paul's argument in 2.10-12. In the MT the "Spirit of the Lord" is the direct object, the one measured by an individual (מי־תכן את־רוח יהוה ואיש עצתו יודיענו). The verb תכן carries the idea of "measuring" or "balancing," an idea that relates well with Paul's concept of discernment—i.e. examining two or more things together and recognizing, in a rational way, their harmony or interrelatedness. Thus it seems strange that Paul does not rely on this reading when making his case in 2.6-16. Why then does he use the LXX instead of the MT? While it might be tempting to say that Paul was either unfamiliar with the MT or he simply favored the LXX over the MT,[46] these options are far from provable with any degree of certainty.[47] It is more likely that Paul follows the LXX because he uses it more

---

[44] See Davis, *Wisdom and Spirit*, 128.

[45] Heil suggests that it not only "comes from Isa 40:13 but is [also] reminiscent of many other OT texts with a similar form and content [which] heightens the likeliness that the implied audience recognizes it as an allusion to scripture" (*The Rhetorical Role of Scripture in 1 Corinthians* [Atlanta: Society of Biblical Literature, 2005], 74-75).

[46] Lindemann favors the idea that Paul was unfamiliar with the MT on the basis that if he was familiar with it, he would have recognized that רוח makes a better case (see *Der erste Korintherbrief* [Tübingen: Mohr Siebeck, 2000], 74).

[47] This also applies to the theories that suggest Paul was operating from memory and simply misquoted or remembered badly.

often than the MT,[48] and that he is writing in Greek to a Greek-speaking audience, thus making the LXX a more suitable choice.

However, by considering the overall logic of 2.6-16, we see that the LXX is not only a more suitable text for his audience but also that its particular reading makes better sense of Paul's argument and therefore becomes the more useful source.[49] Before proceeding, we need to examine two key differences that emerge in the LXX: 1) the direct object is "the mind of the Lord,"[50] and 2) the verbal idea is knowing rather than measuring. Thus, the LXX reads: τίς ἔγνω νοῦν κυρίου καὶ τίς αὐτοῦ σύμβουλος ἐγένετο ὅς συμβιβᾷ αὐτόν. From this we can begin to see why Paul uses the LXX version of this passage for his argument. Throughout the argument of 2.6-16 the primary object of discussion has been the wisdom of God; the Spirit of God, as the mediator of divine wisdom is secondary, although that is not to say of lesser value. Moreover, Paul has been dealing with not only a particular kind of wisdom but also its particular source. Thus, if Paul were to quote from the MT the focus would seem to fall on the *mediator* of wisdom (i.e. the Spirit) rather than the *source* of wisdom (i.e. the Lord [God]). This is made more acute by the fact that Paul has stressed the Spirit's role in directing the believer to God as both the source and provider of true wisdom. By employing the LXX, Paul is not only able to maintain the primary focus of the discussion (i.e. the wisdom of God), he is also able to maintain the secondary

---

[48] To say that Paul uses the LXX more often is different from saying he favors the LXX. While it is true that favoring a text can be proven by the amount of use, it is also true that frequent use can occur out of either necessity or familiarity—i.e. the text used is the most readily available.

[49] Cf. Grosheide, *First Epistle*, 74.

[50] It is sometimes argued (e.g. Witherington, *Conflict and Community*, 129; Hays, *First Corinthians*, 47) that the translators of the Septuagint read רוח as synonymous with νοῦς, evidenced by the substitution of the former with the latter, and Paul simply operated with the same flexibility.

concept of knowing the will and ways of God through the means that God provides (i.e. the Spirit).

One further detail needs to be addressed. In both the LXX and the MT, the question in the Isaiah passage assumes a negative response. Thus, whether we read it as "who has measured the Spirit of the Lord" (MT) or "who has known the mind of the Lord" (LXX), the anticipated answer is an emphatic, "no one."[51] This negative response comports well with Paul's earlier analogy in 2.11, and it adds further support to his claim in 2.14. However, with the emphatic conjunction δέ in 2.16 preceding his conclusion, Paul reverses the expected response and suggests that it is possible to "know the mind of the Lord," yet this possibility is contingent upon specific conditions and their appropriate use.[52] One of the stated conditions is the fact that believers "have the mind of Christ" (2.16c); the other, although not explicitly stated in 2.16, is the reception and presence of the Spirit. This brings us to the next topic of our investigation.

4.3.4.2. The "Mind of Christ"

Here we deal with the specific conditions and their appropriate use for knowing "the mind of the Lord." Immediately we are struck by the change from "the mind of the Lord" in the quotation to "the mind of Christ" in the exhortation.[53] This shift did not go unnoticed by later scribes, for a small number of manuscripts read κυρίου instead of Χριστοῦ in 1 Cor 2.16b.[54] However, the use of

---

[51] Cf. Munzinger, *Discerning the Spirits*, 39-40.

[52] So Heil: "Although the 'positive' statement in 2:16b contradicts the expected negative answer of the rhetorical question in the scriptural reference, it does not lessen or eliminate its effects on the audience as a rhetorical question" (*Rhetorical Role of Scripture*, 71 n.8).

[53] For, "we have the mind of Christ" as an exhortation, cf. Collins, *First Corinthians*, 127.

[54] Specifically B, D*, F, G, 81, it, Ambrosiaster, and Pelagius.

Χριστοῦ not only has stronger attestation,[55] it also maintains the flow of Paul's overall argument, specifically its christological focus.[56] In 1.10 Paul admonishes the Corinthians to be united in speech and for their mind and judgment to be restored to perfection (κατηρτισμένοι). This desire appears to be prompted by the news of party-formations among believers in Corinth, specifically the potential of groups rallying around particular names. For Paul party-formations (whether actual or merely potential) carry with them the danger of dividing the church, which Paul equates with the person of Christ (cf. 1.13)—a theme he will continue in chapter 12. However, if we look closely at the structure of his argument in 1.10, we can see the specific focus of Paul's exhortation: the disharmony in speech and behavior (i.e. rallying around names, community divisions) ultimately results from a faulty mind and flawed judgment.

Therefore, Paul's argument is not directed at particular groups or factions (*per se*); instead, he speaks to the underlying cause that provides space not only for disharmonious speech but also flawed judgments concerning the nature and effect of the gospel message. For Paul the nature of the gospel is God's wisdom displayed in the cross of Christ as a means for salvation, and one primary effect of this event is the complete reversal of ideas and how such ideas are judged. In particular, the cross radically alters notions of wisdom and how that wisdom is conveyed, understood, and obtained by believers. Moreover, with this alteration comes a new framework for how those in Christ live their new transformed life. For Paul the transformed life is lived in the light of the cross, for it is by the cross that believers' lives are (re)defined. As Paul says in Phil 2.5-11, a believer's attitude (or mindset) is to reflect not only Christ's

---

[55] See 𝔓⁴⁶, ℵ, A, C, D¹, Ψ, 048, 0289ᵛⁱᵈ, 33, 1739, 𝔐, vg, syr, cop, Epiphanius.

[56] Cf. Schrage, *Der erste Brief*, 1.267.

faithful, humble, and obedient disposition towards the ways of God (i.e. the wise plan of salvation) but also Christ's willingness to endure public humiliation and shame on a cross. Here we discover strong connections between what the cross of Christ represents and how believers are meant to understand and live life. To put this differently, the way in which believers are to view the world and themselves is through the lens of the cross, and those with the mind of Christ will live a cruciform life.[57]

We find a similar emphasis at work in Paul's exhortation to the Corinthians. In particular, the cruciform life defined by the mind of Christ results in unity and not division. Noting the same connections with Philippians, Brown argues: "When the mind of Christ is embraced, unity in the Body of Christ, the church, is regained (Phil 2:5; 4:2). Likewise, in 1 Corinthians, possession of the consciously cruciform mind is what makes possible the unity Paul calls for in 1:10, the mindful servanthood outlined in chapters 3–4".[58] As Paul argues in 1 Cor 2.1–3.4, because he proclaimed the wisdom of God in the cross of Christ and the Corinthians originally accepted it as such, from that point of acceptance they became recipients of the mind of Christ. Accordingly, and ideally, the Corinthians' views of the world and themselves are no longer determined by the standards of the world (i.e. human wisdom), standards that were rendered impotent and foolish by the cross.

---

[57] Cf. Garland, *1 Corinthians*, 39. More to the point: "Paul's Christ paradigm is not simply an appropriate pattern for relational power, it communicates something fundamental about the shape of true humanity: that it should be cruciform, following (μιμηταί μου γίνεσθε καθὼς κἀγὼ Χριστοῦ, 1 Cor 11.1) and called into fellowship with Christ (1 Cor 1.9)" (Long, *Paul and Human Rights*, 175).

[58] A.R. Brown, "Apocalyptic Transformation in Paul's Discourse on the Cross," *WW* 16.4 (1996): 435. Cf. Goudge: "If we 'have the mind of Christ,' we must share His character. Spirituality of mind and party-spirit cannot exist together" (*First Epistle*, 23).

Especially crucial for our purposes is Paul's view of the Spirit's role in this entire process. We have already noted Paul's belief that the Spirit was powerfully at work in the proclamation and reception of the gospel, and that a central feature of this work was the Spirit's role in revealing God's wisdom displayed in the cross of Christ. Here we find Paul's belief that the Spirit plays an equally crucial role in providing the framework within which the cross of Christ can be understood as God's wisdom and how that wisdom defines new life in Christ. In particular we see that the notion of having "the mind of Christ" is necessarily linked with the idea of Spirit-given and guided discernment.[59]

4.3.4.3. Presence and Guidance of the Spirit

We come now to the second condition for right discernment, a condition not explicitly stated as such but one inherent to Paul's larger argument. Specifically I am referring to the presence of the Spirit in the lives of believers and the new epistemological framework within which believers understand and live life. According to the claims in 2.11, 12, and 14, knowledge of God's wisdom is dependent upon receiving God's Spirit; without the Spirit it is impossible to know the things of God. In other key Pauline texts, a similar connection between believers having the Spirit and their ability to know and live according to God's ways is emphasized (e.g. Rom 8.5-17; Phil 2.1-11; cf. Eph 3.14-19; 4.1-6). When we recognize this connection, especially in relation to having "the mind of Christ," and apply it to the notion of discernment, we must state clearly the implications of this connection. Specifically, in having "the mind of Christ," given by God's revelation via the Spirit, does this mean the believer's mind is superseded? In other words, when a teacher proclaims an inspired message to others, does the Spirit's activity override or

---

[59] Cf. Litfin, *Theology of Proclamation*, 219.

relegate the teacher's abilities in order to sustain and communicate the inspired nature of the message?[60] Moreover, are those hearing the message able to discern the validity of the message (as inspired by God) through their own reasoning or does the Spirit overshadow their abilities? Or does Paul offer a balance between human ability and divine activity for the entire process, both for the teacher and for the listener? Let us consider two options for dealing with this particular issue before mentioning a more plausible reading.

In one sense we could say Paul envisages a dichotomy of Spirit-revelation and human rationality, especially in view of his earlier polarization of God's wisdom and human wisdom, with the former overturning the latter. Thus, those who have God's Spirit and therefore the "mind of Christ" are no longer operating in accordance with their own abilities or faculties; all inspired messages are formulated, proclaimed, and understood by the work of the Spirit, filtered through "the mind of Christ." Moreover, with "the mind of Christ" representing a standard of wise living, definitions of ethical norms and behaviors are solely the product of divine revelation and therefore can only be understood via the illumination of the Spirit. Accordingly, since God's wisdom in the cross has rendered powerless human wisdom, and since God's wisdom can only be revealed or made known via God's Spirit and apart from human ability, Spirit-revelation and discernment about the cross also render powerless human reasoning.[61] However,

---

[60] Aune helpfully shows that ancient Greek notions of "inspiration" presupposed a displacement of the human mind by the divine voice (see *Prophecy in Early Christianity and the Ancient Mediterranean World* [Grand Rapids: Eerdmans, 1983], 24-33).

[61] Munzinger criticizes Schnabel for "relegat[ing] the use of reason for discerning the will of God to a near irrelevant position, since the external 'binding norms' are sufficient" (*Discerning the Spirits*, 145). Specifically Schnabel contends that standard reason is not "particularly relevant for the

Paul's polemic deals with ways (or modes) of knowing and the success or failure of those employing the respective ways. As a result, the failure or success is not linked with inability or ability on the part of the individual; instead the focus falls on the success or failure of the specific mode of knowing by which an individual seeks to understand. Therefore, since we can say the Spirit is the one who reveals the overturning of human wisdom by God's wisdom as the way of knowing, it does not seem appropriate to say the Spirit's activity necessarily overturns the abilities of human rationality.

In another sense, especially in view of the situation to which Paul writes, we could say Paul advocates a more rational or reasoned approach to discernment vis-à-vis one dependent upon ecstatic spiritual experiences. Thus, because some Corinthians are boasting of spiritual superiority, exemplified in their practice of divinely inspired speech (non-rational utterances?) and their claims for prophetic insight via special revelation (or divine possession),[62] Paul offers balance to the situation through his "insistence on the superiority of rational, nonecstatic behavior and communication."[63]

---

substantiation of Christian moral behavior, since it never provides the final word in questions of Christian life-style, nor cancels or invalidates God's norms and commandments, nor is it relevant for discerning and deciding basic moral questions, as these have been decided already in God's eternally valid revelation. The believer's reason is relevant for questions of minor importance and for deciding how (not whether!) the binding norms of, and the guiding criteria for, moral behavior are to be realized *in actu*" (*Law and Wisdom*, 332). However, the preceding context for Schnabel's argument does not warrant such a criticism, for Schnabel emphasizes the necessary interrelationship between a renewed mind and God's Spirit—especially for discerning the ways or wisdom of God (see Schnabel, *Law and Wisdom*, 329-32).

[62] See A.R. Hunt, *The Inspired Body: Paul, the Corinthians, and Divine Inspiration* (Macon: Mercer University Press, 1996), 71-76.

[63] Hunt, *Inspired Body*, 127. Though he specifically focuses on 1 Cor 14, Callan's arguments on Paul's view of inspired prophecy reach a similar

This becomes particularly relevant for Paul's argument in 1 Cor 14, where he favors intelligible speech, which uplifts the entire community, over unintelligible utterances, which provide no real benefit for the whole and divide the community into parts—e.g. those able to speak in ecstatic utterances, and those who cannot. If, however, prophetic insight or inspired teachings via non-rational speech are going to take place in the community, Paul insists they be made comprehensible through an interpreter or translator. As Aune says: "Rather than reject prophesying out of hand, Paul recommends that [believers] allow the Spirit of God to speak through prophets and then retain that which is good and profitable and reject that which is regarded as evil and worthless." [64] Accordingly, distinguishing between good and evil, profitable and worthless involves a more reasoned or rational evaluation of what is communicated and therefore applicable to the community. When applied to the context of 1 Cor 2.1–3.4, this would suggest the idea of rationally discerning what is of God and what is not; God's wisdom vs. human wisdom.

However, as Munzinger points out, both of these options presuppose an antithesis or dualism between Spirit and mind—or "faith versus reason and the supernatural versus the natural." [65] For Munzinger, this dualism is not only difficult to sustain but also inconsistent with Paul's wider views on Spirit and mind, especially in a soteriological context. [66] We arrive at this by noting some key points. First, Paul insists that God's Spirit is necessarily distinct

---

conclusion to that of Hunt—see T. Callan, "Prophecy and Ecstasy in Greco-Roman Religion and 1 Corinthians," *NovT* 28.2 (1985): 125-40.

[64] Aune, *Prophecy*, 219.

[65] See Munzinger, *Discerning the Spirits*, 146. Cf. also Scott, *Implicit Epistemology*, 58-68.

[66] See Munzinger, *Discerning the Spirits*, 147-84.

from the individual—not to mention that person's mind.[67] Second, while endowed with abilities to reason or rationalize, the human mind is incapable of ascertaining the things or ways of God; only God can reveal such things. Third, the revelation involves the Spirit mediating God's wisdom to the believer, and for Paul this mediation is tied to the proclamation of the gospel. Fourth, while Paul sees the Spirit as working powerfully in the mind of the individual, bringing about a proper understanding of God's wisdom in the cross of Christ, this powerful work is not synonymous with an absolute displacement of human reason or a complete suspension of mental faculties. As intimated in Rom 10.8-15, Paul assumes a conscious decision on the part of the one accepting the gospel of Christ as the message of God's salvation. Moreover, Paul "is keen that his listeners understand his message, and an important criterion for proper worship is that it is conducted in an intelligible manner."[68] Thus, and finally, Paul believes this powerful work of the Spirit includes the transformation or renewing of the mind, the point at which human wisdom is replaced with God's wisdom; "natural" discernment is exchanged for "spiritual" discernment. However, Paul does not view this transformation and exchange as the Spirit supplanting the human mind or reason. Accordingly, this transformation brings with it new ways of thinking and therefore a new understanding for how to live, and Paul expects (or assumes) that all believers operate according to this new standard.

---

[67] As noted in the previous chapter, Paul's arguments in this respect must be contrasted with those of the Stoics, who advocate an essential, inherent link between the individual and the divine.

[68] Munzinger, *Discerning the Spirits*, 152.

4.3.4.4. Summary of Conditions

Thus, for Paul, having the "mind of Christ" not only enables believers to know and rightly discern the wisdom of God (or the things of God) as revealed by the Spirit; it also operates as a new framework for understanding life and knowing how to live according to God's wisdom. Specifically, this new epistemology defines appropriate behaviors and equips believers with the ability to recognize or discern when the boundaries of appropriateness are either confused or transgressed. The believers (or the πνευματικοί) are further equipped to know not only how to correct the faulty behavior but also recognize the process(es) of thought that enabled it to happen. In the case of the Corinthians, their struggles can be seen as emanating from two basic and related problems: 1) a faulty understanding of both wisdom and spirituality, exemplified by the issue of boasting of status, and 2) a faulty criterion for assessing things and persons claiming to be wise and spiritual.

For Paul the solution to both problems comes when the entire community defines and discerns both wisdom and spirituality with the mind of Christ, as given and maintained by the Spirit. Moreover, the results of having this mind and mode of discernment are manifest in how the believers live, not only personally but also with each other as a community. Specifically, for Paul, the life lived is one that is humble, self-sacrificing, and others-focused; it is a life that reflects the reality of the cross.[69] With the argument of

---

[69] As Cox summarises: "the hallmark of those who are truly πενυματικοί is the mind of Christ (νοῦς Χριστοῦ, 1 Cor 2:16), a mind that is not puffed up with γνῶσις but is built up by ἀγαπή θεοῦ (1 Cor 8:1-3). The mind of Christ manifests itself in believers not in liberty that comes from knowledge but self-sacrifice in accordance with Christ's sacrifice (8:7-13)" (*By the Same Word: Creation and Salvation in Hellenistic Judaism and Early Christianity* [Berlin: Walter de Gruyter, 2007], 160). We should also recall Fee's assessment: "This paragraph [1 Cor 2.6-16] has endured a most unfortunate history of application

1 Cor 2.1-5, Paul shows his own apostolic mission as operating within this particular framework, and uses it as an example to be imitated by the Corinthians (cf. 4.16).[70]

4.4. Paul's Use of Spiritual Discernment

When we come to Paul's remarks in 1 Cor 3.1-4, we find him offering an assessment of the Corinthian situation, an assessment that not only appeals to the Corinthians' own experience (both past and present) but also employs the criteria for spiritual discernment he has advocated. In this section of the chapter we will focus on these two features of Paul's assessment. However, before we address these we must be clear about the relationship between this passage and the rest of Paul's argument—specifically, what is its logical or rhetorical function?

---

in the church. Paul's own point has been almost totally lost in favor of an interpretation nearly 180 degrees the opposite of his intent. Almost every form of spiritual elitism, 'deeper life' movement, and 'second blessing' doctrine has appealed to this text. To receive the Spirit according to their special expression paves the way for people to know 'deeper truths' about God. One special brand of this elitism surfaces among some who have pushed the possibility of 'faith' to the extreme, and regularly make a 'special revelation' from the Spirit their final court of appeal. Other 'lesser' brothers and sisters are simply living below their full privileges in Christ. Indeed, some advocates of this form of spirituality bid fair to repeat the Corinthian error in its totality. What is painful about so much of this is not simply the improper use of this passage, but that so often it is accompanied by a toning down of the message of the cross. In fact one is hard-pressed to hear the content of 'God's wisdom' ever expounded as the paradigm for truly Christian living" (*First Epistle*, 120).

[70] As Tuckett argues: "the wisdom that Paul will concede and accept for the mature (2.6-16) is the wisdom that comes from the mind of Christ (v. 16). It is the gospel of Christ crucified, and the claim that this gospel is exemplified in his own apostolic existence, that provides the fundamental basis for Paul's attempt to change the self-understanding of the Corinthians" ("Paul, Scripture and Ethics: Some Reflections," *NTS* 46.3 [2000]: 423-24; cf. Hunt, *Inspired Body*, 93).

4.4.1. Situating Paul's Assessment

Commentators agree that with 1 Cor 3.1 Paul begins a new stage of the argument, signaled by the repeated use of κἀγώ ἀδελφοί (cf. 2.1).[71] Where disagreement occurs is with how this new line of argument relates to what precedes and follows. Bünker, under the assumption that 1.10–4.21 represents an elaborate rhetorical letter, reads 3.1 as initiating the *probatio* of Paul's argument.[72] However, in view of the assumed deliberative and apologetic aims of the argument, Bünker consequently downplays the importance of God's wisdom (as revealed by God's Spirit) so that the issues of party-strife and apostolic authority become the primary foci. Or to say this more negatively: Bünker's reading ultimately severs the necessary connection between a proper understanding of God's wisdom and how that understanding engenders appropriate relations, not just amongst the Corinthians but also the Corinthians and Paul.

Davis, on the other hand, appears to emphasize the relational solidarity that Paul desires. In particular, while there are distinctions between believers and non-believers, because of the presence of the Spirit, no distinction should exist within the body of believers. Thus:

> 1 Co 3.1-4 should be recognized as the natural and integral counterpart to 1 Co 2.14-16. There Paul affirms...that no Christian may be called ψυχικός. For inasmuch as every Christian possesses the Spirit and comprehends the spiritual wisdom contained within the kerygma, that one is

---

[71] Grosheide, *First Epistle*, 77; A. Strobel, *Der erste Brief an die Korinther* (Zürich: Theologischer Verlag, 1989), 74-75; Schrage, *Der erste Brief*, 1.280; J. Kremer, *Der erste Brief and die Korinther* (Regensburger: Verlag Friedrich Pustet, 1997), 66-67; Lindemann, *Der erste Korintherbrief*, 76-77.

[72] Bünker, *Briefformular*, 17-18.

πνευματικός. But in 1 Co 3.1-4, Paul shows up the one-sidedness of a purely sapiential criterion, by affirming that Christians become πνευματικοί, (that is, mature), as they reject the deeds and understanding of the flesh, and pursue the control and enlightenment of the Spirit.[73]

While Davis recognizes the important links between 2.14-16 and 3.1-4, the latter is not merely a counterpart of the former; Paul's remarks in 3.1-4 relate to and expand earlier portions of his argument in crucial ways, and such portions cannot be overlooked. Moreover Davis' treatment deals primarily with specific views of wisdom and only secondarily with the issue of party-strife.

However, Kuck offers a reading for 1.10–4.21 that sees "false valuations of wisdom" and party-strife as "complementary"[74] concerns for Paul. In terms of structure,[75] following the general introduction and thesis (i.e. 1.10-17), Paul addresses the topic of wisdom (1.18–2.16), where he offers a corrective for the Corinthians' distorted view of it. Then, as a reminder of the plea for unity among believers, 3.1-4 functions as a transition from the discussion of wisdom to that of party-strife, the latter being the substance of 3.5–4.5. The remainder of the argument (4.6-21) serves as Paul's attempt to recapitulate his primary concerns, but to do so in the light of what he has just argued. This reading has commendable aspects. As Kuck states, it

> can be used as a key to understanding Paul's analysis of the situation and his rhetorical aim. Paul sees the fundamental

---

[73] Davis, *Wisdom and Spirit*, 130-31.

[74] D.W. Kuck, *Judgment and Community Conflict: Paul's Use of Apocalyptic Judgment Language in 1 Corinthians 3:5–4:5* (Leiden: Brill, 1992), 154.

[75] What follows is a summary of Kuck—see *ibid.*, 154-55.

problem in the Corinthian church to be a tendency for individuals to seek status in the congregation on the basis of their demonstration of spiritual wisdom. One visible result of this pursuit of spiritual status has been a divisive weighing of the community's teachers against one another.[76]

While this reading is able to hold in balance the "complementary" topics of party-strife and faulty views of wisdom, and while we can certainly read 3.1-4 as being a part of that balance, it is not helpful to see it simply as a transitional statement. The content and function of 3.1-4 play an integral role for sustaining the balance of Paul's discussion and why he opposes divisions and faulty views of wisdom. We will keep this role in mind as we proceed.

4.4.2. Appeal to the Corinthians' Present Situation

We now turn our attention to the content of 3.1-4, specifically the appeal to the Corinthians' present situation. Since this letter is not Paul's first contact with the Corinthians, we need to consider which one he likely has in mind and for what reason. It is possible to assume that Paul, in 3.1-4, returns once more to the circumstances of his original visit.[77] This assumption rests not only on the thematic parallels associated with κἀγὼ ἀδελφοί (cf. 2.1; 3.1), but also on the implied time references of the verbal ideas specifically in 3.1-2b. Accordingly, the acts of speaking and giving metaphorical sustenance are portrayed as past events, and given the context of the argument it would make sense to assume that these

---

[76] *Ibid.*, 155.

[77] Cf. Kistemaker, *Exposition*, 100; Collins, *First Corinthians*, 142; Garland, *1 Corinthians*, 105. So also by implication, see Robertson-Plummer, *First Epistle*, 52 (cf. 29).

past events refer to Paul's original proclamation.[78] On the surface, this reading accounts for why Paul says it was impossible for him to speak to the Corinthians then as πνευματικοί—i.e. when he first arrived they had not yet heard or received the gospel and therefore could not be recipients of God's Spirit. However, given the rest of the argument—especially Paul's description of the Corinthians as, ἐν Χριστῷ—this reading seems to create more problems than it solves.[79] Thus we must consider an alternative.

A second possibility would be to assume that Paul has in mind the non-extant letter mentioned in 1 Cor 5.9, a letter that *predates* the composition of 1 Corinthians. Given Paul's summary in 5.9-13, specifically the emphasis on proper treatment of immoral people both within the community and those not identified with it,[80] we could say this lost letter was occasioned by the Corinthians' failure to exercise spiritual discernment properly, a failure resulting from an immature spirituality. The implication of 5.9-13 is that the Corinthians were welcoming and associating with immoral people who call themselves ἀδελφοί, and were therefore obscuring the line between those "in Christ" and those who are not.[81]

This approach would account for not only the past-tense references in 3.1-2b but also Paul's description of the Corinthians as both σαρκινοί and νήπιοι ἐν Χριστῷ. If the summary of 5.9-

---

[78] Cf. Hunt, *Inspired Body*, 93-94.

[79] To paraphrase Fee: one cannot be in Christ and lack God's Spirit (see *First Epistle*, 123).

[80] Cf. Schrage, *Der erste Brief*, 1.388-89.

[81] This obscuring of the line is what raises concerns for Paul about the identity of the community of believers. As Meeks points out, Pauline churches "enjoyed an unusual degree of intimacy, high levels of interaction among members, and a very strong sense of internal cohesion and of distinction both from outsiders and from 'the world' " (*First Urban Christians: The Social World of the Apostle Paul* [New Haven: Yale University Press, 1983], 74; cf. also Tucker, *You Belong to Christ*, 224).

13 is any indication of their behavior or actions since receiving the gospel, then these descriptions are apropos. However, apart from the reference to his past experience with the Corinthians, there is nothing in 3.1-2b that would lead us to conclude Paul is referring specifically to the non-extant letter. If he were thinking of that letter here in 3.1-2b, we would expect a reference similar to what we have in 5.9—i.e. ἔγραψα ὑμῖν ἐν τῇ ἐπιστολῇ.

A third possibility assumes that Paul is referring to the full duration of his 18-month sojourn in Corinth (cf. Acts 18.11),[82] which would include not only the initial proclamation to and the establishment of the ἐκκλησία but also the early stages of its development. With an awareness of and reliance on theories of group formation, Robertson reminds us that "[d]evelopmentally speaking, the Corinthian community at the time of Paul's writing lay far closer to 'brand new' than to 'firmly established' "[83] group. Accordingly, we should not expect to find a perfect community operating according to God's wisdom absolutely, much less employing Spirit-led discernment consistently; there might be some in Corinth who do so, but certainly not all.

Superficially this would seem to bring us back to the issue of a stratification of believers in Corinth. However, as Fee contends, given the context Paul does not intend "to suggest classes of Christians or grades of spirituality, but to get them to stop *thinking* like the people of this present age. [Moreover], he wants them to stop *behaving* like the people of the present age, which is the point at hand."[84] The tension between God's wisdom and the world's and the relationship between thought and behavior are what prevent Paul's remarks from being seen as endorsing levels or tiers of belief. Therefore we should not read the focus as dealing with

---

[82] Grosheide, *First Epistle*, 78; Morris, *First Epistle*, 61.

[83] Robertson, *Conflict in Corinth*, 8.

[84] Fee, *First Epistle*, 122—emphasis original.

internal stratification; instead the focus remains on the distinction between those within the community (believers) and those without (non-believers). For Paul the Corinthians, while ἐν Χριστῷ, are thinking and behaving as though they are not—a result of relying on worldly wisdom rather than God's, mediated by the Spirit.[85]

This reading is preferable for at least two reasons. First, it has the advantage of accounting for the implied time references in the passage. In doing so, it raises an intriguing observation. If it is true that 3.1-2b refers to the whole of Paul's original sojourn, and if the description he provides relates to that 18-month period, it would appear that the Corinthians began to exhibit early on traits not necessarily in harmony with their believing the gospel and receiving God's Spirit. In other words, this reading would suggest that the Corinthians began to think and behave in ways contrary to God's wisdom, or ways not in accordance with the revelation of God's Spirit, while Paul was still with them. Thus, Paul's awareness of the problems in Corinth—specifically faulty views of wisdom and spirituality—came not simply from the reports delivered to him by Chloe's people; his awareness is initially based on first-hand experience, only to be confirmed by the subsequent report. Second, this reading accounts for the specific details of the passage, or how Paul describes the Corinthians and his interactions with them. Let us consider each of these in turn.

---

[85] Both Inkelaar and Tucker, while independent of each other, are helpful on this point when taken together. For Inkelaar, the "conflict [in Corinth] presented in the text is not a conflict between movements, parties, leaders, or traditions but a conflict between two manifestations of wisdom" (*Conflict Over Wisdom*, 20). For Tucker, the manifestation of wisdom would be the criterion by which the Corinthians identify themselves, not only as individual believers but as a community in Christ. The conflict Tucker emphasizes is that some Corinthians "were continuing to identify primarily with key aspects of their Roman social identity rather than their identity 'in Christ'" (*You Belong to Christ*, 2).

4.4.2.1. The Corinthians as σαρκινοί

While some commentators see Paul giving the term a slightly difference nuance in 3.3, his use of σάρκινος here in 3.1 is virtually synonymous with ψυχικός in 2.14—i.e. those without God's Spirit.[86] However, Kuck cautions that we must be careful not to draw too close a parallel between σάρκινος and ψυχικός.[87] The reason for the caution stems from an awareness of what Paul is doing in 3.1-2b in relation to what he does in 2.14-16. While the time reference in 3.1-2b calls to mind Paul's preaching ministry in Corinth, he does not wish to say the Corinthians are now exactly as they were then when he first arrived; something marks them now as changed. The change in view can simply be described as the Corinthians having or receiving the Spirit upon belief. Thus, as Kuck observes, "Paul cannot use ψυχικός, because he does not intend to call their [present] faith into question";[88] rhetorically, the recollection is therefore employed for the sake of comparing the Corinthians' present status with how they were initially.

Moreover, by labeling this present status as σάρκινος instead of ψυχικός, Paul is calling attention to the moral aspects associated with the former in a way that parallels his description of τὰ ἔργα τῆς σαρκός (see Gal 5.19-21). Thus, with regard to the Corinthian situation, the question is not the reality of the Spirit's presence in the believing community but the morality of those claiming to be spiritual. On this reading, the Corinthians' status is portrayed as *spiritual* in the sense that they received God's Spirit when they first believed; yet their *behavior* and ways of thinking

---

[86] See e.g. Robertson-Plummer, *First Epistle*, 36, 49; B.A. Pearson, "Hellenistic-Jewish Wisdom Speculation and Paul," in *Aspects of Wisdom in Judaism and Early Christianity* (ed. R.L. Wilcken; Notre Dame: University of Notre Dame Press, 1975), 64 n.45. *Contra* Fee, *First Epistle*, 124.

[87] See Kuck, *Judgment and Community*, 159-60.

[88] *Ibid.*, 160; cf. Godet, *First Epistle*, 164-65.

give the impression they do not have God's Spirit.[89] Accordingly, for Paul, the Corinthians *appear* to be people of flesh and not of the Spirit.

4.4.2.2. The Corinthians as νηπίοι ἐν Χριστῷ

Admittedly, νηπίοις ἐν Χριστῷ is difficult to interpret for the simple fact that it appears nowhere else in the NT. Commentators therefore offer varying suggestions for how to understand this unique description. Some assume that the phrase relates to an early period of faith in Christ, where the Corinthian believers are simply beginning their process of maturity.[90] This would seem to make sense in the light of Paul's use of τέλειος in 2.6, which serves as the ideal or desired goal of Christian existence. On this reading, one begins as an infant and then progresses toward spiritual adulthood.[91] In terms of how to know when the transition occurs, one scholar interprets "babes in Christ" to mean those "who as yet

---

[89] Cf. J. Francis, "'As Babes in Christ'—Some Proposals Regarding 1 Corinthians 3:1-3," *JSNT* 7 (1980): 41; C.T. Rhyne, "1 Corinthians 3:1-9," *Int* 44.2 (1990): 175-76; N. Watson, *The First Epistle to the Corinthians* (London: Epworth, 1992), 28.

[90] See e.g. C.A.A. Scott, *Christianity According to St Paul* (Cambridge: Cambridge University Press, 1927), 173, 175; L.G. Cox, "Sin in Believers," *Wesleyan Theological Journal* 1 (1966): 30; H.T.S. Blaney, "St Paul's Posture on Speaking in Unknown Tongues," *Wesleyan Theological Journal* 8 (1973): 53, 55.

[91] Wesley employs this analogy when defining the nature of Christian perfection, wrought by the work of the Spirit: "I do not say, that every real Christian can declare with the Marquis de Renty, 'I bear about with me continually an experimental verity, and a plenitude of the presence of the ever-blessed Trinity.' I apprehend this is not the experience of 'babes,' but rather of 'fathers in Christ' " ("On the Trinity," sermon 60 in *Sermons on Several Occasions* [vol. 2; Ne York: B. Waugh and T. Mason, 1836], 24; cf. idem, "Letter VII," in *Original Letters, by the Rev. John Wesley and His Friends* [ed. J. Priestly; Birmingham: Thomas Pearson, 1791], 32; idem, *Christian Perfection* [Cincinnati: Jennings & Pye, 1800], 22, 42, 125).

[have] not manifest the gifts of the Spirit, or who [have] not yet been taken into full membership".[92] This reading, however, creates space for internal boasting of spiritual status—a possibility that Paul rejects. Others suggest a double meaning for νήπιος where on the one hand it refers to how the Corinthians are behaving—i.e. like immature children—while on the other hand it refers to the infancy of their belief.[93] Thus, behaving like immature children is reason enough for believers needing to progress or mature in their faith.[94]

This second option seems to account for the basic features of the metaphor and it harmonizes two key related details: 1) Paul's remarks in 3.1-2b as a description of the Corinthians since the proclamation of the gospel—especially their current status,[95] and thus 2) the distinction between non-belief and belief, and how Paul's use of νήπιος is linked with that distinction and not stages of belief. Syntactically and logically the phrase ὡς νηπίοις ἐν Χριστῷ is intimately tied to the descriptive phrase ὡς σαρκίνοις,

---

[92] Nichols, "Two-Level Christianity," 109.

[93] Koenig, "From Mystery to Ministry," 168; J.D. Ekem, "'Spiritual Gifts' or 'Spiritual Persons'? 1 Corinthians 12:1a Revisited," *Neot* 38.1 (2004): 58.

[94] Cf. T. Engberg-Pedersen, "The Gospel and Social Practice according to 1 Corinthians," *NTS* 33.4 (1987): 567-68.

[95] Deluz's argument in this regard is not entirely helpful: "When Paul came for the first time to preach the Gospel in Corinth, the Christians there were still *babes in Christ*" (*Companion to 1 Corinthians*, 33—emphasis original). In this way, it seems as though the Corinthians were already believers when Paul came to them initially. However, as Hunt contends: "Since, at the time of Paul's initial preaching, the Corinthians could not already have been Christians, Paul clearly could not have spoken to them *then* (cf. λαλέω in 3:1) as he does *now* after their conversion (cf. the same verb in 2:6)....Moreover, before they were Christians, they could not have been πνευματικοί (3:1) since such a term signifies existence in the Spirit" (*Inspired Body*, 93-94—emphasis added; cf. I. Edman, *The Mind of Paul* [New York: Henry Holt and Company, 1935], 178).

with the former being an alternate expression for the latter.[96] Accordingly, since I said σάρκινος refers to the moral or behavioral status of the Corinthians at the time of Paul's writing, I must also say νήπιος describes the same status.

By seeing νήπιος in this way, instead of primarily as a reference to an infantile faith in need of maturing, though that does become a part of it, we are better able to square what Paul says here with what he claims about the Corinthians in 1.5-7. As Francis points out, if we read νήπιος in 3.1 as indicating the Corinthians' *present* failure to advance or grow in faith, this then conflicts with Paul's admonishing them in 1.5-7 for being enriched in all things, lacking in nothing.[97] Thus we would have to say that Paul is either inconsistent in 3.1 when compared with 1.5-7 or he merely feigns gratitude in 1.5-7.[98] If, however, we take νήπιος as a qualitative description of one's moral thinking and behavior, rather than a point on a faith-continuum, then we avoid both the potential inconsistency and the issue of false praise. Or, as Francis puts it: "As an alternative,...Paul is rebuking his readers not because they are babes still, and had not progressed further, but because they were in fact being childish, a condition contrary to being spiritual."[99]

Before proceeding, we should examine at least two reasons for interpreting νήπιος as both qualitative and "a condition contrary to being spiritual" or mature (cf. 2.6). First, semantically, while νήπιος does describe a particular stage in human growth, it also carries the general idea of immaturity or being underdeveloped cognitively or even behaviorally. This type of nuance emphasizes

---

[96] Godet, *First Epistle*, 165.

[97] Francis, "'As Babes in Christ'," 43; cf. Godet, *First Epistle*, 165.

[98] Conzelmann sees a disagreement between 3.3 and 1.5, yet explains the conflict by labelling 3.3 "an *ad hoc* statement" (*1 Corinthians*, 72).

[99] Francis, "'As Babes in Christ'," 43.

or describes the lack of what is desired or should be the case, and when specifically applied to knowledge it bears the pejorative meaning of folly or foolishness. [100] The second reason is theological. When we read the whole of Paul's argument, especially the contrast between folly and wisdom, unbelief and belief, "natural" and "spiritual," we see νήπιος as an appropriate counterpart to τέλειος in 2.6, the latter referring to those who have received God's wisdom by the revelation of the Spirit. As noted earlier, a consequence of this involves a new way of knowing (or discerning)—i.e. it is characterized as Spirit-given and led. Thus, νήπιος maintains the overall contrast that has been at work all along, namely not only the distinction between those who believe and from those who do not but also the manner of thinking and behaving within the distinctive groups. For Paul the distinction therefore is not infant-faith versus adult-faith—a topic that presupposes stages of belief—but incomplete (or foolish) knowledge versus complete (or wise) knowledge.

4.4.2.3. The Diet of γάλα and βρῶμα

In keeping with the idea that 3.1-2b refers to Paul's original sojourn in Corinth, we must examine Paul's metaphor of sustenance and how it relates to his apostolic work. Some commentators read the metaphor of γάλα and βρῶμα as referring not just to levels of content in Paul's teaching but also to when such levels would be appropriately taught. On this reading, γάλα refers to Paul's initial proclamation where the absolute basics of the gospel were presented, and βρῶμα refers to a more intimate or in-depth wisdom teaching reserved for a later period in spiritual

---

[100] This reflects other Pauline texts using νήπιος that refer not only to those ὑπὸ τὰ στοιχεῖα τοῦ κόσμου ἤμεθα δεδουλωμένοι, before the revelation of Christ (Gal 4.3), but also those under the tutelage of blind-guides and foolish teachers (Rom 2.19-20).

maturity. An example of this approach is found in Grosheide who takes γάλα as simple "missionary preaching" and βρῶμα as "preaching to convinced Christians in which it is possible to unfold the full richness, the magnificence of the gospel."[101]

In a slightly more nuanced way, Robertson-Plummer interpret γάλα as the message of Christ crucified in 2.2 and βρῶμα as the explanation of the revelation of God's wisdom to the believer in 2.6-13. [102] The underlying assumption is that this deeper-level teaching (βρῶμα) was not a part of the original proclamation (γάλα); Paul withheld it from the Corinthians until they were able to receive it.[103] However, this reading seems to perpetuate the idea of levels of spirituality in Corinth—or stages of Christian belief— when part of Paul's argument is distinguishing believers from non-believers, especially their respective ways of knowing. In the other part, which can be seen as the thrust of the argument, Paul subverts the claims of those in Corinth who claim spiritual superiority and think they are able to consume true "meat," by calling them "babes" (i.e. inferior) who can only handle "milk".

Other commentators read γάλα and βρῶμα together as referring to nourishment in general rather than competing types or

---

[101] Grosheide, *First Epistle*, 79.

[102] Robertson-Plummer, *First Epistle*, 52.

[103] Cf. Goudge, *First Epistle*, 23; Deluz, *Companion to 1 Corinthians*, 34; Conzelmann, *1 Corinthians*, 71; Talbert, *Reading Corinthians*, 6; Kistemaker, *Exposition*, 101; Mare-Harris, *1, 2 Corinthians*, 33; Keener, *1–2 Corinthians*, 40. Morris appears to argue with the same assumption, however it is admittedly uncertain given the relative vagueness of his treatment (see *First Epistle*, 1986, 61; cf. Soards, *1 Corinthians*, 67). Litfin rightly points out that "Paul never equates βρῶμα with σοφία and it is misleading for commentators to conflate 3.2 with 2.6 in such a way as to make it appear that he does" (*Theology of Proclamation*, 222).

degrees of substance or consistency.[104] Part of the reasoning for taking the terms together as referring to a single action is that the entire phrase represents a zeugma, or an elliptical expression used for rhetorical effect. Since both γάλα and βρῶμα are accusatives for the single verb, ποτίζω, it would make little sense to say, "I did not give you solid food to drink." If Paul were indeed speaking of a distinction between types of teaching, metaphorically distinguished by γάλα and βρῶμα, then we would expect him to supply verbal ideas appropriate to the imagery. In this case, ποτίζω for γάλα and ἐσθίω for βρῶμα (cf. 1 Cor 11.26). Given that he uses only one verb, which technically only applies to one of the accusatives,[105] it makes better sense (on this reading) to say he is referring to something more general—i.e. nourishment.

However, despite the apparent parallel between 1) γάλα and βρῶμα and 2) general nourishment, Paul does seem to indicate a distinction between the *types* of nourishment and that each is conducive for a particular context. This distinction is made apparent by the negative οὐ in 3.2b as indicating what he did not supply to the Corinthians, over and against the affirmative claim in 3.2a.[106] Thus, by stating that he initially gave the Corinthians γάλα and not βρῶμα, Paul stresses the point that he made necessary concessions for the Corinthians by supplying them with food conducive for their maturity—i.e. νηπίοις ἐν Χριστῷ.[107] What is

---

[104] Cf. e.g. M.D. Hooker, "Hard Sayings: 1 Cor 3:2," *Theology* 69 (1966): 20-21; Fee, *First Epistle*, 125-26; Thiselton, *First Epistle*, 291-92; Garland, *1 Corinthians*, 106-08; Fitzmyer, *First Corinthians*, 187.

[105] Conzelmann, *1 Corinthians*, 70 n.4.

[106] Schnackenburg mistakenly reads the "nourishment" of 3.2a as the contents of the letter to the Corinthians (see "Christian Adulthood," 357).

[107] While the initial focus falls on the kind of food given, there is the secondary emphasis that Paul is the one who initially supplied the appropriate food (cf. B.R. Gaventa, "Mother's Milk and Ministry in 1 Corinthians 3," in *Theology and Ethics in Paul and His Interpreters: Essays in Honor of Victor*

problematic now, at the time of writing, is that the Corinthians—despite their own views or perceptions—have not matured and cannot therefore receive solid food. Instead, they have remained as they originally were—i.e. νηπίοις ἐν Χριστῷ, only able to ingest milk. Therefore, once again, Paul must now make concessions to accommodate their present (spiritual) immaturity, despite what their actual spiritual status is—i.e. πνευματικοί.

4.4.2.4. Relevance of the Appeal

The specifics of the initial appeal in 3.1-2b are crucial for our understanding of Paul's larger argument. The function of this appeal is not only to situate the Corinthians' present dilemma, in the sense that they are essentially thinking and behaving as though they lacked God's Spirit, but also to stress the theological tension between what they should be and what they are.[108] Paul achieves this by first reminding them of his original visit and their change of status as a result of that visit—i.e. from non-believers to "in Christ." Moreover, Paul reminds the Corinthians of how he "nourished" them during his sojourn: he fed them in accordance with their need. However, while their past soteriological status

---

Paul Furnish [eds. E.H. Lovering, Jr. and J.L. Sumney; Nashville: Abingdon Press, 1996], 101-13). This imagery is reflected in his later comment in 3.6, when he alters the metaphor and emphasizes his role as the one who supplies (or "plants") the seed—i.e. the gospel. Moreover, the imagery of providing drink and its relationship to initial belief in the gospel is also reflected in Paul's later comments in 12.13: καὶ γὰρ ἐν ἑνὶ πνεύματι ἡμεῖς πάντες εἰς ἓν σῶμα ἐβαπτίσθημεν...καὶ πάντες ἓν πνεῦμα ἐποτίσθημεν. Especially relevant for our purposes are the ties between "drink" and the Spirit noted here in 12.13 and the implications of Paul's argument in 3.1-2, for it was in supplying the Corinthians with "drink" (the gospel) that they received the Spirit and thus became "spiritual" people.

[108] As Schnabel observes: "Der Abschnitt 3,1-4 behandelt die Orientierung der Korinther an menschlichen Maßstäben, die ihrem tatsächlichen Status als ‚Vollkommene' widerspricht" (*Der erste Brief*, 183).

underwent a significant change post-gospel, their present epistemological framework (and by extension, behavior) evidences no recognizable change. Hence, the Corinthians do not exhibit the characteristics of πνευματικοί thus inhibiting Paul from providing suitable nourishment. All of this establishes one side of the contrast Paul seeks to make, a contrast used explicitly to move the Corinthians away from the ways of thinking and behaving that are in opposition to the wisdom of God and the mind of Christ.

4.4.3. Paul Employing Spiritual Discernment

When we come to the second portion of Paul's assessment (3.2c-4), we see him shifting the focus from his original visit to the present situation. This shift is signaled by the emphatic phrase, ἀλλ' οὐδὲ ἔτι νῦν δύνασθε· ἔτι γὰρ σαρκικοί ἐστε (3.2c-3a). These two accusations share a cause-and-effect relationship: at present the Corinthians are unable to receive proper nourishment because (γὰρ) they are still σαρκικοί. Scholars often point out the subtle transition from σαρκινός in 3.1 to σαρκικός here in 3.3 and attempt to tease out its importance for Paul's argument. [109] Accordingly, σαρκινός describes the "stuff" of a person's makeup while σαρκικός refers to the ethical or moral dimension of the person's existence. However, Thiselton objects to this approach because the distinction is made on the grounds of morphology rather than semantics. [110] As an alternative, Thiselton notes both the overlap in essential meaning between the two terms and the distinctive emphases on that essential meaning. Specifically, Thiselton reads σαρκινός as a "descriptive" term while σαρκικός

---

[109] E.g. Fee, *First Epistle*, 124-27 (cf. 121 ns.1, 3); Kistemaker, *Exposition*, 102, 104; Mare-Harris, *1, 2 Corinthians*, 34; Collins, *First Corinthians*, 143-44; Soards, *1 Corinthians*, 66-68; Garland, *1 Corinthians*, 109.

[110] See Thiselton, *First Epistle*, 288-89, 291-93.

is "evaluative";[111] the one defines life as ostensibly without the Spirit, while the other stresses the negative theological consequences of that life.

In this way, σαρκικός carries with it ideas similar to what we see in Paul's use of σάρξ elsewhere,[112] specifically as a way of being that is in opposition to the ways of God.[113] In Rom 8.4-9, Paul emphasizes the fact that, because of the work of Christ, believers are no longer to live in the sphere of the "flesh" or they are no longer to be governed by the ways of the "flesh." Instead, their minds (and by extension their lives) are to operate in accordance with the Spirit (οἱ γὰρ κατὰ σάρκα ὄντες τὰ τῆς σαρκὸς φρονοῦσιν, οἱ δὲ κατὰ πνεῦμα τὰ τοῦ πνεύματος [Rom 8.5]).[114] In Gal 5.16-17 we see Paul stressing the reality that while believers are to live in accordance with the Spirit, the life of the "flesh" continues to be a possibility—i.e. it is possible for believers to slip back into the ways of the "flesh." However, in both Galatians and 1 Corinthians, Paul does not endorse compatibility between the life of the "flesh" and life in the Spirit; the believer cannot live in both worlds.

Thus, with the revelation of God's wisdom via the Spirit and the subsequent result of having "the mind of Christ," Paul expects

---

[111] *Ibid.*, 293.

[112] Watson lists three major ways in which "flesh" language appears in Paul's letters (see *First Epistle*, 28). In one sense, the meaning is benign; it simply refers to a category of being (cf. Rom 4.1; 1 Cor 1.26). In a second sense, it describes the mortality of humanity as a result of separation from God. Accordingly, "flesh" emphasizes the weakness and frailty of human existence (cf. Rom 6.19; 8.3; 2 Cor 4.11). Finally, "flesh" language in Paul stresses the reality and effects of sinfulness, and how the "flesh" manifests that reality in how a person lives—i.e. in opposition to the ways of God (cf. Rom 7.5, 18; 8.3-12). Cf. also Thiselton, *First Epistle*, 288-89.

[113] Cf. B.J. Malina and J.J. Pilch, *Social-Science Commentary on the Letters of Paul* (Minneapolis: Fortress, 2006), 186.

[114] Cf. Keener, *1–2 Corinthians*, 40.

this twofold reality to manifest itself in thought and behavior (cf. Gal 5.22). This expectation becomes the standard against which Paul measures the Corinthians' present situation in 3.2c-4. In other words, Paul compares the ideal picture of the τέλειος/πνευ- ματικός of 2.6-16, an ideal that should be actualized by those who have the Spirit and "the mind of Christ," with the reality that the Corinthians do not at present reflect (nor have they in the past reflected) this ideal picture.

Since Paul's argument thus far has dealt with the question of knowledge (or ways of knowing), the ability to know and how such things affect life in the community and the world, it should not surprise us that Paul's brief comparison addresses a similar connection. Specifically, by calling the Corinthians σαρκικοί, Paul suggests that they are operating according to a standard other than the Spirit—much less the mind of Christ. Instead, the Corinthians are operating according to the standard (or mindset) which they possessed before Paul arrived to proclaim the gospel, a standard that is not "spiritual" but "of the flesh." The fundamental problem for Paul is that this should not be the case, since as a result of the gospel the standard "of the flesh" was replaced with the "spiritual" standard—i.e. the mind of Christ, given by God's Spirit.

It is here that we find Paul stressing the connection between mindset and behavior, specifically when he asks, οὐχὶ σαρκικοί ἐστε καὶ κατὰ ἄνθρωπον περιπατεῖτε; (3.3c). In this instance σαρκικός refers to the mindset at work, and the copulative verb suggests a state-of-being, and περιπατέω refers to the expression or behavior that follows, which Paul further qualifies as κατὰ ἄνθρωπον. The justification (or evidence) Paul gives for his claim is the existence of "jealousy" and "strife" within the community of believers. [115] For Paul, jealousy and strife are recognizable manifestations not of the Spirit or the mind of Christ but of the flesh, which is in opposition to the Spirit (cf. Rom 13.13; 2 Cor 12.20; Gal 5.20). [116]

Moreover, for Paul "jealousy" and "strife" are not endorsed by the gospel; neither are they motivated by love nor concerned with the benefit of the community. Instead, "jealousy" and "strife" are the result of the mindset characterized or even shaped by self-love and self-interest. [117] However, as Paul argues elsewhere, οἱ δὲ τοῦ Χριστοῦ τὴν σάρκα ἐσταύρωσαν σὺν τοῖς παθήμασιν καὶ ταῖς ἐπιθυμίαις (Gal 5.24). It is from this "crucifixion" that those who belong to Christ are granted a new life in Christ via the Spirit, which therefore means this new life is to be lived in accordance with "the mind of Christ" given by Spirit. [118] This expectation drives Paul's present critique of the Corinthians, for it is precisely this expectation that they have failed to meet.

Paul completes this stage of his argument by restating his earlier concern in 1.11-12, although this time he provides an

---

[115] A few key manuscripts add a third term to this list: διχοστασία (see 𝔓⁴⁶, D, G, 33, 614, 𝔐, a, b, syr, Irenaeus, Cyprian). However, a wider manuscript tradition supports the lack of the term (see p¹¹, ℵ, A, B, C, P, Ψ, 0289, 81, 630, 1175, 1506, 1739, 1881, r, vul, cop, Clement, Origen, Ambrosiaster). As Metzger points out, the inclusion of the term is accounted for by a scribe's familiarity with the vice-list in Gal 5.20, which includes διχοστασία (see *Textual Commentary*, 482-83).

[116] Paul at least sees "strife" as influential in the party-spirit noted in 1.11-12, with the result that the body of Christ is being divided.

[117] Cf. Ellis, *Prophecy and Hermeneutic*, 69.

[118] It is worth noting Paul's use of κατὰ πνεῦμα περιπατεῖν in Rom 8.4 and 5, which functions as a conceptual antithesis to the κατὰ ἄνθρωπον περιπατεῖν here in 3.3. Moreover, as Schnabel points out: "the phrase κατὰ πνεῦμα περιπατεῖν...implies that the Spirit is not only the foundation and power of the Christian life but also indicates the 'how' of Christian behavior" (*Law and Wisdom*, 327).

explanation for the dilemma. Specifically Paul asks: ὅταν γὰρ λέγῃ τις· ἐγὼ μέν εἰμι Παύλου, ἕτερος δὲ· ἐγὼ Ἀπολλῶ, οὐκ ἄνθρωποί ἐστε; (3.4). The focus here is not so much on a particular instance in the recent past or a possible future occurrence, nor is it primarily about specific individuals, though that does play a role;[119] rather the focus is on the act itself. For Paul, the moment someone claims allegiance to a person or a specific name is evidence of that person thinking and behaving like a mere human (cf. 2.14) rather than one filled with and guided by the Spirit—i.e. πνευματικός.[120] For in asserting allegiance to a name or another person, that assertion is neither motivated by love nor the benefit of the community as a whole; rather the effects of the assertion are division and selfish admiration or elevation of specific individuals.

All of this, for Paul, is inconsistent with the message of the gospel and the life (and mindset) that is expected of those who have embraced the gospel as God's wisdom (cf. 1.26-31). Moreover, we see Paul continuing to emphasize the links between mindset and expression or behavior, and in the light of his remarks about the "natural" person in 2.14 and the similar terminology employed in an equally similar polemical fashion, we can see Paul's rebuke here in 3.4 as a comparison between what the Corinthians should be and what they are. The force or sting of his argument is that their behavior betrays no difference when,

---

[119] Although it is worth pointing out that the list of options in this regard has been reduced to two, rather than the four mentioned in 1.12. Because of this narrowing of focus, there does seem to be a concern with Paul and Apollos in particular. However it appears as though Paul stresses these names to illustrate or provide specific examples of how the Corinthians' faulty human ways of thinking operate.

[120] A small number of manuscripts replace ἄνθρωποι with σαρκικοί (א[2], Ψ, 𝔐, syr), presumably either to maintain continuity with 3.3 (i.e. οὐχὶ σαρκικοί ἐστε) or to stress the contrast between "spirit" and "flesh".

because of the Spirit (and the assumed transformation of mind and life), there should be a radical difference. However, there appears to be something else at work in Paul's critique of the Corinthian situation, something implicit yet foundational.

4.4.4. Paul's Implicit Expectation and Rebuke

We have established that Paul is addressing the Corinthians' current status, in that he sees them behaving as though they did not have the Spirit. Moreover, I have maintained that Paul is concerned about the type of discernment the Corinthians are employing to assess the gospel and Paul as an apostolic witness. In this case that type of discernment is characterized as "natural" and defined by human wisdom, a form of wisdom that Paul sees as inadequate and inappropriate for judging both the message of God's wisdom in the cross and those who proclaim it.

Within what Paul says, there is an implicit expectation and therefore rebuke in the light of the fact that the Corinthians received God's Spirit when they first believed. The expectation is that the manner of thought or discernment exercised by the Corinthians should be that which proceeds from God's Spirit. Moreover, since the reception of God's Spirit brings with it a new paradigm of thought (or epistemology), and this new paradigm necessarily alters how believers understand and live life, Paul expects the Corinthians, as spiritual people, to live in accordance with "the mind of Christ."

The implicit rebuke in all of this is that the Corinthians have not relied on what they have received from God, and the effect of this can be illustrated in their divisiveness or self-interested desires to rally around particular names. In other words, they are collectively not acting as Spirit-led people, living in accordance with the singular mind of Christ; instead they are acting as mere humans who divide themselves according to status, defined by the categories of human wisdom.

We could also reasonably say their lack of Spirit-led communal discernment, filtered through the cross and the mind of Christ, stands behind the dilemmas they currently face. Thus, another side of Paul's rebuke is that if this Spirit-led communal discernment were operating in Corinth, they could have either prevented or settled the issues they now bring to the Apostle. Consequently, because they have not done this, Paul must respond and he does as an arbiter of internal conflicts and the needed voice of wise counsel. We will explore this theme in the final chapter.

4.5. Conclusions

This chapter set out to explore Paul's differentiation between two types of discernment. We found that Paul sees only one type as appropriate for those who belong to Christ, whereas the other type has no place in the believing community. The appropriateness of the one over the other was demonstrated in the fact that only spiritual discernment can know the things of God, specifically that which is revealed by God's Spirit, which in turn defines the new life in Christ; natural discernment fails on all of these counts.

From this we examined the particular details of Paul's assessment of the Corinthian situation. It was shown here that Paul remained consistent with his own explanation of what constitutes spiritual discernment and how it is exercised. Paul was able to discern the root cause for the dilemma(s) in Corinth and respond accordingly. Implicit in this is the rebuke that if the Corinthians relied on the same spiritual discernment, they would not have formed negative conclusions about the nature of the gospel or Paul's apostolic witness and they would have handled their conflicts appropriately. However, as it is, the Corinthians lack the unity of mind necessary for right discernment of what is God's wisdom and how that wisdom shapes true spiritual life.

Chapter 5
APPLYING SPIRIT-GUIDED, COMMUNAL DISCERNMENT

5.1. Introduction

To conclude this study, I return to some basic questions posed at the beginning that have hitherto gone unanswered, or at least have not received explicit attention. These questions can be divided broadly into two categories: thematic and rhetorical. First, what is the relationship between Paul's pneumatological teaching in 1 Cor 2.1–3.4 and the rest of the letter? Specifically, how do the interrelated themes of Spirit, cross, wisdom, and (communal) discernment apply to the immediate context of 3.5–4.21, which deals with the Corinthians' assessment of the apostolic ministry, and the wider context of chapters 5–15, which addresses the Corinthians' particular communal or ecclesial struggles? Following a summary of thematic relationships, the bulk of this chapter will engage with these questions.

Second, why does the pneumatological teaching of 2.1–3.4 appear where it does in Paul's argument? Why does Paul not articulate this teaching when dealing with the topic of "spiritual things" in chapter 12–14? More specifically, what is the purpose of offering this pneumatological teaching sooner rather than later? What are the rhetorical and theological implications for such an early placement? These questions will be taken up in the final portion of this chapter.

5.2. Summary of Thematic Relationships

This summary serves two functions. First, it consolidates the findings of this entire study on the Pauline themes of Spirit, cross, wisdom, and (communal) discernment. In general, this summary emphasizes the interrelationship of these four themes and in particular the Spirit's essential role in the proclamation of the cross, the mediation of divine wisdom, and the establishment and exercise of communal discernment. Second, this summary provides the basic framework for examining the rest of Paul's argument in 1 Corinthians, especially the way in which the key themes relate to or even influence that argument.

5.2.1. Cross and the Spirit

With the theme of the cross, Paul emphasizes his role as a proclaimer of "the word of the cross" (1.18a), a role that could be classified as a divine (christological) commission (cf. 1.17a-b). Implicit to this emphasis is the link between identity and behavior—i.e. how Paul conducts himself as an apostolic herald follows directly from who he is and what he is called to be. This identity-behavior connection is further bound up with the message he proclaims—i.e. all that Paul does and how he views himself are intimately tied to the gospel of Christ crucified.

And just as the cross is a sign of shame, folly, and weakness in the eyes of the world, so too are Paul's message, person, and manner of preaching. Paul proclaimed God's "folly" of the cross (1.21) and nothing else (2.2), and he recognized the humiliation of the cross and declared it with humble reverence (2.3). Furthermore, Paul's proclamation reflected the unadorned nature of the cross by his unpolished manner of speech (2.1, 4a), for if he relied on eloquent speech he would not only fail to reflect the nature of the cross but also portray it as something other than what it is. Or, as he asserts: to rely on wise, human speech would rob the message of the cross of its divine power (1.17c-d). Instead, he relies on (what he sees as) the only means by which the power of the cross is made manifest: the work of God's Spirit (2.4b).

This powerful work of the Spirit engenders faith in those who hear the gospel message (2.5), a faith that sees (or knows) "the word of the cross" as God's power resulting in salvation (1.18). For Paul this work, faith, and salvation represent the new reality and identity for the Corinthians (1.2). Thus, the Corinthians are to define their identity not in accordance with how the (wisdom of the) world determines such things; their new reality and identity are to be measured and assessed by the nature and power of the cross. Paul illustrates this by combining the world's view of the cross with the world's perception of (many of) those within the Corinthian assembly: just as the cross is a sign of folly, weakness, defeat, and reserved for the lowest of society, God's salvation comes to those without world-defined wisdom, power, and nobility (cf. 1.26).[1]

Moreover, Paul insists that just as the cross (through God's wisdom) became the sign of honor, power, and salvation (1.27-28), so too the believers in Corinth (through the cross of Christ) become persons of divinely chosen worth, a status that is reflected in humble and reverent praise (cf. 1.30-31). Accordingly, because of their new reality and identity, Paul expects the Corinthians to see themselves as reflections of God's work in the cross, made manifest to and established among them by the powerful work of the Spirit.

5.2.2. Wisdom and the Spirit

With the theme of wisdom, Paul stresses his commitment to proclaiming "the word of the cross" as the power and wisdom of

---

[1] Bailey argues that Paul's threefold description of not many wise, not many powerful and not many well-born is not exclusively reserved for the Corinthians; it applies to all churches in the whole of nascent Christianity (see *Paul Through Mediterranean Eyes: Cultural Studies in 1 Corinthians* [London: SPCK, 2011], 82-84; cf. also Héring, *First Epistle*, 1-2).

God, despite the world's criticism of it (cf. 1.18a, 21-23). For Paul
this wisdom represents 1) that which is given by God to those who
believe, and 2) a way of knowing how to define life and live
accordingly. God's wisdom thus becomes an epistemological
framework within which believers understand and live life. This
emphasis on the nature and source of wisdom found original
expression in Paul's proclamation of the cross as God's wise
means of salvation and life, revealed to the Corinthians by God's
Spirit (2.10-12).

Thus, as noted above, the cross functions as the (visible)
standard for how the believers in Corinth should measure or define
themselves as participants in God's new life (or reality). Moreover,
Paul insists that the God-given wisdom is necessarily distinct from
the wisdom of the world (2.12), and that the former has overturned
the latter (1.19, 20d). Furthermore, and as a consequence, those
who receive the Spirit's revelation of God's wisdom no longer rely
on that which is incapable of knowing or ascertaining God's
wisdom, for that which is human cannot know what is divine (2.11,
14). Accordingly, it is only by God's wisdom that believers can
know how the cross 1) has the power to give life and 2) becomes
the standard by which new life is defined; human wisdom sees this
as powerless and utter foolishness.

It was precisely this "foolishness" that Paul says he initially
proclaimed to the Corinthians, and it was this "foolishness" that
they originally believed and accepted as God's (true) wisdom
(1.23-24, 30-31; 2.6-8). Since Paul understands the Spirit to be the
only means by which such wisdom is known to be of God, we are
not surprised by his claim that the Corinthians originally believed
and accepted the gospel because of the powerful work of the Spirit
(2.4-5). Moreover, within this claim Paul emphasizes this point by
noting the distinct and contrasting ways of knowing the wisdom
(or ways) of God. While human wisdom sees sophisticated

reasoning and eloquent speech as hallmarks of (worldly) wisdom, Paul denounces such things as inappropriate (and incapable) means for ascertaining God's wisdom (cf. 2.1-4).

Moreover, while the world sees sophisticated reasoning and eloquent speech as useful for supporting one's claim of possessing wisdom, this support is contingent upon certain presuppositions about wisdom and what it reveals—things which Paul also sees as inadequate (1.20, 27-28). The world expects wise proclamations to be characterized by rhetorical flair, polished eloquence, and even boasting of one's abilities,[2] whereas God's wisdom is revealed by the power of the Spirit, working through plain speech and the speaker's reverent disposition (2.1-3). By referring to and describing his apostolic preaching in the way he does, we can reasonably conclude that Paul's allegiance to the message he proclaims and his faithful reliance on the Spirit's work suggest that he was operating in accordance with the new epistemological framework he advocates.

5.2.3. Discernment and the Spirit

It is only when we near the end of Paul's pneumatological teaching in 2.1–3.4 that we find the emphasis on Spirit-led (communal) discernment. However, considering the flow of the argument the delay is appropriate and understandable. For Paul, spiritual discernment operates in accordance with God's wisdom, as displayed in the cross, and that wisdom is revealed via the Spirit working through the proclamation of the cross. This progression of thought 1) stresses the logical connections between discernment, wisdom, and revelation, and 2) reflects the historical circumstances of Paul's apostolic ministry in Corinth.

With regard to the latter point, Paul uses his argument as both a reminder and a point of contrast. As a reminder, historically

---

[2] Cf. Litfin, *Theology of Proclamation*, 209.

speaking Paul came to Corinth in order to proclaim the message of God's salvific plan for the world (cf. 1.17-18; 2.1). In the wisdom of God, this plan involved an unthinkable yet necessary act to bring about salvation: a crucified messiah. However, this act is only unthinkable or foolish when judged according to human wisdom. Thus, in order for the Corinthians to see this divine act as both wise and essential, they needed an alternative framework of thought and standard of measure (or judgment). For Paul, God provided both of these through the work of the Spirit, and the evidence for this divine provision was the Corinthians' acceptance and belief in the cross as the enactment of God's saving wisdom (cf. 1.18b; 2.5, 9, 10, 15).

Paul therefore uses this historical circumstance (or series of events) as one side of a contrast, and this side represents the basis for measuring the Corinthians' present situation. Specifically, Paul emphasizes the fact that his apostolic ministry displayed humble obedience to his divine commission of proclaiming God's wisdom (cf. 2.3), ostensibly in accordance with God's means (cf. 2.13), and this faithfulness to God's wisdom and means played a vital role in the Corinthians' original belief. However, this does not appear to be the present view of the Corinthians, who now assess and value Paul's apostolic ministry on the basis of human wisdom, a criterion that Paul sees as faulty or inappropriate.

As intimated earlier in the argument, Paul portrays the Corinthians' assessment as faulty because it illustrates the point that human wisdom cannot know and accept the things of God, which are spiritual in nature (2.14; cf. 2.11). To judge the apostolic witness and the gospel message in accordance with human wisdom and discernment is to rely on criteria other than what God provides to those who believe, and relying on such things is characteristic of those not of God. As Paul states, such reliance represents those who are of the flesh and not of God's Spirit (cf. 3.1-4).

However, Paul reveals that this faulty assessment is not limited to his own ministry. The Corinthians have presumably applied the same (faulty) criteria to the ministry of Apollos,[3] which results in the Corinthians ostensibly favoring Apollos over Paul.[4] Therefore, the Corinthians' present faulty assessment (or judgment) of both the apostolic witness and the nature of the message proclaimed forms the other side of the contrast.

5.3. Applications to the Immediate Context (1 Cor 3.5–4.21)

As 1 Cor 3.3-4 indicates, Paul's focus beginning with 3.5 remains on the issue of divisive attitudes in the believing community (cf. 1.10-12). However, a noticeable shift occurs in how Paul deals with this dilemma: whereas in 1.10-12 he merely acknowledges the report of believers rallying around particular names,[5] here in 3.5–4.21 Paul confronts the Corinthians' faulty assessment of the apostolic witness that ostensibly led to the issue of sloganeering. Thus, Paul moves beyond the report *that* believers are rallying around names and instead focuses particularly on the nature, cause, and effects of sloganeering. Specifically, as stated in 3.3-4, Paul characterizes rallying around names as an example of party-strife (ἔρις) and jealousy, characteristics he links with behavior that is "fleshly" and "according to human ways of being" (κατὰ ἄνθρωπον περιπατεῖτε).

---

[3] While he does mention Cephas along with himself and Apollos at 1.12 (and Christ), the primary focus of Paul's argument is the Corinthians' faulty assessment of himself and Apollos.

[4] Litfin might be overstating things when he asserts: "[Apollos] was an ἀνὴρ λόγιος and this had its effect in Corinth. The opponents fell before his eloquence and this in turn pleased and impressed the Corinthians believers" (*Theology of Proclamation*, 241).

[5] Even if there are not actual divisions in the community around specific names, Paul shows an awareness of divisions concerning specific practices (cf. 1 Cor 11.17-34 [esp. 11.18-19]).

Moreover, in the light of his wider aims, Paul shows how party-strife and jealousy are endemic to human wisdom, all of which stand in contrast to God's wisdom (or way of being), characterized by concord and love. In 3.5–4.21, therefore, Paul uses the Corinthians' present assessment of his apostolic ministry and the report of sloganeering as evidence that they are operating in accordance with human wisdom rather than God's. Thus, as will be demonstrated, the goal of Paul's critique is twofold: 1) to show up the faulty judgment of the Corinthians, especially as it relates to assessing the apostolic witness, and 2) to reveal what wise, Spirit-led communal discernment entails and the effects it is to have on community life. We can see this emphasis by first considering the basic shape and content of Paul's argument.

5.3.1. Overview of the Argument

Similarly to how he argues in both 1.14-31 and 2.1–3.4, Paul begins the argument of 3.5–4.21 by recalling the nature and role of the apostolic witness in Corinth. Two notable points of differences with the present argument, in relation to the other two, are worth mentioning: 1) the subjects of comparison and 2) the specificity of Paul's description. With regard to the first point, the stress in 1.14-31 and 2.1–3.4 appears to fall on Paul as a herald of God's wisdom and how he compares to Sophistic orators in Hellenistic culture. Thus, the Corinthians are measuring Paul's abilities against those found in the secular world. However, the stress in 3.5–4.21 appears to fall on how Paul compares to the abilities of Apollos. Therefore, the focus here shifts from the Corinthians comparing Paul with "external" orators to comparing him "internally" with another proclaimer of the gospel. Despite the shift in focus, Paul sees the Corinthians employing the same worldly- (or humanly-) defined criteria in both cases and it is the application of these criteria that is problematic, and it is this problematic application that Paul confronts.

With regard to the second point, in both 1.14-17 and 2.1-5, Paul's definition of the apostolic witness is mostly one of negativity. While positive remarks do emerge,[6] Paul describes his role primarily in terms of what it is not. Moreover, he seems to leave it to the Corinthians to draw the appropriate conclusions, which in both cases should at least be: 1) Paul's ministry is not characterized by baptism, only preaching the gospel, and 2) that he proclaims the gospel not as a rhetorician (or one bound to rhetorical conventions or devices) but as one who, aided by the Spirit, speaks plainly the power of the cross of Christ. By comparison, Paul's two descriptive metaphors in 3.6-15 define (or portray) the apostolic witness clearly and he appears to supply for the Corinthians the necessary implications. Specifically, the apostolic witness is characterized as lowly, dependent, and collaborative and not something to exalt or esteem according to judgments about individual preachers. For Paul, the ability to make this distinction is determined by the criteria used, and right assessments of the apostolic witness prevail only when the Corinthians reject the criteria of human wisdom and adhere to the criterion of God's wisdom as displayed in the cross and revealed by the Spirit.

5.3.2. Paul's Critique of the Corinthians' Assessment

While Cephas' name resurfaces at 1 Cor 3.22, the final question in 3.4 suggests that Paul and Apollos are the true objects of sloganeering in Corinth, or, at the very least, their names are the

---

[6] E.g. "to preach the gospel" (1.17b), "my message and my preaching were...in demonstration of the Spirit and of power" (2.4).

most relevant for the issue at hand.[7] Thus, beginning with 3.5 and signaled by the post-positive conjunction, οὖν,[8] Paul directs his attention to this particular dilemma and especially its underlying cause. This focus on the underlying cause is revealed in part by how Paul broaches the subject. When describing himself and Apollos, Paul begins by surprisingly asking, *"what* is Apollos?" and *"what* is Paul?"[9] rather than the expected (and more natural or appropriate) question, *"who* is?"[10]

---

[7] Moreover, Paul does not say in 4.6 that he applies his argument also to Cephas; he only applies it to himself and Apollos. This would further suggest that Paul does not see Cephas' name as playing as significant a role in the Corinthian "party" dilemma as do the names of Paul and Apollos. On the question of how the Corinthians come to know the name of Cephas, Hogeterp suggests awareness of the name as the result of communication shared between churches in the Diaspora and not necessarily because Cephas ever visited Corinth (*contra* Barrett, "Cephas and Corinth"). Specifically he argues: "These interactions may have provided the Corinthians with information about the Christian Jews of the Jerusalem church who are often called saints by Paul" (*Paul and God's Temple: A Historical Interpretation of Cultic Imagery in the Corinthian Correspondence* [Leuven: Peeters, 2006], 310; cf. also Furnish, *Theology of the First Letter*, 10). Richardson, on the other hand, is skeptical of contact with other churches—especially Jerusalem—and contends for the likelihood "that Apollos and Cephas were themselves considerably greater irritants in the Corinthian situation than is sometimes imagined" ("On the Absence of 'Anti-Judaism' in 1 Corinthians," in *Paul and the Gospels,* vol. 1 of *Anti-Judaism in Early Christianity* [eds. P. Richardson, with D. Granskou; Waterloo: Wilfrid Laurier University Press, 1986], 63, 65). Richardson's case for Apollos being personally responsible is based on a rather tenuous interpretation of key passages, and he offers no compelling proof that Cephas ever visited Corinth other than to cite Barrett's article.

[8] Robertson-Plummer read οὖν as a logical transition, one required by the reference to Paul and Apollos in 3.4 (see *First Epistle*, 56), whereas Barrett takes it as "resumptive" rather than purely "argumentative" (*First Epistle*, 83).

[9] A handful of later MSS transpose the names (cf. D[b], L, Ψ, 6, 88, 104, 326, 915, syr[p,h], arm, eth). "This transposition was obviously made out of deference

Moreover, Paul supplies his own answer by labeling himself and Apollos as (mere) servants, appointed by God. While I am conscious of the risk of mirror-reading, it appears as though Paul employs servant imagery in order to overturn loftier portrayals of himself and Apollos as given by the Corinthians. This, then, would indicate that Paul's concern deals with evaluative assumptions about himself and Apollos as held by the Corinthians, evaluations that ostensibly led to (or fueled) the formation of parties with specific champions.[11] If this is the case, then we should expect Paul's response to be one addressing not specific parties but the (faulty) standard by which the Corinthians judge the apostolic witness and esteem one preacher over another.

5.3.2.1. Apostolic Witness

In the opening metaphor (3.6-9), by characterizing his work as planting and Apollos' as watering, Paul emphasizes a necessary relationship between the two types of work: planting without watering is fruitless, and watering without planting is superfluous. A similar emphasis appears when Paul changes metaphors (3.10-15) and describes his initial work in Corinth as laying a foundation (3.10b), "which is Jesus Christ" (3.11b—i.e. the proclamation of the cross [cf. 2.2]). And while Apollos is not specifically named in this metaphor, his work is no doubt in mind when Paul says

---

to the greater prominence of Paul and because of the sequence in ver. 4" (Metzger, *Textual Commentary*, 483).

[10] For MSS that read τις, see $\mathfrak{P}^{46vid}$, $\aleph^2$, C, D, F, G, Ψ, 1881, $\mathfrak{M}$, syr. For MSS that read τί, see $\aleph^*$, A, B, 0298, 33, 81, 1175, 1506, 1739. Collins sees no substantial difference in effect by using either term (see *First Corinthians*, 145).

[11] My underlying assumption here is that neither Paul nor Apollos were instrumental in the formation of parties or groups in Corinth (cf. Chrysostom, *Hom. 1. Cor.*, 3.4-5).

"another is building on" the foundation he laid (3.10c).[12] In terms of construction, and similar to the logic of the agricultural metaphor, laying a foundation without building upon it is a wasted effort, and attempting to build where no foundation exists is utter folly.

Thus, in both illustrations, Paul acknowledges that his initial work in Corinth was supplemented by the efforts of Apollos and Paul is in no way offended or threatened by this additional work.[13] This appears especially with the building metaphor: as long as the foundation is the same, Paul is not concerned with either how others build upon it or what materials they use (cf. 3.13-15);[14] although, he does encourage considered thought (ἕκαστος δὲ βλεπέτω πῶς ἐποικοδομεῖ [3.10c]).

With these images, Paul rejects any view that sees one type of apostolic work as superior to another and the related assumption that only the superior type is necessary.[15] For Paul, while his work was historically prior to that of Apollos, both types of work are collaborative and compatible with each other. However, Paul stresses the fact that apostolic cooperation is rooted in something more substantial, possibly to avoid claims of superiority based on

---

[12] Given the surrounding context, the pairing of the nominative singular ἄλλος and the third singular ἐποικοδομέω as a contrast to Paul's work of "laying the foundation," Apollos' supplementary work appears to be the immediate referent. Cf. Litfin, *Theology of Proclamation*, 224-25.

[13] Cf. Dodd: "Paul's role cannot be separated from that of Apollos, according to the logic of his argument, as the foundation cannot be separated from what is built on top" (*Paul's Paradigmatic "I": Personal Example as Literary Strategy* [Sheffield: Sheffield Academic, 1999], 56).

[14] Cf. L.G. Cox ("The 'Straw' in the Believer—1 Corinthians 3.12," *Wesleyan Theological Journal* 12 [1977]: 34-38), who argues for the two different categories of material as representing the two different types of believer—i.e. wood, hay, and straw refer to believers governed by the flesh, and gold, silver, and precious stones refer to mature believers.

[15] Cf. Godet, *First Epistle*, 1.176.

chronology. With the diversity of apostolic roles still in view, Paul first describes his and Apollos' particular work as carried out in obedience to the task given to them by God (καὶ ἑκάστῳ ὡς ὁ κύριος ἔδωκεν [3.5d]). We know that Paul views his apostolic role as a commission to proclaim the gospel (cf. 1.17), which relates to laying the foundation of Jesus Christ in Corinth (cf. 3.10-11), and that he fulfilled this role without needing to rely on human wisdom or eloquence. If we accept the testimony of Acts (cf. 18.24-28), we can assume that Apollos' ministry was characterized by open and powerful debates (i.e. διακατηλέγχετο δημοσίᾳ) concerning Jesus' messiahship as demonstrated in the Scriptures.

Thus, if the portrait of Acts is correct with regard to Apollos' ministry, and if we assume that Paul's experience with Apollos mirrored this portrait, then we can reasonably conclude that Paul would see Apollos' role as divinely appointed and Apollos as a faithful steward of that role (cf. 4.1).[16] This would certainly lend support to the supplementary nature of the apostolic tasks (cf. 3.6-9) and Paul's distinction between types of materials used in building upon a single foundation (cf. 3.13-15). Moreover, Paul stresses the point that despite the tasks assigned to him and Apollos, the success of the work performed—in this case the Corinthians' salvation—belongs to God alone. This particular stress would therefore function as a contrast for 1) notions of human capability and 2) identify-formation on the basis of assumed capabilities.

This twofold stress is found specifically in the first metaphor. As Paul states in 3.7, neither his work nor Apollos' is necessarily sufficient for bringing about the desired result (i.e. belief or

---

[16] Horsley makes the passing comment: "While Paul insists that he is an apostle, he never refers to Apollos as an apostle" (*1 Corinthians*, 63; *contra* Héring [*First Epistle*, 1], who thinks Paul "implicitly" applies the title "apostle" to Apollos in 4.6).

salvation); only God causes the growth (3.7; cf. 3.6). Paul emphasizes this point first in how he describes the processes (i.e. a simple aorist is used for the servants' work whereas the imperfect is used for God's work), [17] and second by the simultaneous relegation of the servants and the exaltation of the Lord/Master (3.7).[18] While the servants labor in the field, not only do both the field and the servants belong to God but the field and servants are also dependent upon God for the work that is done, for only God is able to cause the crop to grow.[19] This reflects Paul's earlier claim that neither his word nor message caused the Corinthians to believe in the gospel; it was only by the work of God's Spirit that the Corinthians placed their faith in God's power to save (cf. 2.4-5). If, therefore, the Corinthians are rallying around the names of Paul and Apollos, they are doing so on the basis of faulty views of the apostolic witness, particularly the assumption that the apostles are

---

[17] Cf. Lindemann, *Der erste Korintherbrief*, 81.

[18] It is worth noting not only the number of references to θεός in 1 Cor 3.6-9 (5 times) but also the emphatic placement of θεός in 3.7.

[19] The imagery of people as a field not only has ties with Jewish literature, thus explaining the likely source for Paul's use of such imagery, but also particular eschatological motifs within that literature and imagery. Specifically, Wolff lists the references to God's people (i.e. Israel) described as a field, vineyard, or planted garden (cf. Num 24.5-6; Isa 5.1-7; 60.1-3, 21; Jer 2.21; Ezek 36.9)—see Wolff, *Der erste Brief*, 67, as noted by Thiselton, *First Epistle*, 302. Keener also mentions the passages where "God promised to 'plant' or 'build' his people (Jer 1.10; 24.6; 31.28; 42.10; cf. Sir 49.7; 1QS 8.5-6; 11.8)" (*1–2 Corinthians*, 42). Moreover, Bailey recently stressed the parallels between 1 Cor 3.5-9 and Isa 41.19; 44.3-4; 60.21; and 61.3, where we find descriptions of fields being planted and cultivated—see *Paul Through Mediterranean Eyes*, 124-25. The obvious difference between the two is that in Isaiah God is the primary agent in planting and watering the crop, whereas in 1 Corinthians Paul describes himself as the one who plants and Apollos as the one who waters. Despite this difference, the fundamental similarity is that in both God is the one who produces (or brings about) the crop.

responsible for salvation, which stands in direct conflict with Paul's hope in 2.5.

This faulty assumption results from a faulty understanding of dependence. While the Corinthians are dependent upon the apostolic witness to receive the proclamation of the gospel, the Corinthians are ultimately dependent upon God alone to effect the salvation proclaimed in that gospel. However, because they see themselves as the product of the farmhands' labor and therefore belonging to the farmhands, the Corinthians have implicitly exposed their continued reliance on faulty criteria (i.e. human wisdom) and their implicit rejection of the criteria inherent to their new identity in Christ (i.e. God's wisdom). And because of their continued reliance on human wisdom, the Corinthians have failed to see Paul and Apollos as θεοῦ συνεργοί[20] and themselves as θεοῦ οἰκοδομή, and it is this faulty conception that Paul seeks to remedy.

5.3.2.2. God's (Subversive) Wisdom

The Corinthians' failure to see and discern such things is, according to Paul, due to the more pressing failure of not relying on God's wisdom and relying instead on human wisdom. Evidence for this is found in the Corinthians' decision to celebrate or boast in specific individuals (cf. 3.3b-4, 21) rather than boast in the cross of Christ as God's wise means of salvation (cf. 1.30-31; 3.22-23). For Paul, two basic and related consequences arise with this particular failure. First, by adopting and relying upon human

---

[20] It is possible to read θεοῦ γάρ ἐσμεν συνεργοί as Paul and Apollos working together *with* God, which the NASB suggests (cf. also NIV, ESV, KJV, ASV). However, it is equally possible to read the phrase as, working together *for* God (cf. NRSV). Furnish shows how this decision must be made not on lexical or grammatical grounds but on the basis of Paul's usual meaning of συνεργοί (see "Fellow Workers in God's Service," *JBL* 80.4 [1961]: 364-65). Thus, the rendering given by the NRSV is more appropriate.

wisdom, the Corinthians are trusting a system of thought that is both contrary to and now rendered powerless by God's wisdom. This is reminiscent of what we noted with earlier portions of Paul's argument: just as in 1.18-25 and 2.6-13 Paul stressed the "upside-down"[21] nature and subverting role of God's wisdom, here we find him following a similar line (or pattern) of argumentation.

An important difference, however, is the angle of focus: in the earlier treatments, God's wisdom was portrayed as folly from the perspective of the world; in the present instance (i.e. 3.18-23, esp. 19-20), the wisdom of the world is portrayed as folly from God's perspective.[22] It would appear that Paul highlights this difference in order to accentuate the distinction between pre- and post-belief notions of wisdom. In his earlier claims, Paul stresses God's wisdom as folly when viewed from a pre-faith perspective (i.e. it is foolish by the standards of the world), whereas here the world's wisdom is folly from a post-faith perspective (i.e. it is foolish by the standards of God's wisdom).

Second, by adopting and relying upon human wisdom, the Corinthians operate within an epistemological framework that is both limited in what it contains and incapable of comprehending anything outside of itself. As noted in the earlier analogy in 2.11 and the application in 2.12-13, human wisdom in itself cannot know the things of God. Just as knowledge of the other is dependent upon the other's self-disclosure, the only way in which the things of God are known is through divine revelation, and no amount of human effort or superior (human) wisdom will alter that reality. However, Paul clearly says an alteration has taken place via

---

[21] Cf. Thiselton (*First Epistle*, 321), who refers to Allo and Witherington as describing 1 Cor 3.18 in a similar way.

[22] Litfin makes a similar case, but moves the shift to 2.6-16—see *Theology of Proclamation*, 213-16.

God's Spirit (cf. 2.10, 12) and that this Spirit is distinct from "the spirit of the world" (2.12b).

Moreover, Paul suggests that with this revelation comes a new framework of thought (or a new "mind" [cf. 2.16]), those "in Christ" are able to comprehend what is otherwise unknowable by and incomprehensible to human wisdom (or "the spirit of the world"). Thus, to become truly wise (cf. 3.18) requires the adoption of what is otherwise deemed foolish by the standards of the world (cf. 1.18-23; 3.19a). Therefore, paradoxically, only if anyone's claims to wisdom are measured by the "foolishness" of God can he or she be considered truly wise.[23]

However, by adopting and relying upon human wisdom, the Corinthians' claim to wisdom reveals their folly and by such claims they are identifying themselves not as people of the Spirit but as "merely human" (cf. 2.14), those who think and live childishly and according to the flesh (cf. 3.1-4). Moreover, for Paul, this faulty view has created an attitude and a means of defining community relationships that reflect not God's wisdom in the cross but the wisdom of the world, which is in part characterized by prideful boasting in status and illustrated by rallying around human names.

Thus the Corinthians now fail to see not only the gospel of Christ crucified as God's wise act of sacrificial self-giving love for the world but also how God's wisdom is to shape and define their

---

[23] Paul's aphorism in 3.18 does appear to echo Socratic views of wisdom, which portray self-admitted folly as the beginning and mark of true wisdom (cf. Thiselton, *First Epistle*, 321). However, Paul's focus is not so much about self-deprecation as it is contrasting systems of thought (cf. Fee, *First Epistle*, 151). Thus, Paul's claim here in 3.18 echoes more the Jewish wisdom teachings, which contrast the ways of God with the ways of the world—the former as representing true wisdom and the latter as true folly. Moreover, the qualifying phrase ἐν τῷ αἰῶνι τούτῳ recalls the earlier contrast between God's wisdom and the wisdom τοῦ αἰῶνος τούτου (2.6; cf. wisdom τοῦ κόσμου [1.20])

new life "in Christ," and they fail to see things properly because they are relying on other means for discerning the ways of God. Therefore, Paul's solution is clear: only when the Corinthians rely (once again) upon the wisdom of God, as displayed in the cross and mediated by the Spirit, will they be able to see the gospel message *as* God's wisdom and know how to live as a community "in Christ." And only when the Corinthians rely on God's Spirit— and not the spirit of the world—will they find true wisdom.

5.3.2.3. Spirit-led Communal Discernment

This brings us to Paul's emphasis on the Corinthians' need for Spirit-led discernment and for this discernment to emanate from Spirit-revealed wisdom. In particular, Paul stresses that only through Spirit-led discernment will the Corinthians know their identity "in Christ" and the entailments that come with that knowledge, especially the ability to form right judgments about themselves and others (cf. 3.21–4.13). Thus, if they relied on God's wisdom and exercised wise discernment, the Corinthians would recognize both the compatible and servant role of the apostles and the true nature of their relationship with the apostles. Specifically, the Corinthians would not esteem one apostolic herald over another on the basis of perceived superior abilities or talents. Related to this, the Corinthians would not perceive the apostles to be men worthy of praise but conduits through whom God is exalted (3.21a; cf. 1.31), for the aim of the apostolic work is not to bring glory to the apostles but to allow God's powerful work to manifest itself through their faithful service (cf. 3.7-8; 4.1).

However, following Paul's departure, the Corinthians began to view their new identity "in Christ" (crucified) by other means, and the resultant picture bore little resemblance to the image of the cross. Whereas Paul sees the cross as uniting under one name all who believe, he hears of (some) Corinthian believers dividing themselves and rallying around multiple names (cf. 1.11-12). Furthermore, where the cross represents a sign of weakness, shame, and humiliation, yet is able to impart new life and a new identity for those who believe, some in Corinth take their new life and identity as a sign of power, honor, and prestige (4.10) and a legitimate cause for personal boasting.

Moreover, it appears as though some in Corinth use their faulty notion of new life and identity as the standard by which they can judge the validity of the apostolic witness (3.18-20). In doing so the Corinthians reveal that they rely not on the criterion of the cross given by the Spirit but on one of their own making. For if they relied on the criterion of the cross, the Corinthians would now see Paul and the apostolic witness not only as mere servants and contracted builders (3.6-15), thus inadequate objects of praise, but also the very embodiment of what the cross represents: foolish, weak, without honor, ridiculed, persecuted, and socially on a par with common criminals (4.10-13).

Additionally, the Corinthians would identify the apostles not as external or disconnected from them but as divinely commissioned to and thus united with them (cf. 3.21b-22). Here Paul rejects the notion of the Corinthians belonging to key figures and advocates instead the reality that the apostles belong to the Corinthians.[24] However, for Paul, the sense of belonging to the apostles must be understood within the wider (theological) context of relationships: while the apostles may belong to the Corinthians, in the sense that God commissioned the apostles to Corinth (cf. 3.5, 9), the Corinthians ultimately belong to Christ (cf. 3.23a), about whom the apostles proclaimed and in whom the Corinthians believed (cf. 2.1-5). The implication is: if the apostles were sent by God to Corinth as heralds of Christ crucified, and if the Corinthians belong to

---

[24] This accords with Paul's earlier image of himself and Apollos as farmhands in God's field.

Christ because of their faith in the message proclaimed, the Corinthians' decision to identify themselves with one of the apostles is faulty, inappropriate, and misguided, for such an identification subverts (or inverts) the relationship hierarchy established by God in Christ. Moreover, this decision also limits or reduces the benefits that come to the Corinthians in Christ. For the Corinthians to tie themselves to a particular herald of the gospel is to fail to see that all things belong to them (cf. 3.21-22).

In this way, Paul accuses the Corinthians of failing to judge or discern properly both the role of the apostolic witness and the relational status shared between the two heralds, and they have failed because they rely on faulty criteria in making such judgments. However, Paul indicates that he is not concerned about the faulty judgments laid against him by the Corinthians (4.3), presumably due to their reliance on faulty criteria (cf. 2.14), but because he knows that only God can cast final judgment, which comes only at the eschaton (cf. 4.4-5). This claim reflects Paul's earlier assertion in the second metaphor about one's work being tested (or revealed) in the day of fire (cf. 3.13),[25] and therefore

---

[25] Fishburne sees the metaphor of 3.10-15 as echoing both the vocabulary and theology of *T.Ab.* 13, and that Paul is dependent upon this specific text (see, "1 Corinthians iii.10-15 and the *Testament of Abraham*," *NTS* 17.1 [1970]: 109-115; cf. Davis, who seems to accept this view without reflection [*Wisdom and Spirit*, 220 n.189]). Fishburne makes this connection on the assumption that the *Testament* predates 1 Corinthians (cf. Rowland, who offers the tentative date of c. 50 CE—see *The Open Heaven: A Study of Apocalyptic in Judaism and Early Christianity* [London: SPCK, 1982], 259), *contra* Sanders, who sees the textual history as too prolonged to allow for Paul's literary dependence (see "*Testament of Abraham*. A New Translation and Introduction," in *Apocalyptic Literature and Testaments,* vol. 1 of *The Old Testament Pseudepigrapha* [ed. J.H. Charlesworth; Garden City, Doubleday, 1983], 878 n.54). Sanders concludes: "It seems best to assume a date for the original of c. A.D. 100, plus or minus twenty-five years" (*ibid.*, 875; cf. also G. Boccaccini, *Middle Judaism: Jewish Thought, 300 B.C.E. to 200 C.E.* [Minneapolis: Fortress, 1991], 258; J.J. Collins,

premature judgments made by any one other than God (or the Lord [cf. 4.4-5]) are both haughty and inappropriate.

5.3.3. Concluding Remarks on 1 Cor 3.5–4.21

One of the striking features of pneumatological teaching in 2.1–3.4, and the framework it provides, is that Paul applies it both to himself (and the apostolic witness) and the Corinthians. This is striking for at least two reasons. First, Paul demonstrates not only that his manner of preaching reflects the nature of the cross but

---

Apocalyptic Imagination: An Introduction to Jewish Apocalyptic Literature [Grand Rapids: Eerdmans, 1998], 7, 35, 252). Recently Herms observed: "Allison...has demonstrated that several sections in the longer Greek recension of the *Testament of Abraham* do not appear in the shorter (and older) Greek versions and thereby reflect later 'Christian' insertions into the text. Further, in the specific case of *T.Ab.* 13.12-13, Allison demonstrates that on the basis of its parallelism, the dependence of the *Testament of Abraham* upon Paul's metaphor in 1 Cor 3.14-15 is assured.... Thus, the evidence of date and literary development suggests that Fishburne's proposal is anachraonistic and ultimately unfruitful" ("'Being Saved without Honor': A Conceptual Link between 1 Corinthians 3 and *1 Enoch* 50?," *JSNT* 29.2 [2006]: 190).

Moreover, as Fitzmyer and Kirk have shown, it is more likely that both Paul and the writer of the *Testament* drew from a common Jewish tradition, although Paul develops his point in a different direction—see Fitzmyer, *First Corinthians*, 200; A.N. Kirk, "Building with the Corinthians: Human Persons as the Building Materials of 1 Corinthians 3.12 and the 'Work' of 3.13-15," *NTS* 58.4 (2012): 567-68. For Paul, while the construction is destroyed by fire, the builder does not suffer absolute punishment, whereas in the *Testament*: "The sunlike angel, who holds the balance in his hand, this is the archangel Dokiel, the righteous balance-bearer, and he weighs the righteous deeds and the sins with the righteousness of God. And the fiery and merciless angel, who holds the fire in his hand, this is the archangel Purouel, who has authority over fire, and he tests the work of men through fire. And if the fire burns up the work of anyone, immediately the angel of judgment takes him and carries him away to the place of sinners, a most bitter place of punishment" (*T.Ab.* A13.10-12 [Sanders]). Furthermore, in Paul's argument God performs the act of judgment whereas in the *Testament* it is carried out by specific archangels.

also that his view of life (and in this case, salvation) is shaped by God's wisdom as displayed in the cross of Christ. Moreover, the discernment Paul uses to instruct the Corinthians is the same discernment they should have employed in their present assessment of the gospel, its proclaimers, and their own identity in Christ. In this way Paul reveals that he relies on the spiritual discernment he advocates as he critiques the behaviors and judgments of those causing trouble in the Corinthian church. As Lewis argues, Paul's discernment reflects his instruction to "the Corinthians that Christ's cruciform pattern of self-giving love for others, supremely manifest in his death on the cross, has become the new behavioral standard for both Jews and Greeks in God's new age." [26] Accordingly, this cruciform pattern as the new framework for life becomes the lens through which Paul critiques (and corrects) the Corinthian dilemma(s), a critique that unfolds in 1 Cor 5–15.

Second, the implication of Paul's wider argument is that the Corinthians have failed to reflect the nature of the cross, to be shaped by God's wisdom, and to rely on Spirit-given discernment. With each of the topics addressed in the letter, Paul reveals either how the Corinthians have failed to filter the issues through this new matrix or how they should rightly do so in the future. I will develop this in the next section. What is crucial to recognize now is that in critiquing the Corinthians Paul is (again) employing and relying on the framework of thought he advocates; he does what he desires the Corinthians to do for themselves. And as I have stressed throughout this study, necessary for this critique of the spiritual life is Paul's insistence that only this new framework is appropriate for those "in Christ," for it is the only way for spiritual people to discern spiritual things (cf. 1 Cor 2.15). Or to say this negatively: the life, thought, and behavior of those "in Christ" cannot be

---

[26] Lewis, *Looking for Life*, 37; cf. also Long, *Paul and Human Rights*, 98.

discerned by human (or worldly) wisdom, for such wisdom is not from God and it judges the things of God as folly (cf. 1 Cor 2.14).

5.4. Applications to the Wider Context (1 Cor 5–15)

As should be clear from the preceding argument, Paul stresses the need for the Corinthian believers to exercise wise, Spirit-led discernment rooted in God's revealed wisdom. We do not need to venture too far into the letter to find reasons for this stress, especially as it applies to a variety of situations in everyday life. Beginning with 1 Cor 5.1, Paul transitions from the topic of the Corinthians' relationship with himself and Apollos to topics pertaining to their relationship with society and each other as a believing community. The need for this specific focus relates to Paul's expectations of the Corinthian assembly being what Horsley calls an "alternative society,"[27] one whose identity and life are shaped not by the wisdom of the world but God's wisdom displayed in the cross and revealed by the Spirit.

This emphasis on a distinctive identity follows from Paul's earlier stress on the kind of wisdom that believers possess, a wisdom that is contrary to the wisdom of the world and defines the way in which spiritual persons are to live their new life "in Christ." Accordingly, and beginning with chapter 5, we encounter what could be classified as competing ways of ordering or defining life, especially life that is wise and spiritual. Given the flow of Paul's argument,[28] we can divide his interaction with these competing

---

[27] See R.A. Horsley, "1 Corinthians: A Case Study of Paul's Assembly as Alternative Society," in *Paul and Empire: Religion and Power in Roman Imperial Society* (ed. R.A. Horsley; Harrisburg: Trinity Press International, 1997), 242-52.

[28] I am here assuming the general divisions of 1 Cor 5–15, where the lines are drawn according to the topics discussed. Thus: immoral conduct and lawsuits (5.1–6.20); marriage relations (7.1-40); idol food (8.1–11.1); liturgical practices (11.2-34); spiritual manifestations (12.1–14.40); and resurrection

ways into three sections: 1) wise, communal discernment in every day life in society, 2) proper notions of identity and spiritual expression in worship, and 3) communal hope in the life to come. In what follows, I will survey the cases where Paul illustrates the difference in ways of thinking and does so in a way that reflects (or even assumes) the pneumatological teaching of 2.1–3.4.

5.4.1. Wise Situational Discernment

In this first section (1 Cor 5.1–11.1), Paul addresses a number of issues where the Corinthians should be exercising wise, communal discernment in every day life. Many if not all of these concerns are situational, thus requiring a specific response. As sometimes noted, in this instance we see Paul "thinking on his feet,"[29] but doing so (presumably) in accordance with the Spirit-led discernment he advocates for those "in Christ." Here I will focus on two key responses from Paul: 1 Cor 5–6 and 8.1–11.1. What is particularly telling about these responses is that Paul assumes a degree of pre-existing knowledge on the Corinthians' part, knowledge that would have otherwise assisted them in their own decisions. In some cases, this knowledge is based on his own teaching to them; in others, it refers to traditions or even the

---

(15.1-58). Some scholars, however, move the beginning of 12.1–14.40 to 11.2, partly because both 11.2-34 and 12.1–14.40 deal with matters of ecclesial practice and/or behavior (see e.g. Mitchell, *Rhetoric of Reconciliation*, 258-60; Fotopoulos, "1 Corinthians," in *The Blackwell Companion to the New Testament* [ed. D.E. Aune; Chichester: Wiley-Blackwell, 2010], 427; Perkins, *First Corinthians*, 132). Moreover, as Thiselton points out, the combination of the two units is necessary for seeing chapters 12–14 "within the broader theological framework of 11:2–14:40 in deliberate continuity with 8:1–11:1, and indeed ultimately with 1:1–4:21" (*First Epistle*, 900).

[29] M.D. Hooker, *Paul: A Beginner's Guide* (Oxford: One World, 2008), 32; N.K. Gupta, "The Theo-Logic of Paul's Ethics in Recent Research: Crosscurrents and Future Directions in Scholarship in the Last Forty Years," *CBR* 7.3 (2009): 347.

Hebrew Scriptures; while in some it is more general, in the sense that the Corinthians simply possess it as common knowledge or that which is discernable via the Spirit.

5.4.1.1. Moral Judgments and Secular Counsel (1 Cor 5–6)

The argument here can be divided into three major parts. First, in 5.1-11 Paul confronts the interrelated issues of inappropriate sexual practices and the Corinthians' failure to judge them as such.[30] Paul's reference in 5.9-11 to his previous letter suggests that the problem at hand is an *internal* one,[31] and not one brought into the assembly by a non-believer (or group of non-believers).[32] It is generally assumed that the member(s) engaging in such practices is a powerful or influential patron in the church, one who is abusing his privileged status. It is also assumed that the failure of the Corinthians to correct and/or discipline this patron is rooted in their (selfish) desire to retain the benefits that come from keeping the patron in good standing.[33] However, Paul's argument does not move along such specific lines. What is clear is that Paul opposes the action *in toto* (cf. 5.5), regardless of who performs it, and he admonishes the Corinthians collectively for not repudiating the inappropriate behavior. Moreover, instead of knowing better (cf. οὐκ οἴδατε [5.6b]) and responding accordingly, Paul sees the them as having become arrogant or complacent (πεφυσιωμένοι [5.2; cf. 4.6, 18-19]) in their judgment of what is right behavior for those "in Christ" and as having simply allowed the inappropriate behavior to occur.

---

[30] Cf. Adams, *Constructing the World*, 90.

[31] Cf. *Ibid.*, 86 n.3.

[32] Cf. 1 Cor 5.1b, 12-13, which also suggest that the issue is an internal one.

[33] Cf. J.K. Chow, *Patronage and Power: A Study of Social Networks in Corinth* (Sheffield: JSOT Press, 1992), 139.

Second, in 5.12–6.11 Paul deals with an issue that follows from the preceding part, specifically the Corinthians' failure to rely on God's wisdom in making right judgments. Three times in this argument Paul reminds the Corinthians that they already have the appropriate knowledge and ability to settle their own internal disputes (cf. οὐκ οἴδατε [6.2, 3, 9]). Paul also declares that this knowledge and ability are superior to those of the world, for what they possess is from God whereas that which the world possesses is not. This recalls Paul's earlier argument where he describes believers as recipients of God's Spirit and having the "mind of Christ," which enables them to discern (or judge) all things, while those who have not received God's Spirit are incapable of right discernment—especially of spiritual matters (cf. 2.10-15). If such were the case, then there would be no need for Corinthian believers to seek external (secular) counsel, for there must be at least one in the community who is wise (cf. 6.5). However, the Corinthians fail to rely on the wisdom (or knowledge) they possess via the Spirit, evidenced by their inability to judge properly the life and behavior of their own.[34] More problematic, by desiring secular counsel to settle their disputes, the Corinthians are *de facto* rejecting the wisdom of God and seeking after the wisdom of the world.[35] In this way they are showing themselves to be people of flesh and not led by the Spirit.

Finally, in 6.12-20 Paul anchors his argument to the wider issue of the Corinthians' proper understanding of their new identity in Christ. In the light of what he says in 5.1–6.11, we discover here that Paul is critiquing a particular mind-set and way of knowing or judging, one contrary to what the Corinthians should be following.

---

[34] This inability to judge makes better sense of Paul's language of "judgment" in 5.12–6.11, which does initially seem to carry a nuance of condemnation (or casting guilty verdicts).

[35] Cf. Adams, *Constructing the World*, 127-28.

Scholars see Paul in 6.12a reciting a maxim or behavioral slogan of the Corinthians (πάντα μοι ἔξεστιν),[36] one that 1) enables members to engage in inappropriate actions, and 2) justifies the lack of critical judgment. Paul's immediate rejoinder (ἀλλ᾽ οὐ πάντα συμφέρει), however, introduces the necessary wise consideration that is lacking in the Corinthians' slogan—i.e. while all things are allowable, not all allowable things are inherently good. This is especially the case for those "in Christ" and who now live according to the Spirit (6.15-19; cf. 6.9-11).

Thus, Paul critiques (and rejects) the assumption that goodness is determined by what is sanctioned. Instead, Paul emphasizes the link between what is appropriate (i.e. good) and identity (and its source). In this case the Corinthians are members of Christ's body and their body is the temple of the Holy Spirit (or spirit of holiness), and as such all that they do is to glorify God. This twofold identification recalls Paul's earlier claims about the Corinthians being recipients of God's Spirit (cf. 2.10-12), and thus the temple of the Spirit (3.16), having the mind of Christ (so as to be able to discern all things [cf. 2.15-16]), and living lives distinct from the ways and wisdom of the world, which is under God's judgment (cf. 6.9-10).

5.4.1.2. Idol Food and (Divine) Judgment (1 Cor 8.1–11.1)

The argument here can be divided into three major sections, with the middle one being subdivided further into two parts. On the ends of the argument are Paul's discussions concerning idol food (8.1-13; 10.14–11.1), with the middle portion functioning as a two-part example (9.1-27; 10.1-13) illustrating the wider principle

---

[36] Cf. Lewis, *Looking for Life*, 87; Thiselton, *First Epistle*, 460.

articulated in the surrounding discussion.[37] What is this wider principle? From 6.12, we see that Paul has been exhorting the believers in Corinth to be mindful and discerning of each other and not behave in ways that would cause offense. In this particular instance, since some in Corinth appear to have inflated (and faulty) views of knowledge, which in turn foster attitudes of superiority— or possibly moral exemption (8.1-3; cf. 5.1-11)—Paul emphasizes the need for humility of mind and practice.

Specifically, while it may be true that knowledge of only one God can assuage the consciences of some (8.4-6), not all possess such knowledge to the same degree and effect (cf. 8.7), which implies that not all consciences are equally clear. Thus, while one might eat food sacrificed to pagan idols/gods on the basis that such idols/gods are nothing, and therefore the food is not dedicated to them, another might not be able to make that distinction and thus remain faithful to God alone. Accordingly, as Paul suggests in 8.7-13, to encourage or even require those without this knowledge to eat idol food without fear or moral concern is misguided and destructive. In this way, the behavior and/or practices of those claiming (superior) knowledge are motivated by self-interest and not the needs of the other (cf. 8.1c-d). Furthermore, to behave and instruct in such ways fails to show love for others and fails to reflect the knowledge they claim to possess.

With regard to the latter point, claims to superior or complete knowledge without acts of love do not reflect the manner of revelation. It was through an act of love (i.e. the cross) that knowledge of God became a possibility, and it was because of love for God that the Corinthians came to know the wisdom of God, an ability made possible by the power and revelation of God's Spirit.

---

[37] This basic outline follows the suggestion of Gooch—see *Dangerous Food: 1 Corinthians 8–10 in Its Context* (Waterloo: Wilfrid Laurier University Press, 1993), 49.

And it is because of the work of God's Spirit that the Corinthians received "the mind of Christ" (2.16) by which they understand themselves not only as individual believers but also as a unified body and are able to discern how the body is to function. As Paul will argue later (i.e. 1 Cor 12–14), one of the primary functions of the body is the loving edification—or building up—of the whole, not the elevation of the individual (or certain individuals) because of assumed or perceived knowledge. As Pascuzzi points out: "knowledge is not an unqualified good. It can puff up with pride, whereas love builds up."[38] The ability to discern when knowledge is properly used or when it is being employed in the interest of the self comes from a reliance on God's wisdom.

Paul's first illustration in 9.1-27 reveals how he lives in accordance with the wisdom he proclaims. The reason for emphasizing this relationship seems to be twofold. On the one hand, Paul appears to be mindful of the criticisms made against either himself or his ministry in Corinth (or both), and he uses this illustration to demonstrate the valuelessness of such criticisms. On the other hand, Paul must substantiate not only his role as an apostle but also the way in which he lives out that role if he wants to use (or justify) his own life and ministry as an example worthy of imitation (cf. 9.3-12). To achieve this, Paul first appeals to the entitlements available to him as the community's founding apostle. In this case, Paul is entitled to general provisions as well as food in lieu of payment for labors performed (cf. 9.4-7, 10)—the latter being supported by a Mosaic principle (cf. 9.8-9). Paul even states he has the right to receive these entitlements (cf. 9.11-12a), at least on the basis of usual customs.

However, Paul declares that he foregoes such things "so that we will cause no hindrance to the gospel of Christ" (9.12b). He therefore relinquishes both what is entitled to him and the authority

---

[38] Pascuzzi, *First and Second Corinthians*, 53.

he has to receive such things, and he does so for the sake of the Corinthians and the cause of the gospel. Then, in 9.13-27 Paul supports his case by re-emphasizing the nature of his calling and his faithful obedience to it. The effect of this stage of the argument is that Paul's ministry in Corinth does not resemble or reflect either patrons or even traveling orators, but instead reflects the wisdom of God as displayed in the cross. What Paul does is characterized by self-giving, surrendering acts of love, and he does "all things for the sake of the gospel" (9.23).

Following this illustration, Paul uses Israel's disobedience in the wilderness as an illustration, this time emphasizing what happens when self-interested (or idolatrous) behavior encounters divine judgment (cf. 10.1-10). Such an illustration is required for two reasons. First, the repetition of τινες in the application of the illustration (cf. 10.7, 8, 9, 10) suggests that *some* in Corinth were behaving in ways that reflect Israel's disobedience. The implication is that, like those of Israel, the actions of a few carry devastating consequences that affect the whole community, although not directly. Only those who were truly at fault suffered divine judgment; yet the full weight and meaning of such judgment do not go unnoticed by those who remain.

This brings me to the second reason: leaving the parallel or typology of 10.1-4 aside, the focus of the passage deals with the identity of Israel as God's people. However, this identity alone was not sufficient to protect them from divine judgment if their behavior or actions stood in opposition to the ways of God. Paul provides key examples of such unacceptable behavior—idolatry, immorality, testing/tempting God, or grumbling with discontent (10.7, 8, 9, 10). The implication therefore is quite simple: if some of the Israelites, as God's chosen people, disobeyed God and behaved in ways contrary to God and were not spared from divine judgment, those in Corinth who identify themselves as "in Christ" yet behave in similar ways will also not escape the judgment that is to come. The means of escape, which Paul describes as divinely provided, most plausibly refers to the Spirit-given mind of Christ which enables believers (i.e. those who are truly spiritual) to know how to live in accordance with the ways of God, thus equipping them with the means to resist temptation.

It is worth noting that the incompatibility between the ways of the world and the lives of those "in Christ," illustrated in 10.20-22, reflects Paul's earlier teaching in 6.12-20 about the nature and role of the "body." Specifically, "the body is not for immorality, but for the Lord" (6.13c-d) and the "body is a temple of the Holy Spirit" (6.19) in and through which God is to be glorified (cf. 6.20). Moreover, Paul's teaching in 6.12-20 is prefaced with the two-part assertion, "all things are lawful for me, but not all things are profitable" (6.12a-b) and the climax of his teaching of 10.14–11.1 is the repeated claim, "all things are lawful, but not all things are profitable" (10.23). Taken together we could assume that Paul's remarks on the incompatibility between the ways of the world and the lives of those "in Christ" is anchored to his understanding of believers being the temple of the Holy Spirit, an identity made manifest in their life and behavior.

5.4.2. Community of Believers as Christ's Assembled Body

In this second section (1 Cor 11.2–14.40), Paul moves from dealing in general with situations related to every day life in society to those related in particular to the assembly of believers. However, while there is a shift in focus Paul maintains the emphasis on the need for those "in Christ" to understand their new identity as distinct from those who are not. Linked with this emphasis is Paul's stress on the competing wisdom by which life is defined (i.e. the wisdom of the world vs. God's wisdom) and the Corinthians' need to adhere to God's wisdom alone, since it is only from that wisdom that they receive their identity and know how to be a community. The argument of this section can be (loosely) divided into two major sections. In the first section (11.2-34), Paul deals with what could be classified as "liturgical" matters,[39] in this case prayer and the Lord's Supper. In the second section, (12.1– 14.40), Paul confronts the issue of what is often called, "spiritual gifts."[40] With regard to these two sections, and in the light of Paul's argument, I have decided to (re-)label the first, "Traditions and Communal Meals" and the second, "Communal Worship."

5.4.2.1. Traditions and Communal Meals (1 Cor 11.2-34)

Following the request for the Corinthians to imitate him as he imitates Christ (11.1), Paul moves into a discussion concerning the identity and practices of the believing assembly.[41] Even though there is a shift in focus (i.e. from society in general to the assembly in particular), we see Paul maintaining the emphasis on the need for those "in Christ" to be distinguished from those who are not. More specifically, we see Paul continuing to stress the competing wisdoms by which life is defined (i.e. the wisdom of the world vs. God's wisdom) and the Corinthians' need to be identified appropriately. Paul begins by desiring the Corinthians to know (or understand [θέλω δὲ ὑμᾶς εἰδέναι]) the authority (or headship

---

[39] E.g. R. Oster, *1 Corinthians* (Joplin: College Press, 1995), 243; Fitzmyer, *First Corinthians*, 405, 426. Cf. Pascuzzi (*First and Second*, 62), who limits the designation to only 11.2-16, and Collins (*First Corinthians*, 394-95), who shifts it to chapter 14.

[40] E.g. Robertson-Plummer, *First Epistle*, 259; Conzelmann, *1 Corinthians*, 204; Fee, *First Epistle*, 575-76; Collins, *First Corinthians*, 445; Ekem, "'Spiritual Gifts' or 'Spiritual Persons'," 54-74; Fitzmyer, *First Corinthians*, 456. While most commentators provide the gloss, "spiritual things" for τῶν πνευματικῶν, they nevertheless prefer "spiritual gifts" when referring to the topic of discussion.

[41] Cf. Fee, *First Epistle*, 491.

[κεφαλή]) of Christ (11.3), a teaching that they may have already received in some form (cf. 11.2). By establishing this relationship, Paul is able to confront the specific issue of what is honorable practice in the church for both men and women (cf. 11.4-15). While some read Paul as advocating ecclesial hierarchy on the basis of gender (via the created order),[42] the text suggests that Paul's concern is with maintaining the divinely appointed and necessary compatibility between males and females.[43] This perspective follows the line of reasoning displayed earlier when Paul compared his role in the apostolic mission to that of Apollos' (cf. 3.5-15), and that both were dependent upon God.

However, we should note that Paul's primary emphasis, as intimated in 11.3, is humanity's ultimate dependence upon God (11.12c). Implicit to the passage, we see Paul first anchoring the Corinthians' collective identity (and their perceptions of it) to Christ and it is from that identity they are to assess themselves and define behavior. In this case, they are to recognize what is honorable and what is not and conduct themselves accordingly. Second, and presumably contingent upon abilities via the Spirit's indwelling presence, Paul desires that the Corinthians formulate appropriate judgments on their own in this regard (cf. 11.13-15). He desires this for them primarily because it appears that they are

---

[42] See e.g. Héring, *First Epistle*, 102-10; P.T. Butler, *Studies in First Corinthians* (Joplin: College Press, 1985), 201-05. While it may be true that the Jewish creation story describes man created first and woman created from him, Paul's emphasis is that neither is superior to the other—either by created order or by virtue of inherent traits or abilities.

[43] Cf. Barrett, *First Epistle*, 247-58; Hargreaves, *Guide to 1 Corinthians*, 142-47; Perkins, *First Corinthians*, 138-41. Wire shifts this emphasis so that the advocates of compatibility are those female prophets loyal to the flourishing theological feminism in Corinth—see A.C. Wire, *The Corinthian Women Prophets: A Reconstruction through Paul's Rhetoric* (Minneapolis: Fortress, 1995), 130.

not making such judgments. In fact, the judgments they do make create problems amongst themselves (11.17-18), which brings us to the next example: proper behavior at communal meals (11.20-34), specifically honoring Christ through concern for the other.

Based on the prefatory remarks of 11.19-22, Paul shows his awareness of the inappropriate and divisive behavior in the assembly during communal meals (cf. 11.18: ἀκούω σχίσματα ἐν ὑμῖν), specifically the meal intended to signify their unity. Paul's indictment against the Corinthians is that they have failed to discern their own actions. In particular, some in Corinth fail to see how their behavior does not reflect the nature of the cross, and how this failed identification leads to faulty views of each other. More specifically, some in Corinth appear to be excluding those of lesser socio-economic means (or status) from the Lord's Supper on the basis of that lower status. Not only does such an exclusion fail to recall the Corinthians' own calling (cf. 1.26), it also functions as an extension of the earlier problem of divisions via sloganeering (cf. 1.11-12). In both cases, for Paul, the cause is rooted in faulty notions of wisdom and spirituality, specifically believers who are relying on the wisdom of the world, despite its being overturned by God, rather than relying on God's wisdom revealed by the Spirit. And similar to Paul's earlier exhortation, the solution here in 11.20-34 involves right assessment of each other's place and value in the light of the cross, an assessment that reveals communal unity, and this assessment can only be made by those relying on "the mind of Christ" as given by the Spirit.

5.4.2.2. Communal Worship (1 Cor 12–14)

When we come to chapters 12–14 we discover further examples of internal stratification, only now the categorical distinctions and levels of hierarchy are not socially determined. Instead, we see evidence of distinctions made on an assumed hierarchy of spirituality, one in which those ostensibly on "lower" levels are deemed less important while those on "higher" ones are to be esteemed and imitated by others in the community. How then does this dilemma, as found in the argument of 1 Cor 12–14, relate to our analysis of 2.1–3.4?[44] Given the scope of this final chapter, I can only examine the basic, thematic details of 1 Cor 12–14 and their relationship to 2.1–3.4; I will not be engaging in detailed exegesis of the former argument. Moreover, I will not attempt to engage fully in the scholarly debate on the specific nature, purpose, and/or duration of "spiritual gifts"; to enter that discussion would take me beyond the limits of this study and it would require me to re-tread well-trodden territory.[45] My concern in this section is to

---

[44] Admittedly, pairing 1 Cor 2.1–3.4 with chapters 12–14 for the purpose of critical inquiry is not novel. Hunt previously examined the parallels between 2.6-16 and 12–14, noting the "clear lexical and thematic similarities" in an able fashion (see *Inspired Body*, 109-39—quoted, 109). While much of my study agrees with Hunt's findings, I seek to develop his argument in other ways. In particular, Hunt underplays the relevance of 1 Cor 13, not only for 12–14 but also its relationship with key themes in 2.1–3.4. This is surprising given Hunt's ostensible response to seeing 1 Cor 13 as merely a literary flourish: "Far from being an ethereal, flighty poem, 1 Corinthians 13 is firmly planted in reality and is crucial for a reading of chapters 12 and 14" (*Inspired Body*, 117-18 n.18). However, when it comes to his own discussion, Hunt only gives passing comments on chapter 13—see e.g. *Inspired Body*, 117, 119, 121, 139. Hunt also fails to emphasize both the interplay of Spirit, wisdom, and proclamation, and especially the need for discernment within the "inspired body" as found in 1 Cor 12–14. This interplay of the major themes is not clearly expressed and the specific need for *communal* discernment is only incidental to Hunt's argument. For a more recent and succinct treatment of the links between 1 Cor 1–4 and 1 Cor 12–14, see F. Voss, *Das Wort vom Kreuz und die menschliche Vernunft: Eine Untersuchung zur Soteriologie des 1 Korintherbriefes* (Göttingen: Vandenhoeck and Ruprecht, 2002), 29-40. For a different (though slightly idiosyncratic) perspective on the connections between 1 Cor 1–4 and 12–14, and the reasons that underlie them, see Wire, *Women Prophets*, 39-71, 135-58.

[45] See e.g. H.B. Swete, *The Holy Spirit in the Ancient Church: A Study of Christian Teaching in the Age of the Fathers* (London: Macmillan and Co.,

stress the basic contours of the argument of 1 Cor 12–14 and recognize its leading themes and their possible links with 2.1–3.4.

5.4.2.2.1. Contours of the Argument

Virtually all commentators agree that 1 Cor 12–14 is a single rhetorical unit where Paul addresses a new topic,[46] one signalled by the formulaic περὶ δέ. However, not all agree on how to define the specific and rather ambiguous designation, τῶν πνευματικῶν, which can be read as either a masculine or neuter plural. If we read the phrase as masculine, then the designation refers to spiritual *people*,[47] whereas if read as neuter, it refers to spiritual *things* (or "gifts"). A decision between the two options cannot be made on the basis of Pauline usage, for there are instances in the letter where both forms are used.[48] How are we to decide in this case

---

1912), 359-409; D. Bridge and D. Phypers, *Spiritual Gifts and the Church* (Leicester: InterVarsity, 1974); Dunn, *Jesus and the Spirit*; J. Koenig, *Charismata: God's Gifts for God's People* (Philadelphia: Westminster Press, 1978); R.A.N. Kydd, *Charismatic Gifts in the Early Church: An Exploration Into the Gifts of the Spirit During the First Three Centuries of the Christian Church* (Peabody: Hendrickson, 1984); Martin, *Spirit and Congregation*; Carson, *Showing the Spirit*; S.S. Schatzmann, *Pauline Theology of Charismata* (Peabody: Hendrickson, 1989); idem, "Purpose and Function of Gifts in 1 Corinthians," *SwJT* 45.1 (2002): 53-68; J. Ruthven, *On the Cessation of the Charismata: The Protestant Polemic on Postbilical Miracles* (Sheffield: Sheffield Academic, 1993); M. Turner, *The Holy Spirit and Spiritual Gifts: Then and Now* (Carlisle: Paternoster, 2006).

[46] For a recent analysis on the rhetorical unity of this passage, see J.E.A. Chiu, *1 Cor 12–14: Literary Structure and Theology* (Rome: Editrice Pontifica Instituto Biblico, 2007).

[47] See e.g. Hurd, *Origin of 1 Corinthians*, 194; Schmithals, *Gnosticism in Corinth*, 171-72.

[48] For the masculine, see 1 Cor 2.15; 3.1; 14.37. For the neuter, see 1 Cor 2.13; 9.11; 10.3-4; 14.1b.

whether he is speaking about people or things?[49] The argument of 1 Cor 12–14 shows Paul's concern to be primarily with displays of spirituality and only secondarily with those persons who exhibit or display such things.[50] Moreover, by noting the stages of the argument we see that Paul deals with particular displays of spirituality. Specifically, 12.8-10 and 28-30 offers a list of roughly eleven provisions of the Spirit; in 13.1-3 and 8 the list is reduced to three (although he introduces three others); and in 14.1-40 the discussion focuses on only two: tongues and prophecy.[51]

Furthermore, given this narrowing of focus and the fact that tongues and prophecy are relativized in the longer listing,[52] it would seem that these two are a particular problem in the Corinthian assembly, and Paul seeks to *correct* the faulty views associated with them.[53] However, a deeper problem seems to be at

---

[49] Both Morris (*First Epistle*, 163) and Thiselton (*First Epistle*, 901) appear to be indifferent to this dilemma.

[50] Cf. G.D. Fee, "Gifts of the Spirit," in *Dictionary of Paul and His Letters* (eds. G.F. Hawthorne, R.P. Martin, and D.G. Reid; Downers Grove: InterVarsity, 1993), 341.

[51] Cf. Perkins, who qualifies tongues as "praying in tongues" (*First Corinthians*, 133). However, it is not quite clear why she makes this distinction.

[52] In saying prophecy and tongues are relativized I am merely drawing attention to the idea that Paul relegates them to a lesser position because the Corinthians have unjustly elevated them to signs (or indicators) of spiritual superiority—see Keener, *1-2 Corinthians*, 101; although cf. F.W. Horn, "Holy Spirit," in *Anchor Bible Dictionary* (ed. D.N. Freedman; New York: Doubleday, 1992), 3.273.

[53] This follows Horsley, who says the tone of Paul's argument in 1 Cor 12–14 reveals that it "is corrective, not simply informative: it challenges the Corinthian spirituals' orientation as well as their spiritual practice" (*1 Corinthians*, 166). Fee, on the other hand, take things further than Horsley: "Paul's answer is intended to be *corrective*, not instructional or informational. Thus, even if they presented themselves to Paul with a question (or questions), his response seems to take *exception* to their viewpoint, not simply to inform

work. Given the rhetorical placement of chapter 13,[54] this deeper problem is the absence of self-giving sacrificial love, an absence which contributes to the faulty understanding of "spiritual things" and their misguided implementation in the worship, which in turn leads to the potential for internal stratification. As Mitchell shows, the subject of chapter 14 deals with the edification of the church, which represents a central aim of chapter 12, with chapter 13 being the means by which it takes place.[55] Furthermore, the absence of love represents the Corinthians' failure to reflect the nature of the gospel, which they originally accepted and believed because of their love for God (cf. 1.23-24; 2.2, 4-5, 9-10), which united them all "in Christ." Thus, while Mitchell is right to stress the thematic parallels between unity (or "concord") and love as vital for Paul's wider aims for reconciliation, [56] we cannot overlook Paul's emphasis on the Corinthians' need for their spirituality to reflect that which identifies them "in Christ."

---

them in areas where they lack understanding" (*First Epistle*, 570-71—emphasis original).

[54] A number of scholars see chapter 13 as either a digression or an otherwise separate piece brought into the argument for rhetorical effect. For those advocating the first option, see Robertson-Plummer, *First Epistle*, 285; Witherington, *Conflict and Community*, 264; Collins, *First Corinthians*, 605; cf. Keener (*1-2 Corinthians*, 107), who brackets the rhetorical digression as 12.31–13.13. For those advocating the second option, see Héring, *First Epistle*, 134; Barrett, *First Epistle*, 297. However, I agree both with Fitzmyer, who views the discussion on love as "the *climax* of what Paul has been teaching in chap. 12 about the *pneumatika* and the diverse kinds of them" (*First Corinthians*, 488—emphasis original) and with Horrell, who takes chapter 13 as rhetorically preparatory for what Paul argues in chapter 14 (see *Social Ethos*, 182-83).

[55] Mitchell, *Rhetoric of Reconciliation*, 270.

[56] *Ibid.*, 165-71.

5.4.2.2.2. Leading Themes

In chapter 12 Paul deals with the importance of God, via the Spirit, equipping the members with gifts (of grace) for building up the body of Christ (12.4-7, 24b-25; cf. 2.12; 3.10). Noteworthy is the emphasis in 12.8 and 10c on Spirit-given wisdom and Spirit-given discernment, two gifts that Paul described earlier as characterizing who the Corinthians are and how they should view themselves (2.6, 10, 15-16; cf. 3.16-20). There is, however, a noticeable difference between the two claims, one that relates to the recipients of wisdom and those who practice discernment.[57] While in 2.1–3.4, we are left with the impression that all believers receive God's wisdom via the Spirit and are able to exercise Spirit-led discernment, here in chapters 12–14 Paul suggests that not all are equipped in this way. In fact, it appears as though is Paul declaring that "to one is given the word of wisdom through the Spirit" (12.8a) and "to another the discernment of the spirits" (12.10c), and that "the Spirit works all these things distributing to each one individually just as he wills" (12.11). How then do we address the apparent distinctions between what Paul says in 2.1–3.4 and what he states here in chapter 12?

Part of the solution can be seen in the distinctive emphases in the two passages, specifically in relation to the "word of the cross" as God's revealed wisdom and the Corinthians' identity with that wisdom. While in 2.1–3.4 Paul emphasizes the proclamation of the cross as the means by which the Corinthians' identity was originally formed, in 12–14 Paul stresses the need for their identity to continue to reflect the message of the cross. Paul's specific remarks in 1 Cor 12–14 address matters relevant to worship in the believing assembly, worship ostensibly involving exhortations related to the gospel. Thus, Paul's remarks presuppose not only a

---

[57] Cf. M.J. Cartledge, "Charismatic Prophecy: A Definition and Description," *JPT* 5 (1994): 96.

worship setting but also an awareness of how and why such an assembly exists. Accordingly, it is by the Spirit's revelation that the Corinthians believed and accepted God's wisdom as displayed in the cross and identified themselves with that wisdom (2.4-5, 6). And it is through the Spirit that the Corinthians are able not only to discern how God's wisdom in the cross redefines life but also how to assess their lives as reflections of that wisdom (cf. 12.3-11; 14.1-40).

However, Paul sees the Corinthians at present as reflecting neither the message of the cross nor the new identity it bestows. Instead they reflect a wisdom that is wholly different. As noted above, the argument of 1 Cor 12 suggests an internal stratification based on an assumed definition and hierarchy of spirituality. Moreover, the Corinthians appear to be relying on a faulty criterion to justify this stratification, one that prioritizes ecstatic speech and prophetic utterances as superior displays of spirituality. The effect of this view of spirituality and the valuations applied to it could be seen as the Corinthians attempting to create or establish a uniform spirituality. Thus, all who speak in ecstatic tongues or prophetic utterances reflect what it means to be truly spiritual. However, Paul indicates that not all spiritual things are necessarily from God, despite appearances, and therefore there is a need to discern or test such things in order to determine their legitimacy (cf. 1 Thess 5.19-21). For Paul the test is quite simple (cf. 12.3):[58] all (spirit-inspired) utterances that curse Christ cannot be from God, whereas all utterances that proclaim Christ as Lord are consistent with what the Spirit reveals. It is worth noting that with this "test" Paul is subtly arguing against the Corinthians' faulty notion of spirituality. *All* who curse Jesus are not led by the Spirit (i.e. spiritual), and *all*

---

[58] Cf. Barrett, *First Epistle*, 281. There is debate on whether or not the contrasting expressions noted in 12.3 represent actual claims made in the Corinthian assembly, to which Paul responds.

who confess Christ as Lord are led by the Spirit (i.e. they are spiritual).[59] The implication of tying spirituality to this inclusive confession is that it applies to *all* who believe; spirituality is not the exclusive state of only those who practice ostensibly superior pneumatic abilities.[60]

Related to this is the additional (and more substantial) problem of the Corinthians constructing their own "building" and doing so in accordance with their own perceptions of what it should be. By insisting that the body as a worshipping assembly be characterized by uniformity in spiritual expression, and by encouraging (if not requiring) uniformity, the Corinthians are creating a body that is not functionally unified but deformed. For Paul, this construction is not only faulty in itself but also in direct conflict with God's wisdom and work, and he proves this by way of a metaphor.[61] Just as the human body, *as a body*, cannot function if it exists as only a single member (or body part), the believing assembly, as the body of Christ, cannot operate properly and effectively if it prioritizes one spiritual manifestation over all the others. Such a "body" simply does not work. Moreover, as Paul argues in 12.18 and 24b-26, it is God who organized the body in such a way that harmony of the whole is contingent upon the diverse functions of the parts.

---

[59] As Hays argues: "Anyone who utters that confession (not just mouthing the words but making a self-involving confession of the lordship of Jesus) is ipso facto in the sphere of the Holy Spirit's power" (*First Corinthians*, 208).

[60] As Bassler summarises: "Since Paul is concerned to refute those Corinthians who claim their gift of glossolalia is a special, perhaps unique, demonstration of spirit possession, he opens his response in vv 1-3 by presenting a radically different perspective. Noting the simple baptismal confession, Jesus is Lord, can only be uttered under the influence of the Holy Spirit (v 3b), Paul undermines any pneumatic elitism. All Christians make this confession, thus all Christians, not a tongue-speaking few, are πνευματικοί" ("1 Cor 12:3—Curse and Confession in context," *JBL* 101.3 [1982]: 416).

[61] For a summary on the nature and rhetorical use of the "body" metaphor, see Mitchell, *Rhetoric of Reconciliation*, 157-58; Horrell, *Social Ethos*, 178-79.

This emphasis on God as creator and organizer not only recalls Paul's argument concerning God's preordained plan of salvation and benefits for those who accept it (cf. 2.7-9, 13), but also reflects the appropriate cause for boasting. God's purposeful organization of the body, the specific will of the Spirit when distributing gifts of grace, the divine revelation of the mystery of the cross, and the unlikely calling of the Corinthians all militate against self-boasting (cf. 1.30-31; 6.19-20).

For Paul, the Corinthians' failure to reflect who they are meant to be, their faulty valuations of certain members, and their self-boasting are linked with a much larger and more detrimental problem: their failure to rely on and exhibit love for each other now, a love they collectively exhibited for God when they first believed (cf. 2.9). As we can see from Paul's description in 13.4-7, the love in question is a particular kind—or it is characterized by specific traits or attributes. Horsley suggests that Paul's description of love is an implicit accusation against the Corinthians, in that they have failed to reflect the love that Paul expounds. [62] Specifically, boasting of status, relegation of "lesser" members, prideful claims of knowledge, behaving with little to no regard for others, not condemning unrighteousness (or immoral actions) but allowing them to persist; all of these and more fail to exhibit true, divine love—as displayed in the cross.

It is equally possible that Paul finally articulates the concept of (divine) love, which has been at work throughout the argument—albeit in subtle ways (cf. 2.9; 4.21; 8.1, 3). Moreover, Paul's definition also seems to stand in opposition to the Corinthians' notion of what love is and how it is expressed. Thus, Paul's definition of love functions as a criterion against which the Corinthians' behavior can (and should) be measured. Accordingly, by recalling the argument thus far, it becomes clear that the

---

[62] Horsley, *1 Corinthians*, 177.

Corinthians' behaviors reflect more the ways of the world, or life according to the flesh, and are therefore inappropriate for those who are "in Christ."

They are inappropriate because they do not correspond with the specific definition of love and because they fail to reflect the love of God revealed in the cross and the new life it provides by the power of the Spirit. Moreover, the behaviors are inappropriate because they contradict the love the Corinthians displayed toward God when they first believed, a love that ostensibly reflected the definition in 13.4-7. True love humbly seeks after the things of God in accordance with the ways of God and characterizes those who are "mature," whereas faulty love endeavors to satisfy the self in accordance with what the world deems permissible—or what Paul characterizes as that which is fleshly or childish. However, the implication of the argument in 2.1–3.4 is that the Corinthians, because of their acceptance of the gospel and the reception of God's Spirit, are no longer to be defined by that which is fleshly (i.e. of the world) or childish. In a simple analogy, Paul appeals to himself once again in order to illustrate the needed transition (cf. 13.11). Just as childish limits of knowledge, ways of reasoning, and displays of love are inappropriate for adulthood; the ways of the world are inappropriate for those "in Christ." Thus, we should not overlook the emphasis on the kind of love, types of knowledge, and levels of (spiritual) maturity in chapter 13 as it relates to Paul's earlier critique in 2.6–3.4. As in his earlier remarks, Paul here in chapter 13 admonishes the Corinthians to grow up and live not only in accordance with the ways of God but also with whom they have been called to be. While this admonishment is certainly far-reaching in application, a more immediate concern requires its presence at this stage in Paul's argument.

When we come to chapter 14, it becomes quite clear that Paul's description of love is essential for his critique of the Corinthians'

behavior in their worship. Immediately, we see connections with
what Paul has said about the so-called spiritual gifts in chapter 12
and 13.1-3, specifically how they are empty and meaningless if not
governed by (divine) love, which is the "more excellent way"
(12.31b). In this sense, chapter 14 functions as a further example of
this view. In terms of the wider argument, we also find links with
Paul's aphorism in 8.1c-d. Specifically, Paul is concerned with
how the Corinthians understand spirituality and how that
understanding is being used in destructive ways—i.e. establishing
a hierarchy of spirituality based on faulty criteria, and by extension
marginalizing those who do not operate (or exist) on "higher"
levels. Thus, as chapter 14 reveals, it is the arrogance of
knowledge concerning what it means to be spiritual that divides the
community (according to its own terms), and it is the absence of
love that sustains such divisions. In keeping with the theme of
12.31, chapter 14 shows that the Corinthians are not conducting
themselves in accordance to the "more excellent way."

As the argument of chapter 14 bears out, Paul's concern with
the Corinthians' worship deals with the elevation of specific
"gifts" as defining criteria for spirituality and knowledge of or
access to God's revelation. In particular, the "gifts" in mind are
tongues and prophecy. However, scholars recognize that a closer
examination of the argument suggests that the phenomenon of
tongues was more problematic in Corinth than prophetic speech.[63]
Granting this, it does not alter the focus of Paul's critique, which
confronts a misunderstanding and misuse of tongues as an
indicator or even criterion for defining spirituality. Paul appears to
distinguish circumstances for when tongues can be used, one
involving the individual and the other the believing community,
and both share a singular purpose: edification. Thus, and to speak

---

[63] Cf. Fee, *First Epistle*, 571-74, 597-98; Horrell, *Social Ethos*, 176-77;
Fitzmyer, *First Corinthians*, 509.

in rather broad terms, we can say that Paul's critique of the Corinthians' view of tongues is two-pronged: function and intelligibility. In terms of functionality, Paul identifies the purpose of tongues as edification for the one who speaks it (14.4), which is predicated on the idea that this tongue is spoken only to God by the individual (14.2). This intimacy is reinforced by the qualifier, οὐδεὶς γὰρ ἀκούει, πνεύματι δὲ λαλεῖ μυστήρια (14.2b-c).

If, however, a "tongue" is going to be uttered in a communal worship setting then there must be interpretation, ἵνα ἡ ἐκκλησία οἰδοκομὴν λάβη (14.5e). The structure of this passages reveals that the edification for the whole community is dependent upon the interpretation of what the individual speaks. The logical implication is that edification does not occur where there is no interpretation. Paul supports this in 14.10-11 where he asserts: if speaking in tongues goes without interpretation, then the meaning of what is spoken cannot be discerned, since it is otherwise incomprehensible. And if the meaning cannot be discerned, then the incomprehensible message becomes meaningless or impotent for the edification of the community. Edification only occurs when an inspired message is intelligible. By contrast, not only is the function of prophecy beneficial for the whole community (cf. 14.4b, 12), it also relies on a form of speech that can be readily known and understood by all who hear it (cf. 14.6). However, the prophetic message must still be discerned as in harmony with God's revealed wisdom.

With the allowance for "tongues" in a communal worship setting, Paul suggests an overarching criterion for the practice of such things, yet it is one that has been at work all along. If a single person speaks in a tongue, he or she should also pray for the ability to interpret what is said (cf. 14.13). Thus, we see Paul again stressing the need for intelligibility. This consciousness of speaking in an unknown (angelic?) tongue and the conscious decision to seek interpretation suggests that Paul is arguing against ecstatic speech as being characterized by a disengaged or overturned mind. When Philo speaks of similar experiences, he describes the mind of the individual as being by-passed or subverted.[64] Moreover, what is telling about Philo's treatment is that his emphasis falls on the form and not the content of what is spoken in the ecstatic state. In other words, it seems as though the form determined the legitimacy of an inspired message or utterance and not the message itself.

A similar understanding seems to be at work in Corinth, where either form takes priority over content or speaking by the Spirit is prized over speaking with the mind. Paul appears to be confronting this notion when he claims, ἀλλὰ ἐν ἐκκλησίᾳ θέλω πέντε λόγους τῷ νοΐ μου λαλῆσαι, ἵνα καὶ ἄλλους κατηχήσω, ἢ μυρίους λόγους ἐν γλώσσῃ (14.19). While the idea of "teaching others" certainly relates to Paul's remarks in 14.3, we cannot help but notice the force of his meaning by his use of κατηχέω when contrasting prophecy and tongues. Specifically, Paul is stressing the reality that when seeking to instruct the community in a meaningful and coherent way, only intelligible words can achieve this goal.[65] When a myriad of spiritual words spoken by an individual are unintelligible to the whole, they are not beneficial to the community in a meaningful way. All such spiritual words can do is edify the one who speaks them. Or as Barrett suggests, while a myriad of spiritual utterances might strengthen one's spirituality, that is all they can do and should therefore be expressed to God alone (cf. 14.2).[66]

---

[64] See *Her.* 259, 264-65; *QG* 3.9; *Mos.* 2.188-91.

[65] Cf. Fee, *First Epistle*, 675-76. Fitzmyer states it plainly: "in a Christian liturgical gathering, five words uttered with rational intelligibility will have more hortatory and didactic effect that thousands of twitterings in tongues" (*First Corinthians*, 518).

[66] Barrett, *First Epistle*, 322; Keener, *1–2 Corinthians*, 113.

Following an explanation of how spirituality appears to outsiders (14.20-25), Paul elaborates on the communal function of not just prophecy and tongues but all things spiritual (14.26-40). Specifically in 14.26-33, Paul argues that all things done in the believing community should be done for the edification of the whole; they are not opportunities for personal boasting. This mindfulness of others reflects not only the type of love that is to exist within the community, but also the maturity of mind expected of those "in Christ." It is the childish mind and the lack of (divine) love that lead to immature or even chaotic behavior and a prioritizing of self-interest over the needs of others. For Paul, such things belong to the former way of life; they no longer (are to) have any influence on those who belong to Christ and are living in accordance with God's wisdom, as revealed by the Spirit. Those who believe or live otherwise, and claim spiritual inspiration to do so, are not only misconstruing what God has revealed (cf. 14.38) but also placing themselves under God's judgment. This theme of coming under God's judgment for acting or behaving in accordance with what God has revealed is an intensification of earlier judgment themes (cf. 3.10-15; 10.1-10; 11.27-33). What is striking is that, as with the earlier emphases, the notion of judgment is associated with how the community is identified and functions—i.e. how it is built.

One of the leading reasons why Paul pleads for order in worship relates to how the believing community presents itself to the outside world in such a setting. This emphasis is seen primarily in the argument of 14.20-25. Here Paul alerts the Corinthians to the possible accusation from outsiders of madness, due to the chaotic events and incomprehensible speech that take place in worship gatherings (cf. 14.23). While it is true that in such cases the Corinthians could appeal to Paul's remarks in 2.13-15 (i.e. spiritual persons are immune to the accusations of "unspiritual" people),

Paul's admonition for deference to the "weaker" person would seem to trump such an appeal (cf. 9.1-14). Thus, if those "in Christ" are to be God's called community, identified by the sacrificial, self-giving love of Christ, then this community must prioritize reflecting that identity rather than relishing assumed spiritual immunity. Moreover, if individual members of the community are to show deference in behavior for the struggles of other members so as not to cause a hindrance to faith in the gospel, the same applies to how the community as a whole is to behave before "the world" and for precisely the same reason.

Thus, the need for reflecting the reality that God has created for the world in and through Christ crucified has apologetic value. This becomes more acute when we recall the idea that social structures and/or expectations are to reflect or be in harmony with the (divine) wisdom to which they adhere or profess. Serious consequences result when this harmony fails to be maintained, both by the individual and the community. With regard to the individual, failure to live in harmony with the professed wisdom is perceived as an act of folly at best or subversive to the community at worst. In such cases the seditious person is to be removed in order to preserve the integrity of the community (cf. 5.1-2, 5, 13).

With regard to the community, failure to live in accordance with its professed wisdom creates space for accusations of false or misguided wisdom and weakness or insufficiency with regard to the divine. In effect, the integrity of God is at stake when the community fails in this regard. Thus when Paul claims, οὐ γάρ ἐστιν ἀκαταστασίας ὁ θεὸς ἀλλὰ εἰρήνης (14.33a), he is promoting a reality or standard that the Corinthian believers are to reflect. However, when the Corinthian community conducts its worship (of God) in a chaotic manner and an outsider witnesses such an event, the conclusion drawn about the God worshipped is not "peace" but "anarchy."[67] Moreover, the spiritual experiences or displays noted in 1 Cor 14 are not exclusive to God's people but are practiced in pagan cults in the Greco-Roman world. And since such experiences or displays in these other cults are characterized by ecstasy, frenzy, or chaos, an outside observer of the Corinthian community, when ecstatic tongues are manifold, would see no distinction between it and other pagan services of worship. Yet Paul has already reminded the Corinthians that they are no longer to be characterized by what they once were (cf. 12.1-2); they must be characterized now by their identity in the Spirit (cf. 12.13).

Thus, to engage in practices that both present a false or misguided view of God (and divine wisdom) and show no clear distinction between the "society" God creates in Christ and the "society" of the world, is to offer unconsciously a polemic against rather than an apologetic for the truth of the gospel. However, by living in accordance with God's wisdom as displayed in the cross and revealed by the Spirit, the Corinthians (ideally) become what Horsley terms, an "alternative society"[68] in and through which the legitimacy of the gospel is made manifest. In effect the Corinthians become the evidence that through the cross of Christ God is redeeming the world and bringing about its restoration.

5.4.3. The Hope of the Resurrected "Spiritual" Body

Some commentators describe 1 Cor 15 as Paul abruptly initiating a new topic,[69] one that appears to be only loosely related to what precedes it.[70] This designation seems natural when

---

[67] For translating ἀκαταστασία as "anarchy" rather than the softer term, "confusion," see Mitchell, *Rhetoric of Reconciliation*, 172-73.

[68] See Horsley, "Paul's Assembly as Alternative Society," 242-52.

[69] See e.g. Fee, *First Epistle*, 713; Garland, *1 Corinthians*, 682.

[70] Schmithals represents an extreme position when he sees chapter 15 as canonically misplaced. In its present location, Schmithals argues, it "breaks the connection of 16:1 (περὶ τῆς λογείας) with the statement περὶ τῶν

comparing the way Paul introduces this discussion with how he begins his treatment of earlier topics. Ordinarily in the letter, Paul starts with an acknowledgement of the issue being addressed, whether this awareness came about in oral or written form (cf. 5.1; 7.1; 8.1; 11.18; 12.1; 16.1, 12). However, Paul does not directly state how the issue discussed in chapter 15 came to his attention.[71] Moreover, it is not immediately clear what the issue is precisely, because Paul's discussion begins without the topical marker, περὶ δέ κτλ.[72] We have to wait until 15.12 before Paul introduces the topic—i.e. some in Corinth are "saying that there is no resurrection of the dead" (15.12c)[73]—but even then we can only guess at the true nature of the problem.[74] One suggestion is an (over-)realized eschatology, whereby some in Corinth believe they now live in a resurrected state. As Lincoln points out: "Their life in the Spirit

---

πνευματικῶν in chaps. 12–14" (*Gnosticism at Corinth*, 91). For Schmithals, chapter 15 belongs after 11.34.

[71] Voigt rejects the idea that, in this particular instance, word came to Paul in *written* form, and merely entertains the possibility that Stephanas, Fortunatus, and Achaicus relayed the report—presumably in oral form (see *Gemeinsam*, 133; cf. also Barrett, *First Epistle*, 335; J.R. Asher, *Polarity and Change: A Study of Metaphysics, Rhetoric, and Resurrection* [J.C.B. Mohr (Paul Siebeck), 2000], 65 n.118).

[72] A detail particularly troubling for Hurd (see *Origin of 1 Corinthians*, 91-92).

[73] Thiselton argues: "Most commentators believe that few if any [in Corinth] denied the resurrection of *Christ*; but some failed to follow through the eschatological and ethical entailments of what it meant to share in Christ's resurrection, not least corporately as his body" (*First Epistle*, 1176—emphasis original).

[74] Thiselton (*First Epistle* 1172-76) lists the four leading opinions within scholarship: 1) some in Corinth fail to grasp the notion of a post-mortem existence; 2) some in Corinth believe that the resurrection already occurred; 3) some in Corinth are baffled by the notion of a *bodily* resurrection; and 4) various groups of believers in Corinth each hold different (mis)understandings of the resurrection, likely either one or an amalgam of the other three suggestions.

with its abundance of charismatic gifts seemed to them proof that they were already enjoying the eschatological blessings of freedom and fullness associated with its consummation."[75] The effects of this belief seems to branch off in two directions.

On the one hand, this eschatological view of the self leads to a sense of moral freedom, whereby the behaviors of the one "in Christ" are immune from judgment because the individual is already perfected (spiritually). In this sense, we can see how Paul's remarks throughout 1 Cor 5–14 confront not only the specific dilemmas addressed but also this eschatological view that stands behind the dilemmas. On the other hand, the (over-)realized eschatology leads to denying the future resurrection of believers (cf. 15.12), although they do not deny the past resurrection of Christ. In fact, Christ's resurrection is essential for their belief: it is because of Christ's past resurrection that the spiritual elite in Corinth can claim to be living in a perfected state of spiritual existence now, and that they will continue to do so (unchanged) at the (future) parousia of Christ.[76] However, Paul counters this view first by labeling Christ's past resurrection as ἀπαρχή (15.20), which implies a subsequent resurrection (at least in this case for τῶν κεκοιμημένων), and second by asserting ὅτι σάρξ καὶ αἷμα βασιλείαν θεοῦ κληρονομῆσαι οὐ δύναται (15.50b), which means an ontological change must occur before the one "in Christ" can live in spiritual perfection.[77] Since the final resurrection has not yet occurred, no one claiming to be spiritual exists in the (anticipated) perfected state.

---

[75] A.T. Lincoln, *Paradise Now and Not Yet: Studies in the Role of the Heavenly Dimension in Paul's Thought with Special Reference to His Eschatology* (Cambridge: Cambridge University Press, 1981), 33.

[76] Cf. *ibid.*, 35-36.

[77] I use the phrase, "ontological change" in the light of Paul's argument in 15.50-54, where he describes the necessary transformation from perishable to imperishable bodies, and from mortal to immortal bodies.

By considering the way in which Paul makes his case, we can discern a twofold line of argument where he seeks to 1) expose the absurdity of denying the resurrection, along with its logical and theological consequences, and 2) articulate the appropriate understanding of resurrection and its effects on life. Following what is often called the *narratio* (15.1-11),[78] the argument of chapter 15 divides generally into two parts: 15.12-34 and 15.35-57.[79] In the first part, Paul addresses the faulty perceptions of the resurrection as an experienced event (15.12-19). Specifically, and on the basis of the report given to him (cf. 15.12), Paul articulates the results of denying the resurrection of the faithful. He then counters this by explaining the consequences for the future, given the reality of Christ's resurrection (15.20-28),[80] and how those

---

[78] While Eriksson and others define it as 15.3-11 (*Traditions as Rhetorical Proof: Pauline Argumentation in 1 Corinthians* [Stockholm: Almqvist & Wiksell, 1998], 249; D.F. Watson, "Paul's Rhetorical Strategy in 1 Cor 15," in *Rhetoric and the New Testament: Essays from the 1992 Heidelberg Conference* [eds. S.E. Porter and T.H. Olbricht; Sheffield: JSOT Press, 1993], 236; Witherington, *Conflict and Community*, 292; W. Schrage, *Der erste Brief an die Korinther* [Neukirchen-Vluyn: Neukirchen Verlag, 2001], 4.17) and Collins limits it only to 15.3b-5 (*First Corinthians*, 526), Thiselton and others see the whole of 15.1-11 as the *narratio* (cf. *First Epistle*, 1177; Keener, *1-2 Corinthians*, 122-23; Fitzmyer, *First Corinthians*, 540-41, 544).

[79] This general two-part division of the argument follows the reading of most commentators—see e.g. Robertson-Plummer, *First Epistle*, 329-30; Fee, *First Epistle*, 714; Horsley, *1 Corinthians*, 197; Schrage, *Der erste Brief*, 4:108, 266; Keener, *1-2 Corinthians*, 125, 129. Conzelmann (*1 Corinthians*, 263-93) and Fitzmyer (*First Corinthians*, 540) advocate three parts following the *narratio*: 15.12-34, 35-49, 50-58 (cf. Mitchell [*Rhetoric of Reconciliation*, 286], who includes the *narratio* in the first part—thus, 15.1-34).

[80] Cf. Asher, who suggests: "The doctrine that Paul is presenting here is probably his own innovation.... The doctrine of the eschatological resurrection in second temple Judaism apparently consisted of only a one-time, collective resurrection (Dan 12:1-3 and 2 Macc 7:9-14). The doctrine of a two-stage resurrection (Christ's and the eschatological) is probably a development of

consequences have present-life implications (15.29-34).[81] In the second part, Paul addresses the specific issue of the nature (or form) of the future transformed, resurrected body and how it is even possible (15.35-49), before stressing the necessity of this transformation for believers living in God's eschatological kingdom (15.50-57).

While the problem of (over-)realized eschatology might be at work in Corinth, the twofold construction of his argument indicates that Paul confronts the wider problem of the Corinthians relying on faulty notions of wisdom and spirituality that produce this faulty eschatology. This means we once again encounter the twofold dilemma of how the Corinthians at present are defining life and the inappropriate criteria they employ to do so. A leading emphasis throughout is the proper understanding of what it means to be spiritual, especially in the light of Christ's work on the cross and subsequent resurrection. Specifically, while the spiritual life is one that begins at a particular point, its fullness (or perfection) is not an immediate state obtained post-belief and post-reception of God's Spirit. Rather, one's spiritual existence matures throughout his or her life, empowered and guided by the Spirit. At the very least, we can say Paul stresses the point that no one can achieve spiritual perfection prior to the eschaton, for it is only at the eschaton that believers receive imperishable, immortal, (true) spiritual bodies. To stress this distinction Paul employs the contrasting language of ψυχικός and πνευματικός (cf. 15.42-46) which appeared earlier in 2.14-15, although with a slightly different emphasis.

Pauline Christology and, as such, is unique to the early Christians" (*Polarity and Change*, 61 n.101).

[81] Walker recently argued for this portion as another "non-Pauline interpolation" (see "1 Corinthians 15:29-34 as a Non-Pauline Interpolation," *CBQ* 68.1 [2007]: 84-103).

In 2.14-15 Paul uses ψυχικός and πνευματικός to differentiate between the one without and the one with God's Spirit, thus making a (soteriological?) distinction in terms of identity. On the basis of his preceding analogy on different types of "flesh" (σάρξ) in 15.39-41, here in 15.42-46 Paul isolates two types of bodies: one related to the present age and the other kept for the age to come, thus making an ontological distinction between the types (cf. 15.44b).[82] In this instance, ψυχικός is the body (σῶμα) reserved for life in this present age whereas πνευματικός is the body (σῶμα) reserved for life in the age to come. While much debate surrounds whether the "spiritual body" is the "natural body" reconstituted or an entirely new form of existence,[83] we can be sure that Paul (at least) believes that the "natural body" cannot inhabit the age to come.[84] This is borne out when we examine the descriptions Paul gives to the two types of body (15.42-43): the "natural body" is perishable, dishonorable, and weak, whereas the "spiritual body" is imperishable, glorious, and powerful. From the perspective of God's wisdom, the characteristics of the "natural body" reflect the nature of the present age while those of the "spiritual body" reflect the age to come. Therefore, since the present age is passing away and the future age is dawning, and since that future age can only be inhabited by a "body" suited specifically for it, a transformation must take place; one cannot simply transfer from one state of existence to another in the same "body."

Thus, while maintaining the separate nuances with these terms in their particular contexts, two vital points should be considered. The first point deals with the force of Paul's argument in both

---

[82] The specific construction of the claim (i.e. εἰ ἔστιν...ἔστιν καί) bears out this distinction.

[83] For a summary of this debate, see Fitzmyer, *First Corinthians*, 593-94.

[84] A similar emphasis is found in 15.50.

places. While the precise meaning of ψυχικός and πνευματικός might differ in 2.14-15 and 15.42-46, the function of the distinction remains the same in both texts. For Paul, just as the "natural" person cannot claim to be "spiritual," because he or she lacks that which would identify him or her as such (i.e. the indwelling presence of the Spirit), a person in this age cannot claim to possess a "spiritual" body, because the time when such a body is required and given has not come. The second point of consistency relates to the role of the Spirit in the life of the believer and the relationship of the Spirit's work to the person of Christ. In 2.14-15, with regard to the soteriological distinction, it is only by the presence of the Spirit that one can know and discern the (mysterious) things of God (i.e. salvation in the cross), an ability that is characteristic of (only) those who are identified with and have the mind of Christ. In 15.42-46, with regard to the ontological distinction, it is only by the "last Adam" (i.e. Christ), the one who is the "life-giving spirit," that one can partake in the new age of God's wise (mysterious) plan (cf. 15.50-52), because he or she is the recipient of Christ's Spirit, who gives new life and exercises the power of transformation for this age and the age to come.[85]

Along with these specific links is a larger thematic connection, one that brings me back to the question of chapter 15's logical relationship to the rest of the letter. Earlier it was noted that scholars often describe this chapter as seemingly disconnected from what precedes it. However, in 15.1-5 Paul reminds the Corinthians of the thematic (and theological) connection between cross and resurrection, a series of events that Paul sees as inherent to the gospel, and stresses that this gospel is precisely what they believed and accepted during his first sojourn. Moreover, earlier in his argument Paul reminds the Corinthians of their response of faith to the gospel (1.17-18, 21, 23; 2.4-5; 4.15; cf. 15.1-2, 11) and

---

[85] Cf. Thiselton, *First Epistle*, 1284.

that the result of this faith is an on-going movement toward salvation (1.18; 4.5; cf. 15.22), which culminates in eternal life in God's new age. This indicates another type of relationship between chapter 15 and the rest of Paul's argument, and in this case it is theological. Specifically, as Barth points out,[86] the argument of chapter 15 functions as the culmination of both God's restorative power in the cross and the eschatological themes that have pervaded the argument (cf. 1.7-8; 3.10-15; 4.5; 6.13-14; 7.29-31; 11.26), of which the cross is a vital one.

5.4.4. Concluding Remarks on 1 Cor 5–15

Paul's critique of the Corinthian believers' situation, as given in 1 Cor 5–15, suggests a failure not only to live out the wisdom of God but also to allow the transformative power of the Spirit to work within and amongst them. Instead of living in the light of the cross and in humble anticipation of the resurrection, Paul sees the Corinthians as claiming a perfected existence (i.e. a spiritual resurrection) while their behaviors or practices resemble those that the cross has already condemned. The inconsistency between word and deed represents only part of the problem; Paul's leading concern is the Corinthians' line of thought that justifies such an inconsistency. Paul is concerned because such thinking is not in

---

[86] See K. Barth, *Resurrection of the Dead* (trans. H.J. Stenning; Eugene: Wipf & Stock, 2003), 101. More recently, Ackerman nuanced this view by stressing the intended ethical effect of this rhetorical construction. Specifically he argues: "Throughout the letter, Paul focuses upon the *present* behaviors and beliefs of the Corinthians. He refers to the *past* specifically in chapters 1–4 and the *future* in chapter 15 in order to influence the *present* situation in Corinth. The divine plan was *revealed* in the past (*apekalypsen*, 2:10) with Christ's death and resurrection and will be *completed* in the future (*telos*, 15:24) with Christ's coming again and the resurrection of those 'in Christ.' Paul's expressed purpose for the Corinthians, then, is for them to live as believers in communion with Christ in the *interim* time between these two points in history" (*Lo, I Tell You a Mystery*, 3—emphasis original).

agreement with what God has revealed through the Spirit, nor is it consistent with the transformation of mind and thought which the Spirit provides for those who embrace God's wisdom. Paul throughout his argument has shown the Corinthians' failure to rely on Spirit-led, communal discernment in both their public life and life as a believing community. Rather than seek God's available wisdom so as to govern their lives in a manner worthy of the cross, they have sought after a wisdom that, while rendered futile (by God in the cross), is accommodating to their faulty spirituality. As a result, this futile wisdom carries the potential of rendering belief in the complete gospel message vain and foolish (cf. 15.1; 1.17), for it legitimates belief according to criteria that necessarily denigrates the true nature of the gospel.

Thus, Paul's argument is framed by a reminder of the life that begins at the cross and hopes for the life that comes with resurrection, and the life lived in between reflects this tension, a tension that scholars define as, "cruciformity." Cruciformity describes the new life in Christ, whereby the believer carries the "dying of Jesus" (2 Cor 4.10) and endures "the process of dying yet living." [87] Moreover, it is a cross-shaped existence made possible by the transformation of life and mind wrought by the Spirit. As Munzinger argues: "For Paul the Spirit is the sine qua non of the new life. Not that the individual but the πνεῦμα is ultimately responsible for the new set of attitudes of the 'cruciform' character."[88] Cruciformity also allows the believer to see beyond the temporality of "the process of dying yet living" and to be assured of the eternality of true life that begins with the resurrection.[89]

---

[87] Gorman, *Apostle of the Crucified Lord*, 390.

[88] Munzinger, *Discerning the Spirits*, 173.

[89] Cf. Barth: "The dignity of the cross is provisional, indicating the provisional nature of the Christian existence and all sanctification. The crown of

5.5. Summary of Rhetorical Relationships

At the beginning of this chapter I asked: why does the pneumatological teaching of 2.1–3.4 appear where it does in Paul's argument? Why does Paul not articulate this teaching when dealing with the topic of "spiritual things" in chapter 12–14? More specifically, what is the purpose of offering this pneumatological teaching sooner rather than later? What are the rhetorical and theological implications for such an early placement? To answer these questions we must return to the details concerning the occasion for Paul's letter, specifically the dilemma(s) in Corinth that emerged after his departure. I have argued that Paul's letter confronts faulty notions of divine wisdom and spirituality, and that these notions affect not only the Corinthians' assessment of Paul and his preaching but also themselves as spiritual people, recipients of God's wisdom and Spirit.

In one sense, these two "problem" areas establish the basic framework for Paul's response—i.e. chapters 1–4 deal with the Corinthians' post-departure view(s) of Paul, and chapters 5–15 deal with the Corinthians' subsequent view(s) of themselves. Close examination of the text reveals that in both parts of this framework, Paul's answer is the same: the dilemmas exist because the Corinthians are neither relying on God's wisdom as revealed to them by the Spirit nor exercising wise, communal discernment; they are instead relying on a wisdom and a self-interested form of

---

life is more than this. It is of the very essence of the cross carried by Christians that it has a goal, and therefore an end, and therefore its time. It signifies the setting of a term. That is why is it so bitter. But this limitation is not itself ultimate. Borne in participation in the suffering of Jesus, it will cease at the very point to which the suffering of Jesus points in the power of His resurrection, and therefore to which our suffering also points in company with His. It is not our cross which is eternal, but, when we have borne it, the future life revealed by the crucifixion of Jesus" (*Church Dogmatics* [trans. G.W. Bromiley; eds. G.W. Bromiley and T.F. Torrance; Edinburgh: T&T Clark, 1958] 4.2: 613).

judgment that are inappropriate for those "in Christ." Thus, in this first sense, the pneumatological teaching appears early in order to anchor Paul's response to the twofold dilemma.

In another sense, the two "problem" areas also reveal a present cause-and-effect relationship that is contrary to the one that characterized the Corinthians' original experience—i.e. the start of their new life in Christ. When Paul originally came to Corinth and proclaimed the message of Christ crucified, the Corinthians not only accepted Paul as an apostolic witness but also believed and accepted his message as God's wisdom. For Paul, this belief and acceptance came about not through rhetorical display or eloquence but by the demonstrable, powerful work of the Spirit (2.1, 4-5). This work also involved an epistemological transformation enabling the Corinthians to know how to interpret their new life "in Christ" and live in accordance with God's wisdom, a transformation and ability made possible by the work of the Spirit.

However, the Corinthians began to rely on human wisdom (or the wisdom of the world) in order to judge the validity of both Paul and his message as representative of wisdom (cf. 1 Cor 1–4). Moreover, they started to rely on the criteria established by human wisdom so as to identify or even define themselves and others as "wise" and "spiritual" (cf. 1 Cor 5–15). Paul's answer to both problems is clear: the Corinthians must recall their original beginning as God's (spiritual) people, defined by God's wisdom, revealed by the Spirit, and no longer seek to be identified by anything else (cf. Gal 3.3). Thus, in this second sense, the pneumatological teaching appears early so as to reflect the historical circumstances of the Corinthians' original experience, in contrast to their present situation.

Accordingly, if the Corinthians were exercising or adhering to wise (communal) discernment now, then their assessments of both Paul and themselves would be filtered through the Spirit-given criterion of "the mind of Christ." As I have argued, for Paul "the mind of Christ" represents both an identity and way of knowing shaped by the cross, for it is through the wisdom of the cross and by the power of the Spirit that believers are united under the name of Christ. Thus, if the Corinthians were relying on Spirit-guided discernment, an ability resulting from their acceptance of God's wisdom, revealed by the Spirit in the proclamation of the cross, Paul's corrective and his plea for unity would be unnecessary. However, since Paul sees the Corinthians relying on a wisdom other than God's and seeking to define what it means to be spiritual through a criterion other than that given by the Spirit, and this twofold choice ostensibly creates space for divisive problems to emerge, Paul's corrective response is necessary.

However it must be said that this response is more than a plea for unity amongst believers: Paul's focus seeks to articulate the wisdom and means by which it is known appropriate for those "in Christ." Therefore, I contend that Paul's early emphasis on the Spirit's role in the proclamation of the cross, the mediation of divine wisdom, and the exercise of wise, communal discernment shapes how the argument of 1 Corinthians unfolds.[90] In saying this I am not ignoring or downplaying the crucial themes of unity and concord; instead I am simply emphasizing the point that this pneumatological teaching functions as Paul's explanation for *how* unity and concord are re-established in the Corinthian assembly.

5.6. Conclusion

This discussion about the pneumatological teaching appearing at an early stage in the argument of the letter underlines what this dissertation as a whole has claimed about the significance of this teaching as Paul's response to the Corinthian situation. As noted

---

[90] This follows from my earlier argument concerning the theological nature of Paul's response.

throughout, the teaching functions as a corrective to the faulty notions of divine wisdom and spirituality. In summary, the pneumatological teaching of 1 Cor 2.1–3.4 is meant to address the Corinthians' views about the apostolic message (and messenger), the nature and scope of divine wisdom, and what it means to be a spiritual and single-minded community, whose identity, life, and behavior are to be defined by the wisdom of God in the cross of Christ. For Paul, such a community is made possible not through "a wisdom of this age" (2.6) nor through "the spirit of the world" (2.12) but only by the essential, wise, and powerful work of the Spirit of God.

BIBLIOGRAPHY

PRIMARY SOURCES

Most of the non-biblical Greek and Latin references, quotations, and translations below are from the Loeb Classical Library. The OT Pseudepigrapha, the Dead Sea Scrolls, and the Gospel of Thomas were taken from the following:

Charlesworth, J.H., ed. *The Old Testament Pseudepigrapha*. 2 vols. Garden City: Doubleday & Co., 1983-1985.

Martínez, F.G., ed. *The Dead Sea Scrolls Translated: The Qumran Texts in English*. 2nd edition. Leiden: Brill, 1996.

Kirby, P. "The Gospel of Thomas." Early Christian Writings. Retrieved from http://www.earlychristianwritings.com/thomas-fifth.html, 2010.

SECONDARY SOURCES

Ackerman, D.A. *Lo, I Tell You a Mystery: Cross, Resurrection, and Paraenesis in the Rhetoric of 1 Corinthians*. PrTMS. Eugene: Pickwick Publications, 2006.

Adams, E. *Constructing the World: A Study in Paul's Cosmological Language*. SNTW. Edinburgh: T&T Clark, 2000.

Alford, H. *The Greek Testament: With a Critically Revised Text*. Vol. 2. London: Rivingtons, 1865.

Anderson, R.D. *Ancient Rhetorical Theory and Paul*. CBET 18. Leuven: Peeters, 1999.

Arnold, C.E. *Powers of Darkness: Principalities & Powers in Paul's Letters*. Downers Grove: InterVarsity, 1992.

Asher, J.R. *Polarity and Change: A Study of Metaphysics, Rhetoric, and Resurrection*. HUT 42. Tübingen: J.C.B. Mohr (Paul Siebeck), 2000.

Aune, D.E. *Prophecy in Early Christianity and the Ancient Mediterranean World*. Grand Rapids: Eerdmans, 1983.

_____. "Introduction." Pages 1-14 in *The Blackwell Companion to the New Testament*. Edited by D.E. Aune. Chichester: Wiley-Blackwell, 2010.

_____. "The World of Roman Hellenism." Pages 15-37 in *The Blackwell Companion to the New Testament*. Edited by D.E. Aune. Chichester: Wiley-Blackwell, 2010.

Bailey, K.E. *Paul Through Mediterranean Eyes: Cultural Studies in 1 Corinthians*. London: SPCK, 2011.

Baird, W. "'One Against the Other': Intra-Church Conflict in 1 Corinthians." Pages 116-36 in *The Conversation Continues: Studies in Paul and John. In Honor of J. Louis Martyn*. Edited by R.T. Fortna and B.R. Gaventa. Nashville: Abingdon, 1990.

Barclay, J.M.G. "1 Corinthians." Pages 1108-33 in *The Oxford Bible Commentary*. Edited by J. Barton and J. Muddiman. Oxford: Oxford University Press, 2001.

_____. "Πνευματικός in the Social Dialect of Pauline Christianity." Pages 157-67 in *The Holy Spirit and Christian Origins: Essays in Honor of James D.G. Dunn*. Edited by G.N. Stanton, B.W. Longenecker, and S.C. Barton. Grand Rapids: Eerdmans, 2004.

Barrett, C.K. "Cephas and Corinth." Pages 1-12 in *Abraham unser Vater: Festschrift für Otto Michel*. AGSU 5. Edited by O. Betz, M. Hengel, and P. Stuhlmacher. Leiden: Brill, 1963.

_____. *A Commentary on the First Epistle to the Corinthians*. BNTC. 2nd edition. London: Adam & Charles Black, 1971.

Barth, K. *Church Dogmatics*. Vol. 4.2. Translated by G.W. Bromiley. Edited by G.W. Bromiley and T.F. Torrance. Edinburgh: T&T Clark, 1958.

_____. *Resurrection of the Dead*. Translated by H.J. Stenning. Eugene: Wipf & Stock, 2003.

Barton, S.C. "1 Corinthians." Pages 1314-52 in *Eerdmans Commentary on the Bible*. Edited by J.D.G. Dunn and J.W. Rogerson. Grand Rapids: Eerdmans, 2003.

Bassler, J.M. "1 Cor 12:3—Curse and Confession in Context." *JBL* 101.3 (1982): 415-18.

Baur, F.C. *Paul: The Apostle of Jesus Christ. His Life and Work, His Epistles and His Doctrines*. 2 vols. 2nd edition. Translated by E. Zeller and revised by A. Menzies. London: Williams and Norgate, 1876.

Beet, J.A. *A Commentary on St Paul's Epistles to the Corinthians*. London: Hodder and Stoughton, 1882.

Beker, J.C. *Paul the Apostle: The Triumph of God in Life and Thought*. Edinburgh: T&T Clark, 1980.

_____. *The Triumph of God: The Essence of Paul's Thought*. Minneapolis: Fortress, 1990.

Betz, H.D. *II Corinthians 8 and 9: A Commentary on Two Administrative Letters of the Apostle Paul*. Edited by G.W. MacRae. Hermeneia. Philadelphia: Fortress, 1985.

Billroth, J.G. *A Commentary on the Epistles of Paul to the Corinthians*. Translated by W.L. Alexander. Edinburgh: T&T Clark, 1837.

Bird, M.F. and P.M. Sprinkle. "Jewish Interpretation of Paul in the Last Thirty Years." *CBR* 6.3 (2008): 355-76.

Blaney, H.J.S. "St Paul's Posture on Speaking in Unknown Tongues." *Wesleyan Theological Journal* 8 (1973): 52-60.

Boccaccini, G. *Middle Judaism: Jewish Thought, 300 B.C.E. to 200 C.E.* Minneapolis: Fortress, 1991.

Bockmuehl, M. *Revelation and Mystery in Ancient Judaism and Pauline Christianity*. Grand Rapids: Eerdmans, 1997.

Boise, J. *Four of the Earlier Epistles of the Apostle Paul, viz First and Second Thessalonians, First and Second Corinthians: Greek Text with Explanatory Notes*. New York: Appleton and Company, 1890.

Bouter, H. *Christ the Wisdom of God: Reflections on 1 Corinthians 2*. London: Chapter Two, 1998.

Branick, V.P. "Source and Redaction Analysis of 1 Corinthians 1–3." *JBL* 101.2 (1982): 251-69.

_____. "Apocalyptic Paul." *CBQ* 47.4 (1985): 664-75.

Bridge, D. and D. Phypers. *Spiritual Gifts and the Church*. Leicester: InterVarsity Press, 1974.

Brodeur, S. *The Holy Spirit's Agency in the Resurrection of the Dead: An Exegetical-Theological Study of 1 Corinthians 15,44b-49 and Romans 8,9-13*. TGST 14. Rome: Editrice Pontificia Universita Gregoriana, 1996.

Brown, A.R. *The Cross and Human Transformation: Paul's Apocalyptic Word in 1 Corinthians*. Minneapolis: Fortress Press, 1995.

_____. "Apocalyptic Transformation in Paul's Discourse on the Cross." *WW* 16.4 (1996): 427-36.

Bruce, F.F. *1 & 2 Thessalonians*. WBC 45. Waco: Word, 1982.

Bullmore, M.A. *St Paul's Theology of Rhetorical Style: An Examination of 1 Corinthians 2.1-5 in Light of First Century Greco-Roman Rhetorical Culture*. San Francisco: International Scholars Publications, 1995.

Bultmann, R. *Theology of the New Testament*. Vol. 1. Translated by K. Grodel. New York: Charles Scribner's Sons, 1951.

_____. *Primitive Christianity in its Contemporary Setting*. Translated by R.H. Fuller. London: Thames & Hudson, 1956.

_____. "Karl Barth, *The Resurrection of the Dead.*" Pages 66-94 in *Faith and Understanding I*. Edited by R.W. Funk. Translated by L.P. Smith. London: SCM Press, 1969.

_____. *The Second Letter to the Corinthians*. Translated by R.A. Harrisville. Minneapolis: Augsburg, 1985.

Bünker, M. *Briefformular und rhetorische Disposition im 1 Korintherbrief*. GTA 28. Tübingen: Vandenhoeck & Ruprecht, 1983.

Butler, P.T. *Studies in First Corinthians*. Joplin: College Press, 1985.

Caird, G.B. *Principalities and Powers: A Study in Pauline Theology*. Oxford: Clarendon, 1956.

Callan, T. "Prophecy and Ecstasy in Greco-Roman Religion and 1 Corinthians." *NovT* 28.2 (1985): 125-40.

Carr, A.W. "The Rulers of this Age—1 Cor ii:6-8." *NTS* 23.1 (1977): 20-35.

Carson, D.A. *Showing the Spirit: A Theological Exposition of 1 Corinthians 12–14*. Grand Rapids: Baker Book House, 1987.

Cartledge, M.J. "Charismatic Prophecy: A Definition and Description." *JPT* 5 (1994): 79-120.

Carver, F.G. *2 Corinthians: A Commentary in the Wesleyan Tradition*. Kansas City: Beacon Hill, 2009.

Chance, J.B. "Paul's Apology to the Corinthians." *PRSt* 9.2 (1982): 145-55.

Chester, S.J. *Conversion at Corinth: Perspectives on Conversion in Paul's Theology and the Corinthian Church*. London: T&T Clark, 2003.

Chiu, J.E.A. *1 Cor 12–14: Literary Structure and Theology*. AnBib 166. Rome: Editrice Pontifica Instituto Biblico, 2007.

Chow, J.K. *Patronage and Power: A Study of Social Networks in Corinth*. JSNTSup 75. Sheffield: JSOT Press, 1992.

Ciampa, R.E. and B.S. Rosner. "The Structure and Argument of 1 Corinthians: A Biblical/Jewish Approach." *NTS* 52.2 (2006): 205-18.

_____. "1 Corinthians." Pages 695-752 in *Commentary on the New Testament Use of the Old Testament*. Edited by G.K. Beale and D.A. Carson. Grand Rapids: Baker Academic, 2007.

_____. *The First Letter to the Corinthians*. PilNTC. Grand Rapids: Eerdmans, 2010.

Clark, D.L. *Rhetoric in Greco-Roman Education*. New York: Columbia University Press, 1957.

Clarke, A.D. *Secular and Christian Leadership in Corinth: A Socio-historical and Exegetical Study of 1 Corinthians 1–6*. Leiden: Brill, 1993.

Coffey, D. *"Did You Receive the Holy Spirit When You Believed?": Some Basic Questions for Pneumatology*. Père Marquette Lecture in Theology. Milwaukee: Marquette University Press, 2005.

Collins, J.J. *The Apocalyptic Imagination: An Introduction to Jewish Apocalyptic Literature*. 2nd edition. Grand Rapids: Eerdmans, 1998.

Collins, R.F. "Reflections on 1 Corinthians as a Hellenistic Letter." Pages 39-61 in *The Corinthian Correspondence*. Edited by R. Bieringer. Leuven: Leuven University Press, 1996.

_____. *First Corinthians*. SP 7. Collegeville: Liturgical Press, 1999.

_____. *The Power of Images in Paul*. Collegeville: Liturgical Press, 2008.

Conzelmann, H. *1 Corinthians: A Commentary on the First Epistle of St Paul to the Corinthians*. Hermeneia. Edited by G.W. MacRae. Translated by J.W. Leitch. Philadelphia: Fortress Press, 1975.

_____. *Der erste Brief an die Korinther*. KEK 12. Göttingen: Vandenhoeck & Ruprecht, 1981.

Copleston, F.C. *A History of Philosophy*. Vol. 1. London: Search Press, 1946.

Coppens, J. "'Mystery' in the Theology of Saint Paul and its Parallels at Qumran." Pages 132-58 in *Paul and Qumran: Studies in New Testament Exegesis*. Edited by J. Murphy-O'Connor. London: Geoffrey Chapman, 1968.

Cousar, C.B. "1 Corinthians 2:1-13." *Int* 44.2 (1990): 169-73.

_____. *The Theology of the Cross: The Death of Jesus in the Letters of Paul*. Minneapolis: Fortress Press, 1990.

Cox, L.G. "Sin in Believers." *Wesleyan Theological Journal* 1 (1966): 27-32.

_____. "The 'Straw' in the Believer—1 Corinthians 3.12." *Wesleyan Theological Journal* 12 (1977): 34-38.

Cox, R. *By the Same Word: Creation and Salvation in Hellenistic Judaism and Early Christianity*. BZNW 145. Berlin: Walter de Gruyter, 2007.

Crenshaw, J.L. *Old Testament Wisdom: An Introduction*. Louisville: Westminster John Knox, 1998.

Cullmann, O. *Christ and Time: The Primitive Christian Conception of Time and History*. Translated by F.V. Filson. London: SCM Press, 1951.

Dabney, D.L. "*Pneumatologica Crucis*: Reclaiming *Theologica Crucis* for a Theology of the Spirit Today." *SJT* 53.4 (2000): 511-24.

Dahl, N.A. "Paul and the Church at Corinth According to 1 Corinthians 1:10–4:21." Pages 313-35 in *Christian History and Interpretation: Studies Presented to John Knox*. Edited by W.R. Farmer, C.F.D. Moule, and R.R. Niebuhr. Cambridge: Cambridge University Press, 1967.

Davis, J.A. *Wisdom and Spirit: An Investigation of 1 Corinthians 1.18–3.20 Against the Background of Jewish Sapiential Traditions in the Greco-Roman Period*. Lanham: University Press of America, 1984.

de Boer, M.C. "The Composition of 1 Corinthians." *NTS* 40.2 (1994): 229-45.

de Vos, C.S. *Church and Community Conflicts: The Relationship of the Thessalonian, Corinthian, and Philippian Churches with Their Wider Civic Communities*. SBLDS 168. Atlanta: Scholars Press, 1999.

Deluz, G. *A Companion to 1 Corinthians*. Edited and translated by G.E. Watt. London: Darton, Longman & Todd, 1963.

Dibelius, M. and W.G. Kümmel. *Paul*. Translated by F. Clarke. Philadelphia: Westminster Press, 1953.

Dodd, B. *Paul's Paradigmatic "I": Personal Example as Literary Strategy*. JSNTSup 177. Sheffield: Sheffield Academic Press, 1999.

Dods, M. *The First Epistle to the Corinthians*. London: Hodder & Stoughton, 1909.

Donahoe, K. "From Self-Praise to Self-Boasting: Paul's Unmasking of the Conflicting Rhetorical-Linguistic Phenomena in 1 Corinthians." Ph.D. diss. University of St Andrews, 2008.

Dunn, J.D.G. *Jesus and the Spirit: A Study of the Religions and Charismatic Experiences of Jesus and the First Christians as Reflected in the New Testament*. London: SCM Press, 1975.

_____. *1 Corinthians*. NTG. Sheffield: Sheffield Academic Press, 1995.

_____. *Unity and Diversity in the New Testament: An Inquiry into the Character of Earliest Christianity*. 3rd edition. London: SCM Press, 2006.

du Toit, A. *Focusing on Paul: Persuasion and Theological Design in Romans and Galations.* BZNW 151. Edited by C. Breytenback and D.S. du Toit. Berlin: Walter de Gruyter, 2007.

Dutch, R.S. *The Educated Elite in 1 Corinthians: Education and Community Conflict in Greco-Roman Context.* JSNTSup 271. London: T&T Clark, 2005.

Ebojo, E.B. "How Persuasive is 'Persuasive Words of Human Wisdom'?" *Bible Translator* 60 (2009): 10-21.

Edman, I. *The Mind of Paul.* New York: Henry Holt and Company, 1935.

Edwards, T.C. *A Commentary on the First Epistle to the Corinthians.* New York: A.C. Armstrong & Son, 1886.

Ekem, J.D. "'Spiritual Gifts' or 'Spiritual Persons'? 1 Corinthians 12:1a Revisited." *Neot* 38.1 (2004): 54-74.

Ellicott, C.J. *Critical and Grammatical Commentary on St Paul's First Epistle to the Corinthians.* Andover: W.F. Draper, 1889.

Ellis, E.E. *Prophecy and Hermeneutic in Early Christianity: New Testament Essays.* Grand Rapids: Eerdmans, 1978.

Engberg-Pedersen, T. "The Gospel and Social Practice according to 1 Corinthians." *NTS* 33.4 (1987): 557-84.

Erdman, C.R. *The First Epistle of Paul to the Corinthians: An Exposition.* Philadelphia: Westminster Press, 1928.

Eriksson, A. *Traditions as Rhetorical Proof: Pauline Argumentation in 1 Corinthians.* ConBNT. Stockholm: Almqvist & Wiksell, 1998.

Fatehi, M. *The Spirit's Relation to the Risen Lord in Paul: An Examination of Its Christological Implications.* WUNT 2.128. Tübingen: Mohr Siebeck, 2000.

Fee, G.D. *The First Epistle to the Corinthians.* NICNT. Grand Rapids: Eerdmans, 1987.

_____. "Gifts of the Spirit." Pages 339-47 in *Dictionary of Paul and His Letters*. Edited by G.F. Hawthorne, R.P. Martin, and D.G. Reid. Downers Grove: InterVarsity, 1993.

_____. *God's Empowering Presence: The Holy Spirit in the Letters of Paul*. Peabody: Hendrickson, 1994.

_____. *Paul, the Spirit, and the People of God*. Grand Rapids: Baker Academic, 1996.

_____. *Pauline Christology: An Exegetical-Theological Study*. Peabody: Hendrickson, 2007.

Findlay, G.G. *The First Epistle of Paul to the Corinthians*. EGT. Vol. 2. Edited by W.R. Nicoll. London: Hodder & Stoughton, 1897.

Finney, M.T. "Conflict in Corinth: The Appropriateness of Honour-Shame as the Primary Social Context." Ph.D. diss. University of St Andrews, 2004.

_____. "Honor, Rhetoric and Factionalism in the Ancient World: 1 Corinthians 1–4 in Its Social Context." *BTB* 40.1 (2010): 27-36.

_____. *Honor and Conflict in the Ancient World: 1 Corinthians in its Greco-Roman Social Setting*. LNTS. London: Bloomsbury T&T Clark, 2012.

Fiore, B. "'Covert Allusion' in 1 Corinthians 1–4." *CBQ* 47.1 (1985): 85-102.

Fishburne, C.W. "1 Corinthians iii.10-15 and the *Testament of Abraham*." *NTS* 17.1 (1970): 109-15.

Fitzgerald, J.T. *Cracks in an Earthen Vessel: An Examination of the Catalogues of Hardships in the Corinthian Correspondence*. SBLDS 99. Atlanta: Scholars Press, 1988.

Fitzmyer, J.A. *First Corinthians: A New Translation with Introduction and Commentary*. AYB 32. New Haven: Yale University Press, 2008.

Forbes, C.B. "Paul and Rhetorical Comparison." Pages 134-71 in *Paul in the Greco-Roman World: A Handbook*. Edited by J.P. Sampley. Harrisburg: Trinity Press International, 2003.

Fotopoulos, J. "1 Corinthians." Pages 413-33 in *The Blackwell Companion to the New Testament*. Edited by D.E. Aune. Chichester: Wiley-Blackwell, 2010.

Francis, J. "'As Babes in Christ'–Some Proposals Regarding 1 Corinthians 3:1-3." *JSNT* 7 (1980): 41-60

Freese, J.H. "Introduction." Pages vii-xxvii in *The Art of Rhetoric*. Translated by J.H. Freese. London: William Heinemann, 1926.

Fretheim, T.E. *Jeremiah*. SHBC. Macon: Smyth & Helwys, 2002.

Funk, R.W. "Word and World in 1 Corinthians 2:6-16." Pages 275-305 in *Language, Hermeneutics and the Word of God: The Problem of Language in the New Testament and Contemporary Theology*. New York: Harper & Row, 1966.

Furnish, V.P. "Fellow Workers in God's Service." *JBL* 80.4 (1961): 364-70.

_____. *The Theology of the First Letter to the Corinthians*. NTT. Cambridge: Cambridge University Press, 1999.

_____. "Letters in the New Testament." Pages 1268-76 in *Eerdmans Commentary on the Bible*. Edited by J.D.G. Dunn and J.W. Rogerson. Grand Rapids: Eerdmans, 2003.

Garland, D.E. *2 Corinthians*. NAC 29. Nashville: Broadman & Holman, 1999.

_____. *1 Corinthians*. BECNT. Grand Rapids: Baker Academic, 2003.

Gärtner, B.E. "The Pauline and Johannine Idea of 'to Know God' Against the Hellenistic Background." *NTS* 14.2 (1968): 209-31.

Gaventa, B.R. "Mother's Milk and Ministry in 1 Corinthians 3." Pages 101-13 in *Theology and Ethics in Paul and His Interpreters: Essays in Honor of Victor Paul Furnish*. Edited by E.H. Lovering, Jr. and J.L. Sumney. Nashville: Abingdon Press, 1996.

Georgi, D. *The Opponents of Paul in Second Corinthians.* Philadelphia: Fortress, 1986.

Gill, D. "In Search of the Social Elite in the Corinthian Church." *TynBul* 44 (1993): 323-37.

Gladd, B.L. *Revealing the Mysterion: The Use of Mystery in Daniel and Second Temple Judaism with its Bearing on First Corinthians.* BZNW 160. Berlin: Walter de Gruyter, 2008.

Godet, F. *Commentary on St Paul's First Epistle to the Corinthians.* Vol. 1. Translated by A. Cusin. Edinburgh: T&T Clark, 1889.

Gonzáles, J.L. *Acts: The Gospel of the Spirit.* New York: Orbis, 2001.

Gooch, P.D. *Dangerous Food: 1 Corinthians 8-10 in Its Context.* Studies in Christianity and Judaism 5. Waterloo (Ontario): Wilfrid Laurier University Press, 1993.

Gooch, P.W. *Partial Knowledge: Philosophical Studies in Paul.* Notre Dame: University of Notre Dame Press, 1987.

Gorman, M.J. *Apostle of the Crucified Lord: A Theological Introduction to Paul and His Letters.* Grand Rapids: Eerdmans, 2004.

Goudge, H.L. *The First Epistle to the Corinthians: With Introduction and Notes.* London: Methuen & Co., 1911.

Gould, E.P. *Commentary on the Epistles to the Corinthians.* Philadelphia: American Baptist Publication Society, 1887.

Goulder, M.D. *Paul and the Competing Mission in Corinth.* Library of Pauline Studies. Peabody: Hendrickson, 2001.

Gräbe, P. *The Power of God in Paul's Letters.* WUNT 2.123. Tübingen: Mohr Siebeck, 2000.

Green, G.L. *The Letters to the Thessalonians.* PilNTC. Grand Rapids: Eerdmans, 2002.

Greenberg, M. *Ezekiel 1–20: A New Translation with Introduction and Commentary*. AB 22. Garden City: Doubleday, 1983.

Grosheide, F.W. *Commentary on the First Epistle to the Corinthians*. NICNT. Grand Rapids: Eerdmans, 1954.

Gunkel, H. *Influence of the Holy Spirit: The Popular View of the Apostolic Age and the Teaching of the Apostle Paul*. Translated by R.A. Harrisville and P.A Quanbeck II. Philadelphia: Fortress Press, 1979.

Gupta, N.K. "The Theo-Logic of Paul's Ethics in Recent Research: Crosscurrents and Future Directions in Scholarship in the Last Forty Years." *CBR* 7.3 (2009): 336-61.

Gustafson, J.M. *Moral Discernment in the Christian Life: Essays in Theological Ethics*. Louisville: Westminster John Knox, 2007.

Haacker, K. *The Theology of Paul's Letter to the Romans*. NTT. Cambridge: Cambridge University Press, 2003.

Haenchen, E. *The Acts of the Apostles: A Commentary*. Translated by B. Noble and G. Shinn. Oxford: Blackwell, 1971.

Hall, D.R. *The Unity of the Corinthian Correspondence*. JSNTSup 251. London: T&T Clark, 2003.

Hargreaves, J. *A Guide to 1 Corinthians*. London: SPCK, 1978.

Harris, M.J. *The Second Epistle to the Corinthians: A Commentary on the Greek Text*. NIGTC. Grand Rapids: Eerdmans, 2005.

Hays, R.B. *Echoes of Scripture in the Letters of Paul*. New Haven: Yale University Press, 1989.

_____. *First Corinthians*. Interpretation. Louisville: Westminster John Knox, 1997.

Heil, J.P. *The Rhetorical Role of Scripture in 1 Corinthians*. Atlanta: Society of Biblical Literature, 2005.

Héring, J. *The First Epistle of Saint Paul to the Corinthians*. EC. Translated by A.W. Heathcote and P.J. Allcock. London: Epworth, 1962.

Herms, R. "'Being Saved without Honor': A Conceptual Link between 1 Corinthians 3 and *1 Enoch* 50?" *JSNT* 29.2 (2006): 187-210.

Herrick, J. *The History and Theory of Rhetoric: An Introduction.* Boston: Allyn and Bacon, 1997.

Hodge, C. *An Exposition of the First Epistle to the Corinthians.* New York: Robert Carter & Brothers, 1860.

Hogeterp, A.L.A. *Paul and God's Temple: A Historical Interpretation of Cultic Imagery in the Corinthian Correspondence.* Biblical Tools and Studies 2. Leuven: Peeters, 2006.

Holladay, C.R. *First Letter of Paul to the Corinthians.* Living Word Commentaries 8. Austin: Sweet Publishing Company, 1979.

Hooker, M.D. "Hard Sayings: 1 Cor 3:2." *Theology* 69 (1966): 19-22.

_____. *Paul: A Beginner's Guide.* Oxford: One World, 2008.

Horn, F.W. "Holy Spirit." Pages 260-80 in *Anchor Bible Dictionary.* Vol. 3. Edited by D.N. Freedman. New York: Doubleday, 1992.

Horrell, D.G. *The Social Ethos of the Corinthian Correspondence: Interests and Ideology from 1 Corinthians to 1 Clement.* SNTW. Edinburgh: T&T Clark, 1996.

Horsley, R.A. "Pneumatikos vs. Psychikos: Distinctions of Spiritual Status Among the Corinthians." *HTR* 69 (1976): 269-88.

_____. "Wisdom of Word and Words of Wisdom in Corinth." *CBQ* 39.2 (1977): 224-39.

_____. "Gnosis in Corinth: 1 Corinthians 8.1-6." *NTS* 27.1 (1980): 32-51.

_____. "1 Corinthians: A Case Study of Paul's Assembly as an Alternative Society." Pages 242-52 in *Paul and Empire:*

Religion and Power in Roman Imperial Society. Edited by R.A. Horsley. Harrisburg: Trinity Press International, 1997.

_____. *1 Corinthians*. ANTC. Nashville: Abingdon, 1998.

Hug, J.L. *An Introduction to the Writings of the New Testament*. 2 vols. Translated by D.G. Wait. London: C. & J. Rivington, 1827.

Hughes, P.E. *Paul's Second Epistle to the Corinthians*. NICNT. Grand Rapids: Eerdmans, 1962.

_____. *A Commentary on the Epistle to the Hebrews*. Grand Rapids: Eerdmans, 1988.

Hunt, A.R. *The Inspired Body: Paul, the Corinthians, and Divine Inspiration*. Macon: Mercer University Press, 1996.

Hurd, J.C. *The Origin of 1 Corinthians*. London: SPCK, 1965.

Inkelaar, H.-J. *Conflict Over Wisdom: The Theme of 1 Corinthians 1–4 Rooted in Scripture*. CBET 63. Leuven: Peeters, 2011.

Jarratt, S.C. *Rereading the Sophists: Classical Rhetoric Refigured*. Carbondale: Southern Illinois University Press, 1991.

Jewett, R. *Paul's Anthropological Terms: A Study of Their Use in Conflict Settings*. AGJU 10. Leiden: Brill, 1971.

Kaiser, W.C. "A Neglected Text in Bibliology Discussions: 1 Corinthians 2:6-16." *WTJ* 43.2 (1981): 310-19.

Kammler, H.-C. *Kreuz und Weisheit: Eine exegetische Untersuchung zu 1 Kor 1,10–3,4*. WUNT 2.159. Tübingen: Mohr Siebeck, 2003.

Karenga, M. *Maat: The Moral Ideal in Ancient Egypt. A Study in Classical African Ethics*. African Studies. New York: Routledge, 2004.

Käsemann, E. *New Testament Questions of Today*. Translated by W.J. Montague. Philadelphia: Fortress Press, 1969.

Keener, C.S. *The IVP Background Commentary: New Testament*. Downers Grove: InterVarsity, 1993.

_____. *1–2 Corinthians*. NCamBC. Cambridge: Cambridge University Press, 2005.

Kennedy, G.A. *New Testament Interpretation Through Rhetorical Criticism*. Chapel Hill: University of North Carolina Press, 1984.

_____. *A New History of Classical Rhetoric*. Princeton: Princeton University Press, 1994.

_____. *Comparative Rhetoric: An Historical and Cross-Cultural Introduction*. New York: Oxford University Press, 1998.

_____. *Classical Rhetoric and Its Christian and Secular Tradition from Ancient to Modern Times*. Chapel Hill: University of North Carolina Press, 1999.

_____. "Historical Survey of Rhetoric." Pages 3-37 in *Handbook of Classical Rhetoric in the Hellenistic Period: 330 B.C.–A.D. 400*. Edited by S.E. Porter. Boston: Brill Academic, 2001.

_____. "The Genres of Rhetoric." Pages 43-50 in *Handbook of Classical Rhetoric in the Hellenistic Period: 330 B.C.–A.D. 400*. Edited by S.E. Porter. Boston: Brill Academic, 2001.

Kim, Y.S. *Christ's Body at Corinth: The Politics of a Metaphor*. PCC. Minneapolis: Fortress, 2008.

Kirk, A.N. "Building with the Corinthians: Human Persons as the Building Materials of 1 Corinthians 3.12 and the 'Work' of 3.13-15." *NTS* 58.4 (2012): 549-70.

Kistemaker, S.J. *Exposition of the First Epistle to the Corinthians*. NTC. Grand Rapids: Baker, 1993.

Klauck, H.–J. *Ancient Letters and the New Testament: A Guide to Context and Exegesis*. Waco: Baylor University Press, 2006.

Kling, C.F. *The First Epistle of Paul to the Corinthians*. New York: Charles Scribner's Sons, 1868.

Klutz, T.E. "Re-Reading 1 Corinthians after *Rethinking Gnosticism*." *JSNT* 26.2 (2003): 193-216.

Koenig, J. "From Mystery to Ministry: Paul as Interpreter of Charismatic Gifts." *USQR* 33.3/4 (1978): 167-74.

_____. *Charismata: God's Gifts for God's People*. Biblical Perspectives on Current Issues. Philadelphia: Westminster Press, 1978.

Kovacs, J.L. "The Archons, the Spirit and the Death of Christ: Do We Need the Hypothesis of Gnostic Opponents to Explain 1 Cor 2.6-16?" Pages 218-36 in *Apocalyptic and the New Testament: Essays in Honor of J. Louis Martyn*. JSNTSup 24. Edited by J. Marcus and M.L. Soards. Sheffield: JSOT Press, 1989.

Kremer, J. *Der erste Brief and die Korinther*. RNT. Regensburger: Verlag Friedrich Pustet, 1997.

Kuck, D.W. *Judgment and Community Conflict: Paul's Use of Apocalyptic Judgment Language in 1 Corinthians 3:5–4:5*. NovTSup 66. Leiden: Brill, 1992.

Kwon, O.–Y. "A Critical Review of Recent Scholarship on the Pauline Opposition and the Nature of its Wisdom (σοφία) in 1 Corinthians 1–4." *CBR* 8.3 (2010): 386-427.

Kydd, R.A.N. *Charismatic Gifts in the Early Church: An Exploration Into the Gifts of the Spirit During the First Three Centuries of the Christian Church*. Peabody: Hendrickson, 1984.

Lambrecht, J. "The Fragment 2 Cor vi 14–vii 1: A Plea for Its Authenticity." Pages 531-49 in *Studies on 2 Corinthians*. BETL 102. Edited by R. Bieringer and J. Lambrecht. Leuven: Leuven University Press, 1994.

_____. *Second Corinthians*. SP 8. Collegeville: Liturgical Press, 1999.

Lamp, J.S. *First Corinthians 1–4 in Light of Jewish Wisdom Traditions: Christ, Wisdom and Spirituality*. SBEC 42. Lewiston: E. Mellen, 2000.

Lampe, P. "Theological Wisdom and the 'Word About the Cross': The Rhetorical Scheme of 1 Corinthians 1–4." *Int* 44.2 (1990): 117-31.

Lang, F. *Die Briefe an die Korinther*. NTD. Göttingen: Vandenhoeck & Ruprecht, 1994.

Lee, S.M. *The Cosmic Drama of Salvation: A Study of Paul's Undisputed Writings from Anthropological and Cosmological Perspectives*. WUNT 2.276. Tübingen: Mohr Siebeck, 2010.

Lewis, J.G. *Looking for Life: The Role of "Theo-Ethical Reasoning" in Paul's Religion*. JSNTSup 622. London: T&T Clark International, 2007.

Lias, J.J. *The First Epistle to the Corinthians*. Cambridge: The University Press, 1897.

Lichtheim, M. *Moral Values in Ancient Egypt*. OBO 155. Göttingen: Vandenhoeck & Ruprecht, 1997.

Lietzmann, H. *An die Korinther I-II*. HNT 9. Edited and supplemented by W.G. Kümmel. Tübingen: J.C.B. Mohr (Paul Siebeck), 1969.

Lim, T.H. "'Not in Persuasive Words of Wisdom, But in the Demonstration of the Spirit and Power'." *NovT* 29.2 (1987): 137-49.

Lincoln, A.T. *Paradise Now and Not Yet. Studies in the Role of the Heavenly Dimension in Paul's Thought with Special Reference to His Eschatology*. SNTSMS 43. Cambridge: Cambridge University Press, 1981.

_____. "Liberation from the Powers: Supernatural Spirits or Societal Structures?" Pages 335-54 in *The Bible and Human Society: Essays in Honor of John Rogerson*. JSOTSup 200. Edited by M.D. Carroll R., D.J.A. Clines, and P.R. Davies. Sheffield: Sheffield Academic Press, 1995.

Lindemann, A. *Der erste Korintherbrief*. HNT 9.1. Tübingen: Mohr Siebeck, 2000.

Lioy, D. "Divine Wisdom versus Human Wisdom: An Exegetical-Theological Analysis of 1 Corinthians 1:10–2:16." *Cons* 8 (2009): 35-61.

Lipson, C.S. "Ancient Egyptian Rhetoric: It All Comes Down to *Maat*." Pages 79-97 in *Rhetoric Before and Beyond the Greeks*. Edited by C.S. Lipson and R.A. Binkley. Albany: State University of New York, 2004.

Litfin, A.D. *St Paul's Theology of Proclamation: 1 Corinthians 1–4 and Greco-Roman Rhetoric*. SNTSMS. Cambridge: Cambridge University Press, 1994.

Locke, J. *A Paraphrase and Notes on the Epistles of Galatians, First and Second Corinthians, Romans and Ephesians*. Cambridge: Brown, Shattuck, and Company, 1832.

Logan, A.H.B. *Gnostic Truth and Christian Heresy: A Study in the History of Gnosticism*. London: Continuum, 1996.

Long, A. *Paul and Human Rights: A Dialogue with the Father of the Corinthian Community*. BMW 26. Sheffield: Sheffield Phoenix Press, 2009.

Long, F.J. *Ancient Rhetoric and Paul's Apology: The Compositional Unity of 2 Corinthians*. SNTSMS 131. Cambridge: Cambridge University Press, 2004.

Lothian, W. *Expository Lectures on Paul's Epistles to the Corinthians*. Edinburgh: Waugh & Innes, 1828.

Lüdemann, G. *Paul, Apostle to the Gentiles: Studies in Chronology*. Translated by E. Stanley Jones. Philadelphia: Fortress Press, 1984.

MacDonald, M.Y. *The Pauline Churches: A Socio-historical Study of Institutionalization in the Pauline and Deutero-Pauline Writings*. SNTSMS 60. Cambridge: Cambridge University Press, 1991.

Mack, B. *Rhetoric and the New Testament*. Minneapolis: Fortress, 1990.

Malina, B.J. and J.J. Pilch. *Social-Science Commentary on the Letters of Paul*. Minneapolis: Fortress, 2006.

Mare, W.H. and M.J. Harris. *1, 2 Corinthians: The Expositor's Bible Commentary with the New International Version*. Grand Rapids: Zondervan, 1995.

Marshall, P. *Enmity in Corinth: Social Conventions in Paul's Relations with the Corinthians*. WUNT 2.23. Tübingen: J.C.B. Mohr (Paul Siebeck), 1987.

Martin, D.B. *The Corinthian Body*. 2nd edition. New Haven: Yale University Press, 1999.

Martin, R.P. *New Testament Foundations: A Guide for Christian Students*. Vol. 2. Grand Rapids: Eerdmans, 1978.

_____. *The Spirit and the Congregation: Studies in 1 Corinthians 12–15*. Grand Rapids: Eerdmans, 1984.

Matlock, R.B. *Unveiling the Apocalyptic Paul: Paul's Interpreters and the Rhetoric of Criticism*. JSNTSup 127. Sheffield: Sheffield Academic Press, 1996.

McComiskey, B. *Gorgias and the New Sophistic Rhetoric*. Carbondale: Southern Illinois University Press, 2001.

McConnell, D.W.M. *Paul as Teacher of Discernment: The Ethical Paradigm of 1 Corinthians 7*. New York: General Theological Seminary, 1983.

McFadyen, J.E. *The Epistles to the Corinthians with Notes and Comments*. London: Hodder and Stoughton, 1911.

McLean, B.H. *Cursed Christ: Mediterranean Expulsion Rituals and Pauline Soteriology*. JSNTSup 126. Sheffield: Sheffield Academic Press, 1996.

Meeks, W.A. *First Urban Christians: The Social World of the Apostle Paul*. New Haven: Yale University Press, 1983.

Menzies, R.P. *The Development of Early Christian Pneumatology with Special Reference to Luke-Acts*. JSNTSup 54. Sheffield: JSOT Press, 1991.

Merklein, H. *Der erste Brief an die Korinther: Kapitel 1–4.* ÖTK 7.1. Gütersloh: Gütersloher Verlagshaus Gerd Mohn, 1992.

Metzger, B.M. *A Textual Commentary on the Greek New Testament.* 2nd edition. Stuttgart: Deutsche Bibelgesellschaft, 1997.

Meyer, H.A.W. *Critical and Exegetical Handbook on the Epistles to the Corinthians.* Vol. 1. Translated and edited by W.P. Dickson and F. Crombie. Edinburgh: T&T Clark, 1878.

Mihaila, C. *The Paul-Apollos Relationship and Paul's Stance Toward Greco-Roman Rhetoric: An Exegetical and Socio-historical Study of 1 Corinthians 1–4.* LNTS 402. London: T&T Clark/Continuum, 2009.

Miller, G. "ἀρχόντων τοῦ αἰῶνος τούτου—A New Look at 1 Corinthians 2.6-8." *JBL* 91.4 (1972): 522-28.

Minor, M.L. *2 Corinthians.* SHBC. Macon: Smyth & Helwys, 2009.

Mitchell, M.M. "Concerning ΠΕΡΙ ΔΕ in 1 Corinthians." *NovT* 31.3 (1989): 231-56.

_____. *Paul and the Rhetoric of Reconciliation: An Exegetical Investigation of the Language and Composition of Corinthians.* Louisville: Westminster John Knox, 1991.

_____. "The Corinthian Correspondence and the Birth of Pauline Hermeneutics." Pages 17-54 in *Paul and the Corinthians: Studies on a Community in Conflict. Essays in Honor of Margaret Thrall.* Edited by T.J. Burke and J.K. Elliott. Leiden: Brill, 2003.

_____. *Paul, the Corinthians and the Birth of Christian Hermeneutics.* Cambridge: Cambridge University Press, 2010.

Moffatt, J. *The First Epistle of Paul to the Corinthians.* New York: Harper and Brothers, 1890.

Morris, L.L. *The First Epistle of Paul to the Corinthians: An Introduction and Commentary*. TNTC. Leicester: InterVarsity Press, 1986.

Moule, C.F.D. *The Holy Spirit*. London: Mowbrays, 1978.

Munck, J. *Paul and the Salvation of Mankind*. Study edition. Translated by F. Clarke London: SCM Press, 1959.

Munzinger, A. *Discerning the Spirits: Theological and Ethical Hermeneutics in Paul*. SNTSMS 140. Cambridge: Cambridge University Press, 2007.

Murphy-O'Connor, J. *Paul the Letter-Writer: His World, His Options, His Skill*. GNS 41. Collegeville: Liturgical Press, 1995.

Nichols, D. "The Problem of Two-Level Christianity at Corinth." *Pneuma* 11.2 (1989): 99-111.

O'Brien, P.T. *Gospel and Mission in the Writings of Paul: An Exegetical and Theological Analysis*. Grand Rapids, Baker, 1995.

Økland, J. *1 Corinthians Through the Centuries*. Blackwell Bible Commentaries. Chichester: Wiley-Blackwell, forthcoming.

Olshausen, H. *Biblical Commentary on St Paul's First and Second Epistles to the Corinthians*. Translated by J.E. Cox. Edinburgh: T&T Clark, 1851.

Oster, R. *1 Corinthians*. College Press NIV Commentary. Joplin: College Press, 1995.

Pagels, E.H. *The Gnostic Paul: Gnostic Exegesis of the Pauline Letters*. Philadelphia: Fortress Press, 1975.

Paige, L. *First and Second Epistles to the Corinthians*. Boston: Universalist Publishing House, 1867.

Pascuzzi, M.A. *Ethics, Ecclesiology and Church Discipline: A Rhetorical Analysis of 1 Corinthians 5*. TGST 32. Rome: Editrice Pontificia Universita Gregoriana, 1997.

_____. *First and Second Corinthians*. NColBC. Collegeville: Liturgical, 2005.

Pathrapankal, J. "From Areopagus to Corinth (Acts 17:22-31; 1 Cor 2:1-5): A Study on the Transition from the Power of Knowledge to the Power of the Spirit." *MSt* 23.1 (2006): 61-80.

Pate, C.M. *The Reverse of the Curse: Paul, Wisdom and the Law*. WUNT 2.114. Tübingen: Mohr Siebeck, 2000.

Patte, D. *Paul's Faith and the Power of the Gospel: A Structural Introduction to the Pauline Letters*. Philadelphia: Fortress, 1983.

Pearson, B.A. *The Pneumatikos-Psychikos Terminology in 1 Corinthians*. Missoula: University of Montana, 1973.

_____. "Hellenistic-Jewish Wisdom Speculation and Paul." Pages 43-66 in *Aspects of Wisdom in Judaism and Early Christianity*. Edited by R.L. Wilcken. Notre Dame: University of Notre Dame Press, 1975.

_____. *Gnosticism, Judaism, and Egyptian Christianity*. SAC. Minneapolis: Fortress, 1990.

_____. "Philo, Gnosis and the New Testament." Pages 73-89 in *New Testament and Gnosis*. Edited by A.H.B. Logan and A.J.M. Wedderburn. London: T&T Clark/Continuum, 2004.

Penna, R. "The Gospel as 'Power of God' According to 1 Corinthians 1:18-25." Pages 169-80 in *Paul the Apostle*. Vol. 1. Translated by T.P. Wahl. Collegeville: Liturgical Press, 1996.

Perkins, P. *Gnosticism and the New Testament*. Minneapolis: Fortress, 1993.

_____. *First Corinthians*. Paideia. Grand Rapids: Baker Academic, 2012.

Pernot, L. *Rhetoric in Antiquity*. Translated by W.E. Higgins. Washington: Catholic University of America Press, 2005.

Peterson, B.K. *Eloquence and the Proclamation of the Gospel at Corinth*. SBLDS 163. Atlanta: Scholars Press, 1998.

Philip, F. *The Origins of Pauline Pneumatology: The Eschatological Bestowal of the Spirit upon Gentiles in Judaism and in the Early Development of Paul's Theology*. WUNT 2.194. Tübingen: Mohr Siebeck, 2005.

Pickett, R. *The Cross in Corinth: The Social Significance of the Death of Jesus*. JSNTSup 143. Sheffield: Sheffield Academic Press, 1997.

Pogoloff, S.M. *Logos and Sophia: The Rhetorical Situation of 1 Corinthians*. SBLDS 134. Atlanta: Scholars Press, 1992.

Polhill, J.B. "The Wisdom of God and Factionalism: 1 Corinthians 1–4." *RevExp* 80.3 (1983): 325-29.

Rabens, V. *The Holy Spirit and Ethics in Paul: Transformation and Empowering for Religious-Ethical Life*. WUNT 2.283. Tübingen: Mohr Siebeck, 2010.

Reinmuth, R. "LAB 40,4 und die Krise der Weisheit im 1 Korintherbrief: Ein Beitrag zu den hermeneutischen Voraussetzungen der paulinischen Argumentation." Pages 471-78 in *The Corinthian Correspondence*. BETL 125. Edited by R. Bieringer. Leuven: Leuven University Press, 1996.

Reitzenstein, R. *Hellenistic Mystery-Religions: Their Basic Ideas and Significance*. PTMS. Translated by J.E. Steely. Pittsburgh: Pickwick Publications, 1978.

Rhyne, C.T. "1 Corinthians 3:1-9." *Int* 44.2 (1990): 174-79.

Richardson, P. "On the Absence of 'Anti-Judaism' in 1 Corinthians." Pages 59-74 in *Paul and the Gospels*. Vol. 1 of *Anti-Judaism in Early Christianity*. SCJ 2. Edited by P. Richardson, with D. Granskou. Waterloo (Ontario): Wilfrid Laurier University Press, 1986.

Rickaby, J. *Notes on Paul: Corinthians, Galatians, Romans*. London: Burns and Oats, 1898.

Riggs, J. and H. Reed. *Epistles to the Corinthians*. New York: Macmillan Company, 1922.

Robertson A. and A. Plummer. *A Critical and Exegetical Commentary on the First Epistle of St Paul to the Corinthians*. ICC. Edinburgh: T&T Clark, 1911.

Robertson, C.K. *Conflict in Corinth: Redefining the System*. Studies in Biblical Literature 42. New York: Peter Lang, 2001.

Rosner, B.S. *Paul and the Law: Keeping the Commandments of God*. Downers Grove: InterVarsity Press, 2013.

Roukema, R. *Gnosis and Faith in Early Christianity: An Introduction to Gnosticism*. Translated by J. Bowden. Harrisburg: Trinity Press International, 1999.

Rowland, C. *The Open Heaven: A Study of Apocalyptic in Judaism and Early Christianity*. London: SPCK, 1982.

Rudolph, K. *Gnosis: The Nature and History of Gnosticism*. Translated and edited by R. McL. Wilson. Edinburgh: T&T Clark, 1987.

Ruef, J.S. *Paul's First Letter to Corinth*. PNTC. Harmondsworth: Penguin Books, 1971.

Runia, D. *Philo of Alexandria and the Timaeus of Plato*. Leiden: Brill, 1986.

Russell, B. *History of Western Philosophy*. Reprint. London: Routledge, 2004.

Ruthven, J. *On the Cessation of the Charismata: The Protestant Polemic on Postbiblical Miracles*. JPTSup 3. Sheffield: Sheffield Academic Press, 1993.

Rylands, L.G. *A Critical Analysis of the Four Chief Pauline Epistles: Romans, First and Second Corinthians, and Galatians*. London: Watts & Co., 1929.

Sadler, M.F. *The First and Second Epistles to the Corinthians: With Notes Critical and Practical*. London: George Bell and Sons, 1898.

Salles, R. "Introduction: God and Cosmos in Stoicism." Pages 1-19 in *God and Cosmos in Stoicism*. Edited by R. Salles. Oxford: Oxford University Press, 2009.

Sanders, E.P. *"Testament of Abraham*. A New Translation and Introduction." Pages 871-902 in *Apocalyptic Literature and Testaments*. Vol. 1 of *The Old Testament Pseudepigrapha*. Edited by J.H. Charlesworth. Garden City, Doubleday, 1983.

Schatzmann, S.S. *A Pauline Theology of Charismata*. Reprint. Peabody: Hendrickson, 1989.

_____. "Purpose and Function of Gifts in 1 Corinthians." *SwJT* 45.1 (2002): 53-68.

Schenck, K. *A Brief Guide to Philo*. Louisville: Westminster John Knox, 2005.

Schenk, W. "Der Korintherbrief als Briefsammlung." *ZNW* 60 (1969): 219-43.

Schiffmann, L.H. *From Text to Tradition: A History of Second Temple & Rabbinic Judaism*. New York: KTAV Publishing, 1991.

Schmithals, W. *Gnosticism in Corinth: An Investigation of the Letters to the Corinthians*. Translated by J.E. Steely. Nashville: Abingdon, 1971.

_____. "Die Korintherbriefe als Briefsammlung." *ZNW* 64 (1973): 263-88.

_____. *The Theology of the First Christians*. Translated by O.C. Dean. Louisville: Westminster John Knox, 1997.

Schnabel, E.J. *Law and Wisdom from Ben Sira to Paul*. WUNT 2.16. Tübingen: Mohr Siebeck, 1985.

_____. *Der erste Brief des Paulus an die Korinther*. HTA 4. Wuppertal: R. Brockhaus, 2006.

Schnackenburg, R. "Christian Adulthood According to the Apostle Paul." *CBQ* 25.3 (1963): 354-70.

Schnelle, U. *Apostle Paul: His Life and Theology*. Translated by M.E. Boring. Grand Rapids: Baker Academic, 2005.

Schnökel, L.A. *A Manual of Hermeneutics*. Translated by L.M. Rosa. Edited by B.W.R. Pearson. Sheffield: Sheffield Academic Press, 1998.

Schoeps, H.J. *Paul: The Theology of the Apostle in the Light of Jewish Religious History*. Translated by H. Knight. Philadelphia: Westminster Press, 1961.

Schrage, W. *Der erste Brief an die Korinther: 1Kor 1,1–6,11*. EKKNT 7.1. Neukirchen-Vluyn: Neukirchener Verlag, 1991.

_____. *Der erste Brief an die Korinther: 1Kor 15,1–16,24*. EKKNT 7.4. Neukirchen-Vluyn: Neukirchener Verlag, 2001.

Schütz, J.H. *Paul and the Anatomy of Apostolic Authority*. SNTSMS 26. Cambridge: Cambridge University Press, 1975.

Schwager, R. *Must There Be Scapegoats?: Violence and Redemption in the Bible*. Translated by M.L. Assad. 2nd edition, reprint. New York: Crossroads Publishing, 2000.

Schweitzer, A. *The Mysticism of Paul the Apostle*. Translated by W. Montgomery. New York: H. Holt and Company, 1931.

Scott, C.A.A. *Christianity According to St Paul*. Cambridge: The University Press, 1927.

Scott, I.W. *Implicit Epistemology in the Letters of Paul*. WUNT 2.205. Tübingen: Mohr Siebeck, 2006.

Scott, J.M. *2 Corinthians*. NIBC. Peabody: Hendrickson, 1998.

Scott, R. *The Pauline Epistles: A Critical Study*. Edinburgh: T&T Clark, 1909.

Scroggs, R. "Paul: ΣΟΦΟΣ and ΠΝΕΥΜΑΤΙΚΟΣ." *NTS* 14 (1967): 33-55.

Selby, G.S. "Paul, the Seer: The Rhetorical Persona in 1 Corinthians 2.1-16." Pages 351-73 in *The Rhetorical Analysis of Scripture: Essays from the 1997 London Conference*.

JSNTSup 146. Edited by S.E. Porter and T.H. Olbricht. Sheffield: Sheffield Academic Press, 1997.

Sellars, J. *Stoicism*. Reprint. Durham: Acumen, 2010.

Sevrin, J.–M. "La gnose à Corinthe. Questions de méthode et observations sur 1 Co 1,17–3.3." Pages 121-39 in *The Corinthian Correspondence*. BETL 125. Edited by R. Bieringer. Leuven: Leuven University Press, 1996.

Shupak, N. *Where Can Wisdom Be Found? The Sage's Language in the Bible and in Ancient Egyptian Literature*. OBO 130. Fribourg: University Press, 1993.

Smit, J.F. *"About the Idol Offerings": Rhetoric, Social Context and Theology of Paul's Discourse in First Corinthians 8:1–11.1*. CBET 27. Leuven: Peeters, 2000.

_____. "Epideictic Rhetoric in Paul's First Letter to the Corinthians 1–4." *Bib* 84 (2003): 183-201.

Soards, M.L. *1 Corinthians*. NIBC. Peabody: Hendrickson, 1999.

Stamps, D.L. "Rhetorical Criticism of the New Testament: Ancient and Modern Evaluations of Argumentation." Pages 129-69 in *Approaches to New Testament Study*. JSNTSup 120. Edited by S.E. Porter and D. Tombs. Sheffield: Sheffield Academic Press, 1995.

_____. "The Christological Premise in Pauline Theological Rhetoric: 1 Corinthians 1:4–2.5 as an Example." Pages 441-57 in *Rhetorical Criticism and the Bible*. JSNTSup 195. Edited by S.E. Porter and D.L. Stamps. Sheffield: Sheffield Academic Press, 2002.

Stanley, A. *The Epistles of St Paul to the Corinthians: With Critical Notes and Dissertations*. London: John Murray, 1882.

Stanley, C.D. *Paul and the Language of Scripture: Citation and Technique in the Pauline Epistles and Contemporary Literature*. SNTSMS 74. Cambridge: Cambridge University Press, 1992.

_____. *Arguing with Scripture: The Rhetoric of Quotations in the Letters of Paul*. New York: T&T Clark International, 2004.

Sterling, G.E. "'Wisdom Among the Perfect': Creation Traditions in Alexandrian Judaism and Corinthian Christianity." *NovT* 37.4 (1995): 354-84.

Stowers, S.K. "Social Status, Public Speaking and Private Teaching: The Circumstances of Paul's Preaching Activity." *NovT* 26.1 (1984): 59-82.

Strecker, G. *Theology of the New Testament*. Translated and edited by F.W. Horn. Louisville: Westminster John Knox, 2000.

Strobel, A. *Der erste Brief an die Korinther*. ZBNT 6.1. Zürich: Theologischer Verlag, 1989.

Stuhlmacher, P. "The Hermeneutical Significance of 1 Cor 2:6-16." Pages 328-47 in *Tradition and Interpretation in the New Testament: Essays in Honor of E. Earle Ellis for His 60th Birthday*. Edited by G.F. Hawthorne. Grand Rapids: Eerdmans, 1987.

Sumney, J.L. *Identifying Paul's Opponents: The Question of Method in 2 Corinthians*. Sheffield: Sheffield Academic Press, 1990.

Swete, H.B. *The Holy Spirit in the Ancient Church: A Study of Christian Teaching in the Age of the Fathers*. London: Macmillan and Co., 1912.

Talbert, C.H. *Reading Corinthians: A New Commentary for Preachers*. London: SPCK, 1987.

Theissen, G. *The Social Setting of Pauline Christianity: Essays on Corinth*. Edited and translated by J.H. Schütz. Edinburgh: T&T Clark, 1982.

_____. *Psychological Aspects of Pauline Theology*. Translated by J.P. Gavin. Edinburgh: T&T Clark, 1987.

Therrien, G. *Le discernement dans les écrits pauliniens*. Paris: J. Gabalda, 1973.

Thiselton, A.C. "Realized Eschatology at Corinth." *NTS* 24 (1978): 510-26.

_____. *The First Epistle to the Corinthians: A Commentary on the Greek Text*. NIGTC. Grand Rapids: Eerdmans, 2000.

Thomas, R.L. *Understanding Spiritual Gifts: A Verse by Verse Study of 1 Cor 12–14*. Grand Rapids: Kregel, 1999.

Thompson, J. *The Second Letter of Paul to the Corinthians*. LWC. Austin: R.B. Sweet Co., 1970.

Thrall, M. *The First and Second Letters of Paul to the Corinthians*. Cambridge: Cambridge University Press, 1965.

_____. *2 Corinthians 1–7*. ICC. 2nd edition. London: T&T Clark, 2004.

Tibbs, C. *The Religious Experience of the Pneuma: Communication with the Spirit World in 1 Corinthians 12 and 14*. WUNT 2.230. Tübingen: Mohr Siebeck, 2007.

Tillich, P. *Systematic Theology*. Vol. 3. Digswell Place: James Nisbet & Co. Ltd., 1964.

Tucker, J.B. *You Belong to Christ: Paul and the Formation of Social Identity in 1 Corinthians 1–4*. Eugene: Pickwick, 2010.

Tuckett, C.M. "Paul, Scripture and Ethics: Some Reflections." *NTS* 46.3 (2000): 403-24.

Turner, M. *The Holy Spirit and Spiritual Gifts: Then and Now*. Studies in Pentecostal and Charismatic Issues. 2nd reprint. Carlisle: Paternoster, 2006.

Unger, M.F. *The Baptism and Gifts of the Holy Spirit*. Chicago: Moody Bible Institute, 1974.

van Roon, A. "The Relation Between Christ and the Wisdom of God According to Paul." *NovT* 16.3 (1974): 207-39.

van Unnik, W.C. *Newly Discovered Gnostic Writings: A Preliminary Survey of the Nag Hammadi Find*. SBT 30. London: SCM Press, 1960.

Verhoef, E. "The Senders of the Letters to the Corinthians and the Use of 'I' and 'We'." Pages 417-25 in *The Corinthian Correspondence*. BETL 124. Edited by R. Bieringer. Leuven: Leuven University Press, 1996.

Voigt, G. *Gemeinsam glauben, hoffen, lieben: Paulus an die Korinther 1*. BTS 4. Göttingen: Vandenhoeck & Ruprecht, 1989.

Volf, M. *Exclusion and Embrace: A Theological Exploration of Identity, Otherness, and Reconciliation*. Nashville: Abingdon Press, 1996.

Voss, F. *Das Wort vom Kreuz und die menschliche Vernunft: Eine Untersuchung zur Soteriologie des 1 Korintherbriefes*. FRLANT 199. Göttingen: Vandenhoeck and Ruprecht, 2002.

Walker, W.O. "1 Corinthians 2.6-16: A Non-Pauline Interpolation?" *JSNT* 47 (1992): 75-94.

_____. "1 Corinthians 15:29-34 as a Non-Pauline Interpolation." *CBQ* 69.1 (2007): 84-103.

Waterfield, R. "Introduction." Pages xi-xxxiii in *The First Philosophers: The Presocratics and the Sophists*. Translated by R. Waterfield. Oxford: Oxford University Press, 2000.

Watson, D.F. "Paul's Rhetorical Strategy in 1 Cor 15." Pages 231-49 in *Rhetoric and the New Testament: Essays from the 1992 Heidelberg Conference*. JSNTSup 90. Edited by S.E. Porter and T.H. Olbricht. Sheffield: JSOT Press, 1993.

Watson, N. *The First Epistle to the Corinthians*. EC. London: Epworth, 1992.

Weiss, J. *Der erste Korintherbrief*. EKKNT 5. Göttingen: Vandenhoeck & Ruprecht, 1910.

Welborn, L.L. "On the Discord in Corinth: 1 Corinthians 1–4 and Ancient Politics." *JBL* 106.1 (1987): 85-111.

_____. *Paul the Fool of Christ: A Study of 1 Corinthians 1–4 in the Comic-Philosophic Tradition*. JSNTSup 293. ECC. London: T&T Clark International, 2005.

Wesley, J. "Letter VII" in *Original Letters, by the Rev. John Wesley and His Friends*. Edited by J. Priestley. Birmingham: Thomas Pearson, 1791.

_____. *Christian Perfection*. Cincinnati: Jennings & Pye, 1800.

_____. "On the Trinity." Sermon 60 in *Sermons on Several Occasions*. Vol. 2. New York: B. Waugh and T. Mason, 1836.

Whiteley, D.E.H. *The Theology of St. Paul*. Oxford: Basil Blackwell, 1964.

Wilckens, U. *Weisheit und Torheit: Eine exegetisch-religions-geschichtliche Untersuchung zu 1. Kor 1 und 2*. BHT 26. Tübingen: J. C. B. Mohr, 1959.

_____. "Das Kreuz Christi als die Tiefe der Weisheit Gottes: Zu 1 Kor 2,1-16." Pages 501-37 in *Theologia Crucis-Signum Crucis: Festschrift für Erich Dinkler zum 70 Geburstag*. Edited by C. Anderson and G. Klein. Tübingen: Mohr, 1979.

Williams, H.H.D. *The Wisdom of the Wise: The Presence and Function of Scripture in 1 Cor 1.18–3.23*. Leiden: Brill, 2001.

Williams, M.A. *Rethinking "Gnosticism": An Argument for Dismantling a Dubious Category*. Princeton: Princeton University Press, 1996.

Willis W. "'The Mind of Christ' in 1 Corinthians 2,16." *Bib* 70.1 (1989): 110-22.

Wilson, R. McL. *Gnosis and the New Testament*. Oxford: Basil Blackwell, 1968.

_____. "How Gnostic Were the Corinthians?" *NTS* 19.1 (1972): 65-74.

_____. "Gnosis at Corinth." Pages 102-14 in *Paul and Paulinism: Essays in Honor of C.K. Barrett*. Edited by M.D. Hooker and S.G. Wilson. London: SPCK, 1982.

Winter, B. *After Paul Left Corinth: The Influence of Secular Ethics and Social Change*. Grand Rapids: Eerdmans, 2001.

_____. *Philo and Paul Among the Sophists: Alexandrian and Corinthian Responses to a Julio-Claudian Movement*. Grand Rapids: Eerdmans, 2002.

_____. "Philodemus and Paul on Rhetorical Delivery (ὑπόκρισις)." Pages 323-42 in *Philodemus and the New Testament World*. NovTSup 111. Edited by J.T. Fitzgerald, D. Obbink, and G.S. Holland. Leiden: Brill, 2004.

Winter, M. *Pneumatiker und Psychiker in Korinth: zum religionsgeschichtlichen Hintergrund von 1 Kor 2,6–3,4*. Marburger theologische Studien 12. Marburg: N.G. Elwert, 1975.

Wire, A.C. *The Corinthian Women Prophets: A Reconstruction through Paul's Rhetoric*. Reprint. Minneapolis: Fortress Press, 1995.

Witherington, B. *Conflict and Community in Corinth: A Socio-Rhetorical Commentary on 1 and 2 Corinthians*. Grand Rapids: Eerdmans, 1995.

_____. *The Paul Quest: The Renewed Search for the Jew of Tarsus*. Downers Grove: InterVarsity, 1998.

Wuellner, W. "Haggadic Homily Genre in 1 Corinthians 1–3." *JBL* 89.2 (1970): 199-204.

Yamauchi, E.M. "Pre-Christian Gnosticism, the New Testament and Nag Hammadi in Recent Debate." *Them* 10.1 (1984): 26-31.

Yates, J.W. *The Spirit and Creation in Paul*. WUNT 2.251. Tübingen: Mohr Siebeck, 2008.

Zeller, E. *Outlines of the History of Greek Philosophy*. Translated by L.R. Palmer. Revised by W. Nestle. New York: Meridian, 1955.

PRIMARY SOURCES

GRECO-ROMAN

Aetius 46a, *171*
Ambrosiaster
   Ad Cor Prim 2.9, *126*
Aristotle
   Rhet. 1.2.5, *59*
   Rhet. 1.3.3, *55*
   Rhet. 1.4.1–1.15.33, *55*
   Rhet. 1.9.7-12, *59*
   Rhet. 2.2.1–2.11.7, *59*
   Rhet. 2.12.1–2.17.6, *57*
   Rhet. 2.24, *82*
   Rhet. 3.1–19, *59*
   Rhet. 3.5.6, *4*
   Rhet. 3.13.1, *56*
   Rhet. 3.13.1-4, *56*
   Rhet. 3.13.3, *56*
   Rhet. 3.14.1-12, *57*
   Rhet. 3.14.7, *57*
   Rhet. 3.16.8, *58*
   Rhet. 3.17.1-4, *58*
Cicero
   De or. 1.137-47, *55*
   De or. 2.115, *61*
   Inv. 1.1, *60, 72*
   Inv. 1.5.7, *55*
   Inv. 1.9, *60*
   Inv. 1.31-33, *58*
   Inv. 27, *56*
   Nat. Gods 2.19, *171*
   Nat. Gods 2.24, *171*
   Part. or. 27, *56-57*
   Top. 24.91, *55*

Dio Cassius
   Rome 52.4.3, *171*
Dio Chrysostom
   Or. 8-9, *64*
   Or. 8.9, *65*
   Or. 9.4, *65*
   Or. 12, *64*
Diogenes Laertius 44b, *171*
Epictetus
   Diss. 1.14.13-14, *171*
   Diss. 2.8.11-13, *171*
Euclid
   Elem. 5. Prop. 8, *82*
Eusebius
   H.E. 5.22, *115*
Herodotus
   Hist. 1.1.0, *81*
   Hist. 1.136.1, *81*
   Hist. 1.207.7, *81*
   Hist. 2.101.1, *81*
   Hist. 2.148.2, *81*
   Hist. 7.50.2, *82*
   Hist. 8.101.2, *82*
Hippolytus
   Haer. 9.9, *4*
Irenaeus
   Adv. Haer. 1.23.2, *115*
John Chrysostom
   Hom. 1 Cor. 3.4-5, *245*
   Hom. 1 Cor. 6.3, *82*
Josephus
   A.J. 8.2.8, *82*
   A.J. 8.4.1, *81*

Ps 97.10, *125*

Ps 102.26, *5*

Ps 104.29-30, *5, 191*

Ps 107.18, *130*

Ps 112.6-10, *130*

Ps 119.155, *130*

Ps 121.2, *5*

Ps 104.24, *5*

Prov 1.7, *130*

Prov 2.6, *5*

Prov 2.13, *130*

Prov 2.18, *130*

Prov 2.21-22, *130*

Prov 3.33, *130*

Prov 4.18-19, *130*

Prov 5.5, *130*

Prov 6.6, *5*

Prov 7.27, *130*

Prov 8, *6*

Prov 9.9, *5*

Prov 10.1–18.24, *130*

Prov 10.8, *129, 130*

Prov 10.14, *130*

Prov 10.21, *130*

Prov 12.15, *130*

Prov 12.18, *5*

Prov 12.23, *130*

Prov 13.14, *5*

Prov 13.20, *130*

Prov 14.12, *130*

Prov 14.16, *130*

Prov 14.24, *130*

Prov 15.2, *130*

Prov 15.5, *130*

Prov 15.7, *130*

Prov 15.14, *130*

Prov 15.20, *130*

Prov 16.21, *129*

Prov 16.22, *130*

Prov 16.23, *129*

Prov 18.2, *130*

Prov 18.15, *129*

Prov 19.20, *5*

Prov 19.29, *130*

Prov 20.20, *130*

Prov 21.12, *130*

Prov 21.18, *130*

Prov 21.29, *130*

Prov 24.7, *130*

Prov 24.16, *130*

Prov 25.26, *130*

Prov 28.4, *130*

Prov 28.12, *130*

Prov 28.28, *130*

Prov 29.2, *130*

Prov 29.7, *130*

Prov 29.16, *130*

Eccl 1.13, *129*

Eccl 1.16, *129*

Eccl 1.17, *129*

Eccl 2.3, *129*

Eccl 2.14, *130*

Eccl 2.26, *5*

Eccl 6.4, *130*

Eccl 7.15, *130*

Eccl 8.5, *129*

Eccl 8.14, *130*

Isa 5.1-7, *248*

Isa 6.9, *129*

Isa 6.9-10, *129*

Isa 10.13, *5*

Isa 11.2, *91*

Isa 19.16, *95*

Isa 28.5, *91*

Isa 28.5-6, *91*

Isa 32.3, *129*

Isa 32.15, *91*

Isa 40.12-25, *5*

Rom 8.4, *230*
Rom 8.4-9, *228*
Rom 8.5, *228, 230*
Rom 8.5-17, *206*
Rom 8.26, *95*
Rom 8.36, *122*
Rom 9.13, *122*
Rom 9.19, *95*
Rom 9.33, *122*
Rom 10.8-15, *210*
Rom 10.15, *122*
Rom 11.8, *122*
Rom 11.26, *122*
Rom 11.33, *138*
Rom 12.19, *122*
Rom 13.13, *230*
Rom 14.1, *95*
Rom 14.2, *95*
Rom 14.11, *122*
Rom 15.3, *122*
Rom 15.9, *122*
Rom 15.13, *85*
Rom 15.19, *85*
Rom 15.21, *122, 126*
1 Cor 1–3, *39*
1 Cor 1–4, *1, 2, 7, 24, 26-27, 31, 35-44, 47-49, 79, 109, 111, 120, 269, 290, 292-93*
1 Cor 1–6, *40*
1 Cor 1.1, *154*
1 Cor 1.1-9, *46*
1 Cor 1.1–4.21, *258*
1 Cor 1.2, *237*
1 Cor 1.4-17, *154*
1 Cor 1.5, *222*
1 Cor 1.5-7, *222*
1 Cor 1.7, *143*
1 Cor 1.7-8, *290*
1 Cor 1.9, *205*

1 Cor 1.9–2.5, *27*
1 Cor 1.10, *10, 40-46, 204-055*
1 Cor 1.10-11, *42*
1 Cor 1.10-12, *241*
1 Cor 1.10-13, *41*
1 Cor 1.10-17, *42, 46, 214*
1 Cor 1.10–3.23, *111*
1 Cor 1.10–4.21, *40-41, 43, 46, 213-14*
1 Cor 1.11, *46*
1 Cor 1.11-12, *8, 9, 230, 253, 268*
1 Cor 1.11–4.15, *40*
1 Cor 1.12, *11, 17, 231, 241*
1 Cor 1.12-13, *46*
1 Cor 1.13, *44, 204*
1 Cor 1.14, *46*
1 Cor 1.14-17, *46-47, 243*
1 Cor 1.14-31, *47, 242*
1 Cor 1.14–3.4, *47, 130*
1 Cor 1.17, *39, 44, 51, 73, 74, 87, 94, 100, 142, 155, 236, 243, 247, 291*
1 Cor 1.17-18, *79, 240, 289*
1 Cor 1.17-31, *104*
1 Cor 1.17–3.2, *41*
1 Cor 1.18, *45, 74, 84, 102, 133-34, 152, 154, 163, 178, 236-38, 240, 290*
1 Cor 1.18-20, *93, 166*
1 Cor 1.18-21, *90, 161*
1 Cor 1.18-23, *251*
1 Cor 1.18-25, *45, 47, 104, 120-21, 134, 161, 250*
1 Cor 1.18-31, *39, 43, 44*
1 Cor 1.18–2.5, *43, 44, 45, 46*
1 Cor 1.18–2.13, *195, 199*
1 Cor 1.18–2.16, *214*
1 Cor 1.18–3.4, *44, 192*

Post-NT
Gos. Thom. 17, *127*

Modern Authors

Subjects

18913904R00209

Printed in Poland
by Amazon Fulfillment
Poland Sp. z o.o., Wrocław